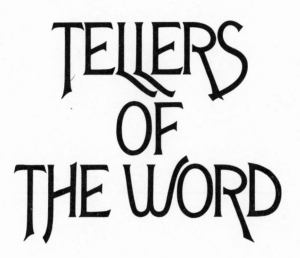

TELLERS OF THE WORD

JOHN NAVONE, S.J., AND FR. THOMAS COOPER

TELLERS OF THE WORD

John Navone, S.J., and Fr. Thomas Cooper

LE JACQ PUBLISHING INC.
NEW YORK

TABLE OF CONTENTS

Foreword

Theological research and the communication of that research are essentially a collaborative effort. Gone are the days when one person could be expected to master all the disciplines that must cross-fertilize one another if the theological tree is to remain fruitful. *Tellers of the Word* is the result of two theologians pooling their resources. Since this book has two storytellers, each with his own story, it will be easier if this foreword, like any life story, starts by differentiating the primordial "we" into two distinct subjects before resolving into the "we" of united existence.

Thomas Cooper and I corresponded and collaborated for four years on matters concerning the theology of story before meeting each other in Rome in February 1981. Our names first appeared together in *The Clergy Review* when, in May 1977, Tom referred to my work on the theology of the story in his article "Communicating the Incommunicable." Exactly a year later he reviewed my book *Towards a Theology of Story*. Later still I asked him to write the preface to my next work, *The Jesus Story: Our Life as Story in Christ* (1979). In response to an interviewer's request for ten axiomatic propositions about the theology of story, I embarked on a systematic approach to this field of study. I solicited Tom's views on the ten axiomatic propositions that I had written. Rather than write a gloss on the pages I had sent him, he simply rewrote them in a way that brought out their meaning, retaining and yet enhancing what I had written. Encouraged by the accomplishment of someone who was manifestly an alter ego, I invited him to continue collaborating with the hope that we might eventually produce a book that would advance the theology of story by systematizing it. Our Thomistic and Lonerganian background, evident throughout this book, facilitated our collaborative attempt to systematize previous efforts. It served as a key to appreciating the work of others in this field who shared the same background: John S. Dunne, John Haught, and Michael Novak, to name just a few.

Our collaboration might be described as Anglo-American and Roman. Thomas Cooper is English; I am American. Tom studied philosophy and theology at the Gregorian University from 1964 to 1971; I have studied and taught at this university since 1963. Our Roman roots go even deeper. Tom is from a Northern English family that, on his mother's side, can claim two beatified martyrs in the unbroken story of its Catholicism. My parents are Italian-born, from cities founded by the Romans. Roman, for both of us, represents universalism, the integration of all stories within the universal story that is the gift of God's love for all.

* * *

John Navone's work first came to my attention when I was preparing a lecture to be delivered to the Society of Catholic Artists, a lecture that was to find publication as "Communicating the Incommunicable." As a student in Rome, I had been profoundly influenced by the work of Father Frank O'Farrell, S.J., who communicated to his students an aesthetic delight in the ontology of St. Thomas Aquinas. He was later to give me invaluable bibliographical advice when, under the direction of Father Sixto Cartechini, S.J., I first attempted to write at some length on the problems of theological aesthetics. Six years of parochial ministry—the *materia prima* for most if not all theological reflection—led me to search for some overarching method that could unify for me what Alfred North Whitehead called the bagatelle of transient experience. I found such a method in the writings of Bernard Lonergan and in its application to the writings of Sigmund Freud, Carl G. Jung, and Frank Lake. I discovered in my reading of Lonergan the truth that there is nothing quite so practical for the problems of daily living and loving as a good and rigorous theory. My account of how I discovered Lonergan has amused enough people to perhaps be worth recording. In the early days of my parochial experience I used to sit for hours at a time in a confessional box while a trickle of people made their visits. Needing to fill in the time between penitents I decided to study Lonergan's *Insight*. I quickly discovered that Lonergan's insight into the scotomas, the flights from understanding, the general and the particular bias of common nonsense was an invaluable aid to understanding the stories people told me in the confessional. "Communicating the Incommunicable" was a first attempt to share something of what I had found. Its fruit, like all grace, was an unexpected and unmerited offer of friendship and the revelation that I had been "acting better than I knew": unbeknown to myself I had been writing a theology of story.

John has already outlined the story of the conception, gestation, and birth of this book. William Wordsworth in "The Tables Turned" wrote that

> One impulse from a vernal wood
> May teach you more of man,

Of moral evil and of good,
Than all the sages can.

Every author has his or her own vernal wood: that little band of persons whose love, affection, and criticism are present on every page, even where, and perhaps especially where, it is not acknowledged in the footnotes. In presenting my first book to a wider public, I gratefully acknowledge the trees that make up my own personal wood, imputing to them none of the responsibility for the times I have responded inadequately to their impulse: the Very Reverend Professor Denis J. M. Bradley of the Oratory; the Reverend John Koenig, Norah Edwardes, and last, but very far from least, Sally Louise Casey.

*   *   *

Unlike Humpty Dumpty, the authors are able to put themselves together again; we return to the "we" from which we came. Friendly critics of our first draft pointed out that the narrative flow of the main part of the book, Part Two, is a little uneven. This is largely inevitable in a work born out of a dialogue between two persons a thousand miles—and two sometimes inefficient postal services—apart. We decided to leave it as it stood, a witness to the dialogical story of its composition. In *The Jesus Story* the attempt was made to raise the questions: What is the theology of story? Who are the theologians of story, and what are they doing? In this book, the result of our collaborative effort, we attempt the beginnings of a systematic answer to those questions.

We have been especially encouraged by the recognition that James J. Gill, S.J., M.D., the editor of *Human Development*, has given our work. We are most grateful to him for having brought it to the attention of our publisher, Louis F. Le Jacq. We also thank Robert Spitzer, S.J., for both his keen interest in our work and his excellent suggestion that we provide three propaedeutic chapters for our readers.

John Navone, S.J.
Gregorian University
Rome, Italy
April 5, 1981

Thomas Cooper
University of Lancaster
Lancaster, England
April 10, 1981

Introduction

When Hollywood decided to make a movie of Fulton Oursler's *The Greatest Story Ever Told,* they very wisely used the same title. The picture was perhaps objectionable because of its sentimentality and ultimate trivializing of its subject, but the choice of title showed an unerring instinct for the truth about the meaning of Christ's life. The life of Jesus is a story. It is the universal story of all men and women, whether they explicitly know it or not. Bernard Lonergan has described the shift from a classical understanding of theology to the modern understanding as a change in the very conception of what the theologian does—". . . while theology used to be defined as the science about God, today I believe it is to be defined as reflection on the significance and value of a religion in a culture."[1]

Theology is no longer, as Richard Hooker thought, the "science of things divine," but the sustained reflection of the theologian on the way in which men and women react to and appropriate the story of Jesus into their own stories. If theology is words or talk about God (*theo-logos*), then the center of attention is no longer the words being used—a conceptual system of affirmations about God— but the activity of talking itself. The second half of the word "God-talk" is not a substantive but a verb; we are interested in how, through talking (whether it be about God or about the seemingly secular concerns of our neighbor), God is disclosed as present and redemptive in the very talking itself. To open one's mouth to talk is to enter a relationship with a listener, however superficial. Even when, lonely and dejected, we talk to ourselves we are witnessing to our essential being as talkers-relators.

The theology of story is a theology about the human and divine subjects who speak, tell stories, spin yarns, and relate to one another through the ceaseless babble and chatter that make up the world in which we live. In the world of today, with its noise and ease of communications, when television projects pictures into every home and when to speak to someone in Rome an Englishman has only to dial thirteen digits, we perhaps appreciate more than ever that "Silence Is Golden." But if Jesus left the hurly-burly of the crowds to be alone with God and if preachers and theologians increasingly feel obliged to remind their congregations and their readers that the life of prayer requires periods of withdrawal and silence, the aloneness and the silence are there in order that we may attend to Someone who speaks.

If all talking and telling of stories is a relating of the speaker to her or his audience, then the greatest story will be the greatest relating; the story that undergrounds all other stories will be a story of love. The theology of story attempts to bring into sharp relief the self-investing love of God made manifest in Jesus, a love that creates, sustains, and brings to fulfillment all the partial, incomplete, and imperfect stories that men and women tell one another. When a man or woman withdraws completely from the world of relationships that make up a truly human life, he or she does not fill the air with cries of hatred or abuse but lapses into catatonia—a terrible, all-negating silence. In *The Screwtape Letters* the Anglican theologian C. S. Lewis speaks of how Satan's greatest weapon is to remain silent; in the Gospel stories Jesus makes the devils speak as a prelude to their being cast out. The image of a total silence, a total absence of storytelling, is an image of absolute evil, the total negation of God, who, through Jesus and in the Spirit, is a Word spoken and a Love shared.

The first three chapters by John Navone provide an historiographical, literary, and philosophical propaedeutic to contextualize the nine moments in the theology of story that make up the main part of the book. They preface the authors' attempts to show that a theology of story excludes any modernist or reductionist interpretation of theological anthropology, which seems to suggest that theological doctrines are to be viewed as statements about merely human realities. Rather, it is based on the position that humankind is for God, that religion is intrinsic to authentic humanism, and that in theology the theocentric and the anthropocentric coincide; so it is that all theological statements are to be matched by statements of their meaning in human terms. Theology of story employs the category of story to bring to life theological truth through a contemporary apprehension of personal and social reality in all its concreteness. It aims to provide us with a wealth of new insights into what it means to be human.

The first three chapters of this book are a propaedeutic on three levels to a theory of storytelling. We have chosen to write a *theology* of storytelling because we are convinced that all stories are implicitly meant to communicate interpersonal relationships that ultimately are embraced by the value and mystery of God. All stories are meant to be "theological." Humankind needs theological stories because human beings are fundamentally interpersonal and because, if the Christian God's promise is true, then humankind is fundamentally related to God as person. Since story is the only means by which the interpersonal reality of humankind can be expressed in its cognitive and affective fullness and since our relationship to God is fundamentally interpersonal, it follows that storytelling and storylistening provide the most appropriate means of enabling us to live this relationship.

In chapters 4 through 12, a work of joint authorship, we present nine moments in the theology of story. The first three moments delineate a phenomenology of storytelling; in forty foundational theses we treat of storytelling as the mode in which human beings live in the world. The first moment reveals human beings as the subject of their stories. The second moment analyzes how human beings tell stories. The third moment considers the meaning of human stories, a meaning that intends the story of Jesus as the subject of the next six moments. Moments four through nine apply the phenomenology of storytelling to the revelation of God in Christ. The fourth moment considers how the universal story of God is revealed through human stories. In the fifth moment we consider Christian conversion as the gift of God's love through the Holy Spirit. The sixth moment considers the Jesus story as sacrament of our friendship with God, while the seventh moment deals with the Jesus story as foundational for the story of his community, the Church. The eighth moment speaks of the amazing quality of God's interventions in the stories told by human lives, and in the ninth moment we pass to a consideration of the Blessed and Undivided Trinity as the beginning, the middle, and the end of all human storytelling.

Appendix I, the work of John Navone abridged by Thomas Cooper, considers the storytelling of Mark the evangelist as a model for all who wish to tell the story of Jesus. Although not the earliest of the New Testament writings, the four Gospels are narrative models for all who seek to tell the Good News of Jesus. The first example of any literary genre functions as a kind of breakthrough. The first to compose a novel or a play in a particular fashion acts as the model for all who follow. By understanding how the writer of the first Gospel sets about his task, we come to a greater understanding not only of how to read his work but also how in our turn to tell the story of Jesus.

Appendix II, the work of Thomas Cooper, functions as a brief guide—almost a checklist—to the ways in which contemporary tellers of the Jesus story can prepare themselves for their task.

Appendix III widens the collaborative effort to include suggestions from a colleague and our students as to what other theses or questions we might have overlooked.

The nine moments that make up the main part of this book consist of one hundred twenty theses arranged in clusters. They are numbered according to a decimal system; the number before the point is the number of the moment. The numbers after the point group the theses in clusters, 1.3, for example, being the third thesis of moment 1; 1.31 being the first thesis associated with 1.3. It should be noted that the numbering of the theses does not of itself indicate the relative importance of a thesis in the minds of its authors but is an indication of the relationships between theses, how one throws further light on or develops from another.

1. Bernard J. F. Lonergan, *Philosophy of God, and Theology: The Relationship Between Philosophy of God and the Functional Specialty, Systematics* (London: Darton, Longman & Todd, 1973) p. 33.

Theses for the Theology of Story

A. A Phenomenology of Storytelling

1   Human beings as the subjects of their stories
1.1   People are storytelling animals.
1.2   People are storymaking animals.
1.3   The self is conscious as the subject of a verb.

    1.31   The self is a particular agent that is known and revealed in its life story.

    1.311   Every human life story shares the three temporal dimensions of past, present, and future, which are respectively called to mind by memory, awareness, and anticipation.

    1.312   The meaning of (life) stories is seen from the end.

    1.3121   Human stories involve both a process (promise) and a term (fulfillment).

    1.3122   The beginning of a human story is the promise of its ending or fulfillment.

    1.3123   We organize our storymaking around the conclusion that we have chosen for our stories, or around what we believe must be their conclusion.

1.4   The art of storytelling expresses the art of living.

    1.41   A condition for sanity is the ability to tell our stories.

1.5   What human life stories mean to us depends on what kind of person we are.

    1.51   Human life stories are their own interpretation inasmuch as they are the product of the understanding that people have of themselves, their situation, their role, the human condition. The interpretation interprets the interpreter.

    1.52   Of the symbols with which we spontaneously but uncritically express our life story, a privileged place is occupied by parental imagery.

    1.521   These spontaneous symbols, because they are spontaneous, are in need of critical reflection.

1.6   Our storylistening prepares us for our storymaking: we are storylisteners before we become storytellers.
1.7   There are two poles to the horizon of every story.
1.8   Human security is grounded in the stories we hear and tell.

    1.81   The movement from one stage of storytelling to another stage, accompanied by the threat to the subject's sense of security, is confirmed as a law of human development by the developmental psychologies of Erikson and Kohlberg.

    1.82   The story told by a human life is not exclusively a story of peak experiences.

    1.821   Patience is a precondition for all divine and human storymaking.

2   The craft of telling stories
2.1   Like a teacher, a craftsperson, or an artist, the storyteller must use techniques and skills adapted for his or her purpose.

2.11   We cannot do what we cannot, at least in some way, imagine or envision.

2.111   Authentic lives evidence authentic vision.

2.12   The art of the storyteller is measured by his or her ability to master complexity: the more that he or she is able to unify within his or her story, the greater his or her art as a storyteller.

2.121   The excellence of human stories is measured by the demands they make of their authors.

2.2 The storyteller is implicitly a teacher inasmuch as she or he creates a story that moves the listener to decision.

2.21   Stories are a mutual creation of the teller and the listeners.

2.3 The author of a story has an attitude toward the subject of the story.

2.31   The author of a story has an attitude toward his or her audience.

2.4 The true meaning and value of human stories are determined by their context.

2.5 There is no human story without limits.

2.6 The human action that defines a story is a declaration of a basic faith.

2.61   We seek to live by the stories that embody our basic faith.

2.611   Since the communication and expression of faith transcends all conceptual knowledge, both its expression and communication lie in the symbolic mode of consciousness, symbol being defined as the best possible expression of an unknown content.

2.6111   Because the symbolic is rooted in the psychic depths of the personality there is need of a critical mediation of symbols. Because the critical intellect can never comprehend the mystery of God, there is a need for a return to the symbolic.

2.62   Images, and the stories that contain them, provide models and motives for the decisions and actions that shape our lives.

2.621   Human conduct is more story or model abiding than it is principle or law abiding.

2.6211   Law-abiding behavior can itself be a mode of storytelling.

2.63   A human life story is not exclusively a matter of self-determination.

3   The meaning of human stories

3.1 That every person who has ever lived has lived out a story of storytelling and storylistening posits a comprehensible universe with a permanent meaning at the heart of things.

3.11   Stories express the horizon of their author's vision.

3.12   Human stories are implicit answers to the fundamental questions that arise concerning life and death.

3.13   Human stories raise questions about the answers that they imply with regard to the basic questions about life and death.

3.2 God is ultimately intended by every human life story.

**B. The Universal Story of God Told
in the Life Story of Jesus**

4   God is revealed through human stories
4.1   God is a particular agent that is known and revealed in his story.
    4.11   The transcendent Spirit of God is, and is known, where it acts in the self-transcending faith and hope and love through which it transforms our lives.
    4.12   Inasmuch as God is the giver of all human life stories, they are manifestations of his grace and are measured by the demands of his intention.
    4.13   Human stories are implicitly coauthored with God and neighbor.
4.2   The story in which God is known and revealed is the Word of God.
    4.21   The universal story, together with every human life story, is God's primary word.
    4.22   The stories of God told by prophets, priests, apostles, evangelists, and others are God's secondary word.
4.3   Jesus the Storyteller redeems all human storytelling.
    4.31   Every human life story will reflect the presence of evil in the world and in men's lives.
    4.311   The guilt that attends every life story must not only be experienced but also understood and judged.
    4.312   Guilt is not absolved by observing that the person "meant well."
    4.32   As storymaking animals we are responsible for our failure to tell our story authentically.
    4.33   The true meaning and value of a human story are precarious; it can be lost through a misinterpretation of the meaning and a noncommitment to its value.
    4.331   Sin consists in the deliberate distortion of our life stories in order to take them out of their proper context in the universal story.
    4.34   Jesus Christ's making and telling of stories summon all humankind to share his filial responsibility for the making of their stories.
    4.341   The divine Storymaker unifies all creation within his universal story.
4.4   The way in which we envision God is always determined from the start by the way we love and treasure the things presented to us within the context of our life's story.
    4.41   The way that Jesus Christ loved and treasured the things presented to him within the context of his life story reveals to Christian faith the meaning of authentic love and the true vision of God.
4.5   The meaning of Jesus Christ is seen as the outcome of his life story.
    4.51   The vision of the Beloved Sonship symbolized in the baptism of Jesus is further revealed as the foundation of the Christian story by Jesus' Way of the Cross.
    4.52   The story of Christ's life reveals the necessity of suffering in every human life story.

4.521   The Way of the Cross as disclosed in the story of Jesus reveals the nature of authentic suffering.

4.522   The cross reveals to Christian faith the extent to which the divine Storymaker is committed to the excellence of his universal story.

4.6   Because our faith is preconceptual our telling and listening to God's story will be a communication of the incommunicable and an expression of the inexpressible.

4.61   The symbols with which we spontaneously express the life story of God are taken from our own unthematized expression of our life story.

5   The gift of God's love through the Holy Spirit of Jesus Christ grounds the story of Christian conversion

5.1   The telling and the hearing of the Gospel story are the work of the same Spirit working in both the teller and the hearer.

5.11   Christian conversion is a gift of God that enables us to hear the story of Jesus and his Church.

5.12   Christian conversion is a gift of God that enables us to tell the story of Jesus and his Church.

5.2   The materials of the Gospel story point to distinctive understandings of God's gift of his love manifested in Jesus and to the dimensions of discipleship associated with them.

5.21   In appropriating the story told by the four Gospels we appropriate our own life story.

5.22   The Gospel story calls its hearers to return (be converted) to themselves in the process of being converted to God.

5.3   Four versions of the Gospel story serve the Church as four manuals for the attainment of Christian maturity.

5.31   The story as told by Mark prepares the catechumen for the sacramental celebration of the first moment of conversion.

5.32   The story as told by Matthew illuminates the way for the newly baptized to enter into fellowship.

5.33   The story as told by Luke, both in his Gospel and in Acts, aids the newly converted and mutually strengthened Christian to enter into a life of missionary commitment.

5.34   The story as told by John serves the mature and contemplative Christian as a manual for ascertaining and attaining the full development of the Christian life.

5.35   Bernard Lonergan's theology of conversion allows us to understand the progressive unfolding of the Christian story from Mark through John.

5.4   The death of Jesus outside the "camp" or "city" symbolizes Christian conversion as a breakout from our self-imposed imprisonment.

5.41   The Church employs the four stories of Mark, Matthew, Luke, and John as a means for communicating and cultivating its foundational experience of the love of God in Christ Jesus and in his Spirit that has been given us.

5.42   Basic to our experience of conversion is the felt judgment that we are loved.

5.421   The world disclosed by Jesus in his Sonship of God defines each Christian storyteller as one who has been trusted.

5.43   The different ways of telling the story of Jesus correspond to the diverse ways in which God can tell us that we are loved.

5.431   The names of Jesus connote the ways that God's gift of his love transforms our lives and constitutes the life story of the church.

5.5 Christian conversion is worked out in a process of self-transcendence, in a lifetime's death in love and self-surrender.

5.51   The truths of the Gospel story evoke Christian conversion both as event and as process.

5.52   The division of the Scriptures into Old and New Testaments and the story of Jesus as told by Luke-Acts symbolize the presence of continuity and discontinuity in stories of Christian conversion.

5.53   The story of Jesus being in agony in the garden discloses the inescapable presence of tension in the life of Christian conversion.

5.6 Christian conversion is sacramentally signified by the grace of matrimony.

5.61   The charism of celibacy for the Kingdom reflects the narrative quality of our life in Christ.

5.7 The story of Judas as portrayed by the Gospel writers discloses ultimate human failure as the betrayal of the divine offer of friendship.

6   Jesus Christ is the Sacrament who transforms human life stories

6.1 The categories appropriate to a critical understanding of the Gospel story are aesthetic rather than classically scientific.

6.11   The claim to universal validity of the judgment of taste provides a fruitful analogy for understanding the claim to universal validity made by the Gospel story.

6.12   The claim to universal validity implicit in the judgment of taste provides a fruitful if imperfect analogy for understanding how, through the Incarnation, we love the God whom no human eye has seen.

6.2 Human life stories function as icons of the divine life story.

6.21   The life story of every human storyteller functions as an icon of that storyteller's faith.

6.22   The life story of the crucified-risen Jesus is the primordial sacrament of God's gift of his love, experienced by the Christian as underlying and informing all human life stories.

6.23   The Gospel stories function as sacramental symbols evoked by the feeling for Christ of their writers and evoking the feeling for Christ of their readers or listeners.

6.24   The Resurrection is the key to the Christian interpretation of the divine and human coauthoring of the Jesus story, the story of the Church and the universal story of the world.

7   The Jesus story as foundation for the story of his community, the Church

7.1 Persons communicate and relate to one another by the stories they tell.

7.11   There can be no community life, no consensus, and thus no common action without participation in a common understanding of the meaning of a common story and without a common commitment to that story's value.

7.12   The life story of a community is the common good of those who call to mind its meaning and value by memory, awareness, and anticipation.

7.13   The tradition of a community or society is the story of its life.

7.14   Authentic storytelling is the creation of a community of love.

7.2   The members of a society benefit from its common story only to the extent that they allow themselves to be governed by it.

7.21   Every society has limits to its tolerance for the diversity of its members' interpretations of its common (foundational) story.

7.3   Preparation is required for grasping the meaning of human stories.

7.31   Our experience of the Jesus story is conditioned by our experience of the world.

7.32   Our understanding of the Jesus story, the Good News, is conditioned by our participation in the living communities of Christian faith that tell the story.

7.33   The tradition of the Church is the life story of Christians.

8   The Jesus story reveals that human beings are ever to be "surprised by joy"

8.1   The Gospel stories witness the amazing quality of God's grace.

8.2   Christ's story of the Good Samaritan challenges our a priori assumptions about the mode in which God will reveal himself to us.

9   The Blessed Trinity and Undivided Unity of God is the beginning, the middle, and the end of all our storytelling

9.1   The mystery of the Blessed Trinity and Undivided Unity, symbolically present in human consciousness, points to God as the deepest fulfillment of the human Spirit.

9.2   The human experience of telling and listening to stories provides a fruitful if imperfect analogy for the Blessed and Undivided Trinity.

9.3   The interpersonal dynamics of the life story of Jesus Christ as disclosed in his life of universal friendship function as a fruitful model for understanding the interpersonal dynamics of our life in Christ.

9.4   The interpersonal life of Jesus Christ—his relationships to God and to his fellow humans, to divine and human persons—is the prime analogate for the Christian community's experience and understanding and judgment of its own interpersonal relationships with divine and human persons, and of the relationship between the universal story and the Blessed Trinity.

PART ONE

A Threefold Propaedeutic to the Theology of Story

A Story of Storytelling: A Historiographic Propaedeutic to a Theology of Storytelling

The human desire to understand historical experience takes the form of storytelling. In fact, the history of historiography is a story about storytellers and their talent for storytelling.

In Egypt (Manetho, third century B.C.), Mesopotamia, and China, historical records appear immediately after the appearance of writing, for kings wished to record their triumphs for posterity. There was interest in the remote past, especially genealogical interest in the glorification of royal ancestors and their achievements. There appears, too, an ethical and a religious interest in showing the lessons of history for the attainment of human righteousness.

The Jewish historiography of the Old Testament is based on written sources such as the chronicles of the kings of Judah and Israel, on oral traditions, knowledge of contemporary affairs, codes, songs, poems, and hymns. Jewish writers exhibited a feeling for the dramatic and exalted the role of the individual in relation to the life of the people. They attempted to show that their history, as shaped by God, contained lessons for the shaping of contemporary and future events. God, the Lord of the past and present and future, manifested his purpose in historical events. These historical sections of the Old Testament were written from about the ninth to the fourth century B.C.

In the period from Homer to Herodotus (c. 484–425 B.C.) the Homeric epics satisfied the historical interest of many generations. Mythological tradition was elaborated, chronologically arranged, and systematized. Historical inquiry was stimulated by the interest in colonization. Local city histories and geographical guidebooks appeared. The *logographoi* (middle of the sixth century), the first prose writers, wrote mostly myths, genealogies, legends, and the chronicles of cities. The Ionian prose writers recorded "sayings" (*logoi*). Herodotus, often called the Father of History, collected his data from his own observations, eyewitnesses, old family legends and traditions, oracles, lists of satraps, Egyptian priests, and the earlier logographers. He did not credulously record, without criticism or evaluation, the vast amount of material communicated to him. Although he believed in the gods, he was cautious in relating tales of their interventions in human affairs. He died about 425 B.C. and was followed by Thucydides (c.445–c.400 B.C.). Thucydides introduced speeches into his narrative of the Peloponnesian War to present his analysis and interpretation of the forces and issues that shaped it. With Thucydides this literary device became an essential part of Greek historiography. Thucydides was the first to apply to the writing of history the scientific methods of the Hippocratic school of medicine. He sought the causes of events in a critical study of men, their actions and emotions. Xenophon (434 – 354 B.C.), Polybius (c.198 – 117 B.C.), and Dion or Cassius Dio Coccianus (c.155 – c.235 B.C.) were other outstanding Greek historiographers. The writing of Greek historical biographies reached its culmination in the *Parallel Lives* of Plutarch (A.D. c.50 – c.120). These accounts of the lives of forty-six Greeks and forty-six Romans, arranged in pairs, are the work of a moralist who sought to present the personalities of the world's great and thus inculcate a desire for virtue and excellence.

Among the Roman historians, Julius Caesar (c.100–44 B.C.), in seven books that describe his activities in Gaul from 58 to 52 B.C., tried to justify his actions and positions to the Romans. Sallust (87–c.35 B.C.) wrote brilliant monographs in a moralistic tone that decried the venality, the selfishness, and the evil habits that wealth, luxury, and power brought to the governing aristocracy of his day. Livy (59 B.C.–A.D. 17), in the tradition of Herodotus, invokes the intervention of the gods to explain cause and effect. His *History of Rome* extols the civic virtues of the founders and upholders of the Republic and recalls the qualities of the national character that had made Rome the ruler of the world. Tacitus, who wrote in the first century A.D., employed historiography to instruct the statesmen of the future by relating the experiences of others, to give praise where it was due, and to show the evil consequences of malicious and immoral acts.

Augustine of Hippo (354 – 430), the greatest of the Latin Fathers, wrote his *City of God* after the sack of Rome by Alaric the Goth (410) in reply to the accusation that Rome had fallen because the worship of the Roman gods had been abandoned in favor of an oriental superstition. His work developed from a controversial pamphlet into a vast synthesis that embraced the history of the whole human race and its destinies in time and eternity. Augustine theologically interprets the history of the world as the unfolding of

God's will; the earth is the scene of perpetual conflict between two cities or states. The earthly one is composed of all who seek their ultimate reward and happiness on this earth; the heavenly one is composed of all faithful Christians who are but pilgrims in this world. All human history leads to the Last Judgment, the end of the conflict between these two polities, where the citizens of the *City of God* will obtain immortality and blessedness while those of the city of unrighteousness will be condemned. Augustine traced the history of the earthly city from the secular records as found in Cicero, Varro, Jerome's version of Eusebius's *Chronicle,* Plato, Sallust, Pliny the Elder, Vergil, and others; he traced the history of the heavenly city from the Scriptures. Augustine commissioned his scholarly researcher, Orosius, to write a more orderly complement to his own discursive *City of God.* Orosius's summary of world history, completed about 418, drew from the work of earlier Christian writers such as Eusebius and of pagan historians such as Livy and Suetonius. It became the standard textbook on universal history for a thousand years; it was translated into English by King Alfred. It represents the first attempt at a history of the world. For all its defects, according to R. L. P. Milburn,[1] it is a history that accords reasonably well with the demand of the ancient theoreticians that narrative should be concise, clear, and truthful. Until the final disintegration of the medieval world view in the eighteenth century, world chronology had to be fitted into the sacred history of the Bible, as it had been since the time of Orosius in the early fifth century.

Medieval historiography tended to divide into two types. One was the universal history, inspired by Augustine, Orosius, and Isidore of Seville (c. 560 – 636). The other was chronicle, ranging from the simple annals of local monasteries to more organized accounts such as those of Saxo Grammaticus, Otto of Freising (d.1158), Matthew of Paris (d.1259). The two forms were often mixed. Attempts at broader histories of peoples such as that of the Goths by Cassiodorus (c.485–c.580) and that of the Franks by Gregory of Tours (538 – 594) were early achievements that had few successors. Gregory, the historian *par excellence* of the Merovingian age, rigorously observed the order of events. He draws from recounted facts, the stories of the oral tradition, and the testimony of eyewitnesses; he writes at a time when there are few contemporary written sources. The Venerable Bede (673 – 735) employs anecdotes and stories in his *Ecclesiastical History of the English People.* He does not think of starting with the Deluge as the chroniclers did. He begins with the "profane" fact of Caesar's expeditions; however, he is not writing "profane" history. Everything becomes Church history because the Church encompassed the whole of life. Bede enumerated his written sources; he tested his oral traditions by asking old people preferably, trustworthy persons, or several witnesses at once. Paul the Deacon, born between 720 – 730 of a Lombard family, wrote the first "national" history of his people. His *History of the Lombards* in six books is a more "secular history" than that of Bede, even though both were Benedictines. He was the first professional historian of the Middle Ages; he resided at the royal court of Charlemagne between 782 – 786.

One learns most about the political history of Italy and Germany in the medieval period from the *Liber Pontificalis* ("the Papal Book"), a collection of early papal biographies, begun in the sixth century. By the eighth century it became the major archivistic source for Roman life and for the relations between the religious and lay powers. Jean de Joinville's *Histoire du roi Saint Louis* (1309) represents the first vernacular classic of lay biography. The emergence of the secular historian continues with Jean Froissart (c.1335 – c.1405), who traveled throughout Europe to gather material for his chronicles, covering the more considerable European countries from 1325 to 1400. Most of his material was based on the stories of eyewitnesses. Philippe de Comines (c.1447 – c.1511), whose *Memoirs* are of merit, frequently saw events develop so differently from human plans and abilities that he regularly attributed the inexplicable and the unexpected to divine intervention. In the interpretive and critical sense, little history was studied, written, or read, not even in the thirteenth century, when the study of philosophy reached a height not attained since fifth-century Athens.

Unlike the medieval historians, the Renaissance humanists tended to regard the millennium between the collapse of the Roman Empire in the West and the fifteenth century as an era of prolonged decline. The concept of the Middle Ages was thus introduced for this intervening period. The scholarship and literary activity of the Florentines established their city as the intellectual center of Italy. Thus Leonardo Bruni (1369 – 1444), instructed in Greek by Chrysologas, became the author of the first humanistic history. He destroyed legends surrounding Florentine history, and he no longer attributed to Divine Providence events in history. Poggio Bracciolini (1380 – 1459) and his contemporary Niccolò de Niccoli searched for surviving Greek and Roman manuscripts and thus recovered for posterity invaluable sources for ancient history. Niccolo Machiavelli (1469 – 1527) and Francesco Guicciardini (1483 – 1540), both experienced diplomats and rejected office seekers, exposed the self-interested motives of contemporary leaders in their histories of Florence and Italy.

The Florentine historiographers were interested in the past as human experience; they subjected it to examination on the basis of their own personal aspirations. Their purposes were diverse. Bruni thought of history as a vehicle for rhetoric; Guicciardini, as a way of providing wholesome instruction; Machiavelli (in *The Prince*), as a means for uniting Italy. Flavio Biondo (1388 – 1463) explored the ruins of classical foundations. He and Bernardo Giustiniani studied the origins of Venice. Humanist historians insisted on the choice of definite, clearly delimitative subjects and on a more coherent organization of material. Machiavelli hit upon a method of historical analogy. Comparing the Rome of Titus Livius (Livy) with Florence, he deduced principles and precepts for political action. This use of the past became a model for others. Analysis by analogy dominated historical thinking until the end of the eighteenth century. From the fifteenth century the city and new national governments and private families engaged in business and made records of what they did. Increasingly these were preserved. The great modern collections of manuscripts and books, so necessary for historical research, were also beginning. The Vatican Library was founded in the fifteenth century.

As a rule, humanist historiographers north of the Alps thought that history belonged to the field of moral philosophy. History was teaching philosophy by examples. It made concrete what the able moral philosopher already knew. Sir Philip Sidney argued that since history dealt with individual events, it was inferior to poetry, which could (like philosophy) present truths of universal importance. The historiography of successful men of affairs could supply others with practical wisdom.

The main theme of historians during the sixteenth and seventeenth centuries was the Christian Church. The Reformation influenced historiography. Protestants sought to prove that the Church of the Medici popes was not that of the early Christians and to show how degeneration had taken place. They had to retell in a new way the entire history of Christianity. Disagreements arose when they tried to pinpoint the moment when the Church took the fatal turn away from God's true purpose. While the radical sectarians considered that the papacy had always been corrupt, less extremist Protestants were prepared to accept the earlier popes and to argue that the rot set in at some date between the time of Eusebius (died c.340) and the seventh century. Catholics, for their part, attempted to confound their enemies by revealing facts of which they were unaware. The Roman Curia directed Cardinal Baronius to prepare an exhaustive refutation of the *Magdeburg Centuries* (a Lutheran version of the first thirteen centuries of Church history) and placed the Vatican archives at his disposal. Religious controversy stimulated storytelling. Catholicism, more than Protestantism, rested its authority on tradition. For Catholic scholars such as Mabillon, the defense of history became a defense of their religion.

Enlightenment historians, writing in the era from about 1715 to 1780, told more about trade, industry, social life, cultural developments, and the interrelation among these forces, than had been customary in the old political and theological histories. Montesquieu, Voltaire, and William Robertson included Asia and America in their historiography. To write history as a *philosophe* meant to write it in the service of the Enlightenment creed of nature, reason, progress, and humanity. Enlightenment historians were propagandists for a new value system that reflected their upper middle class prejudice. The past, for Voltaire, was shrouded in crimes, follies, dogmatisms, credulity, and ignorance. He failed to make clear how the enlightened eighteenth century could have evolved from such a past. Sharing Voltaire's contempt for the past was Condorcet, an early prophet of the doctrine of endless progress of mankind and a pioneer historian of European civilization, who was a member of a French parliamentary commission that in 1792–93 deliberately destroyed some of the royal records as comprising relics of past servitude.

Historians have had to face restrictions on the access to documents and on the liberty to announce results. When an archivist was appointed in East Friesland in 1729, he was informed by his employers that "after learning the secrets of our house he must carry them to the grave and reveal them to nobody."[2] No one was allowed to use the archives at Stuttgart without the express permission of the duke. The title of court historiographer possessed a real meaning when its holder was regarded as the defender of the glory and dignity of the dynasty. In France, Louis XIV in 1714 imprisoned Nicolas Fréret in the Bastille for alleging (correctly) that the Franks were originally a confederacy of German tribes and not descendants of more illustrious ancestors. Mézeray was deprived of his pension for some comments on the fiscal expedients of the predecessors of Louis XIV.

During the eighteenth century it was safer and easier to publish controversial works of history than it had been in the past. The *philosophes* reenacted the role of the Sophists in the Athens of Socrates' day, with equally unsettling results so far as traditional religious ideas were concerned. It was they, and not the men of science themselves, who first put about the notion that there is a conflict between science and religion. Although Voltaire and his school blamed the Middle Ages for not thinking modern thoughts, they translated Christian dualism, eschatology, and universalism into their secularized historiography. Inverting the Augustinian two cities, they depicted the Church as the earthly force of darkness obscuring the heavenly light of reason and science. The struggle between God and evil became the struggle between reason and unreason. The Christian hope of a fulfillment in the historical process of God's promises of salvation was secularized into a belief in the goal of history as a fulfillment of humankind's power to achieve ultimate happiness on earth by its own science and wisdom. Just as universal Christian church histories had put religious faith above nationality or state loyalty, it was felt that history would best serve the cause of philosophy and reason if it were written on a scale broader than national history.

Enlightenment historiography set forth the new rationalistic world view as the self-authenticating judgment of "all reasonable men," of "modern man." The Age of Reason loved the story of the noble savage, born free and as yet untrammeled by the institutions of society. Voltaire idealized the Chinese, the Mohammedans, and the Indians, whom he represents as being nearer to that religion of nature that all men had originally practiced and that had been sadly obscured in Christendom by the superstitious prejudices (such as the teaching on Original Sin and the need for Redemption), which had been invented for their own ends by a cunning and avaricious priestly caste. Such things as despotism in China or sutteeism in India were due to the thwarting of the noble ideals of the Mandarins and Brahmans by the superstition of a stupid populace. Enlightenment rationalists wrote history as literature to point a moral. The most that historical evidence could provide was the corroboration of truths that reason had independently discovered about humankind. The incidental truths of history could never impinge upon the necessary truths of reason.

Giovanni Battista Vico (1668 – 1744) was appointed historiographer to Charles III (1734) of Naples. His book, *Scienza nuova*, was one of the first attempts to expound a philosophy of history. He criticized the nonhistorical rationalism of Descartes and stressed that man was a historical being in society who made his own history and therefore could understand it. He analyzed the evolution of languages, fables, poems, laws, and religions to reconstruct the intellectual, political, economic, and social development of early man. He saw Homer, Romulus, Zoroaster, Lycurgus, and others as the symbolizers of civilizations. He influenced J. G. Herder, K. Marx, B. Croce, J. Michelet, and J. de Maistre.

Where Descartes had begun with the disjunction of fact and idea, Vico as a historian began with the given facts of the past; to these facts he brought a critical method and principles for the establishment of historical knowledge.

Vico divided history into periods and taught that these periods tended to occur again and again in a certain order; he believed that he had found a pattern to history. The recurrence of historical periods was not a rigidly conceived cyclical movement, self-enclosed, as it had been for later pre-Christian thought, but rather a spiral movement, preeminently one of ascent. Vico was a Christian who believed that history had a beginning and an end, that periodization did not mean the cyclical trap of an enclosed eternal recurrence, but he did believe that in history one could trace through these periods observable phases and laws. Because this motion of history was envisioned as spiral, the historian could not, from his knowledge of the patterns, predict the future; each state of history possessed its own peculiar qualities. Vico believed that divine Providence was a law immanent in history. Historical process reflected the gradual unfolding of the divine Will. In addition, history provided abundant evidence of human freedom. The twofold existence of human freedom and divine Providence forbade any certain predictions of the future. The development that exists in the stages of human history is real development in which the eternal law of God emerges; but this law (Providence) is also continually opposed by the evil disposition of human persons. The universal story that Providence intends is not accepted by all persons.

Romanticism was another spring of historical understanding that arose to oppose rationalism. It stressed the supernatural, tradition, individual differences, and folkways in contrast to reason, science, the common nature of man, and natural law. Rousseau (1712–1778), the first important representative of this movement, wrote little history, but his emotion, his love of the primitive, his disdain for the classical and formal were shared by two generations of philosophers, poets, novelists, and historians and became the source of persistent tradition (in the writings of Michelet, T. Carlyle, and F. Parkman) in Western culture. Nor was the early German romanticist Johann Gottfried von Herder (1744 – 1803) primarily a historian, but his *Outlines of a Philosophy of the History of Man* portrayed all life as an organic unity and history as the continuous education of humankind. A little later, Friedrich Karl von Savigny (1779 – 1861) reached far back into medieval law to reveal how, through continuous development, the past had led to the present. The ideas of Herder and Savigny were harbingers of much future historical narrative and historiography.

The adherents of the French Revolution of 1789, believing in its principles and in their own classical Roman virtues, wrote tracts, memoirs, and histories to praise or defend what happened (or what they thought had happened) and what they had done. Their opponents, often Romanticists, believing that the revolution was a crime that broke with tradition and violated the organic unity of society, attacked its principles through appeal to historical precedent.

New historical experience necessitates new interpretations of history. The demand for a new history (the telling of a new "story") is most urgent in times of rapid and far-reaching social and political change. The age of the French Revolution was just such a period, and a man who achieved a new understanding of history in that age was Edmund Burke (1729 – 1797). Burke was a Whig who desired to preserve the values that had been established by the conservative English Revolution of 1688 and that were obviously jeopardized by the success of the radical French Revolution of 1789. To understand those values, as enshrined in such institutions as Parliament itself, was to understand their history, and this carried Burke's study back into the time of their beginnings in the Middle Ages. In its turn, this meant seeing the Middle Ages with new eyes: what had been for Gibbon "the rubbish of the Dark Ages" became for the new historians (adversaries of the revolution) the cradle of European civilization. The rediscovery of the Middle Ages now became one of the most exciting enterprises of the Romantic Age.

The word "Gothic" ceased to be an epithet of abuse (not only in architecture), and novelists, painters, church builders, and railway architects were soon vying with historians in re-creating the "enchantments of the Middle Age." The verdicts of Enlightenment historiographers had to be revised because the perspective of a new age had focused the attention of historians upon materials that hitherto only the antiquarians had turned to. Through the centuries a sense of real historical development had been born. Henceforth historians were to become increasingly aware that their task consisted not in the creation of an "ultimate history," (the final settlement or interpretation of all questions concerning the past), and not even primarily in discovering new "facts," but in the never-ending task of the reappraisal of past history in the light of new experience. (During the nineteenth century the constant reappraisal of the French Revolution itself was a compulsive preoccupation of historians.)

Both the revolutionaries and their adversaries searched diligently for justification of their ideas and for the origins of their nations and national institutions. Out of revolution and reaction, Romanticism and nationalism, arose unprecedented concern for historical study. History would become the mark of the nineteenth century as philosophy had been for the eighteenth. Historiography, in the eighteenth century, was rarely connected with universities; however, from the early nineteenth century, it began to develop in a radically different way. The organized teaching of history in schools and universities became a matter of national importance, first in Prussia and then in other parts of Germany. As universal education spread to most European countries in the course of the nineteenth century, history was an obligatory subject in schools. For the first time the bulk of historical writing came to be done by professional historians, for whom it became a condition of securing academic appointments or of consolidating their standing as university professors. Historiography became an increasingly cooperative enterprise. The achievements of past historians could be used systematically by their successors.

The new historiography of the nineteenth century was created chiefly by the Germans, who, in reaction to the ungodly and iconoclastic Enlightenment, extolled the uniqueness of their fatherland through the whole course of German history. These developments in German historiography derived, in part, from the writings of Johann Gottfried von Herder. Herder denied that the purpose of history was to trace the progress of the human mind; it was, rather, to reconstruct history as it had been. This meant that all countries and periods of history were equally deserving of study. This view anticipated the aim of Leopold von Ranke (1795 – 1886) to describe what has actually happened and his conviction that the description of all human history displays the workings of God's providence.

Ranke believed that from history one has the duty of judging the past, to serve the needs of the world for instruction concerning the future. Ranke aspired to more than just reconstruction of the past. A Prussian patriot, he was also a Protestant idealist who professed to see the workings of God in history. Through careful research on and intuitive contemplation of unique events, Ranke wanted to write universal history, history that would have meaning for all humankind. Through his numerous students and use of the seminar method (from 1830), Ranke began modern historical study. He emphasized research in manuscripts and documents (not just the reading of earlier historians). His superlative students spread his doctrines. The Ranke school prided itself on the scientific precision of its methods, on its determination to get all the facts right, and on the scrupulous quotation of sources. Ranke and his disciples assumed that they were writing presuppositionless history in which the facts were speaking for themselves. Ranke presided over the vast and thorough historical enterprise of searching out the facts and presenting them in an objectively scientific form, the form of "ultimate history," free from all bias and presupposition. The Rankean view of history was characterized by Lord Acton as something that was detached from the questions on which persons differ— religion, politics, philosophy, literature.[3] It was a laying-out of a story on which all persons and all parties can form what judgments they like when they have read it, but they will not be able to dispute the facts themselves. The science of history deals with what must be true for all interpreters.

The nationalism formulated in Hegel's philosophy and dramatized by Bismarck's triumphs led many German historians of the Ranke school to compromise their scientific detachment by becoming the protagonists of Prussian patriotism. They eulogized the Hohenzollerns, proclaimed the historic necessity of a German empire and the mission of Prussia, the most perfect state, to create a German fatherland that would become the highest expression of human reason, an ideal political system. The Prussian school included Friedrich Dahlmann (1785–1860), Maximilian Duncker (1811–1886), Johann Gustav Droysen (1808–1884), Heinrich von Sybel (1817–1895), and Heinrich von Treitschke (1834–1896). The defeat in 1848 of the German aspiration to national unity inspired Ranke's student Wilhelm von Giesebrecht (1814–1889) to write the history of the medieval German empire to remind his countrymen of their past glories. While Ranke presided over historiography in Germany, the Bismarck myth was born; the historians were making history in the twentieth century in the very act of writing history in the nineteenth.

Friedrich Meinecke, born in 1862, was brought up in the tradition of Ranke and became its historian; he occupied Ranke's chair at Berlin from 1914 – 1928. He criticized Ranke's tradition of scientific history ("Historismus"), asserting that historical reality cannot be apprehended by a method that leaves out value (especially political and ethical). Meinecke did not believe that the historian could write presuppositionless history. The historian serves others by making the past useful for the present. In his *Die deutsche Katastrophe* (1946), Meinecke affirmed that the events of recent German history profoundly affected our understanding of the historian's task, more particularly concerning his responsibility to society for the story he tells. The historical myths of the superiority of Aryans and the Third Reich as the bulwark against Communism were not overthrown in the German mind by historians, but by events. Furthermore, it was not merely historical myths that were destroyed: a theory about the nature of historiography itself, the view of scientific history to which all orthodox historians, with few exceptions, had subscribed for a hundred years, was discredited. As the searching reappraisal of German history since 1945 has demonstrated, it is not merely a new history (a new story or myth) that is demanded, but a responsible, new historiography, one that takes account of human values and does not open the door to demogogues by assuming that historians, being scientists, are not to be concerned about moral issues.

Reappraisals of history are generally undertaken with the deepest sense of urgency following periods of radical historical change. As far back as 1921 Carl Becker had written that, when times are out of joint, historians will be disposed to cross-examine the past to find out why it did not usher in a better state of affairs—approving or disapproving in the light of present discontents. The past is a screen upon which each generation projects its vision of the future, and so long as hope springs in the human breast, the "new history" will be a recurring phenomenon.[4]

What would be the new image of Germany and its history that would follow upon World War II? How is the postwar generation of historians to discharge its responsibility to society? Behind this question debated by German historians since "the catastrophe" lies the more fundamental question of the nature of historiography, the storytelling of historians. One quotation suffices to illustrate some of the lines of approach discussed; it is taken from the Swiss historian Walther Hofer (b.1920):

Though concealed in the conception of history is the notion

that we have in our mind a picture of the historical past, the theory of historiography has long since recognized that we should not take "picture" here in the sense of faithful copy of the past. Naive historical realism, according to which something like recognition of an historical object "in itself" (*an sich*) is possible, has long since been overcome. The picture that we form of the past must not be compared to a photograph but to a painting. And, just as we can see a landscape only from a given place, similarly all historical vision is determined by that place from which we view it. It means seeing in *perspective.* Broadly conceived, a historical problem, therefore, is always a question by the present to the past. Hence, in point of fact the questioner's interest and principle of selection, and in the final analysis his value system and his ideology, are decisive factors in the definition of the question. An understanding of history is never achieved by cognition without prior assumptions, but with understanding of specific assumptions. Only when these assumptions enter into our calculations as conditions can we speak of historical objectivity.[5]

The experience of the present lies behind the activity of the historian. Every generation must write history afresh in the light of its own experience and interests. The ideas of Charles Darwin (1809 – 1882) on evolution, for example, combined with those of Henry Thomas Buckle (1821 – 1862) on progress, provided a new basis for the selection, organization, and interpretation of facts. Not all historians read Darwin and Buckle, but the views they held became part of the intellectual climate and the conceptual systems of historians: evolution, the influence of environment in shaping persons and societies, the probability that the human family, through science and education, would make great progress in development. Human transformation and development became a key concern of the "new history" that took definite form in the decade of the 1880s. It stressed scientific method, exhaustive research, and the production of analytical, monographic studies.

The historian is more than a collector of data and an examiner of documents. He or she is a narrator who tells where and when who (persons, peoples) did what (public life, external acts) to enjoy what success, suffer what reverses, exert what influence (basic history). In their special histories, historians tell of movements whether cultural (language, art, religion, literature), institutional (family, mores, society, education, state, law, church, sect, economy, technology), or doctrinal (mathematics, natural science, human science, philosophy, history, theology).[6] They express their understanding of the past from their perspective of the present and their orientation to the future ("The past is prologue"). Historiography represents our attempt to grasp our historical experience. It represents persons who believe in the sense that they cannot have before their eyes the realities of which they speak; they depend on one another's critically evaluated work and participate in an ongoing collaboration for the advance of knowledge. A historian's value judgments make his or her work a selection of things that are worth knowing, even though such judgments are not his or her specialty.

Although recovering the past as it actually was had been the ideal of historians, its full realization is impossible because the surviving records, especially of ancient times, are scanty; the records of modern times, though partial and incomplete, are so vast that historians can but sample them; the records were created by persons who may or may not give an accurate, but never do give a full account of a happening; historians themselves are conditioned by their times and the biases of their culture; and historians cannot, even imaginatively, fully transport themselves out of their own present into the lives of persons in earlier times, for they acted and thought in ways partly beyond historians' comprehension. Historians seek to recover as much of what happened as they are able, but they cannot fully recover the past. What can be known of the past is always less than what happened, as the knowledge reflects both the incomplete and faulty nature of the records as well as the limitations of the historian. What is thought about the past may be more than persons of the past had recognized as significant. The historian attempts to make the past meaningful to himself, his readers, or his students and seeks answers to questions arising out of his own culture, questions that earlier persons of different cultures could not have asked or answered. The problems of historiographers reflect those of all hearers and tellers of stories.

The establishment of the Communist regime in Russia led, at first, to the rejection of most pre-1917 history as a fit subject for schools and universities. This decision was reversed in the 1930s, and from 1945 Communist countries were encouraging a form of historiography especially concerned with economic history and the class struggles of the past. The subordination of historical study to the ends of the Party involves the assumption that the Soviet period in world history is something new and apart from the past, while springing from it, and that each act of the Party reilluminates the past while serving the future. Objectivity in the Western sense was denounced in 1946 by Andrei Zhdanov, a member of the Politburo. He held that politics was the true function of historiographers.

Karl Marx (1818 – 1883) and his conception of history challenge every other view of history. Marx was not only interested in understanding history, he was equally desirous of shaping it. He brought the concept of social dynamics, a desire to use history for certain ends, to his systems. Marxism became under his guiding genius an amalgam: the inverted idealism of Hegel, the empiricism of Voltaire, the positivism of Comte (French philosopher, 1798 – 1857), and his own intense practical interest in the uses of history.

Marx believed that the only real influence that existed in human history was economics. No serious historian since Marx has been able to ignore the economic influence upon the course of history. More than a system of conceiving history, Marxism is a faith in the inexorable processes of history, in the certainty of the ultimate term of history in the socialist reality. It reminds us that the achievements of historiography express the basic faith of the historiographer. There is no telling of a story, at any level, apart from the teller's convictions about ultimate reality. Historiography derives from the historiographer's meaning system, from his or her set of underlying convictions about the ultimate nature of reality. Histories symbolize our interpretation of our historical experience; they implicitly transmit our meaning system for coping with the complexity of the human condition. Marxist and Christian historiographies are, implicitly, confessions of conflicting faiths.

To be a historian is to accept the challenges of history, to be committed to an interpretation of history that is based on our decision and action in the present and our hopes for the future. Historical interpretations (myths or stories) are not "read off" from the records of the past, but are chosen by persons in the light of their present experience and their determination to shape the future. Each person is free to choose to be what he or she is and to believe what he or she believes, though he or she is never wholly free of conditioning factors. To assert that all interpretations of historical experience (histories, stories) are equally subjective is to assert that moral experience is an illusion and that no way of life is better than another. All persons are challenged by their historical experience to commit themselves to moral (intellectual, religious) decision and action; all are responsible for the stories (historiographies, life stories, etc.) they choose to make their own. We find ourselves active participants in the life stories of many others. We are addressed and challenged by our historical experience of others and their stories to become more than mere spectators or detached observers. Our basic faith seeks to find, compose, and communicate the narrative quality of our response to this challenge. Our life stories, no less than our historiography and other forms of narrative, "tell" our response and reveal our basic faith. Our life stories, together with the various forms of stories that we choose to tell, symbolize our basic faith and hope.

1. R. L. P. Milburn, *Early Christian Interpretations of History*, Brampton Lectures of 1952 (New York: Harper & Bros., 1954), p. 92.

2. G. P. Gooch, *History and Historians in the Nineteenth Century* (London: Longmans, Green and Co., 1958), pp. 12f.

3. See Herbert Butterfield, *Man on His Past* (Cambridge: Cambridge University Press, 1955), p. 94. This view, sometimes called scientific history, is also called technical history. *Ibid.*, pp. 137 – 141.

4. In a review in the *American Historical Review*, 26 (July 1921), of H. G. Wells' *Outline of History* (1920), a rationalist piece of propaganda history aimed (not unsuccessfully) at the younger generation.

5. Walther Hofer, "Towards a Revision of the German Concept of History," in Hans Kohn, ed., *German History: Some New German Views* (London: George Allen and Unwin, 1954), p. 188.

6. Bernard Lonergan, *Method in Theology* (London: Darton, Longman & Todd, 1971), p. 128.

CHAPTER 2

The Work of Symbolizers: A Literary Propaedeutic to a Theology of Storytelling*

Historiography, like all storytelling, is implicitly autobiographical and biographical. Suetonius *is* in his *Lives of the Caesars*. Machiavelli, no less than his hero, Cesare Borgia, is in *The Prince*. The narrators are in their narratives about others, just as others are in their narratives about themselves.

It was Tertullian (c.150 – c.230) who coined the phrase, *anima naturaliter christiana*. This means that in the innermost depth of every human being there is alive a sort of natural religion with its standards of true and false, good and evil; it means that we are preprogramed to a sense of wonder and awe before the mystery of our existence and meaning within the universe.

Literature implies this basic truth of our openness to the transcendent when our dreams are seen to surpass both our personal resources and those of our society for their attainment, yet dream we must. In fact, our dreams may become more real for us than any other reality of our historical condition, bearing witness to that reality that underlies human awareness and, nevertheless, transcends human definition.

Sometimes the dream is associated with madness when a person tragically deluded and mistaken about the meaning of his or her life, destroys himself or herself in an attempt to force reality to conform to the shape of illusions. There is a profound pathos in a person's faithful response to a destructive illusion, to the wrong dream; even this, however, is perhaps better than no dream at all. In any case, literature reveals much about humankind and the quality of our dream; it reveals how we and our society can be transformed for better or for worse by them.

We live by our dreams and hopes, defining ourselves by our expectations. Hope is the force and power behind the dreams that influence our lives, whether at the personal or at the social and political level. There is hope in the possibility of realizing the

---

* For a more ample treatment of this subject, see the preface to John Navone's *Everyman's Odyssey* (Rome: Gregorian University Press, 1974), pp. 11–18.

dream, in the power of the dream, when realized, to transform and fulfill our lives. Dreams give concrete expression to hope, and are ultimately judged by that hope. If the dream fails to satisfy that hope, if hope stretches beyond the dream, then the dream is rejected by the very hope that first brought it into being. It is shown to be an illusion, a false dream.

Literature (and drama) is one of the many means that we have created for communicating our dreams. Expressing our experience of the world around us and of the world within us, literature (and drama) is a form of myth, embracing the many-sidedness of humans, revealing the simultaneous disparity and coherence of that which ought to be. However implicitly, literature communicates the experience of what the writer believes to be most real in the world.

Significant literature inevitably reflects our odyssey through time in which we search for answers to the mystery of our existence. It may invite us to experience a new way of living, of becoming a new person with a new horizon. It may lead us to experience a type of personal completion through a higher vision of reality.

Everyman's odyssey seeks the fulfillment of a dream for some kind of personal integrity: the writer expresses this in the symbols and categories of his or her cultural milieu, creating myths (stories) for his or her time.

Myth is a tissue of symbolism clothing the mystery of everyman's odyssey. There are mythic qualities in any world view because the ultimate mystery of human living is never completely accessible to discursive reason. There are cultural, psychological, and spiritual realities that underlie myth and that have fascinated many scholars. Their theories recognize myth as a symbolic expression of truths about human life and thought; they have noted the parallels between myths and dreams and have seen in them projections of, or objectifications of, our inner strivings and desires. Myths, they conclude, express our understanding of our basic self-others-world-Mystery relationship. We identify ourselves through the myths (stories) that we have made our own.

According to modern scientific research, myth is not merely a story told but a reality lived; it is not an idle tale, but an active force in human living. It not only represents a vital meaning and value for people, but also gives a cultural and social coherence to a people whose unity would disintegrate with the loss of a common mythological heritage of foundational stories. Myth expresses the experience of what is most sacred and preeminently real in the lives of individuals and societies. Through our mythmaking (story-telling) we express our feelings and concerns about our position in a mysterious universe. Mystery is a given. It raises questions that our mythmaking is forever attempting to answer. Involvement in a story characterizes all human life.

The existentialist philosophers affirm that myth is closely related to the question of finding a personal identity or of gaining that self-understanding inherent in our very mode of existence. Together with modern literature, their works express an awareness of the tensions and paradoxes that are constitutive of our being as persons who know in themselves freedom, finitude, guilt, hope, and the imminence of death. In different ways, both philosophers and authors of literature (dramatists) wrestle with the mystery of our existence and try to find answers to its apparent contradictions: the theories of the former and the myths of the latter focus on the paradox of the human person as one who, according to Alexander Pope's *Essay on Man,* is "in doubt to deem himself a god or beast."

Literature (and drama) express in a mythic way what philosophy attempts to express scientifically. Both are concerned with the mystery of existence, finitude, love, and truth. Both deal with problems arising out of the very structure of human existence, with the self-questioning that underlies our quest for personal integrity and the fulfillment of our deepest aspirations.

From the standpoint of Rollo May, we cannot live without myth. May asserts that myth is an expression of our self-consciousness. Myths reveal our capacity to transcend the immediate concrete situation and to see life in terms of "the possible." This capacity is one aspect of our experiencing ourselves as human subjects having a world. Through myths with a transcendent meaning, May believes that society furnishes its members with symbols that enable them to overcome the normal crises of life.[1] The powerful truth of the Gospel story of the crucified and risen Jesus has given persons of Christian faith the courage to live through such crises without succumbing to despair.

From the standpoint of anthropology, the death awareness expressed in myth is a basic constituent of our being that marks us from the animal. The theologian might interpret this awareness as the eschatological character of myth. The awareness of living in face of the end is not primarily a question of speculations about the end of the world; rather, it concerns attempts to find some framework of meaning within which to set the transience and mortality of human existence. It implies a certain realization that we already have an ineluctable relationship to death. Our existence is inevitably related to the mystery of death, the end of our historical odyssey.

The truth or falsity of the dream the writer (or dramatist) clothes in myth is a question implicitly treated by Michael Novak in his essay, "Philosophy of Fiction," where he states that falsity occurs with the presentation of a viewpoint that is no more than a rationalization, or that shows only the most superficial penetration.[2] Only persons can judge personal authenticity. The truth or falsity of the author's world view and concept of self-fulfillment is not judged as directly as the truth or falsity of a scientific theory, for they are established at a level prior to science. The truth or falsity of the dream is verified in living one's own life: live in the horizon of the writer and see how it meets the tests of life.

The dream or hope or image of fulfillment that a literary work implies would, for Novak, not so much describe the human condition so that we can look into and see ourselves; rather, it invites us to enter into a new horizon. It re-creates the standpoint and furnishes the pointers by which we live through a way of conceiving our lives. The writer is not so much interested in articulating his or her experience as in living through it by means of his or her artifact. A writer is interested in the skillful re-creation of an experience within a certain horizon, so that readers (or audience) may likewise experience it within his or her mythmaking or storytelling. Unlike the philosopher, who tries to speak about experience in a system of propositions, the writer of literature re-creates the horizon of the self within which his or her own search for personal integrity occurs. What the writer depicts is less the exterior world than his or her own inner reality and reaction to what is most important in life.

Literature implicitly spells out different ways in which we seek wholeness and dignity. By the same token, it implies the different ways in which we hope to avoid meaninglessness and disintegration. The narratives of literature symbolize how we define ourselves by whatever we are seeking, whether the goal be simply insight of a human kind or some transcendent ideal such as peace. They remind us that, whatever we are seeking, we cannot help taking certain attitudes and forming certain judgments that imply a dream, a vision, a concept of and a search for wholeness. Such attitudes are "theological" in the broadest sense of the word inasmuch as they imply that there is more to ourselves and to our images, symbols, and stories than meets the eye. They imply this whether there is any explicit awareness of the need for suprahuman aid in the achievement of personal fulfillment or not.

Literature symbolizes an author's reaction to his or her own historical experience. It implies what is most sacred to him or her: what is of genuine value and what is specious in the quest for the fulfillment of the author's own deepest desires. A work of literature embodies the author's vision of human fulfillment according to which persons are judged fortunate or unfortunate, admirable or contemptible, reasonable or absurd, human or less than human. The failure to give substance to this vision will—from the standpoint of the author—be rooted in some flaw that reveals something of human insufficiency. The flaw need not be fatal. Without the possibility of healing, there would be no myth (drama or story). The healing of the flaw may be seen in purely human terms or in terms of divine assistance. It is the possibility of such healing that grounds the hope pervading the search for whatever one is seeking. The author's story discloses the quality of his or her dreams and hopes.

Arthur Miller, for example, symbolizes his reaction to his society in his play *The Death of a Salesman*. He indicts society for its failure to provide its members with a worthy vision of life. Willy Loman has the wrong dream (hopes, ideals), and is destroyed by it. His dream is associated with the belief in untrammeled individualism and with the worship of success. Willy is profoundly incapable of warding off the shame and suffering that derive from a vision of life that he cannot make work. The competition of the business world is too much for him. The pressures of a success-oriented society, wherein respect must be constantly earned by endless achievements, eventually drive him out of his mind. In such a society, where respect is never gratuitously bestowed on anyone, failure is unbearable. To be successful comes to mean that a person is loved and approved; to fail is to find oneself alone and not worthy of love and attention. The "phony dream" of success, the ideal of Willy's society, not only makes Willy peculiarly vulnerable to suffering and eventually madness; it finally leads him to suicide.

The myths (stories) of drama and literature symbolize the dreams of the times the religious and moral leaders—like the Bible's Joseph in Egypt—seek to interpret. It is important to discern what is of genuine value and what is illusory because the wrong dream may destroy a person and a society. Literature expresses and reveals a basic stance, attitude, orientation to decision and action. It both evokes and is evoked by our feelings for our basic self-others-Mystery relationship. Inasmuch as feelings are an orientation to decision and action, no author can evade the responsibility for symbol-forging activity. Symbolizing can be symbol evoking with regard to the influence on other human lives. The affectivity and aggressiveness that storytellers and mythmakers elicit raise the question of responsibility.

If a symbol is an image of an object that evokes feeling, narrators are symbolizers of themselves and others. Their stories, implicitly or explicitly, express their felt images of themselves and others. When these images communicate a feeling for the sacred, they function as sacraments.

Persons (life stories) act as symbols when their lives affect us. Leaders are symbolizers of profoundly felt values for their followers. A sacrament symbolizes the sacred: an apprehension of the supreme goodness of God. When lives of persons communicate a sense of the sacred, their symbolizing is that of a sacrament.

When Paul addresses Christians as saints, he is calling them to make their lives sacraments of the supreme goodness of God for others. Christian authenticity is a matter of symbolizing the goodness of the sacred as revealed in Jesus Christ and his community of faith and hope. This does not mean that the goodness of God that is sacramentally symbolized in Jesus Christ and his followers will be recognized and accepted. One must know a language to recognize and follow it. One must be in touch with the sacred through religious conversion to be aware of it in others who are living as God's sacraments. Such living, Christians believe, is participating in God's life as revealed and transmitted in Jesus Christ. This is infinitely more than merely imitating Jesus or acquiring values.

Literature expresses our vision of our basic self-others-God relationship. Human subjects generate autobiographies, biographies, histories, and the stories of literature. We project our basic relationship in all these narrative forms. To the extent that the supreme goodness of God is a felt experience in our lives, our narrative forms will inevitably express it: they will be sacraments.

1. Rollo May, *Symbolism in Religion and Literature* (New York: George Braziller, Inc., 1961).
2. Michael Novak, "Philosophy of Fiction," *Christian Scholar* 47 (1964), p. 109.

CHAPTER 3

Memories Make the Future: A Philosophical Propaedeutic to a Theology of Storytelling*

Remembering is essential to the life of the people of God.[1] Commemoration is a Christian obligation: "Do this in commemoration of me" (Lk. 22:19). The eucharistic celebration reenacts Christ's sacrifice and actively expresses the Church's remembering: "This is my body which shall be given up for you; do this in remembrance of me" (1 Cor. 11:24).

Through faith, Christians share the same memories, the same history. Their sacred memories unite them as a people. For the people of God the way of recalling the past is essential for its continued existence as a community.[2] The future of the Church is promising because it remembers a past of promises: "Anyone who does eat my flesh and drink my blood has eternal life, and I shall raise him up on the last day" (Jn. 6:54). Memories make the future. Only he or she can anticipate the wonderful works of the Lord, the *magnalia Dei*, who remembers them; if they are not already a part of our history, they cannot be seen as a part of our future. We share in the life of the Church, the people of God, if we share its memories. We belong to a chosen people only if we remember that God has chosen us; we live in a promised land only if we remember that God had promised it. To forget this, to view the past in a different way, is to have a different history; it would be to separate ourselves from the Church and its future in the fulfillment of the promises made to it. The cohesion of the people of God perdures in shared historical memories created and sustained by faith.

There is a sense in which our memories possess us and determine what we are. An immigrant coming to the United States, for example, has really become an American when he or she inadvertently remarks, "In 1776 *we* defeated the British." This new way of remembering the past indicates that he or she has become different: he or she has become an American because he or she now shares the

---

* With the exception of footnotes 5 and 7 and the sections on Sassoon and the British budget film—the work of Thomas Cooper—this chapter is taken from John Navone, *A Theology of Failure* (New York: The Paulist Press, 1974), chap. 6.

memories of the American people. Similarly, Abraham becomes the father of all who, after the Spirit, share in his faith (Mt. 3:9; Lk. 13:16; 16:24, 19:9; Acts 13:26; Rom. 11:1; Gal. 3:29), whereas his sons and daughters according to the flesh may be disinherited (Mt. 8:11 – 12; Jn. 8:39). Even though the ancestors of most Christians had nothing to do with the history of the Hebrew people, they have all been incorporated into it through their faith in and adhesion to Christ. The God of Israel "swore an oath" with Abraham, sealed with promises (Lk. 1:73; Acts 7:5 – 6), and Christians are the "children of the promise" (Gal. 4:28) and its proper heirs (Gal. 3:29). Their God is the "God of Abraham" (Mk. 12:26; Acts 7:32). This same God acts on behalf of Christians; he has "glorified his servant Jesus" (Acts 3:13). Abraham is an essential part of Christian history: "Merely by belonging to Christ you are the posterity of Abraham, the heirs he was promised" (Gal. 3:26).

Existentialist insights into history help us to understand what it means to have sacred memories and lead us directly into the heart of history as a constituent of human life. Both Gabriel Marcel and Martin Heidegger have written about the meaning of care within the economy of man's existence. Historians who care about history organize their material around principles and events, persons and crises they are interested in. Historical time is structured. For Heidegger history takes its start not from the present nor from what is real only today, but from the future. The selection of what is to be an object of history is made by the historian, in whom history arises. *Humankind organizes its past around the direction of its future.* This insight into the nature of the historian's craft has obvious implications for the way in which the people of God recall their sacred memories in terms of the *eschaton* and the second coming. The eucharistic commemoration is forward looking: "*Until the Lord comes*, therefore, every time you eat this bread and drink this cup, you are proclaiming his death . . ." (1 Cor. 11:26).

Psychiatry illustrates the Heideggerian insights into time in a way that deepens our appreciation of our sacred history and liturgical commemoration.[3] The existential analyst notes that a sign of mental deterioration and psychic trauma is the patient's inability to organize the past. Even though the patient is often aware of what actually happened and capable of giving an objective account of his or her life, he or she cannot select the important and ignore the trivial; she or he can record only with a monotonous accuracy. The patient's past has become a chaos because she or he has no future, no direction, no will to live. Time shrivels to the spatial limits of the hospital cell so that real time has departed from the patient's life, and she or he is tyrannized by all-limiting space. A condition for sanity is the capacity to organize the past in the direction of the intentional thrust toward the future, a thrust that is not added to humankind but that constitutes each one of us as the unique being that each is. If Israel's past made sense in the light of its present under God, pointing toward a future that would transcend history, so too does the past of every sane person receive its significance in the light of his or her present, which, like an arrow, is aimed at the future. An aimless life is not a human life; it cannot be.

Conversion illustrates Heidegger's insight into historical time. What was once little more than a chaos of circumstance and events, the bucket of ashes that the secular mind denominates as the past, suddenly coalesces and stiffens into a unity for the man or woman blessed with the gift of faith. All sorts of random events now take on a new meaning in which they are understood as having led this person to this supreme moment in which he or she has received the grace of God. The grace itself is a call to his or her future, which gives meaning to his or her past and unifies life into a significant whole. Our hopes, motives, and ideals stir us into action; they create our style of life, giving meaning and direction to our past.[4]

We will find in the past whatever we seek for the future. If what we seek is trivial, the past we discover will be trivial. If what we seek is noble, what we find will be splendidly human. Thus the Christian, seeking his or her divinization with and in the risen Christ at the second coming and the beatific vision of God, finds a past that is sacred, marvelously transcending the purely human with its wonderful works of the Lord, the *magnalia Dei*. The Christian is tending toward the gift of God; consequently, his or her past is also the gift of God, a sacred memory of divine interventions in his or her history. The divine gift has made the Christian capable of having this kind of history, of finding this meaning for his or her past. In our liturgical remembering, we recognize both our past and our future as the gift of God, anticipating the resurrection of the just in Christ and the beatific vision.

Through remembering the past we can transcend failure. We are what we will to remember, and our memories make the future. Among some there is an ineluctable tendency to cherish only the ugliest elements that the past can offer. No degree of courtesy, friendliness, or any other form of positive change in a formerly unpleasant relationship outweighs their bitter memories because the past they choose to remember blinds them to any good the present might offer. Their minds have become frozen with a past vision of wickedness, and the goodness or beauty of the present will remain eternally inaccessible to them.

For example, what some Germans did several decades ago becomes the basis for suspecting all Germans today. And anti-Semites are often blinded by the same principle: what a few Jews did to Christ many centuries ago blinds them to the fact that Jesus was a Jew. Thus the past becomes the basis for an overriding hate-memory directed against all Jews in every age.[5] Likewise, anti-Christian feeling among Jews has been based on the same type of hate-memory, on what some "Christians" have done to Jews. Where there is a will to hate, there is a way to sufficient evidence for hating any group. History is full of hate-evidence for those who want it, and it continues to poison human relationships with distrust through the centuries.

Hate-memories perpetuate evils and human failures. The tendency to abstract only the worst of German history has produced a general apathy over German reunification. The bigot begins with the aprioristic conviction that Germans are not to be trusted and concludes that German reunification is undesirable. The bigot's security depends upon the weakness of the "untrustworthy." The evidence of the past proves for this simplistic mind that Germans are basically dangerous—in fact, *the* basically dangerous people. It never occurs to such a mind that its vision is limited to the worst elements of German history. Were such a mind to approach French and British history, in the same way, it would undoubtedly be forced to the same conclusion: the French and British are dangerous and cannot be trusted. In the poem "At the Cenotaph," prophetically published in 1933, the English poet Siegfried Sassoon, who had fought in the trenches in the First World War, beautifully summed up the dangers of the mind suffused by hate-memories. In his poem he sees Satan standing with bared head by the Cenotaph, the British national war memorial in Whitehall:

> Unostentatious and respectful, there
> He stood, and offered up the following prayer.
>   "Make them forget, O Lord, what this Memorial
>   Means; their discredited ideas revive;
>   Breed new belief that War is purgatorial
>   Proof of the pride and power of being alive;
>   Men's biologic urge to readjust
>   The map of Europe, Lord of Hosts, increase;

> Lift up their hearts in large destructive lust;
>   And crown their heads with blind vindictive Peace.''
> The Prince of Darkness to the Cenotaph
> Bowed. As he walked away I heard him laugh.[6]

The hate-memory focuses on the worst of any nation's or group's past as a rationalization for the incapacity to love others. It is a rationalization for the inability to create personal friendship with peoples of different races, religions, classes, and nations. It takes the form of the one-word definition, the unnuanced viewpoint, perpetuating hatreds for centuries and misery for millions. For this mind, German means Nazi, Italian means Mafia, Christian means pogrom, Jew means deicide, middle class means hypocrisy, Southerner means racist, Negro or black means crime, Catholic means poor and prolific, and Protestant means conservative. Friendship requires a personal creative power and effort. This is not something that just happens. The hate-memory absolves one of this responsibility.

The hate-memory also absolves one from the responsibility of accepting the possibilities for guilt in one's own life. The hated person becomes a dustbin or garbage can in which one can jettison the unacceptable parts of one's own lacking in what it takes to be fully human. A small budget film made in Britain, *It Happened Here*, is instructive in this regard. The basic story was that Hitler's invasion plans had succeeded and the Germans had invaded Britain in 1940. The film charted the history of occupied Britain: German troops guarded Buckingham Palace, British collaborators denounced British Jews, wholesome English girls—"English roses"—dressed in the uniform of the British Red Cross administered lethal injections in euthanasia clinics. The main film distributors and the television companies considered that the film was so disturbing to the British myth of indomitable courage—the "Dunkirk spirit"—that they refused to screen it. Where it was shown, to small audiences, it was largely received as a pleasant fantasy. The images of SS Troops goose-stepping in Trafalgar Square were a pleasant fantasy.[7]

When the film was shown in Hamburg, however, the audience reaction was so hostile that the police had to be called and the film withdrawn. Because of a diet of British and American war films where Errol Flynn and John Wayne win the war single-handedly, the caricatures of German soldiers were not seemingly offensive to the audience, so removed were they from reality. In *It Happened*

Here the German audience was more aware than the British audience that it could indeed happen here, whereas the British audiences knew that it had not happened; it was "only a film." The realistic portrayal of the nice girl next door behaving in such a nasty fashion was a different story from that of the usual unrealistic British-American myth.

When times are out of joint, men and women will be especially disposed to cross-examine the past to discover why it did not usher in a better state of affairs. The past is a kind of screen upon which each generation projects its vision of the future. Historians, for example, were creating the history of the twentieth century in the very act of writing history in the nineteenth century. Similarly, each generation's judgment of the past expresses an attitude existing in the present and perduring in the future. Consequently, if the past is merely a collection of hatreds, the future can promise nothing more than the perpetuation of these hatreds. In this way, our vision of the past, whether it be our own personal past or the history of other groups, nations, races, and religions, adumbrates the quality of our individual or collective future. Every woman and every man and every society are therefore responsible to future generations for the way in which the past is viewed. To remember only the crimes of others is to prepare a future of vendettas, reprisals, and recriminations or, at best, of tranquil hostility.

The character and humanity of the martyred Jews of our time merit far greater emphasis than the depravity of those who killed them. They died as men and women with faces, men and women who preserved their character and identity at the price of death. Had they been less gifted, less remarkable, less distinguishable from the mediocrity surrounding them, this would never have happened to them. Inhuman perversity will martyr only the godlike, because they are in their very being and existence a reproach to mediocrity. The perverse Cain murdered his brother "simply for this reason, that his own life was evil and his brother lived a good life" (1 Jn. 3:12). It would be tragic to forget six million martyrs only to immortalize the hatred of those who killed them. In remembering the tragedy of those times we should never dwell upon the memory of the evildoer's deeds lest the image of God in which even the evildoer was created and which can never entirely be extinguished should be profaned.

In the long run, to immortalize the hatred would only be to perpetuate its destructive power. What deserves remembrance is the humanity of those who suffered. If for Christians and Jews alike a martyr is one who dies giving witness to the one true God of all, then the six million are the martyrs of our time. For if, as we believe, the very identity of the Jewish people consists in their being the people of the Messiah, then, in some way, the six million killed for no other reason than their identity as Jews died giving witness to the one true God and his Messiah. They are the people whom God has "identified," chosen, called into being. Like the Messiah, they were falsely accused and killed without cause. In reverencing them we reverence not only the image of our common Father, the One Who Is (Yahweh) for Jew and Christian alike, but we reverence also the likeness of the one who sprang from them and whom we Christians believe God has made both Lord and Christ.

Like the Messiah whom Christians accept, they were killed because of what they were, because of their identity. They died, therefore, because of their witness to the God who had identified them as his people. And their deaths, in turn, bore witness to the one true God who, as Paul tells us, still identifies them as his people and who will never turn his face from those whom he has eternally chosen (Rom. 11).

Perhaps it is truer to say that women and men are martyred because they are saints, rather than to say that they become saints because they were martyred. They are hated, tortured, persecuted, and killed because of that to which they give witness. Saints are not what the world wants, but what the world needs. The only sound way of remembering the past is a positive, constructive, human way—a way in which we may construct a far-more-human future for ourselves and future generations. Hate-memories will cease to produce their lethal results only when we have the good will to learn a new way of remembering, the way the people of God recall their martyrs and those who killed them. The deeply Christian way of remembering the martyrs (and their tormenters) is by sharing on earth the banquet of thanksgiving that they share already in the Kingdom; by celebrating the mass in their honor. This is the way of the Spirit of God within the Church and within the heart of every man and woman of good will. It is a way of remembering—a way that wills to recall and to immortalize only what was, is, and forever shall be lovable.

1. God remembers certain persons and shows them his grace and mercy (Gen. 8:1; 19:29; 30:22; Ex. 32:13; 1 Sam. 1:11, 19; 25:31). God's remembering is an efficacious and creative event, which enables humankind to remember God.
2. Deuteronomy especially develops a theology of remembering (Dt. 5:15; 7:18; 8:2, 18; 9:7; 15:15; 16:3, 12; 24:18, 20, 22; 32:7). Israel should especially remember its trials in

Egypt (Dt. 15:15; 16:12; 24:18, 20, 22) and should learn a new obedience and trust from them and avoid disobedience and arrogance.

3. *Anamnesis* (recollection or recalling to memory) is a technical term in both eucharistic theology and psychiatry.

4. The importance of the future is studied by N. Cohn in *The Pursuit of the Millenium: Revolutionary Messianism in Medieval and Reformation Europe and Its Bearing on Modern Totalitarian Movements* (New York: Harper & Row, 1961). If we believe that the future of an act (the images, visions, heavens, and all forms of perfect commonwealth) determines, along with the past, how we act in the present, then we ought to study visions of the future, as we do those in which we "recapture" the past. As Mannheim made clear, a Utopian as much as a conservative style of thought affects how we act. And as Dewey and Mead taught, we envision a future to make action in a present possible. Although each present has its future, there are few histories of these futures. Cohn's book indicates how much could be gained from the study of future visions of ideal societies.

5. On anti-Semitism in Christian theology, see Charlotte Klein, *Anti-Judaism in Christian Theology* (London: S.P.C.K., 1978). The bigoted anti-Semitic mind, of course, conveniently overlooks the part played by the goyim in encompassing the death of Christ. Pilate was no Jew, and the Christ-baiters in the Praetorium were Romans. By a curious psychological defense mechanism many Christians are willing to accept solidarity with a Jew, accepting that his death has saved us, while rejecting solidarity with Jews "who killed him." As several people remarked to one of the present authors after he had given a series of homilies on the Jewish background of Jesus: "Why do you pretend that the Jews could have something to teach us? We're Catholics!" The same phenomenon can be observed in reactions to Genesis; that Adam's sin can be transmitted to the rest of us is felt to be unfair, but no one ever questions the fairness of the Second Adam (Christ) giving his life for the rest of us.

6. From "At the Cenotaph" from *Collected Poems* by Siegfried Sassoon. Copyright 1918, 1920 by E. P. Dutton & Co.; copyright 1936, 1946, 1947, 1948 by Siegfried Sassoon. Reprinted by permission of Viking Penguin Inc.

7. It is interesting in this regard to note the large audience ratings achieved in recent years by a popular soap opera on British television whose subject was the German occupation of the Channel Islands, the only British soil to be occupied by the Nazis. By and large the British were portrayed as gentle, ordinary people heroically suffering. The Germans were either evil or ineffective bumblers.

PART TWO

Nine Moments in the
Theology of Story

A PHENOMENOLOGY OF STORYTELLING

THE FIRST MOMENT

Human beings are the subjects of their stories

There can be no stories unless someone tells them. They would never be told unless there was someone to listen. *Cor ad cor loquitur*; heart speaks to heart, or subject speaks to subject. In this moment we discover the human subject in his or her telling of and listening to stories. We tell not so much of things unknown as of things that bring home the familiar; ultimately, our appeal is to the common facts of human experience. Like the Delphic oracle, this moment seeks to aid each reader to know himself or herself; by nature we are all of us tellers of stories.

1.1 *People are storytelling animals.*

Common experience shows that men and women delight in the telling of stories. Children demand a bedtime story. Fishermen tell stories of the catches they have made, veterans of the battles they have fought, travelers of the lands they have seen. The elderly tell all who will listen the tales of their youth, of what it was like to live in such bygone days. A lover tells a beloved the story of his or her life before they met. The contents of our television screens are largely made up of stories: the fictional stories of cops battling with robbers; cowboys with Indians; husbands with wives; the factual stories of the newscasts and the "in-depth" documentary.

Traditionally man was defined as *zoon logikon*, as an animal endowed with reason. Today, as Bernard Lonergan has argued, man is more concretely defined as a symbolic animal.[1] Prior to what might be termed the posterior logos of scientific understanding and scholarly writing, there is the prior logos of narrative discourse. People tell stories of the creation of the world long before they

begin to construct a mathematical physics. Speech, the articulation of words (*logos*), is that which distinguishes humankind from
all other species. Insofar as the logos of story precedes the logos of
theoretical discourse, the *zoon logikon* of Greek philosophy may be
translated as storytelling animal.

At the root of both prior and posterior logos, the word as narrative and the word as theorem, lies a pure and unrestricted wonder.
Thus the philosopher, that is every theoretician, is related to the
storyteller in that he must be *philomythes, amator fabulae.*[2] The
daytime child tires adult companions by unceasing questioning.
The questions concern concept-formation: What is it? From the
questions *Quid sit?* there proceed questions for judgment: *An sit?*
At night, before the loss of waking consciousness, the child asks for
a story. Inchoatively the child is raising these latter questions. Stories of trolls and people-eating tigers, of wolves dressed as grand-
mothers, and giants who live above beanstalks all take place "once
upon a time," *in illo tempore,* and in faraway places, *illo loco,* and
not in the here and now of a warm and cosy bed. The stories of
frightening times and dreadful happenings circumscribe the bed
with a barrier over which the evil spirits may not cross. They allow
the child to affirm, albeit unself-consciously, that the here and now
is safe, that he or she is not vulnerable to unknown and hostile
forces. In a word, the stories we tell our children at bedtime exor-
cise the unknown so that the known may be affirmed as safe and
good. At the same time they invite further exploration in that they
suggest that reality, the here and now world of the child, does not
exhaust the possibilities of what may be the case.[3]

The roots of story lie in that wonder that Aristotle posited as
underlying the manifold differentiations of intellectual consciousness, in that which Scholasticism termed the natural light of the
intellect. Thus, as Hillman rightly observes, economic, scientific,
and historical explanations are all different sorts of story.[4] If the
ability to relate and to listen to stories were to atrophy, it would be
because the wonder that grounds all knowing, the dynamism that
leads from perception to understanding to judgment to decision,
had evaporated. Story is constitutive of consciousness; it is definitive of what a human being is.[5]

1.2 *People are storymaking animals.*

The fact that men and women tell stories does not exhaust the
"storicity" of the human animal. Men and women make stories as

well as tell them. They are responsible for the stories they tell. Where knowing is an extroversion to the already-out-there-now real, where what is real is what can be seen, felt, tasted, heard, and smelled, finding the story to tell becomes a matter of looking in a book. We tell other peoples' stories. Only if the story I hear is recognized as my story do I become responsible for the story I tell. In such a case *illo tempore* becomes my time; *illo loco* becomes my place. Eliade speaks of the "Great Time," *illud tempus,* where the deeds of gods and heroes take place. The telling of the stories of that time, *illius temporis,* brings them into the here and now of my time.[6] The traditional beginning of each Gospel pericope with the words *"in illo tempore"* brought the events that happened not "once upon a time" but in the time "when Pontius Pilate was governor of Judea, Herod, tetrarch of Galilee, his brother Philip, tetrarch of the lands of Ituraea and Trachonitis" (Lk. 3:1 – 2) into relation not with all time, understood as an abstraction or as a time outside of time, other time, but with the time of every succeeding generation. Where knowing is taking a look, so that revelation, the Word of God, becomes that which is contained in the Book, as occurs in Fundamentalism, the story of God's deeds becomes the story of things that happened *illo tempore,* the once-upon-a-time-out-there-then, instead of a story that is happening here and now. Thus there arises the problem of the search for the personal Savior.

In the words of Carl Jung, "the bridge from dogma to the inner experience of the individual has broken down."[7] As a consequence, men and women look back to another time, the *illo tempore* of childhood, to provide for them the experience they cannot experience for themselves. Whence arises the propensity for sentimentality, the illegitimate idealization of the childish? Humans cannot live in the already-out-there-now-reality, the world of extroverted, animal consciousness, forever. If the *chairos,* the call to conversion, is refused; if the pleasure principle is not transcended by the reality principle; if the first naivete is not sublated by a critical exigency that grounds a second naivete; if the phantasm is not so much returned to as never left; then the child in the adult cries out to his or her long-lost mother to "tell me the old, old story." The Sankey and Moody telling of that old, old story remains a telling but never becomes a making since it evokes the memories of the telling of the story in childhood and not the making of that story in and through the life of its hearer. The sentimental telling of the story ensures that the old rugged Cross stays securely upon its hill, where it can be looked at out-there-then, rather than being made a reality in the heart.

Where, on the contrary, revelation is conceived as a disclosure that occurs *"in iudicio intellectus prophetae,"*[8] so that what is required is not a telling of the story in the words of Paul or John, but a making of the story as John and Paul in their own way believed and lived and made it,[9] then there occurs not only a telling but also a making of the story. A bridge is thrown across from dogma to the inner experience so that in the telling (Haggadah) of the story in every single generation a man can so "regard himself as if he had gone forth from Egypt."[10] The story is only truly told where it is also made.

1.3 *The self is conscious of itself as the subject of a verb.*

Verbs are the foundation blocks of speech. Meaning can be expressed by verbs alone. *"Veni, vidi, vici"* is a perfectly grammatical sentence. It is composed entirely of verbs. Although the first word articulated by a baby may be mama or dada, both of which are names or substantives, the infant has already expressed himself or herself in the nonarticulated verbs of crying, screaming, chuckling. "I hurt," "I hunger," "I need," "I am content" are the meaning of these primary sounds.

Because the first articulated words are names, there is a tendency to reify the world, to believe that all words refer to things. Consequently, people have feelings but no longer feel, have thoughts but no longer think, have wishes but no longer wish. At a further stage the feelings, thoughts, and wishes take on a life of their own. A bad feeling came on me; a thought came into my head; I am the prey of my evil desires. Grammatically, the feelings, thoughts, desires are now the subjects of the sentences. The person has become an object even to himself or herself. Consciousness is then confused with a looking back upon oneself, a reflexive turning of the mind's eye to look upon the self as an object distinct from the looker. Thus am I made an alien to myself. I become, as it were, a theater in which things happen to a me that is not truly I.

In the fully human act I experience myself, as Cardinal Wojtyla has argued, as an acting person. I am conscious of myself as an actor, as the subject of a verb, of the act as being my act for which I am responsible.[11] I am conscious of acting though my knowledge of what it is that acts, as opposed to who it is who acts, that is, my knowledge of myself, is known through understanding not the subject of the acts but the acts themselves. The self is conscious of itself as the subject of a verb; the self knows what the self must be by attending to the verbs of which it is the subject, by understanding those verbs and by judging that they are indeed the case.

Verbs are intrinsically narrative. "I came, I saw, I conquered" is the story told by Caesar. "I came from the Father . . . and now I leave the world to go to the Father. I am going away, and shall return" (Jn. 16:28; 14:28) is the story told by Christ. Who is Caesar? He is the one who came and saw and conquered. Who is Christ? He is the one who came, who comes, who will come. What is a Jew? He or she is one who has come through the Red Sea. What is a Christian? He or she is one who has come through the waters of baptism. I am consciously a subject and knowingly a self. Thus we can say that:

1.31 **The self is a particular agent that is known and revealed in its life story.**

Agents are known in their activities; they are defined by their life stories. As subject I am present to myself. I am conscious that I am typing these words. I know from memory that it was I who typed the previous sentence. To know the self I must know the manifold acts or verbs of which I was, or am, or will be the subject. Since no one act can exhaust the possibilities of acting, to know the self requires that one know the successive acts or verbs of which one is the subject. Persons, therefore, are agents whom we know through the story of which they are the subject. Unlike concepts, their definition is not to be found in dictionaries. The life of every person, or agent, tells a story. Persons make decisions and act; to act is to be the author of a life story, to declare one's identity, meaning, and role. The basic faith of a person is manifested in the decisions and actions that tell his or her life story. What a person believes to be of ultimate meaning and value motivates the action that tells the story. Life stories reveal their authors: how they see the world in which they live, who they think they are, and what they actually care about.

1.311 **Every human (life) story shares the three temporal dimensions of past, present, and future, which are respectively called to mind by memory, awareness, and anticipation.**

From the present in which our stories are told we reach into our past by memories and into our future by anticipations. Besides our individual memories, we enjoy the shared memories of the group, which we celebrate in song and story, and which we preserve in written narratives, in monuments, and in every other trace of the group's tradition. Our anticipations are not only the prospective objects of our hopes and our fears and our desires but also the carefully considered estimates that we have based on our experience or the rigorously calculated forecasts of applied science. The meaning of the human (life) story that we call to mind by memory, awareness, and anticipation may be lost respectively by forgetfulness, ignorance, and despair. Individuals and groups may forget their true story; they may ignore its present meaning, the true meaning they ought to know; they may despair of its true possibilities for any ultimate meaning or value. The past, present, and future must be truly called to mind and held together for the sake of our integrity and authenticity and sanity. We cannot reject any one of these dimensions without impairing the truth and unity of the human story, the story of each of us, of the Church, and of the world.[12]

Each teller of the Christian story is newly created in Christ "to live the good life as from the beginning he had meant us to live it."[13] By telling my story I make myself what (and who) I am. I am responsible for the shaping of my life story. Only insofar as I am responsible for what I make of my story may my storytelling be judged ethically or morally. Storytelling is a *poiesis*, a making. Customarily, moral and ethical behavior has been classed with artistic production as an activity of the practical reason. Insofar as there is an artistry of living, an analogy between the "art of loving" (and all authentic living is loving) and the art of making pictures, verses, plays, artifacts, novels, music, and the like, thus far we may find in the canons of literary criticism clues to the way in which we should make moral judgments and conceive moral and ethical principles. Moral philosophy and moral theology are illuminated by a comparison with literary criticism.[14]

Ethical and religious principles are derived from human life stories that have come to term in ethical and religious excellence. Human maturity, intellectual, psychological, moral, and religious—the excellence of the "finished product"—is the norm for judging what it is that should characterize the process that constitutes an authentically good life story. The meaning of human life stories is disclosed in their term or conclusion: that which made the story good for its author to tell. Individual details in a painting and individual incidents in a novel or play must be judged in the context of the whole work; likewise, the individual actions of a person's life must be judged in the context of his or her whole life story.

Human freedom shapes both the process and the term of human stories, even though it is always a limited or finite freedom. The *poiema* of our life story is coauthored by two authors: the human subject and God. Authors (and human subjects of life stories) are free within limits to choose and shape the stories they make their own. Inevitably, they are in search of an ending. That search for an ending constitutes the process of human storytelling with respect to both the parts (phases, episodes, stages, chapters) and the whole of a story. Turning points, conversions, and shifts of the storyteller's horizon represent endings and new beginnings within the whole process of telling a story.

Mark's Gospel is called "The *beginning* of the story of how Jesus Christ, the Son of God, brought the good news to humankind" (cf. 1:1), with the implication that the story is still in the process of being told by those who accept it as their own; that the story has not yet reached its conclusion or ultimate fulfillment. The story that God has begun in Jesus Christ and in his Church culminates with the fulfillment of the universal story and the resurrection of the just.

In some plays and novels the central character is so conceived that his or her name becomes the name of the whole play or novel. *Hamlet* is not the story only of the Prince of Denmark but of Polonius, Ophelia, Rosencrantz, Guildenstern, and others. Hamlet is both a man and a story made up of the stories of other men and women. In a somewhat analogous fashion, the story of Jesus Christ is both the story of a rabbi from Nazareth and the stories of other women and men. His name becomes the name of a whole story.[15] The stories of Polonius and Ophelia, of Banquo and Malcolm, of Goneril, Regan, and Cordelia are told only because of their relation to Hamlet, Macbeth, or Lear. Every human life story, insofar as it is related to Jesus of Nazareth, becomes not the individual story of Tom or Dick or Harry or of Mary, Alice, or Jane but the story of the Whole Christ. The story of Hamlet or Lear becomes the pattern for the stories of the lesser characters insofar as without the central character Shakespeare would not have bothered to invent a supporting cast. Even more so does the story of Jesus become the pattern of all other stories. In Jesus of Nazareth the universal story of humankind is present in the story of a human individual. Newman wrote of "the glory and beauty of His (Christ's) eternal excellence," and Manigne compares the Incarnation to a work of art in that the totality of meaning becomes present in contingence, not by diminishing the contingency, but by making this contingency totally meaningful.[16] The excellence of Christ's story becomes the norm and pattern and vision of what human excellence can and should be.

1.312 *The meaning of (life) stories is seen from the end.*

The meaning of a process emerges and is grasped when it reaches its conclusion. Histories are written by those who know the end of a process of growth and development (or of decay and dissolution) and can thus see the significance of the beginning from the end. All historical interpretation necessarily involves the seeing of the significance of the beginning from the end. The wisdom or the unwisdom of decisions is seen at the term of the process they initiated. The outcome of a process manifests its meaning. The conclusion of a human life story provides the ultimate context for its interpretation. There can be no final judgment about a story until all the evidence is in.

1.3121 *Human stories involve both a process (promise) and a term (fulfillment).*

Human stories are incomplete or unfinished without their conclusions; they are not properly stories until they have reached their endings. The wholeness of the story is achieved in its culmination. To be the author of a story is to originate a process that must be brought to completion. By starting to tell a story the author implicitly promises to bring it to its fulfillment or term. The story of Jesus Christ expresses the Christian understanding of the divine author's intention for the process and term of all human life stories. Jesus Christ is the divine author's intention made visible; he is the revelation of God's promise to bring all human stories to their ultimate fulfillment.

In his letter to the Ephesians, Paul makes use of aesthetic categories when he speaks of Christians as being God's work of art (*poiema;* 2:10).

1.3122 *The beginning of a human story is the promise of its ending or fulfillment.*

"In my beginning is my end," wrote Eliot, "time future (is) contained in time past."[17] Promise and fulfillment find their counterparts in the beginning and the ending of every story. The resolution of a piece of music is already contained in the body of the piece: if the melody were to be resolved in a different way or a different key, it would usually be the resolution not of this melody but of another. It is the musical genius who can resolve a tune in a totally unexpected and surprising way while at the same time satisfying us. The composer of such a resolution surprises us by finding an unexpected way of resolving, a resolution that is as much contained in the melody as the one we were expecting.[18] To begin telling a story is implicitly to promise to bring it to a conclusion. A storyteller betrays his or her listeners if he or she leaves the tale unfinished. A musician once described hell as the perfect performance of a Bach fugue where the Devil shouted *"da capo!"* at the end of the penultimate bar. When we fail to complete a story—as happens, for example, when a joke falls flat because we forget or mangle the punch line—the lack of an appropriate ending is itself a kind of ending that can be distinguished from fulfillment. No story that is told in time goes on forever; inevitably it has an ending.

Every human life story promises an ending from the moment of its beginning. When a man or woman "dies before his or her time," we say that a life has been cut short. The young poet killed in war or the brilliant young scholar struck down by cancer is said to have been taken before his or her promise had, to human eyes at least, been fulfilled. The ending that appears unsatisfactory to human eyes, the promise that seems unfulfilled, may in God's sight be a startling fulfillment. From one point of view, the death of Christ is a death "before his time," but from the viewpoint of faith it is a death "in the fullness of time." Not every human story ends with the hero (usually with a heroine) living happily ever after; the ending may be what J. R. R. Tolkien called a eucatastrophe, the revelation of God's power brought to perfection in human weakness.[19] The short and humanly unfulfilled life of a child born seriously handicapped or the tragedy of the young person taken in the springtime of promise, can be the quasi-sacramental sign of a special conformity to the Passover mystery of Christ. In one of his letters to the Christians of Thessalonica, Paul told his listeners to comfort their mourning brothers and sisters with words of faith in the Resurrection of Jesus.[20] To the ear of faith the Word spoken becomes the declarative form that effects the matter of physical death into the sign of Christ's loving and abiding presence. A young child of eight lost his father through death. Later, as a young adult he faced, with the help of Jungian analysis, his previously unacknowledged feelings of resentment and loss. Later still he came to realize that the early loss of his father had been instrumental in making him who he was. His reaction to the early chapters of his life story had shaped and molded his subsequent storytelling. He was brought, as a thirty-year-old, to the place where he could publicly give thanks to the gracious purpose of God in taking his father to himself. Like Francis Thompson in *Ode to the Setting Sun,* he was able to

> . . . give thanks even for those griefs in me,
> The restless windward stirring of whose feather
> Prove them the brood of immortality.

The end lies in the beginning. The depth psychologist pays attention to the traumas and events of childhood. Many trace the events of later life to their roots in the process of being born. Genius, like that of Mozart or Einstein, often shows itself early. The Gospel of Luke gives us an infancy narrative where the later history of the child is prefigured in the opening chapters of the story. The ending to which each storyteller brings his or her own life story is not inevitably the fulfillment of the promise with which he or she started. Stories can fall flat. The narrator may lose the thread of the narrative, may give disproportionate attention to one or another element in the story so that the whole goes out of focus, can lose heart or lose interest and give up speaking altogether. The story may lack all resolution and, unless it is taken up by the Cross of Jesus and finished by God, as it were, from "notes that the author left," it may come to an ending that leaves the listener wondering whether the story had had any meaning at all. Hell is the refusal to give meaning to our stories.

Some stories are left unresolved because they are written to be completed and resolved by a further narrative. *Paradise Lost* is resolved by *Paradise Regained.* Some stories are, in their own terms, resolved but attain a higher resolution in their sequel. The Gospel of Luke is satisfactorily resolved by the disciples returning to the Temple (Lk. 24:53). Luke's Gospel as the story of a journey to Jerusalem is satisfactorily resolved by Christ's arrival and death in that city and by his disciples returning there from the outskirts of Bethany. There is no need to read on further; the movement of the Gospel is complete. From the perspective of Acts, however, the apostolic sojourn in the temple appears not as a goal but as a starting point from which they have to break away. The early pages of Acts appear to relate a number of false starts, each one followed by a return to the temple (cf. 2:46; 3:1; 5:12, 25, 42). Even after they have been taken from the temple by the summons of the Sanhedrin, they return to the temple. Even though a bitter persecution breaks out in Jerusalem (8:1) so that Christ's disciples have to flee to other places (8:4), still Luke shows them as returning back to the temple from which they came (8:25). It is only with the revelation of Christ to the chief persecutor, Saul, and Peter's satisfying the Jerusalem Church about the authenticity of his dream (11:18) that the narrative begins to show a definitive movement from Jerusalem and its temple into a mission that will reach to the ends of the earth. Acts can be seen as a story that undoes the resolution of the story told by Luke's Gospel and resolves it in a "higher key" by leading the reader into a deeper appreciation of the story of Christ. Analogously we may conceive the story that is told in eternity. Human life stories (fully or partially resolved in earthly terms) are resolved in a fulfillment that is not static (all earthly stories come to an end and lapse into silence) but dynamic: a fulfillment that completely satisfies while it leads on into an ever-deeper acceptance of the mystery of God.

1.3123 *We organize our storymaking around the conclusion that we have chosen for our stories, or around what we believe must be their conclusion.*

Writers commonly write their forewords or prefaces after their book has been written. The writer of detective stories scatters clues throughout the course of the narrative intending to resolve them in the book's dénouement. Unless the author of a thriller knows who the murderer will be, he or she will fail to scatter the correct clues that mystify the reader during the course of the story but are believable once the ending is known. If Shakespeare had not already decided that Macduff's mother had had a cesarean and that he would attack the castle at Dunsinane, the apparitions in the witches' cavern would never have been written. The prophecy of act 4 presupposes the ending of act 5. Like the stories told in books and plays, the stories told by our lives are shaped in large measure by the ending we envision for them.

It is the vision of a completed book selling well in the shops that encourages writers to study the material, shape the discourse, and put their thoughts together. If the writer is convinced that the book will not get written, the book will not get written. The idea of living in a beautiful home with affectionate children or of being footloose and fancy free will explicitly or implicitly affect our choice of a life partner or our decision to live without one. How we expect our life to turn out largely shapes the way we attempt to live it. Comedies are anticipations of happy endings; tragedies anticipate tragic endings. Viktor E. Frankl, writing of his experience in the death camps of Germany, tells us that men and women "can only live by looking to the future—*sub specie aeternitatis.*"[21] He tells the story of those prisoners who had lost faith in the future, men and women who could no longer envision a happy ending. This loss of faith in the future, usually happened quite suddenly and exhibited recognizable symptoms. Frankl tells the story of a man who in February 1945 dreamed that liberation would come on March 30.

> When F—— told me about his dream, he was still full of hope and convinced that the voice of his dream would be right. But as the promised day drew nearer, the war news which reached our camp made it appear very unlikely that we would be free on the promised date. On March 29, F—— suddenly became ill and ran a high temperature. On March 30, the day his prophecy had told him that the war and suffering would be over for him, he became delirious and lost consciousness. On March 31, he was dead. To all outward appearances, he had died of typhus.[22]

The prisoner had lost hope in a happy outcome for his story and started to live (and die) accordingly. Although the terminology in such a context might appear strange or unfeeling, rightly understood we might say that the prisoner's changed expectation of what would be the ending had moved him from the comic to the tragic mood of living.

People who expect a trivial outcome to their lives will live in a trivial fashion. Anticipating a trivial ending trivializes the story. If we tell our children that "Baby Jesus died on the Cross because he was kind to little children," then we are trivializing the awesomeness of the *kenosis* of our God. It has been said that much of the popular conception of morality among Catholics has been a case of believing that God might damn a person for all eternity where a hanging judge in a human court would give the person only twenty years. The story preserved in the eighth chapter of John's Gospel about the adulterous woman reveals the *Judex venturus* as more merciful than the judgments of human legalities. The unjust are not judged by Christ but stand judged already by their failure to live authentically according to his word (cf. John 12:47f). To believe that one is cut off from the eucharistic banquet because one has swallowed a peanut when one should have been fasting is to bear witness not to the holiness of God, nor to the inexorableness of his demands, but to the shallowness of one's conceptions of God's justice and forgiveness. To believe in the frequency and quasi-inevitability of mortal sins is a trivialization of sin and, ultimately, an almost blasphemous trivialization of God and the death his Son died. The chronic anxiety and scrupulosity exhibited by a narrow legalism, where it does not stem from psychopathological causes beyond the individual's present control, can often be a symptom of a refusal to accept the possibility of the presence of real evil in our life.

A schoolteacher with responsibility for the religious education of more than a hundred children was an alcoholic who physically battered her husband and made the lives of her own children miserable. On the eve of temporarily being detained in a drug-addiction unit, she spontaneously abreacted her birth trauma while confessing, under the influence of a great deal of alcohol, to the great sin of her life: as a teenager she had occasionally masturbated. The alcoholic, oral satisfaction compensated for the pain of fearing eternal damnation. In her preparation of children for first confession and Communion she habitually exhibited a trivialized picture of God and Redemption. The children were taught that eating ice cream within an hour of mass would make Baby Jesus have a cold head, that doing handstands in the playground was sinful because passers-by might see their knickers, and that failing to kneel upright during mass was a mortal sin. Any attempt to suggest a more adult conception of God met with furious resistance. Her whole lifestyle and her religious teaching suggested an almost systematic trivialization of the Gospel message. By inventing a tyrannical God, a screen idol on which she could project her own fears of growing up and taking responsibility for her lifestory, she had succeeded in creating a rigid "religious" system she secretly despised. Christ's Cross, for her, was a salvation from infantile peccadilloes; her own responsibility for the ravages caused by anger and alcohol in her family was totally denied. In her own eyes she was a victim of circumstance.

The trivialization of sin and therefore of Redemption as a defense mechanism against admitting the depth of what Jung called the shadow can be seen in the case of the adulterous husband. A priest was called to a house where the husband had gone beserk. Maddened with drink he had returned from the house of his mistress, physically broken up the matrimonial home, and caused grievous bodily harm to his wife. Arriving to find the wife bloodstained and battered and the furniture broken beyond repair, the priest remonstrated with the husband. The husband looked amazed: "Father, it is not me you should condemn but my wife. She uses contraceptives." By trivializing the redemptive death of Jesus, by expecting the rewards and the punishments associated with infantile transgression of not yet understood and therefore arbitrary rules, we succeed in trivializing the demands of God's righteousness and shut out his healing power from the areas of our life that need it most. In psychotherapy an analogous situation appears when we systematically denigrate the therapist's understanding and methods and, by expecting that we will not get better, ensure that we do not. Conversely, the saints who have the highest expectations of God are those who most readily admit the reality of their sinfulness, and the patients who are nearest being healed are those who most fully accept responsibility for the shadows of their personality. Shallow gods have shallow religions, and trivial endings are preceded by trivial stories.

1.4 *The art of storytelling expresses the art of living.*

Human stories express their authors' way of being in the world and of relating to it. They imply the extent to which an author has mastered the art of living attentively, intelligently, reasonably and responsibly, courageously, compassionately, generously, and in love with God and neighbor. The human stories of individuals, communities, societies, and nations disclose their way or art of living. They belong to human persons who, individually or collectively, are responsible for their way of being in the world and of freely relating to it. In this respect, human persons are the authors of their life stories, the subjects of their appropriated life stories in autobiographies, biographies, histories, legends, and other narratives. More profoundly, human persons are coauthors of their stories, working them out in a grace-filled world where they are necessarily answering or resisting the call of their Creator no matter how implicitly it is experienced. Their life stories are the historical shape that their response to this call assumes; consequently, they are coauthored. Their stories are called forth from beginning to end by Eternal Life; they imply the art of living in response to that call.

1.41 A condition for sanity is the ability to tell our stories.

Psychotherapeutic treatments usually start with an anamnesis of the patient's history. Freudian psychoanalysis in large part requires the patient to tell his or her story. Though the patient's understanding of his or her own subjectivity may be erroneous and the behavior neurotic and irresponsible, nevertheless he or she can give some narrative account of his or her life. Catatonia, severe schizophrenia, is often if not always associated with an inability to tell any story at all. In the terms of narrative ability, the difference between neurosis and psychosis (granted that the division of mental states signified by these terms is open to question and that the varieties of mental dysfunction are perhaps best conceived as points on a continuum) might be expressed as the difference between telling a story badly and being unable to tell one at all.[23] In amnesias and fugue states the mind blots out those parts of its story that it neither wishes to tell nor acknowledge; in hysterias and paranoias the subject tells a story from the past as if it were in the present and the *dramatis personae* from one play are imported into a quite different drama; in schizoid neuroses the person refuses to tell his or her story to the assembled listeners and splits off the chapters that he or she does not like; and in the psychoses the narrative ability becomes impaired, bizarre, and in extreme cases, mute altogether. The ability to organize one's memories, present reality, and future expectations, the ability to experience one's self as the single subject of a continuous narrative, in short, the ability to tell one's story, is a sine qua non of mental health. The ability to tell some sort of story, however badly, is an essential condition for sanity; the ability to tell one's story truthfully and responsibly is an essential condition for mental and moral maturity and growth.

1.5 What human life stories mean to us depends on what kind of a person we are.

Our appreciating the values that others represent, our criticizing their defects, and allowing our living to be challenged by their words and deeds, depend on what kind of person we are. Our interpretation of stories depends on our self-understanding. The transformation of our self-understanding through conversion (intellectual, moral, psychological, and religious) modifies our understanding and appreciation of stories. We find and appreciate in them what fits into our horizon; we have little ability to notice what we have never understood. Our understanding and evaluation of stories (of persons as life stories or of narratives or histories) are self-revealing; the interpretation interprets the interpreter (ourselves). A true understanding and appreciation of the meaning of Jesus is self-revealing; for nobody can recognize the movement of the divine presence in the Son unless he or she is prepared for such recognition by the presence of the divine Father in himself or herself: "No one can come to me unless he is drawn by the Father who sent me" (Jn. 6:44). That prior drawing is a listening and learning with regard to the interior word that the Father speaks directly to the heart: "To hear the teaching of the Father, and to learn from it, is to come to me" (Jn. 6:45). The true meaning of Jesus is not revealed through information tendered by Jesus, but through a person's response to the fullness of the presence in Jesus of the same God by whose presence each believer is initially moved in his own existence. The external word of Jesus' preaching comes to us as a word we have already heard in our hearts. What the story of Jesus means to us entails the interplay of an inner faith and an outer belief, of gift and its outer expression.

A true story may clarify this. In a prison for young offenders, most of whom had received little if any religious formation, the chaplain was recounting the story of the Passion and death of Jesus. He had arrived at the point where Jesus was on trial before Pilate. At this moment the bell rang, calling the prisoners to lunch, and the chaplain announced that he would continue the story later in the week. At this one of the prisoners begged him to continue, remarking "Please don't leave us in suspense; we want to see whether he gets off." This young offender clearly identified with the spectacle of a man on trial. He had not previously heard the Jesus story. His attitude was of one who treated the business of courts and justice as a game, a kind of "cops and robbers," in which justice was irrelevant, if not a meaningless concept. The idea that a just and innocent man might be unjustly condemned was not shocking to him; he presumed it happened all the time. To be unjustly condemned was an acceptable hazard of playing the game. The young offender could identify with Christ the defendant in a criminal trial, but not, or so it seemed, with Christ the victim freely offering himself for the sins of humankind. Without the prior love of the

Redeemer as Redeemer, without a previous hearing of the wordless witness of God in the heart, the outward word of Christ's story remained on the level of a television courtroom drama.

1.51 **Human life stories are their own interpretation inasmuch as they are the product of the understanding that people have of themselves, their situation, their role, the human condition. The interpretation interprets the interpreter.**

Every person embodies an interpretation (vision) of God, the world, others, and himself or herself that is attained in the concreteness of experience and, in turn, is expressed at every level of one's being and becoming. The storyteller is in his or her story telling.

Both our life story and the stories we tell express the cognitive and affective reality of our inner being: the vision that permeates our thoughts, desires, interests, ideals, imagination, feelings, and body language. Life stories are the product of our world view, our sense of life, our basic faith, our way of grasping the complexity of life. Stories are interpretations that provide the evidence for our interpreting their authors. By their stories we shall know them.

1.52 **Of the symbols with which we spontaneously but uncritically express our life story, a privileged place is occupied by parental imagery.**

The patterns of perception and response laid down in infancy form a substrate of later-learned patterns. The interaction between parents and their offspring colors the later interactions between their offspring and other persons. Such interactions, though cognitive as well as affective, are always highly charged or affect laden. A baby, for instance, who is frequently left with his or her cries unanswered, particularly where the baby suffers transmarginal stress, will frequently in later life, even though if explicitly a Christian believer, have difficulty in believing that God cares and that there is any use in praying. Unanswered prayer in infancy tends to a decrease in expectation that any prayer will be answered. Parent-infant transactions that contribute to a disturbed capacity to form relationships will affect the relationships to all other persons, human or divine. From their testing of school children and adult religious, Godin and Hallez saw a relationship in the variable but crucial part played by the images formed of our parents and the formation of our images of God, at least in Western society, though the importance of such images tended to fade with age.[24] Our parental figures are the horizon in which we first take up a cognitive and an affective stance vis-à-vis reality. All subsequent confirmations or rejections of that stance are modifications of a first basic relationship with the world of truth and value.

> *1.521* **These spontaneous symbols, because they are sponta-neous, are in need of critical reflection.**

That which is spontaneous is that which is without critical reflec-tion. Without critical reflection there is no control over the mean-ing our life stories and the symbols that reflect them express. While we remain on the level of spontaneous living, responding to feelings as if they were perceptions, the symbols with which we sponta-neously express our life story will bear witness to the conflicting and contradictory values we spontaneously cherish. At the level of animal extroversion, where knowing is a kind of looking, the out-ward appearance of particular goods or values can hide or mask the real good or value. The child's questioning of value is a ques-tioning of the value *quoad nos* and not a questioning of value *quoad se.* "Is it good?" means "Is it good *for me?*" (See thesis 1.1 on p. 35.)

Consequently, the sum total of the things we value, the values we cherish, will be an admixture of real values apprehended and trea-sured as valuable, real values misapprehended and rejected as lacking in value, false values misapprehended and misvalued as true values, and false values apprehended and rejected as value-less. The symbols with which we spontaneously express our life story will, therefore, compound truth with falsehood and value with worthlessness. Hence there arises the kitsch symbolism with which there is expressed the kitsch values of a kitsch life story.

> *1.6* **Our storylistening prepares us for our storymaking: we are storylisteners before we become storytellers.**

We learn to speak by hearing others talk. Deafness impairs our ability to speak. James Hillman affirms that those who have not been told stories in childhood experience difficulty in telling their own stories in later life.[25] The masterpieces of classical Greek drama were the product of their authors' desire to retell the ancient myths and stories they had heard. The stories we hear in childhood shape the stories we tell as adults. Battered wives are most often the victims of child batterers grown up; they repeat the stories they have learned to tell. Without understanding we are condemned to repeat past (hi)stories. Who I am depends in large part upon who I am told I am. The creative freedom to shape my own self-identity, the ability to take responsibility for the story my life is telling, is a faculty that comes only with increasing maturity. The law allows no criminal responsibility to be imputed to a child; the child is able to repeat only the stories he or she has been told, to play out the scenes he or she has observed. Minors below a certain age are not allowed to marry; they have not yet attained an age where we may presume that they have the ability to take for themselves such a story-shaping decision. All countries have a minimum age for voting in an election; we may reasonably presume that people below that age have not yet attained the ability to take their part in the shaping of the nation's story. We must hear the myths of our community before we can shape the myths our children will hear.

We learn who we are through the stories we hear from our parents; and later, from the stories that teachers, companions, and other significant persons tell us about ourselves, about the world, and about God. We become aware of ourselves and of our being part of a community in the stories we hear. As storylisteners, we embark on our lifelong quest for our true story. We are storylisteners before becoming storytellers because we are affected by the stories lived and told by others before we become capable of putting together our own stories. Whatever stories we tell emerge from our conscious, affective, critical reaction to our experience of the stories in which we live and breathe.[26]

We tell our stories in the games we play. Eric Berne's transactional analysis depends upon the idea that in the games played out in adulthood we can sense the games and scenes of a childhood that should have been outgrown and transmuted. Children play at being grown up. When a child plays at keeping house, or plays at soldiers, or plays at saying mass, he or she is learning to tell the stories the adults around him or her are telling. It is a pedagogical mistake of the highest magnitude to talk down to children. If we tell them baby stories they will learn to tell baby stories; if we tell them adult stories they will grow in their ability to comprehend and to tell adult stories themselves.[27] Taking a child to the Trooping of the Color on Horseguards Parade will teach him or her more about England than a watered-down disquisition on the constitutional position of the queen. The child will thrill to the sound and sight of the marching troops as they march past the queen to salute her birthday and will probably enact the scene when playing at home. If the child is playing with friends there may well be a squabble as one or another insists on being the queen or the color subaltern or the colonel of the guard. The children are beginning to tell for themselves the stories they have heard.

A child of nonbelievers watched when he was four years old a Corpus Christi procession through the streets of his town. He saw the priest carrying the monstrance, a point of stillness in the midst of the bustle of the parade. Turning to his mother he said, "I want to be that man." In the ensuing weeks he played at Corpus Christi processions in the garden of his home. He knew nothing of the doctrine of the Eucharist and little about the person of Christ. Seventy or more years later, as a consultor at the Holy Office, he retold the story in the homily of his golden jubilee mass.

Modern catechetical methods rightly make use of every means that developmental and pedagogical psychology reveals as adapted to the mentality and capabilities of children. No one in his or her right senses would deliver a disquisition on Sabellianism to children. Nevertheless, it is equally a mistake to pitch the homily, the ceremonies, the prayers, and the rituals of a parish Sunday mass at a level falsely imagined as suitable for children. Children are the future generation of the Church. They need to see and hear the present generation of adult Christians "acting their age" so that they in turn may learn to enact the saving story of Christ. The stories from Shakespeare told by Charles and Mary Lamb are nowhere near so captivating for children as the plays themselves when they are acted with consummate mastery. The religious educator—whether he or she be the liturgical president, the parochial catechist, or the parent in the home—needs to achieve what Paul Ricoeur calls the second naiveté; having achieved a critical understanding of the Christ myth, he or she returns from the mountain of doctrines and systematics to retell in an intelligent, adult, and responsible way the myths, stories, and symbols that articulate the truth of the Story-made-flesh.

The early Apocryphal gospels are filled with charming stories of the Infant Jesus shaping birds of clay and making them fly by his almighty power. The God plays at being the child. Such gospels betray not only a superficial and unorthodox understanding of the Incarnation but also a mistaken understanding of the ways of children. The canonical Luke imagines the hidden life of Nazareth more truly than the Apocryphal Thomas when he places the child in the temple among the doctors of the Law. From what we know of children, it is more probable to imagine Jesus as playing at being a carpenter or a rabbi in the synagogue. A more authentic Christian midrash would be an image of Jesus the Child holding aloft in his play the Torah scroll as he had seen it held aloft by his elders in the Sabbath service. Luke records Jesus as proclaiming that he had come to set fire to the earth (Lk. 12:49); John's Gospel records Jesus as understanding himself to be the light of the world; Mary's weekly kindling of the Sabbath lights in the home at Nazareth must have impressed itself deeply on the mind and psyche of the child.[28] Jesus listened to the stories of his people before he himself preached to the House of Israel. Jesus listened to the story of Moses before he himself preached upon the mount. The Apocryphal gospels show us God playing at being a child; the Gospel of Luke hints at a Child who plays at being God.

The Christian life may be described as a continuous and lifelong process of reaching up to the mind of Christ. If the stories told by Christ and about Christ are bowdlerized and brought down to a supposedly child-oriented level they run the risk of becoming childish. The human being is born with a dynamic curiosity that unceasingly asks questions; the child reaches out spontaneously to learn and explore. An effective catechetics, like any effective education, must foster the spontaneous reaching out of the child so that he or she may have the mind of Christ and grow according to the measure of the maturity of the Son of God.

1.7 *There are two poles to the horizon of every story.*

The horizon metaphor links the subject and his or her world in a mutually defining relationship on the premise that what we know of the world is known only through consciousness, and we are conscious only through being in a world. Self and world exist in regard to each other only when united by a conscious act. The subject and its world do not exist for each other until they are consciously intended. One pole of our horizon is the range of all that we can experience, understand, evaluate, and do. The other pole is the subject of those activities of experiencing, understanding, evaluating, doing. Neither the objective nor the subjective pole can be attended to without reference to the other. Each pole is conditioned by the other, existing only in mutual relation. Neither pole can change separately without some influence from and on the other. The subjective pole (the knowing subject) is specified by the four activities of experiencing, understanding, evaluating, doing. The objective pole (the object known) is specified by the symbols through which those activities are given shape and effect, by the objectification or thematization of the meanings the subject has found. Cultural institutions, according to Michael Novak, ordinarily provide us with the symbols by which we shape our activities.[29] They are the creation of question-asking and symbol-making humans; they are objectifications of human self-understanding, implicit answers to the questions "Who are we?" or "What is our task?" and "How do we cooperate?" or "What is the story that we are acting out?" (See also thesis 3.11 on p. 94.)

1.8 *Human security is grounded in the stories we hear and tell.*

Frightened infants are calmed by a bedtime story. Stories of salvation, of rescue from hostile and unknown forces, speak to the profoundest depths of the human psyche. The stories we tell and the stories that are told to us express our self-understanding. Such a self-understanding may be that of freed men and women as told in the stories of Exodus, or it may be that of slaves and manipulated victims as told in the stories of juvenile delinquents. It is always a story that expresses our understanding of who we are, and that self-understanding, whether as individuals or as societies, grounds our sense of security. "I do not know who I am," that is, "I do not know what story to tell" is the classic cry of the insecure adolescent. The unknown terrifies. We are not secure with what we do not understand. Our views, our convictions, our very understanding of who we are, are undermined or built up by the stories we tell and hear. Instinctively, we welcome the human stories that affirm us, and we defend ourselves from those that threaten us.

We may build up for ourselves a false security. Where understanding fails and yet the need for security is overwhelming, we can make illegitimate and obscurantist appeals to the presence of mystery (where mystery is used as a *Deus ex machina* and not as pointing to a *Deus absconditus*), and to the authority of Church or party or state or scientific and cultural establishment. We need not only stories that affirm us as securely held but also stories that can liberate us from the false securities in which we imprison ourselves. The function of such stories is soteriological or liberating.

The parables of Jesus aimed at such liberation. To be without a story is to be unable to relate either to oneself, or to others or to the world or to God. We may name such a state of being without a story a state of pathological and radical insecurity. Anxiety and storylessness show themselves in the grim determination to hang on at whatever cost to the crumbs and fragments of story that we have and in the emotional and aggressive rejection of any story that threatens our precarious sense of having a story to tell.

Jesus and his adversaries, as portrayed in the Gospel accounts, had the security of their respective stories or self-understandings. A young man came one day to Jesus. His self-understanding as expressed in his own story was of one who had kept all the commandments from youth. He asked what more he needed to do, implying thereby that he was dissatisfied with his own storytelling. Jesus showed him a new story: "Go and sell what you own and give the money to the poor, and you will have treasure in heaven; then come, follow me" (Mt. 19:16ff).

Jesus' story threatened his own story. The story told by Jesus uncovered the hidden story of the young man's life; he was a wealthy man and had many possessions. The young man acknowledged himself to be a man who sought to be perfect and who had enjoyed spiritual success. Jesus' challenge to live a new story uncovered a conflicting value and a conflicting story in the young man's life. The thought of losing his possessions—the prospect of changing the subject of his story from a man secured by possessions to a man secured by the promise of the Kingdom—made him sad. He turned and went home; that is, he refused to change his life story by joining it to the life story of Jesus and hung on to the story that he had already outgrown but that gave him an illusion of security.

The stories of Jesus posed a threat to the stories told by his adversaries. If his security were true, then theirs was false or inadequate. The story that expressed their understanding of their basic self-others-world-God relationship was false. They dared ask him no more questions (Mt. 22:46) since his replies would threaten their own stories and thus their sense of security. In their fear of asking any more questions lay the urgency of their need to silence him forever by death. Dead men, as the proverb goes, tell no tales. Like Socrates before him and Dante after him, the teller of tales and the raiser of questions must be put to death or exiled lest the whole fabric of his hearers' world collapse about them.

> ### 1.81 **The movement from one stage of storytelling to another stage, accompanied by a threat to the subject's sense of security, is confirmed as a law of human development by the developmental psychologies of Erikson and Kohlberg.**[30]

Piaget discovered the importance of storytelling and story analysis for the understanding of moral development in human beings. Kohlberg further refined our understanding of moral development by identifying six stages of moral development, each one identifiable by studying the responses of children, adolescents, and adults to a series of specially constructed stories that expressed various possible modes of human behavior. By studying the agreement or disagreement of his subjects to the moral reasoning expressed by the stories, Kohlberg was able to identify the stages of moral development and the chronological ages where such stages are normally entered and transcended. According to Kohlberg every human being must, if he or she is to mature, pass from a stage in which the subject is the obedient or disobedient object of punishment to a stage in which the subject is engaged in what might be termed reciprocal self-seeking. From thence the subject passes to a conventional morality based on obtaining approbation as a "good boy" or "nice girl" and to a further stage usually described as "law and order morality." From thence the subject may transcend conventional morality by adhering to a social-contract understanding of ethical behavior, and finally he or she may achieve a state where one acknowledges the need to live by universal ethical principles.

Kohlberg affirms that every individual must pass successively through each lower stage before attaining a higher viewpoint, though any one individual's growth may be arrested at any one stage. He further affirms that one cannot comprehend moral reasoning at a stage more than one stage beyond one's own. Thus an adolescent orientated to being thought a fine fellow or a nice girl is simply incapable of real assent to the propositions of a postconventional, critically grounded moral philosophy. Finally, transition from one stage of moral understanding to another occurs, according to Kohlberg, by the creation of a state of cognitive disequilibrium. The subject's present stage of moral reasoning and understanding can no longer cope with the problems presented to it. The subject's self-understanding is threatened and shown to be inadequate by the new stories or situations he or she comes across.

The developmental psychologists are concerned not so much with the behavior of their subjects, with what they do, as with their understanding of their behavior, with what they think would be the right or wrong way to behave.[31] It is important perhaps at this point to stress that the inability to follow a chain of moral reasoning that is at a level several stages higher than one's own does not necessarily imply that a higher level of acting may not be symbolically appropriated and lived out by one whose moral reasoning is still at a lower level. If one may be in need of forgiveness for not knowing what one does (Lk. 23:34), one may also be in line for a reward though, like the sheep in Christ's parable, being unable to give an account of why one had deserved it. In some lectures Bernard Lonergan gave on the philosophy of education, he affirmed that in judging people morally one should not ask them what they think but rather see what they do.[32] The apparent conflict of methodologies between Lonergan and Kohlberg resolves itself when we advert to the symbolic, narrative quality of moral living.

"Don't do as I do; do as I say" may be the humble admission that one's performance falls short of one's ideals, or it may be a hypocritical letting of oneself off the hook. What one thinks about morality, in a theoretical and conceptual way, is not the sole criterion for assessing one's moral development. Conversely, Lonergan should not be understood as advocating a morality based only on the presence or absence of acceptable behavior. If such were the case, then the police state and the efficient use of drugs would be the ideal method of ensuring the moral development of all citizens. Lonergan rightly affirms that

> a person may be apprehending symbolically a very high morality, even though he seems to be apprehending nothing but the particular good; and he may be living according to a very high morality even though all his explicit thinking is concerned with particular goods . . .[33]

One may do the right thing for the wrong reasons.

Lonergan is affirming that what one does, how one acts, may be a surer guide to understanding the story that one's life is telling than what one explicitly believes to be the "moral" of one's tale. Just as the artist cannot always conceptually translate what he or she means by a painting, so the concrete human subject may live a life of heroic virtue without being able to pass an examination in moral or ascetical theology. Shakespeare's *Hamlet* was written by a man who knew nothing of the Oedipus complex. Two children were playing at "mummies and daddies" and the roles acted out in their play gave the unobserved watcher a startlingly accurate insight into the pathological dynamics of their parents' relationship. Brought up in a family where marital discord and violence were all but institutionalized, the two children knew, on the basis of the only pattern ever presented to them, the "appropriate" way in which to behave as a married couple. The Byzantine twists and turns of the marital relationship were faithfully reproduced and acted out though the child actors could have given no conceptually worked-out explanation of how men and women interreact.

It is a truism to remark that young children cannot understand the novels of a Dostoevsky or of an Austen. The stories such authors have to tell are at a level too high for the child to reach. In a way analogous to the stages of moral reasoning identified by Kohlberg, each of us must pass from one level of storytelling to the next. Each new level of storytelling challenges the narrative patterns of the previous stage. At each transition from one level of storytelling and listening to another, the new story, with its tale of new ways of being a storyteller, challenges and threatens the sense of identity of the listener. Erikson posited as fundamental to development the achievement of trust. The basic trust of the individual allows him or her to weather the temporary disorientation caused by learning to hear and tell stories on a higher plane. The art of the great storyteller lies in confirming the basic trust of the listener while threatening his or her present self-understanding.

Peter's basic trust in Jesus as a storyteller allowed him to live safely through the disorientation of learning a new story. The eucharistic discourse of the sixth chapter of John's Gospel must have been as challenging and disorientating to Peter as it was to those listeners who walked with him no more. A basic trust in the story told by Jesus allowed him to affirm that there was no other storyteller to whom he could go.

Alfred North Whitehead had an experience similar to many who studied theology in the aftermath of the Second Vatican Council. Whitehead had studied and taught at Cambridge in the 1880s. More than 150 years had passed since Descartes and Newton and, in the main, mathematical physics looked sound, solid, and certain. "By the turn of the century," wrote Whitehead, "nothing, absolutely nothing was left, not a single major concept. This I consider to have been one of the supreme facts of my experience."[34]

For many the Second Vatican Council was an event that shattered their previous self-understanding of what it is to be a Catholic. Where before the Church's teaching appeared sound, solid, and certain, by the end of the conciliar period many might have joined Whitehead in saying that, especially in the field of biblical exegesis, nothing seemed certain, not a single major concept. A cognitive disequilibrium ensued. The sense of identity was threatened. The Catholic story seemed to many to have changed. Those, whether they were theologically literate or illiterate, whether they were clerical or lay, who successfully navigated the change were those whose basic trust in the Storyteller—Jesus as mediated through the sacraments, the magisterium, the theological teachers, and the pastors—was not threatened by turning to a new chapter in his story. For example, a couple had ceased attending mass during the pontificate of Pius XII. Years later, when the impediments to the convalidation of their marriage had ceased, they were welcomed back into the community. The pastor worried that they might find the changes too great a shock—mass in English, women serving at the altar, and the like. At the end of mass on the first Sunday back home in the parish community, they joyfully told the pastor, "Nothing has changed." Their faith and basic trust in the Storyteller allowed them to recognize the unchanged Storyteller coming through the changes in his story.

The Rule of St. Benedict shows in this regard an acute understanding of the conditions for human growth. Benedict combined obedience to an abbot and stability within a community (basic trust in the storyteller(s)) with a promise of continual conversion (commitment to learning new stories and storyforms) as the basis of monastic life. The greatest stories, and above all those told by Jesus, are tellable at many levels. The infancy narratives of Matthew and Luke, for example, can speak effectively both to children and theologians, to the exegetically naïve and to the critically sophisticated. Where they are heard and appropriated authentically by the listener at his or her own level of storytelling, the stories contain the seeds of subsequent stage transcendence and sublation to a higher level.

1.82 *The story told by a human life is not exclusively a story of peak experiences.*

The aesthetic categories proper to a theology of story must not be taken to imply that all religious living *in via* is a matter of seeking and prolonging peak experiences. The joy that is the gift and presence of the Holy Spirit is not a mindless euphoria that casts out all vestige of sorrow and suffering. Just as the great tragedies delight us—one can enjoy a great performance of *Hamlet*—so the Spirit is the joy that is present even in the midst of sorrow. The search for a religion that is joyful can be a hysterical refusal to allow God to speak to us in angst and suffering. The theology of story does not affirm that to be religious all experience must be in a narrow sense "aesthetic." Eliot puts this well:

> . . . to apprehend
> The point of intersection of the timeless
> With time, is an occupation for the saint . . .
> For most of us, there is only the unattended
> Moment . . .

These are only hints and guesses,
Hints followed by guesses; and the rest
Is prayer, observance, discipline, thought and action.[35]

The rapture of a symphony or sonata, the momentary identification with Hamlet or the Ancient Mariner, the joy of taking part in Figaro's wedding are transitory joys. Yet, though the moment passes, the man or woman who has heard Beethoven and Mozart and seen Shakespeare and read Coleridge is never the same again. The passing moments of authentic aesthetic experience remain, working on and shaping us even when the superficial memories of the performance have faded. The honeymoon gives way to a

. . . lifetime's death in love,
Ardor and selflessness and self-surrender.[36]

The peak moments of religious rapture are given to us that we may become more capable of hearing the telling of the same Story in the humdrum, the wearisome, and the boring.

1.821 *Patience is a precondition for all divine and human storymaking.*

It takes time to tell a story. Nothing of value can be communicated instantaneously. The teller of stories must be someone with time for others. The storyteller must realize that his or her listeners will get the full impact of the story only when it has drawn to its close. The storyteller must show patience if his or her listeners do not seem to fully comprehend or fully appreciate what he or she is intending to say. Until the story ends, what the teller intends has not yet been fully uttered. The story of salvation is in large measure the story of God's patience in communicating his story to his stiff-necked and uncomprehending people.

If the storyteller is to be a person for others, he or she must first be a person for himself or herself. To have time for another, I must first find time for myself. One third of our day is spent in sleep. It represents the daily pause or silence in the life story or biography of every person—a pause that is omitted in our biographical accounts despite its being an integral and constitutive part of our living. During our sleep, whether waking consciousness remembers it or not, we are engaged in a dialogue with ourselves. If we listen to our dreams we can hear ourselves articulating the desires, long-ings, hopes, fears, and anxieties that in waking life we may ignore or flee. Jesus is sometimes called the man for others, but he was only a man for others because he was also a man for himself. He is shown by the Gospels as leaving the crowds and seeking the silence of the desert and lonely places. Jesus is shown by the Gospel as one who loved the creative pauses of his life. If we speak without paus-ing for breath, running the words and sentences into one another, we cease to be intelligible. The minute silence between words artic-ulates our sentences, it allows each group of sounds to be perceived as a gestalt and thereby to be understood. The silence between notes makes the melody possible. The silence at the end of a reading in church enables the Word of God to sink into the hearts and minds of his hearers. The well-timed pause and the proper punctuation of our speech allow the story to be understood and evaluated. The silent and wordless moments of our life (the prayer between God and humans and between one human and another) allow us to tell our story well.

1. Bernard Lonergan, "Religious Experience," in *Trinification of the World: A Festschrift in Honor of Frederick E. Crowe,* ed. Thomas A. Dunne and Jean-Marc Laporte (Toronto: Regis, 1978), pp. 71–83.
2. Cf. Aquinas, *In Metaphys. Aristot. Lect 3,* 55.
3. On the importance of the "pathological" elements in stories told to children, see James Hillman, "A Note on Story" in *Id, Loose Ends: Primary Papers in Archetypal Psychology* (Zürich: Springer Verlag, 1975), pp. 1–4.
4. *Ibid.,* pp. 1f.
5. The characteristic wanderings of psychotic consciousness might usefully be consid-ered as a dysfunction of the ability to maintain a narrative flow, thus underlining the essential storicity of consciousness. Insofar as the irruptions of what is commonly called the unconscious point to a hidden narrative, they would confirm our thesis that where there is meaning there is story. A man who had suffered two bouts of dreamless coma, amounting in all to twenty-one days, reported that twenty-one days of his life were as if he had not existed: his existence as a subject depended on his ability to "tell the story," even if only inchoatively in dreams.
6. Mircea Eliade, *Patterns in Comparative Religion* (London: Sheed & Ward, 1976), pp. 388–409.
7. C. G. Jung, *Aion: Researches into the Phenomenology of the Self,* in *Collected Works IX ii,* trans. R. F. C. Hull (London: Routledge & Kegan Paul, 2nd ed., 1968), p. 276.
8. Aquinas, *De Verit.* 12, 7 and *In 2 Cor.* 12, 1. Cf. P. E. Persson, *Sacra Doctrina: Reason and Revelation in Aquinas* (Oxford: Blackwell, 1970), p. 45. Also, Frederick E. Crowe, *Theology of the Christian Word: A Study in History* (New York: The Paulist Press, 1978), passim.
9. Bernard Lonergan, *De Deo Trino: Pars Dogmatica* (Rome: Gregorian University Press, 2nd rev. ed., 1964), p. 10.
10. Cecil Roth, trans., *The Haggadah: A New Edition with English Translation, Introduc-tion, and Notes* (London: The Soncino Press, 1959), p. 36.

11. Karol Wojtyla, *The Acting Person,* in *Analecta Husserliana X* (Dordrecht, Holland: Reidel, 1979), pp. 66ff.
12. Denis McBride, "The Unity of Time in the Human Story," *The Month* 12/7 (July 1979), pp. 229–232.
13. *Ibid.*
14. Cf. Joseph Flanagan, "Transcendental Dialectic of Desire and Fear," *Lonergan Workshop, vol. I,* pp. 69–91; J. Fitzpatrick, "Lonergan and Poetry," *New Blackfriars* 59 (1978), pp. 441–450, 517–526.
15. This analogy responds to the famous distinction made by Emile Mersch between the historical Christ and the Whole Christ; cf. his *The Whole Christ: The Historical Development of the Doctrine of the Mystical Body in Scripture and Tradition* (London: Dennis Dobson, 1938).
16. John Henry Newman, *Discourses to Mixed Congregations* (Westminster, Md.: The Newman Press, 1966), Discourse XIV. J.P. Manigne, O.P., *Pour une Poétique de la Foi: Essai sur le mystère symbolique* (Paris: Les Éditions du Cerf, 1969), p. 138f.
17. T. S. Eliot, *Four Quartets:* "East Coker" and "Burnt Norton," (New York: Harcourt Brace Jovanovich).
18. The *tonus antiquus ad libitum (simplex)* of the Gregorian Collect, which resolves the melody by a surprising drop of a fifth when the ear is led to expect a third is an example of the way in which we can be continuously delighted by an unexpected resolution already contained in the melody. See *Graduale Romanum a Solesmensibus Monachis Diligenter Ornatum* (Paris: Desclee & Co., 1957), p. 118.
19. J. R. R. Tolkien, "On Fairy-Stories," *The Tolkien Reader* (New York: Ballantine Books, 1966), pp. 71–72; see John Navone, *The Jesus Story: Our Life as Story in Christ* (Collegeville, Minn. The Liturgical Press, 1979), p. 182.
20. 1 Th. 4:13–18. The Christians should comfort one another with these words *(logois toutois),* that is, words of faith in Jesus as having risen from the dead (14). Ultimately, the sacramental forms are all specifications of the one mystery of faith: that Jesus is risen and appears now to you as he appeared to Simon.
21. Viktor E. Frankl, *Man's Search for Meaning: An Introduction to Logotherapy,* rev. ed. (London: Hodder & Stoughton, 1964, and Boston: Beacon Press, 1959), p. 72.
22. *Ibid.,* p. 75.
23. Cf. W. Mayer-Gross, Eliot Slater, Martin Roth, *Clinical Psychiatry,* 3rd ed. (London: Baillière Tindall, 1977), pp. 286f.
24. A. Godin and M. Hallez, "Parental Images and Divine Paternity," *Lumen Vitae* 19, 1964, English edition, pp. 253–284.
25. Hillman, *op. cit.,* pp. 1–4.
26. Cf. John Navone, *The Jesus Story,* pp. 130f.
27. Cf. Hillman, *loc. cit.*
28. At the lighting of the Sabbath light the mother of the Jewish family prays, "Lord of all creation, I am about to perform the sacred duty of kindling the lights in honor of the Sabbath . . . and may the effect of my fulfilling this commandment be that the stream of abundant life and heavenly blessing flow in upon me and mine . . . and grant that peace, light, and joy ever abide in our home. For with you is the fountain of life and in your light we see light." Whatever the exact form that Mary's prayer took, it must have presented to the child the images and symbols that later he would use in his preaching.
29. Michael Novak, *The Experience of Nothingness* (New York: Harper & Row, 1970), p. 27. Bernard Lonergan, *Method in Theology,* (London: Darton, Longman & Todd, 1972), p. 78, affirms that institutional change involves change of meaning, of idea or concept, of judgment or evaluation, of the order or request.
30. For a brief and readily accessible account of Kohlberg, see Ronald Duska and Mariellen Whelan, *Moral Development: A Guide to Piaget and Kohlberg* (Dublin: Gill & Macmillan, 1975). A fuller account of Erikson and Kohlberg will be found in Walter E. Conn, "Conscience and Self-Transcendence" (Ph.D. diss., Columbia University, 1973; Ann Arbor, Mich.: University Microfilms).

31. Duska and Whelan, *op. cit.,* p. 43.
32. Bernard Lonergan, *The Philosophy of Education,* transcribed and edited by James and John Quinn (Toronto: Lonergan Center, Regis College, 1979) p. 123.
33. *Ibid.,* p. 123.
34. Quoted *in extenso* by Karl Stern in his introduction to Görres, *The Methods and Experience of Psychoanalysis* (London and New York: Sheed & Ward, 1962).
35. T.S. Eliot, "The Dry Salvages," *Four Quartets.*
36. *Ibid.*

CHAPTER 5

THE SECOND MOMENT:

The craft of telling stories

Poiesis, poetry or literature, is in the first instance something created or made. *Poiesis* is an art, a craft, the making of something. Stories are the creation of their storytellers. *Omne agens agit simile sibi*, by understanding the subject in his or her telling of stories, the art and skill with which the storyteller plies her or his art, we come to a deeper understanding of the meaning of stories.

2.1 *Like a teacher, a craftsperson, or an artist, the storyteller must use techniques and skills adapted for his or her purpose.*

It is sometimes argued that to tell the story of Christ effectively all that is needed is to have one's "heart in the right place" and that the mechanics of the storytelling will take care of themselves. Usually this argument takes the form of brushing aside dogma and systematic theology, scriptural exegesis and ascetical theology, psychology, and the other human sciences. It is not how you think about your neighbor that matters, so the argument runs, but how you treat him or her. The argument commonly issues in a devaluation of theology, of catechetics, and of the liturgical homily. Armed with such a view, the presiding celebrant, for example, approaches the altar with what Lonergan calls an empty head.[1] The texts of the liturgy will speak for themselves and require little or no preparation on the part of the celebrants. In religious schools great stress may be placed on "getting the children involved" and in providing a "Catholic atmosphere," while the critical appropriation of doctrine (other than by rote learning) is almost systematically ignored. In a parochial school where the teachers laid strident claim to providing a "Catholic atmosphere," the teacher responsible for the preparation of candidates for confirmation was unable to look up a biblical reference because, it transpired, he knew neither the names of the books of the Bible nor the fact that it was divided into chapters and verses. An informal check among the staff revealed to the school chaplain that none of the teachers had even heard of Kohlberg or Piaget.

Those who are called to tell the Christian story, especially those who are called to tell that story in the name of the whole community—ministers of the word, catechists, teachers—can tell the story with effect only insofar as they have understood that story critically and reflected on its meaning within their own cultural context (theology), appropriated that story responsibly as the story of their own life (prayer and sacramental living as founding a life of loving self-giving), *and* understood and become practiced in the effective use of the means of communication. To take but one example, all things being equal, the elder who has learned how to use language by immersing himself or herself in literature, and especially poetry, will be a more effective communicator of the Word than one who despises or ignores the literature of his cultural inheritance. The one who appreciates the value and function of drama will better appreciate its limits also and will be a better "performer" of the liturgical drama.

2.11 *We cannot do what we cannot, at least in some way, imagine or envision.*

Believing, hoping, loving, deciding—all are fundamental activities at the heart of every human life story. These activities involve human motivation. Vision is essential to human life stories, inasmuch as it is an orientation to decision and action. We cannot do what we can in no way imagine or envision. In Johannine theology no one can come to Christ unless the Father draw him (6:44) but to have seen Christ is to have seen the Father (14:9). Christ is the icon, the image through which the Father draws each particular storyteller to make his or her story. In the measure that each storyteller's image of Christ is in or out of focus, is more or less oblique, in that measure will the life story reflect explicitly or implicitly the universal story. Every human life story bears witness to a basic vision; this vision includes images of ourselves, others, the world, human integrity and failure, God, and so on. However unclear, distorted, or false our vision (or images), there is no human life story without it. Vision, including all the images associated with it, is integral to human motivation; it shapes human life stories.

2.111 *Authentic lives evidence authentic vision.*

Human authenticity bespeaks a sound relationship with the true goodness of the transcendent being of God, which is its ultimate measure. The truthfulness of authentic human lives evidences the truth of their vision of themselves, others, the world, and God. Traditionally, the quality of Israel's life at every level had been interpreted as the index of its truly seeing God:

> Whenever the Israelites saw God they became virtuous. They saw him at the Red Sea and became virtuous. They saw him at Sinai and became honest . . . . They saw him in the tabernacle and became just.[2]

When the Israelites were attacked by serpents in the desert they were preserved from harm by their unwavering gaze upon the brazen serpent that Moses had made. Christ, lifted up like the serpent in the desert, becomes the source of healing for all who see him. He becomes the vision that draws our life story authentically to become the bearer and revealer of the universal story of God. In the vision of the crucified and exalted Savior there is given the effectiveness of response, sanctifying and elevating grace, which draws all parts and aspects of our life story into harmony with the life story of Christ. Thus Bonhoeffer, commenting on the command not to lust after women, rightly says:

> Jesus does not impose intolerable restrictions on his disciples, he does not forbid them to look at anything, but bids them gaze on him. If they do that he knows that their gaze will always be pure, even when they look upon a woman.[3]

The beatitude of the pure of heart, who see God, is witnessed by the authenticity of their lives. The integrity of the well-ordered love that governs the pure of heart is evidence of the true vision— even though in a glass darkly—of Ultimate Reality and of all related reality. The vision of the pure of heart who see God as he truly is, is born of love: God's gift of his love purifies the heart to see what it could not otherwise see and to become what it could not otherwise become.

2.12 *The art of the storyteller is measured by his or her ability to master complexity: the more that he or she is able to unify within his or her story, the greater his or her art as a storyteller.*

Jacques Maritain mentions, in one of his books on art, the criterion of Italian Renaissance masters for determining the comparative achievement of artists: the more detail an artist is successfully able to integrate (master or unify) within a work of art, the greater the artist. This principle was extrapolated from the Christian doctrine of creation. God is the Supreme Artist. He unifies all that is within the universe that he has created. Likewise, God is the Supreme Storyteller. He unifies all that is in his universal story. Human storytellers approximate to the Supreme Storyteller to the extent that they can master the complexity of their experience within the comprehensibility and truthfulness of their storytelling. The excellence of the storyteller is manifested by the degree to which he or she is able to truly interpret and evaluate all the elements and levels of meaning and value that are relevant to the story he or she seeks to tell.

2.121 *The excellence of human stories is measured by the demands they make of their authors.*

The greater the storyteller or author, the greater will be his or her story. The greatest stories will be told by those who are richly endowed with acute perception, rich imagination, insightful understanding, refined taste, and depth of affectivity. Great courage may be required to tell a story. The cost to the storyteller, in terms of self-sacrifice and suffering, may be high. Prophets often end by being martyrs. The martyr is willing to die for a truth that must be told and a value that must be affirmed at all costs. Freely and courageously, storytellers have chosen to tell their story with the full awareness of the possible dire consequences. Radical adherence to the truth of his or her story is witnessed by the willingness of the storyteller to die for it. Such total self-investment in one's story represents the ultimate demand that the truth and goodness of the author's story can make of him or her.

We must not, however, be naive about martyrdom. I can die for a cause that is hopeless or wrongheaded. My commitment to my story may have been tragically misguided; the truth of my story may have been an illusion and its goodness trivial. I may be sincere but wrong. It is not enough that the martyred storyteller was doing his or her best, that he or she meant well; the story must have been worth telling.

A great story demands greatness in the author. Self-discipline, willingness to learn, patience with self and with others, preparation, commitment to self-transcendence and self-investment are essential to the telling of a good story. The great storytellers confront the demands of the complexity within human experience in order to master it through the art of their storytelling. They are neither overcome by the complexity of human experience nor do they try to evade it. Rather, they have the courage and the maturity to come to grips with life's complexity, accepting its challenge and bringing it to judgment for themselves and for others. Great storytellers make demands of their listeners.

2.2 *The storyteller is implicitly a teacher inasmuch as she or he creates a story that moves the listener to decision.*

Inasmuch as the storyteller articulates and names the authentic subjectivity of humankind, thus far does she or he summon the listener to decide for or against his or her own authentic subjectivity as a human person. To tell a story I must take a stance for or against the truthfulness and value of my experience. I speak about the things I know and love. Not only do I affirm in my storytelling the truthfulness and value of my experience (understood as my perceptions, understanding of and judgments about those perceptions as objective experience) but, more importantly, I affirm the truthfulness and value of my *experiencing*. I affirm the goodness of my *experientia experiens* as well as my *experientia experta*. It is not so much a question of communicating knowledge about and love of particulars (though this too may have its place), so that the deepest work of the storyteller is not overtly didactic, but that in the authentic telling of a story the universal value of human subjects is articulated and shared.

In communicating my experience of what it is to be the subject of a story and, ultimately, of the universal story, I can communicate my meaning only insofar as I have understood it. Where my grasp of the meaning is partial, my communication will be partial. We do not always fully grasp the meaning of what we are relating to others. In regard to the communication of the experience of being a subject of the universal story (whether implicitly or explicitly in its relation to the definitive communication of that experience in Christ) we can never express all that we are and know. We know more than we can say. Our communication of the story will always be partial. This is not the same as to say that our communication need always be inauthentic. Paul, like the rest of humankind, saw only in part, but his communication of what it is to live in Christ bore fruit in those who heard him. Like other women and men, he saw only as though through a darkened glass, but his telling of the story was an authentic telling because it was born of an authentic gift of the Father's love. Even when we do not know the words, in order to tell the story properly, the Spirit himself tells the story in a way too deep for words. Where a heart has been flooded by the gift of God's love, a gift born of the outpouring of the Spirit, then the tale that heart tells will be a tale born of that same love, and the telling will tell more than the discursive mind can grasp. On the other hand, our outward telling of the story may be "word perfect," but our living of it may be seriously defective, the fruit of a lack of love or of inauthentic loving. The religious formalist, for example, knows the words of the story but misses its true meaning. His or her telling of the story will be an inauthentic telling, and the hearers of that particular telling of the story will sooner or later see through it.

2.21 *Stories are a mutual creation of the teller and the listeners.*

Telling stories is a mutually creative art. Both the storyteller and the listener cooperate in making the story happen. Together the teller and his or her hearers enter a world pieced together by creative imagination. You cannot tell a child the story of Little Red Ridinghood unless the child is willing to believe, at least for the duration of the story, in wolves that speak.

If the storyteller and the listener are to create a story together they needs must speak the same language. To recite the parables of Jesus in Aramaic to a British or North American congregation would not be to tell a story. At a profounder level, the teller and her or his audience must not only speak the same language in the sense that English or French or Swahili are languages, but must also share a common language of images and symbols. There must be a common fund of affective connotations to the words they speak. Where an American will criticize something for being "homely," a Briton will praise it for the same quality! The affective connotations of the image of Mary, the Mother of God, are different for an Irish or Polish Catholic and a Bible Belt Baptist. A French general may address his soliders as *"mes enfants,"* but for an American or a British general to do so would be insufferably patronizing.

Common to the whole human race are those words that Karl Rahner calls primordial and that Jung identifies as archetypal representations.[4] Jung, writing on the relationship of analytical psychology to poetry, quotes Gerhart Hauptmann as saying that "Poetry evokes out of words the resonance of the primordial word."[5] Rainer Maria Rilke conceived the poet's task (and the task of every human being) as the telling of "purely untellable things."[6] Ultimately we are here to utter the name of creation:

> Sind wir vielleicht hier, um zu sagen: Haus, Brücke, Brun-nen, Tor, Krug, Obstbaum, Fenster,—höchstens: Säule, Turm . . . aber zu sagen, verstehs, oh zu sagen so, wie selber die Dinge niemals innig zu sein (. . .)
> Hier ist die Säglichen Zeit, hier seine Heimat. Sprich und be-kenn.[7]

Like Adam and Eve in the Garden we are led by God to name creation. And in naming creation we name ourselves. Rilke puts into the mouths of women a song addressed to the poet:

> Mit uns geht das Unendliche *vorbei.*
> Du aber sei, du Mund, daß wir es hören,
> du aber, du Uns-Sagender: du sei.[8]

Here the storyteller expresses his or her listener as she or he expresses himself or herself. She or he is an "us-expresser." Similar tales emerge in cultures and civilizations remote from one another. Leitmotifs and story patterns arise in diverse lands and nations. The storyteller in his or her uttering of the primordial word expresses not only the transient experiences that may or may not be common to the storyteller and the audience, but expresses also what it is to be human. Gerardus van der Leeuw affirms that the poet "stands in close relation to the prophet."[9] Martin Heidegger tells us that the poet "nennt das Heilige": names what is holy.[10] The storyteller names the holy as spokesman or spokeswoman (prophet) for God; or, better, the storyteller expresses us implicitly or explicitly in the name of God. When the storyteller authentically articulates himself or herself as the subject of a human story (that is, as an authentic part of the universal story) she or he expresses the common subjectivity of men and women. Inasmuch as the storylistener makes his or her own the story she or he hears, so does he or she enter a common world of meaning with the teller and creates, together with the teller, a world in which she or he can return to the self and ultimately come home to God.

2.3 *The author of a story has an attitude toward the subject of the story.*

As authors relate their own or another's experience, they reveal their response toward that experience. When John in his first letter tells us that his subject is life, a subject that he has experienced with his own eyes, he exhibits his own response to that subject: a mood of joy and confidence (cf. 1 Jn. 1:4; 5:14). Our experience is both cognitive and affective. We may refer to the affective dimension of an author's experience as the mood of his or her storytelling. The author reveals how she or he feels and how he or she is affected by her or his subject through his or her articulation and description of her or his experience. The storyteller's response may convey sadness, joy, anger, happiness, bitterness, indignation, acceptance, rejection, fear, dread, outrage, and the like. The storyteller's mood may vary from the comic to the tragic, from optimism to pessimism, and from exasperation to serenity; but in the story as a whole we can find a dominant mood or spirit, a prevailing way of being in the world and of relating to it. The author may have a casual attitude to his or her subject or a deeply reflective one.

The sensitive and observant listener can often detect a hidden mood coming through the overt mood of the storyteller. The most obvious example is the forced gaiety and laughter that try, usually unsuccessfully, to hide a deeper anxiety or nervousness. The unrelieved jollity of some forms of shared prayer makes the more critical observer suspect a deeper level of unresolved guilt and anxiety than the participants would ever acknowledge. It is not all those who cry "Praise the Lord" who are necessarily sufficiently healed to enter the Kingdom. The words we habitually choose to express our experience may reflect a preverbal experience at odds with our expressed mood. Frank Lake, commenting on Christopher F. Mooney's book on Teilhard de Chardin, affirms that "it would be open to a serious student of anxiety to ask whether much of this "contemporary," "existential" anxiety is not, in fact, a defense by *projection from repressed birth experiences on to adult existence, rather than anything teleological, ethical, social, or ultimate in any theological or philosophical sense.*"[11] Certainly, Mooney's analysis of de Chardin's preferred metaphors and imagery makes a strong *prima facie* case for suspecting that de Chardin's mood was one of deep-felt anxiety.

J. Murtagh in an article on animus and anima in St. Peter and St.

John makes an interesting suggestion about the authorship of the Book of Revelation. Murtagh assumes an identity between the author of the Letters of John and the Apocalypse and John the son of Zebedee, an assumption that is exegetically extremely dubious but that allows him to uncover a facet of authorship that biblical hermeneutics overlooks at its peril.[12] Let us accept, for the purposes of our argument, Murtagh's unargued assumption that the Letters and the Apocalypse come directly from the pen of John the disciple. It is frequently overlooked that an author may write in different moods or styles depending on his present mood or even his sense of fun. Thus Ronald A. Knox wrote two very amusing pieces, one about birth control in the style of a Dryden epic, and the other about parish jumble sales in the style of a *quaestio* of Aquinas.

Murtagh notes the ancient traditions concerning John in old age being unable to preach anything but "Love one another." Such a tradition squares with the mood of the Letters and, indeed, of the Fourth Gospel. The John of Luke's Gospel is portrayed as naturally violent, as one who merited the nickname Son of Thunder (cf. Lk. 9:51 – 56). In the Letters and the Gospel all "the thunder of his early life that had earned him his nickname seems to have disappeared; his harshness has given way to extreme tenderness." Murtagh sees this as proof of the Spirit's working in the soul of John, whereas a psychiatrist might as easily suspect the maudlin sentimentality so often the obverse of the violent temperament.[13]

Even if we accept that the pentecostal life of John had transformed him from a quick-tempered person into one who is loving and solicitous, nevertheless the Book of Revelation purports to be a *dream*. If we accept the Jungian notion of dreams as compensatory to the attitudes of waking consciousness, then we will not be surprised if the one who found great joy that his children had been living the life of truth (cf. 2 Jn. 4) is also capable of relating with great relish the plagues of the seven angels and the fate of the scarlet whore (cf. Rev. 16:1 – 18:24). Indeed, these three chapters of the Apocalypse sound very like an extended "midrash" on Luke 9:51 – 56. Murtagh, on the basis of his identification, comments, "There is evidence, too, that John's basic natural tendency to strength and violence remained with him despite his growth in tenderness. . . . The contents of the Book of Revelation leave us in no doubt concerning what was repressed in the conscious mind of John, violence. . . ."

Whatever our judgment about the validity of Murtagh's thesis as applied to the historical son of Zebedee or the Johannine corpus, it illustrates the indisputable fact that the underlying mood of a story may accurately reflect the conscious but nonobjectified affects that our waking consciousness would fail to recognize as our own or would even with horror reject. It also serves to remind us that the meaning of revelation or ecclesial tradition must not be simplistically restricted to the conscious intent of the scriptural writer or the pope or bishops in council. God's power can shine through even our psychic weakness.

2.31 *The author of a story has an attitude toward his or her audience.*

An author may exhibit the same attitude toward his or her audience as he or she does to his or her subject. In such a case the author invites the listener to share her or his mood. John writes to his audience so that they, like him, may be filled with joy by union with God in Christ (cf. 1 Jn. 1:3 – 4). On the other hand, the attitude of the author to his or her subject may differ considerably from her or his attitude to the audience. Christ's welcome to the children is meant as a reprimand to his disciples. The parables of Jesus frequently contain a "sting in the tail." His attitude to the prodigal son is quite other than his attitude to the hostile Pharisees who hear his telling of the story. John Steinbeck in his novel *The Grapes of Wrath* expresses sympathy for migrant workers and points an accusing finger at the reader who is responsible for their plight. The biblical John in his first letter is affectionate to his readers while hostile to the Antichrist and those whose sin is lethal.

2.4 *The true meaning and value of human stories are determined by their context.*

Human stories occur within a context. Our basic self-others-world-God relationship, our *Sitz-im-Leben* or *Sitz-in-Erzählung*, constitutes the context of our story, inasmuch as every author implicitly communicates an understanding or interpretation and evaluation of his or her relationship to self, to others, to the world, and to God. The author inevitably communicates his or her attitude to her or his context: namely, the "audience" composed of self (when we tell stories we are aware of what we are doing), of others, of the world, and of the mystery (the known-unknown we call God), which is the ultimate background, ground, and foreground of every human story. Storytellers intend their storytelling for storylisteners, for their context or audience. Storytellers "hear" their own stories; in this sense, they are also storylisteners, constituent parts of their own context or audience. Their storytelling is meant or intended for themselves no less than for others. It is the way they freely choose to relate themselves to themselves, the way they choose to be. Their freedom is, of course, always a limited freedom. It is limited to the resources of the storyteller's context, of his or her basic self-others-world-God relationship, of her or his historical and cultural context. Inasmuch as human stories are a way of relating to a context, their true meaning and value cannot be grasped apart from it.

Fundamentalism is largely a matter of attempting to take a story or part of a story out of its context. It is not restricted to biblical Fundamentalism. The Fundamentalist rips a saying of Jesus out of the context of his life, of his immediate hearers, of his world and, ultimately, of his God. The Fundamentalist attempts to set up the signs of other times and other places as the signs of this time and this place. The Fundamentalist refuses to enter the world of the storyteller so that he or she may truly "hear" what is being said. There is a fundamentalism of papal and magisterial pronouncements (Denzinger theology) as there is of biblical texts. There is a fundamentalism of morality that seeks to rip individual actions from the context of the life stories that enshrine them, which results in an inability to "hear" what such actions (which may well indeed be aberrant or sinful) are saying about the actor's relationship to self, to others, to the world, and to God. We fail to interpret the Scriptures, the Creeds, the pronouncements of popes, and the behavior of other persons when we prescind from the context in which the sayings or actions took place.

The storyteller's context has two poles: the knower (the storyteller) and the known (the storyteller's self-others-world-God relationship as thematized in his or her storytelling or as unthematized in his or her life story). The truthfulness—or lack thereof—of her or his storytelling ultimately derives from the authenticity of her or his basic relationship to the ultimate context (background, ground, and foreground) of all human stories. All are implicitly meant and intended for that context and derive their true meaning and value from it.

2.5 *There is no human story without limits.*

Tragedy, at least in its classical Greek sense, depends for its effect upon the portrayal of a basically just man ruined by a fatal flaw. In *The Trial* Kafka expressed the impossibility of any person's being able to claim with truth that his or her existence was flawless. Even if we do not know the crime of which we are accused, we cannot truthfully refuse to plead guilty to the indictment. The psalmist expressed the same truth: "If you, O Lord, should mark our guilt, Lord, who would survive?" (Psalm 130). Paul articulates the same theme: "all have sinned and fall short of the glory of God" (Romans 3:23). All human lives are marked by failure. The vehemence and emotional strength with which persons who deny this thesis deny that there is failure or sin in their life itself, attest, perhaps, to the emotional strength required to repress the experience of failure and blameworthiness from conscious experience.

There are tension and conflict at the heart of every human life story. It has perhaps been best expressed by Paul in his letter to the Christians of Rome:

> I cannot understand my own behavior. I fail to carry out the things I want to do, and I find myself doing the very things I hate. . . . In fact, this seems to be the rule, that every single time I want to do good it is something evil that comes to hand. (Rom. 7:15, 21)

It is a fact of common human experience that desire is one thing, performance is another. Where a man or woman could truthfully claim that he or she had successfully achieved all goals, it would be grounds for suspicion that his or her sights are set too low, that is, that they had failed to envision the rich varieties of possibility open to every human life, that they had suffered a failure in their imagination. Where a human person has achieved the knowledge of all he or she wishes to know, there is a failure, an atrophy, of basic wonder—perhaps the worst failure of all. Complete success in the goals we have set ourselves points to the poverty of our aspirations.

Every human life story, as well as testifying to the failures and conflicts in our lives as individuals, will also testify to the failures and conflicts of men and women as members of society. Eliot remarked that

human kind
Cannot bear very much reality.[14]

There results from this what Bernard Lonergan has called the flight from understanding. Not only is there an individual bias, but there is also a group bias. Not only is there a refusal to face reality, to understand intelligently, to judge reasonably, and to act responsibly on the level of each individual person, but there are also failures of attentiveness, of intelligence, of reasonableness, and of responsibility within the life of the group. The limited attentiveness, the limited intelligence, the limited reasonableness, and the limited responsiveness to value of others interact with the limitations of the individual. History chronicles the violence and the indifference with which human beings treat their fellow humans. History is a saga of decline and failure as well as of progress and success. Individual and collective suffering, deportations, massacres, wars, oppression—suffering of every description is reported on every page of history. Every age records the attempts of human beings to respond with schemes and utopias, and every age records the disillusion of idealists as they see their schemes collapse. The idea that there is to be a fulfillment *in* history, that the religious, or social, or political millenium will come in time, rather than at the end of time or outside of time, is debated. Regardless of the position taken in the debate, the fact remains that no age has been without a profound experience of human limits and failures.

Our understanding and appreciation of our own life story are limited; we have limited personal and social resources for discerning both its direction and its most appropriate possibilities. We learn only slowly to cope with our own lives and to attack the real problems of society. Not all the suffering and disorder in human life stories and the world's story spring from human malice. Because of human finitude there is always need for compassion in our response to human stories. Within the historical particularities of our stories, a limited happiness is the only happiness available.

2.6 *The human action that defines a story is a declaration of a basic faith.*

Stories are defined by human action. The completed lives of individuals and of societies trace out a story whose implications reveal their basic faith: what they took the world in which they lived to be, who they thought they were, what in their actions showed their ultimate concerns. Action is a declaration of faith. The action that is the living out of a story derives from a sense of rightness that we cannot put easily into words. It derives from a basic faith that is preconceptual. Just as the infant trusts his or her mother and feels safe in her arms long before he or she can express such feelings in words, so the first movements and the ultimate depths of faith take place at a preconceptual level. Our fundamental convictions retain their preconceptual character; they are never adequately expressible in words, though they shape our lives and guide our thinking, our judging, and our deciding. Our actions are more comprehensive and complex than our capacities for analysis.[15] They are an implicit declaration of our identity and basic faith in response to the mystery that we find in ourselves, in others, and in the world. Our actions, reflected upon, reveal what we really value more accurately than our words about what we value. Our behavior more truly reflects the goals we aim for than the aspirations and hopes we express. Our actions disclose the ground of our basic faith and hope.

2.61 *We seek to live by the stories that embody our basic faith.*

We often sense the rightness or wrongness of a particular human story without being able to articulate why. We possess a connatural knowledge of its quality that is based largely on our "second nature" of habit, instinct, and resonance. We cannot exhaustively state in words everything within the horizon of our awareness; nevertheless, we are able to refer particular stories that serve as symbols to express what we sense to be right or wrong, authentic or inauthentic, human or less than human.

A story may illustrate our meaning. One of the authors had done some work on the medieval conceptualization of God as Mother. A priestly colleague, whose mother had died before he had reached an age where he could remember her, and whose overly sentimental and defensive devotion to Mary was perhaps a reaching out for the lost joys of childhood, could find no sense at all in such a conception. He judged it to be dangerous and "contaminated by feminism." An elderly woman, ignorant alike of medieval theology and modern feminism, instinctively remarked, "I've never been told about the motherhood of God, but that's the God I've always believed in." Confronted by a new and strange symbol, both judged its rightness or wrongness on the basis of their past experience. Like the creative artist, they could give no clear account of their symbols, but they judged them instinctively or connaturally by whether they felt right or wrong.

A life story unfolds according to its basic faith. There is no human story without a basic faith that seeks proper objects, definitions, forms, shapes, persons. We move on to the stage of our basic faith, to stay or go, succeed or fail (or, more frequently, to half-succeed and half-fail) to become its objects and forms. Their life stories intersect with ours. We embrace them as our own to help us in the search that is dynamically rooted in and motivated by our basic faith. Whatever the self is seeking, its basic faith will take the shape of the particular human stories that most illuminate and encourage it. Through their evocative power they convey a latent meaning that is apprehended in a nonconceptual, even subliminal, way. They transform our horizons, integrate our perception of reality, alter our scale of values, reorient our loyalties and aspirations in a way far exceeding the powers of abstract conceptual thought.[16] We live by the stories in which we sense the way to our own true story, the story most appropriate to our own unique possibilities and limitations.

Rollo May tells us that we experience ourselves simultaneously on three levels. One level emerges from the archaic depths, another is made up of the memories and consequences of personal events, and the third level is made up of the general symbols and values of our culture. The symbols that attract or repel us and the stories we tell or listen to are an expression of a unique self-consciousness and of a person's capacity to transcend the immediate *Sitz-im-Leben* by imagining creatively the possibilities of a life of which he or she would be the subject.[17] We judge and, perhaps more importantly feel, connaturally which possibilities most become the telling of a story told by us.

Our success in finding our own true story depends largely on the stories we have embraced as our own, on how accurately we have discerned their true meaning and value with respect to our own unique possibilities for leading an authentically human life in a graced world. There is always the threat of absurdity, the folly of trusting the untrustworthy, the danger of losing the thread to our true story, the gift of God, which culminates in the resurrection of the just. The story of the Church embodies the basic faith of Christians. Its structures exist to communicate the grace and demand of God for discerning and doing his will in the historical particularities of Christian life in every age.

> 2.611 **Since the communication and expression of faith transcend all conceptual knowledge, both its expression and communication lie in the symbolic mode of consciousness, symbol being defined as the best possible expression of an unknown content.**

Faith is more than the sum of a person's information about God. The student of comparative religion may well know more about a particular religion's teaching than many of its adherents, but he does not necessarily have faith in that religion as a divinely revealed way to God. In matters of faith we know more than we can say. We believe more than we can put into words. In the kerygmatic proclamation of our faith and the catechetical instruction into its mysteries, we communicate our faith in the mystery (the known-unknown) of Christ. Scientific, conceptualized thought has an in-built drive toward an increasing clarity and distinctness in its ideas. It is the product of an increasingly differentiated consciousness. It is a mode of thinking that remains firmly in the intellectual pattern of consciousness.

Faith can be described as a falling in love with God, a falling in love in an unrestricted fashion, a being grasped by ultimate concern. In one of the great affirmations of religious faith, we are told that we must love the Lord our God not only with our mind but also with all our heart and with all our soul.[18] Faith is the response of the whole person to the call of the Unknown God. The communication and expression of faith are both interpersonal and intrapersonal. Without the interpersonal communication of the preacher we will never hear the Good News (cf. Rom. 10:14–17). The content of that preaching must tie together (*symbollein*) the intellectual, volitional, and affective response of the preacher to his or her own hearing of the Good News. It must point beyond its own content to something that has not yet entered the hearts of men and women (cf. 1 Cor. 2:9). The joy of the Gospel remains nothing but a bright idea or a pious hope unless it speaks directly and with power to every level of human consciousness. What is required is intrapersonal communication. On the score of one of his pieces, Beethoven wrote that "Heart must speak to heart." Before one heart can speak to another it is necessary that the heart, understood as the ancient Hebrews understood it as the seat of all a person's powers, bodily and spiritual, should be in communication with all the levels—organic, psychic, affective, intellectual, conative—which make up the human person. Lonergan rightly affirms that it is through symbols that "mind and body, mind and heart, heart and body communicate."[19] The symbol ties together and communicates the multilayered response and intent of the whole person. By its very nature a symbol expresses more than can be conceived or grasped by the understanding. Anthony J. de Luca defines symbols as the point of intersection of genesis and *telos*. The symbol incorporates past experience but points to a beyond, to an unknown, an only half-disclosed future.[20] For Jung the symbol is an "intimation of a meaning beyond the level of our present powers of comprehension." In a happy metaphor he calls symbols "the best possible expressions for something unknown—bridges thrown out toward an unseen shore."[21] Insofar as the preacher of faith achieves a mastery of symbolic expression, so does he or she become an authentic *pontifex*, a builder of bridges between the inchoate forms of faith-response that have their genesis in the psychic depths and the unknown telos, which, when raised up on a symbol, draws all men and women to Himself.

> 2.6111 **Because the symbolic is rooted in the psychic depths of the personality, there is need of a critical mediation of symbols. Because the critical intellect can never comprehend the mystery of God, there is a need for a return to the symbolic.**

Ontogeny reflects phylogeny. The development of the individual reflects the development of the race. Just as the human race passed historically from undifferentiated to increasingly differentiated levels of consciousness, from animism through *mythos* to *logos* and thence through classical to postclassical theologies, so too must the individual human being in his or her life pass from undifferentiated, inchoate feelings about the other, through more or less highly articulated symbol systems, to critical reflection on the place and meaning of a theology in a culture.

In his presidential address to the American Academy of Religion, John C. Meagher spoke of theology as not only the curator and commissioner but also as the critic of icons.[22] Because symbolic consciousness is chronologically prior to critical reflection there is a temptation to consider symbolism as nothing but archaic, prelogical thinking.[23] Story is then likely to be conceived as the outworn product of a precritical consciousness. The Greek experiment with theory originated in part as a critique of the anthropomorphic myths about the gods of Olympus. The quest for universal definitions, the scientific and critical calling into question of common-sense notions, threatened the received symbols of the community, and Socrates was thereby put to death in the name of religious piety. The icons humankind spontaneously produces may speak volumes about the persons who produce them, but they may be less than adequate as pointers to the mystery of which they purport to speak. As Meagher puts it, "some icons are decidedly unwholesome."[24] It pertains to theology to reflect upon the significance and meaning of religious icons or symbols within the particular pattern of dramatic living that makes up the culture in which they are expressed.

It is a mistake, however, to conceive of theological discourse as the pure, unadulterated kernel of truth in the husk of narrative and symbol. We demythologize the content of our religious discourse at our peril. Johannes B. Metz has issued a timely warning against the neglect by theology of the value and importance of narrative and symbolic discourse:

> The atrophy of narrative is particularly dangerous in theology. If the category of narrative is lost or outlawed by theology as precritical, then real or original experiences of faith may come to lack objectivity and become silenced, and all linguistic expressions of faith may therefore be seen as categorical objectivizations or as changing symbols of what cannot be said. In this way, the experience of faith will become vague, and its content will be preserved only in ritual and dogmatic language, without the narrative form showing any power to exchange experience.[25]

Once the symbols and narratives we have received have been criticized and reflected upon by theology, and particularly by a theology attuned to the function and significance of human storytelling and listening, there is the need for a return to the image, for the creation of a new and intelligently constructed "midrash" that speaks both to the primary naiveté of the precritical and the second and richer naiveté of those who are morally, religiously, intellectually, and psychically converted. The Council of Nicaea is a watershed in the transposition from mythos to logos. Nicaea produced as its fruit not only a clarification of theological concepts but also the *symbolum nicenum*.[26] Only a jot (*iota*) separates *Homoousion* from *Homoiousion*, yet the fact that human beings were prepared to suffer and cause others to suffer over that jot is proof that more than a conceptual system was at stake or, perhaps more accurately, that the rival conceptions of the christological schools had become powerful symbols in the hearts and minds of their adherents.[27] The teaching office of the Church may perhaps most illuminatingly be seen as a defense of the icons; a charism to judge, by way of theological, conceptual analysis, the claims of conflicting symbol and the narratives that contain them to be more authentic carriers of the Gospel than their rivals.

2.62 *Images, and the stories that contain them, provide models and motives for the decisions and actions that shape our lives.*

In a prison for young offenders there was a young man, about twenty, who had fathered three children by three different women. As juveniles are wont to do, he boasted of his potency and manliness. The chaplain and others responsible for his care spent much time and effort in attempting to help him understand the reality of his situation and the need to behave responsibly. Their efforts were to no avail. The chaplain's lifestyle, beliefs, and ethical stance seemed to exist in a different world from that in which the prisoner lived. The chaplain's words seemed fated to fall upon stony ground. In the prison chapel the chaplain had hung a poster showing a young child in a garden. The child was pretty and was running with uncertain steps toward the camera. On the poster a slogan proclaimed the simple message: All my tomorrows depend on your love. The young prisoner walked into the chapel, saw the poster, and immediately sought out the chaplain. "Sir," said the prisoner, "my children have no father," and he wept. The sight of the poster was to prove a turning point in the young man's life.

Images have a power to move us and to transform our lives. Like the diagram of a geometrical puzzle or the rising water in Archimedes' bath, they help us to achieve an insight into the problems and meaning of our life. Stories, especially those that are told with direct and compelling imagery, have a power to change the lives of those who listen. The story of a stolen sheep gave David an insight into his behavior. The stories of the saints changed the whole course of Loyola's life.

A person lives primarily not by abstract principles but by stories that other lives are telling.[28] We are immersed in a world of stories that actually motivate our behavior before we begin to reflect on who we are and who we choose to become. These stories lie outside our control; they are charged with powers of attraction or repulsion, illumination or depression, expansion or fear. Action precedes reflection. Persons are already acting and have been acting for centuries before they learn the possibilities of ethical behavior through reflection on their actions. We notice significant correlations, understand their importance, judge the validity of our understanding, and decide upon appropriate action long before we undertake the study of cognitional theory. Men were hanging criminals and settling property disputes long before they codified laws and evolved a jurisprudence. As Piaget observed, children playing marbles develop a mechanism for resolving disputes long before they can philosophize about the nature of rules and their application to particular cases.

We act before we begin to reflect upon the appropriateness and direction of our action, or on the concrete life stories of others that we have implicitly chosen as the criteria for our actions. Concrete human models motivate and shape our lives before we begin to reflect on them. Our responsibility concerns which models we choose to value by making them central to our actions.

Through storytelling we express our own orientation to decision and action, our feelings and concerns about what is ultimately fulfilling and the ways in which to achieve such fulfillment. Not only did Jesus hear the stories of his people, listening to the stories of what had gone before, but also he in his turn used stories to perfect and complete the stories he had heard, to communicate his own vision of what the human story might and should be. We tell stories to advise, to persuade, to educate, to encourage, and to transform others. We communicate the horizon of our interests and knowledge through our storytelling. Inasmuch as an horizon is an orientation to decision and action, our storytelling provides models and motives that implicitly invite others to share our own orientation to decision and action. We are storylisteners before we become storytellers. We hear stories, we are motivated by stories, before we begin to reflect on them and responsibly choose them as our own.

2.621 *Human conduct is more story or model abiding than it is principle or law abiding.*

From our earliest years we are shaped by our relationships to our parents and to the significant others whose life stories impinge upon our own. Our earliest conduct is imitative rather than deliberately learned and chosen. Before we can conceptualize our experience and evaluate it discursively, before we can share the experiences of other times and other places through reading, before we can share our own experiences with others through writing, we model our conduct upon those who surround us. Anybody who has been present as a neutral observer in a family will testify how the parents' faults and behavior patterns are imitated and reproduced in their children even though the parents may have verbally forbidden and disapproved of such modes of behavior. Before we become responsible for the models we choose as our own, our openness to truth and our commitment to value have been conditioned by the influence of those upon whom we most depend. We imitate those who surround us. We do not choose the initial models or patterns of human behavior with which we are presented.

Michael Novak affirms that we seldom, if ever, act according to principles and rules stated in words and logically arranged.[29] Rather we act according to models, metaphors, stories, and myths. Young children spontaneously ask their parents to tell the story of their own childhood so that it may shed light upon their own. Our behavior is imitative rather than rule abiding; prior to our intention to obey sets of rules, we are trying to become a certain type of person. The young child obeys his or her father not because parental authority is modeled on divine authority, from which all human fatherhood takes its name, but rather because the child wants to become, or at least wants to be considered, a good little boy or girl.

The self-image through which we act is the story we tell ourselves about ourselves or (quite possibly) the story that our speech evades but our actions reveal.[30] I want to be a good little boy or a good husband or a good priest. I consciously or unconsciously model my behavior and my attitudes imitatively or (possibly) in opposition to my understanding of the models with which I have been presented. A young woman wishes to be a good wife. She has an image of what a good wife is. The image is made up of her memories of her own mother's relationship to her father and of other women's relationships to other men. The way she heard the story of her mother's marriage affects and in large measure shapes the story she herself is trying to tell.

Rules, for Novak, are to stories what single words are to sentences.[31] The same word may have different meanings in different sentences; the same rules may be obeyed differently by persons living out different life stories. The rule binding Catholics to attend Sunday mass, for example, is a rule that binds on all. It is a rule that must figure (even if in some cases as a nonobserved rule) in any life story that in some way claims to be a Catholic life story. The significance and meaning of that rule will be lived out differently in one who by choice attends mass each day of the week and in one who attends only on Sundays. The rule may be understood as a legal expression of the spiritual need to worship in community, to celebrate the Lord's resurrection weekly with and among his body, or it may be understood as a legalistic imposition. We may hear mass in order to meet Christ sacramentally in communion with our fellow Christians, or we may attend mass in order to escape the fires of hell. The story that we are acting out determines our actions more than verbally stated rules that we are following. Novak concludes that to adequately analyze ethical behavior, we must pay attention to a logical category prior to the category of rules, principles, propositions, and codes of behavior—specifically, to the category of story, myth, symbol, and ritual.[32] The aesthetic precedes and undergirds the ethical.

2.6211 Law-abiding behavior can itself be a mode of storytelling.

The narrative demands of the story we are telling are more fundamental in shaping our behavior than the rules we are explicitly obeying. We learn the possibilities for the actions that tell our life story, not through intuition into some abstract realm, but through reflection upon the actual, concrete story that my life is telling and upon the life stories of those upon whom we are modeling them. If the models who are given us (or whom we choose) are rigidly law abiding and legalistic, then our own self-image may become that of a person bound by laws and suffocated by the demands of unreasonable and arbitrary commandments. Dr. Mara Palazzoli affirms from her clinical experience that rigidity of belief and lovelessness are found in those whose excessive devotion to law and order is a means of defense against the excessive demands of rigid and law-abiding parents and grandparents.[33] Where the Ten Commandments are presented as the essence of all religion, where self-sacrifice is presented as the highest of all the virtues, the child becomes law abiding as a result of the self-image he or she is trying to project. It is self-defense by incorporation. Too weak to reject the false life stories presented to him or her as models and patterns for behavior, the child incorporates the false myth of life as a process of law abiding into his or her own self-image. In such cases the law-abiding behavior becomes a mode of storytelling.

In his work among juvenile delinquents, one of the present authors would regularly play a game in discussion groups by asking the delinquents to imagine themselves as members of a commission seeking to improve the prison service. They were asked to suggest ways of improving the penal service generally and specifically to suggest courses of action aimed at reducing the rate of recidivism. Approximately ninety-five percent of those who took part gave as their top priority the tightening of rules and the making of life

tougher for the inmates. It was an underlying aspect of prison philosophy observed by other workers in the field. The young offenders
had an invincible and naive belief that Draconian reforms would
deter them from committing further crimes. Such an attitude suggested an atrophy of the autonomic quality of their life stories.

Life, for these young men, appeared to consist in playing the roles
expected of them by their peers and by the authorities opposed to
them. The self-image was one of being the victim. Expected by my
peers to show my autonomy and freedom by rebelling against the
rules society imposes, I am constrained, or consider myself to be
constrained, to act according to the ways and patterns shown me
by my companions. I seek freedom from such constraint not by
becoming truly autonomous, that is, by critically grounding the
stories I tell, but by hoping that the constraints imposed by authority will be more powerfully coercive than the pressures exerted by
my peer group. The subject of my story remains a victim. I
(mis)understand myself to be the victim of my circumstances and
seek to become a victim of authority. What Erich Fromm affirmed
to be the fear of freedom is the acquiescence by the anxious self in
a story in which he or she is cast in the role of victim. Such a mythic
understanding of oneself as the prey of outside and manipulative
forces underlies the story of the hypochondriac who understands
himself or herself to be the victim of bad health and the prey of
microbial forces outside his or her control. Raised to the level of
scientific, theoretical discourse, the myth becomes the pessimistic
psychophilosophy of Skinner's behaviorism.

We experience human freedom in both our ability to choose concrete human models for our conduct and our ability to live accordingly. Human maturation involves the development of a critical
awareness of the stories on which we are modeling our lives. These
include our stories of God (critically grounded in theology), the
myths or stories of our culture (critically grounded by history) and
the lives of those who are nearest to me (critically grounded by
depth psychologies).

2.63 *A human life story is not exclusively a matter of self-deter-
mination.*

We do not ask to be born. We were not consulted when our parents conceived us. Before our very birth the raw material of our
characters was formed. Some obstetricians maintain that incipient

character differences can be observed already in unborn twins. Before Jeremiah was formed in the womb God knew him and had appointed him a prophet to the nations (Jer. 1:5) and the psalmist acknowledges the givenness of his life when he says to God:

> It was you who created my being,
> knit me together in my mother's womb . . .
> Already you knew my soul,
> my body held no secret from you
> when I was being fashioned in secret
> and moulded in the depths of the earth. (Ps. 139)[34]

We are born virtually not absolutely unconditioned. The sum total of necessary conditions for the coming into being of an individual, a species, a phylum, or life itself is not logically nor historically identifiable with the individual, or species, or phylum, or life. Each one of us is a conditioned of which the conditions have been fulfilled. We are neither the authors nor the masters of those conditions. We are neither the absolute creators of our life stories, nor do we possess them fully. Our life stories are a work of joint authorship in which we and others, both known and unknown, are the writers together with One Other, who is at the same time known and unknown.

We originate as gift. Our life story begins with three dots and an "and." In recounting our life story we are rarely able to account for more than the immediate others in the long and wide web of ancestors that have been the indispensable conditions for our existence. Like Melchizedek we soon run out of genealogy. Through the lives of our ancestors we have received a biological and cultural inheritance; we have been called into a particular world that, although presented to us for our free acceptance or rejection, we have not chosen for ourselves.

We must freely accept our nature as being predetermined, for we have not called ourselves into existence. The world into which we have been called confronts us as something that has been determined before we freely begin to make the decisions that shape our life story. This world can never be manipulated to the extent that we are eventually dealing only with material we have chosen and created. Accepting what has been predetermined in our own being is a basic task of our free moral existence. Rahner affirms that when these aspects of our life are not "accepted with confidence in patience and humility as the gift of an incomprehensible love," we will be subject to total neurosis, to a restless and futile struggle with our own destiny.[35]

An illegitimate woman whose mother had subsequently married and had children by another man once remarked to one of the authors how much better it would have been if her mother's husband had been her real father rather than her stepfather. If such had been the case she herself would never have existed; her place in the family would have been occupied by somebody else. A young man often sat in the church where one of the present authors was once an assistant pastor. A diagnosed schizophrenic, controlled and made harmless by drugs, he had been born on the same day as the Prince of Wales. His story, which, like the Ancient Mariner, he would tell to all he could waylay, was that there had been a mix-up at the hospital where he had been born and that he was the rightful heir to the throne of England and the man in Buckingham Palace was really John Doe from Wellingborough. Daydreaming that one could have been born more beautiful or clever or noble or wealthy is a pleasant and, within limits, harmless enough, parlor game; spending one's whole life wishing or, in extreme cases, believing that one were somebody else is tragic.

The great dramas of ancient Greece were written as competition pieces; the characters and the plot were given, the individuality of the playwright's imprint was shown forth in the skill and beauty with which he shaped his material and told the familiar story. The great icon painters were bound by strict canons governing theme, composition, material, and style, yet the individual genius of Rublev is always distinguishable from the works of other painters. In the same way, our life story has been launched within certain limits of possibility long before we can choose for ourselves. We do not entirely invent our own story; in part we discover it as we learn our true possibilities and limitations. The characters in our story, the plot, and the scenery are largely given us; the dramatic unities of time and place are largely imposed upon us; but the resulting completed story bears the unmistakable imprint of our own individuality. We are given the material for our life story; it is up to us to make it our own.

1. On the "Principle of the Empty Head" *see* Bernard Lonergan, *Method in Theology* (London: Darton, Longman & Todd, 1972), p. 157f.
2. H. Strack and P. Billerbeck, *Kommentär zum NT aus Talmud und Midrasch* (Munich, 1922–8 and 1956, 2nd ed.), p. 213, quoted in *Encyclopedia of Biblical Theology III*, Johannes B. Bauer, ed.; see also Rudolph Schnackenberg, "Vision of God" (London: Sheed & Ward, 1970), p. 951.

3. Dietrich Bonhoeffer, *The Cost of Discipleship* (London: SCM Press, 1964), p. 120.
4. Karl Rahner, "Priest and Poet," *Theological Investigations III* (London: Darton, Longman & Todd, 1972), pp. 294 – 317. The archetypal representations should not be confused with the archetypes, which are not innate images or words but "inborn possibilities of ideas that set bounds to the boldest fantasy"; C. G. Jung, *The Spirit in Man, Art, and Literature*, in *Collected Works*, vol. XV (London: Routledge & Kegan Paul, 1966), p. 81; cf. *Id, The Structure and Dynamics of the Psyche*, in *Collected Works*, vol. VIII (London, 2nd ed., 1969), pp. 213f.
5. C. G. Jung, *The Spirit in Man, Art, and Literature*, p. 80.
6. Rainer Maria Rilke, *Duino Elegies: The German Text with an English Translation, Introduction and Commentary by J. B. Leishman & Stephen Spender* (London: The Hogarth Press, 4th ed. 1968), Elegy IX: "lauter Unsägliches."
7. "Maybe we're here to say: House, / Bridge, Spring, Gate, Pitcher, Fruit tree, Casement,— / at best: Column, Tower . . . but to say, you understand, / O to say in such a wise as these things in their inmost being never believed themselves to be (. . .) / Here is the time for the tellable, here its home. / Speak and proclaim." Trans. by Thomas Cooper.
8. Rainer Maria Rilke, *New Poems: The German Text, with a Translation, Introduction, and Notes by J. B. Leishman* (London: The Hogarth Press, 1964), pp. 70f. Trans. by Thomas Cooper: "The infinite passes *us* by. / But *you* are the mouth through which we hear it; / but you, you Us-expresser: you are."
9. Gerardus van der Leeuw, *Sacred and Profane Beauty: The Holy in Art* (Nashville, Tenn., & New York: Abingdon, 1968), p. 122.
10. Martin Heidegger, *Was ist der Metaphysik?* in *Existence and Being*, trans. by R. F. C. Hull and Alan Crick (Chicago: Henry Regnery Sons, 1949).
11. Frank Lake, *Clinical Pastoral Care in Anxiety and Related Conditions: Phobic Reactions, Automatic Reactions, Dissociative Reactions, Depersonalization and Conversion Reactions* (Nottingham, Eng.: The Clinical Theology Association, 2nd ed., 1970), pp. 16ff; Christopher F. Mooney, S. J., *Teilhard de Chardin and the Mystery of Christ* (London: Collins, 1964), pp. 17ff.
12. J. Murtagh, "Animus and Anima in St. Peter and St. John," *Irish Theological Quarterly* 37 (1970) pp. 65 – 70. The present authors take up no position here in the exegetical debate over the authorship of the Johannine corpus. Even if Murtagh's assumptions are wrong, the point he makes is valid: one cannot rule out a common authorship of the Apocalypse and the other writings *solely* on the basis of different moods.
13. The connection between sentimentality and violence has been well portrayed by Bogarde and Rampling in the film *The Night Porter*. The fact that one cannot hear the tone in which St. John would speak his frequent apostrophe of his readers as "children" highlights the difficulties of accurately judging the mood of a writer from his written words alone. The ease with which Mark 10:14 and Luke 18:16 may be sentimentalized should serve as a warning to all interpreters of the mood of Scripture.
14. T. S. Eliot, "Burnt Norton," *Four Quartets*.
15. Michael Novak, *Ascent of the Mountain, Flight of the Dove*, (New York: Harper & Row, 1971), p. 63.
16. Avery Dulles, *Models of the Church* (Garden City, N.Y.: Doubleday & Co., 1974), p. 18.
17. Rollo May, "The Significance of Symbols" in *Symbolism in Religion and Literature*, Rollo May, ed., (New York: George Braziller, 1961), pp. 11 – 49. esp. pp. 22, 33.
18. The Deuteronomic version of the Sh'ma Yisroel, which Matthew records Jesus as quoting, enjoins the love of God with all one's strength. The response of faith is bodily as well as mental.
19. Bernard Lonergan, *Method in Theology*, p. 67. On the meaning of the word "heart," cf. Jean Lévêque, "Interiorité—I," *Dictionnaire de Spiritualité, Ascétique et Mystique*, vol. 7 (Paris: Beauschesne, 2nd ed., 1971), coll. 1877 – 1889; also Edith Stein, *The Science of the Cross: A Study of St. John of the Cross* (London: Burns & Oates, 1960), pp. 118 – 119.

20. Anthony J. de Luca, *Freud and Future Religious Experience* (Totowa, New Jersey: Littlefield, Adams & Co., 1977 ed.), p. 144.
21. C. G. Jung, "On the Relation of Analytical Psychology to Poetry," in *Collected Works,* vol. XV, p. 76.
22. John C. Meagher, "Pictures at an Exhibition: Reflections on Exegesis and Theology," *Journal of the American Academy of Religion* 47 (1979), p. 17.
23. Such a view of symbolic consciousness is omnipresent in Freud, and it appears to mar some of Lonergan's writings on symbolism. For a development of Lonergan's thought on symbolism to a perhaps more nuanced position, see the important article by Robert M. Doran, "Psychic Conversion," *The Thomist* 41 (1977), pp. 200 – 236.
24. Meagher, *op. cit.,* p. 18.
25. Johannes B. Metz, "A Short Apology for Narrative," *Concilium* 85 (1973), p. 85.
26. Cf. C. G. Jung, *Aion: Researches into the Phenomenology of the Self,* in *Collected Works,* vol. IX, ii (London: Routledge & Kegan Paul, 2nd ed., 1968), p. 73.
27. Cf. Paul Tillich's remark that even abstract concepts can become symbols, "The Religious Symbol" in Rollo May, ed., *Symbolism in Religion and Literature,* p. 76.
28. Michael Novak, *Ascent of the Mountain,* p. 67. Also *Id, The Experience of Nothingness* (New York: Harper & Row, 1970), pp. 68 – 70.
29. Novak, *The Experience of Nothingness,* p. 23.
30. *Ibid.,* p. 87.
31. *Ibid.,* p. 23.
32. *Ibid.,* p. 24.
33. Mara S. Palazzoli, *Self-Starvation: From the Intrapsychic to the Transpersonal Approach to Anorexia Nervosa* (London: Chaucer, 1974), pp. 75, 242; Thomas Cooper, "On Praying to God in English," *The Clergy Review* 65 (1980), pp. 41 – 51.
34. From *The Psalms: A New Translation.* By permission from The Grail (England).
35. Karl Rahner, "The Problem of Genetic Manipulation," *Theological Investigations IX,* pp. 243 – 244.

—————————— CHAPTER 6 ——————————

THE THIRD MOMENT:

The meaning of human stories

O sage, Dichter, was du tust? — Ich rühme.
Aber das Tödliche und Ungetüme,
wie hälst du's aus, wie nimmst du's hin?—Ich rühme.
Aber das Namenlose, Anonyme,
wie rufst du's, Dichter, denoch an?—Ich rühme.[1]

Rainer Maria Rilke

God's utterance of himself in himself is God the Word, outside himself is this world. This world then is word, expression, news of God. Therefore its end, its purpose, its purport, its meaning is God, and its life or work to name and praise him.[2]

Gerard Manley Hopkins

3.1 **That every person who has ever lived has lived out a story of storylistening and storytelling posits a comprehensible universe with a permanent meaning at the heart of things.**

Pointless stories are irritating. To be a proper story every story must have a point. Storytellers are trying to communicate a meaning by their stories. People whose stories ramble on and get bogged down in unnecessary and irrelevant details so that we find it hard to follow their drift eventually find themselves talking to deaf ears. The fact that our lives are spent telling and listening to stories implies that we are called to live truly meaningful lives in a universe that is essentially benign and comprehensible.[3] The narrative quality of human experience posits coherence in the universe. What Whitehead called the bagatelle of transient experience is shaped and given meaning by our stories. Our ability to comprehend our experience in the spontaneous ordering of our experience in storytelling reveals our fundamental self-others-world-mystery relationship. Both our storylistening and our storytelling intend a coherent universe on the premise that order ultimately prevails over chaos. Our narrative consciousness is operative in a world that is already ordered. Our ordering minds grasp such a world; the permanent inability to have or to participate in any story is in some cases a sign of psychic disorder or disturbance. Every person who has ever lived has lived out a story of a basic self-others-world-mystery relationship. Our storylistening and storytelling are interpretations of this basic relationship, of this fundamental order, coherence, and comprehensibility at the heart of things.

3.11 *Stories express the horizon of their author's vision.*

The stories that authors tell express the patterns of selection in their attention. Authors cannot express everything. What do they select? What do they neglect? What lies beyond the range of their knowledge and interests is simply beyond the horizon.[4] What lies within the authors' horizon is in some measure an object of interest and knowledge. Stories that we call to mind are valued and understood within the limits of our horizon. We attend to those dimensions of the story (e.g., life stories of individuals, communities, nations, etc.) that are within the range of our horizon. What does not fit will go unnoticed or, if called to our attention, will seem irrelevant or unimportant, both in our storylistening and in our storytelling. Inasmuch as story expresses the sweep of an author's interests and knowledge, it can be the fertile source of further knowledge and care. All known reality is part of a human horizon; it is known by and through human subjects. Our story expresses our horizon.

3.12 *Human stories are implicit answers to the fundamental questions that arise concerning life and death.*

The stories told by men and women raise basic questions. All storytelling may be analyzed in terms of the following questions: Who is telling the story? To whom are they telling the story? Where and when does the storytelling take place? What is being told, what is the theme of the story, and what are the contents of the story? Why is the story being told? What is the motive and intent of the author? How is the story told? In what tone of voice is it told? What attitudes of the author does it betray? What is the spirit and mood of the narrative? To what effect is the story told? How does its audience react? What impact does it have on them? How does it affect their subsequent living? Other questions, related to the former, may be mentioned. What is the storyteller's point of view? What is the form and structure discernible in his or her story? What kind of language does the author employ? What are the connotations, the emotional associations, that the story conjures up? What figures of speech does the storyteller employ for evoking his or her intended response? Does he or she delight in irony, paradox, metaphor, or simile? What kind of symbolism does the author use? What does the author's preferred symbolism tell one about the author's own attitudes? The author's key words, images, and repetitions are clues that point to her or his underlying meaning.[5]

The answers we make to these and similar questions reveal to us both our own understanding of what the author intends and means and also our own intent and meaning as we tell our own life story. Insofar as the author puts himself or herself into his or her work, so far are his or her stories implicit answers to the questions that motivate his or her reflection, decision, and action. My answers to the daily questions raised by life imply, more or less profoundly, and more or less explicitly, my answers to the fundamental questions that occupy me. What my reader "hears" me as saying, what he or she understands me as meaning, in its turn implies the answers that she or he make to the questions that fundamentally exercise him or her.

3.13 Human stories raise questions about the answers that they imply with regard to the basic questions of life and death.

Stories are the form of our answer to the basic questions of life and death; consequently, they raise the question of the authenticity of our answers. The work of John S. Dunne illustrates the role of storytelling as an exploration of questions and answers about life and death.[6] Aged thirty, Dunne found himself, like Dante, in the midst of a dark wood. All men die and in *The City of the Gods* he looked at the answers men had given to the question "What can I do to fulfill my desire to live?" By examining the myths, stories, and legends of the human race, Dunne was able to discern the varying answers men and women had given. The answer was a second question: "Who am I?" Dunne undertook *A Search for God in Time and Memory*. The answer to this search was a new question: "To whom shall we go for a companion on the journey to life?" *The Way of All the Earth* passed over to God as the companion of our journey. A fourth question arose: "How are we to descend from the mountain of solitude to enter again into the fellowship of our brother

and sister humans?" Each answer evokes a further question. Ultimately we face the only question a human being can ask, the question that underlies all other questions. "Who (or what) is this Unknown who (or which) calls me unceasingly as the known-unknown
term of my quest for self-transcendence?"

In all these questions, and the partial answers contained in the
various stories I tell, there arise questions about the authenticity
of my partial answers. Are my questions true or false? Am I asking
the right questions? Or are the questions I ask a cover story to mask
my refusal to ask the questions that really matter? Are the answers
I give to these questions true or false? Are the answers good or evil?
Do my questioning and my answering reveal me as intelligent or
unintelligent? Do I seek insight or fly from understanding? Am I
responsible in my raising of questions and in the answers I give?
Are my answers reasonable or unreasonable? Do my questions and
answers reveal me as loving or as unloving? A human story implies
the author's judgment, convictions, and values. Consequently, it
raises questions about their authenticity. Do the questions I ask
and the answers I give in my storymaking reflect my true self as a
self-transcending lover? Human experience is a call to judgment;
human stories are a form of our response to that call; they are a
form of our judgment of the meaning and value of our human experience; they raise questions about the truth or falsity (adequacy
or inadequacy) of our interpretations and evaluations of human
experience.

3.2 *God is ultimately intended by every human life story.*

Storytelling presupposes a listener. Even when we soliloquize we
are, in a sense, talking to ourselves. In telling a story we relate
what we have done and, more importantly, what we are to a thou.
Thou is the personal pronoun by which we acknowledge and address personal otherness. Otherness is irreducibly mysterious. If
we could fathom and encapture any particular thou it would have
ceased to be other and would thereby have ceased to be thou. In
love we delight in the otherness of the other as present (the *complacentia* of Aquinas) and are drawn to that otherness as the future of
what we could be (love as tending, as transforming).

Storytelling presupposes that we have a story to tell. Even when
we are babbling about nothing we are revealing the poverty of our
reality. We speak of the things we know; even when we speak of the
things we do not know we reveal thereby the truth about ourselves

as lacking in understanding and judgment and knowledge. There is an identity between the thing known and the knower. Truth and the mind that judges truly are convertible. Insofar as I tell my story truly, insofar as I utter truth, I utter self. Truth is in the minds of men and women. Truth is irreducibly mysterious in that humankind is ever unfinished.

Since storytelling intends to utter the truth (that which is) to another, story presupposes beauty because beauty is the perichoresis, the dancing within one another, of truth known and loveliness intended.

God is the loveliness of truth and the truth of loveliness. God is both wholly other and also, as Augustine remarked, *interius intimo meo*, more truly me than I. God, as Father, Son, and Spirit; as Origin, as Word, and as Love Proceeding, is the perichoresis of Otherness and Self-Identity. All that can be affirmed of the Father can be affirmed of the Son, except that the Father is not the Son, nor the Son the Father. By their very otherness to each other (relations of opposition) they constitute each other as other and yet are one. In this God reveals himself as the term of all human longing and questioning.

Human beings are born in symbiotic union with the mother. Early childhood and youth are largely a matter of achieving independence. Yet, if one may put the matter a little colloquially, no sooner is a precarious independence achieved, than one throws it all away by forsaking all others to cleave unto another. The art of loving truthfully consists largely in the art of resolving the inherent conflict between the claims of otherness and identity. Man delights in the otherness of woman; he is drawn to that otherness; yet the risk is that he lose himself. Commonly, humans err either by rejecting the other in order to affirm the self or by losing their own self to the claims of the other.

Humankind longs for union with another self. We long not for union with another made in the image of our own self (possessive love), so that the other has ceased to be other; we long not for union with another so wholly other that we cannot recognize it as a self (love falsely conceived as essentially altruistic). We long for that union that constitutes the other as self and yet as other.

The inner story of God, if one may so speak, reveals God to us as the giving that is also possession, the total union that constitutes I as I and thou as thou, the rest without which our heart is restless.

The Jesus story reveals God as the one who gives his very Self to that which is wholly other (humankind), a Self that in its inmost nature is constitutive of the Other and constituted by the Other. The Jesus story reveals God as the dynamism that underlies all our questioning and all our desiring. God is the question that lies beyond all our particular questions. God is the love that lies beyond all our particular loves. Every human life story is, to a greater or lesser degree, explicitly or implicitly, a raising of questions and a complacent ecstasy in the other. Every human life story intends God, the loveliness of transcendent being and value. And because God is a truth that transcends human questioning and a value that transcends human desires and satisfaction, he transcends all that humankind can imagine.

1. Translation by Thomas Cooper: "Dear Poet, tell me what it is you do?—I praise. / But how do you put up with the deadly and the monstrous? / How do you react to them?—I praise. / But the nameless, the anonymous, / how do you call out to it?—I praise."
2. Gerard Manley Hopkins, unpublished manuscript, Campion Hall, Oxford, England.
3. John Navone, *The Jesus Story: Our Life as Story in Christ* (Collegeville, Minn.: The Liturgical Press, 1979), p. 135.
4. The notion of horizon is treated extensively by Bernard Lonergan in *Method in Theology* (London: Darton, Longman & Todd, 1972), pp. 235–237.
5. For an application of these questions to Gospel Study, see John Navone, "Write a Gospel," *Review for Religious* 38 (1979) pp. 668–678, and *Id*, "Four Gospels: Four Stages of Christian Maturation," *Review for Religious* 39 (1980) pp. 558–567.
6. John S. Dunne, *The City of the Gods: A Study in Myth and Mortality* (London: Sheldon Press, 1974); *Id*, *A Search for God in Time and Memory* (London: Sheldon Press, 1975); *Id*, *The Way of All the Earth: An Encounter with Eastern Religions* (London: Sheldon Press, 1973); *Id*, *Time and Myth: A Meditation on Storytelling as an Exploration of Life and Death* (London: SCM Press, 1979); *Id*, *The Reasons of the Heart: A Journey into Solitude and Back Again into the Human Circle* (London: SCM Press, 1978).

THE UNIVERSAL STORY OF GOD TOLD IN
THE LIFE STORY OF JESUS

CHAPTER 7

THE FOURTH MOMENT:

God is revealed through human stories

Adoro te devote latens Deitas, quae sub his figuris vere latitas. Everything is a parable—*figura*—of God, who is constantly being unveiled yet at the same time constantly concealed in the parable.

Theological Investigation XIII
Karl Rahner

Metaphor is, I believe, the heart of the matter for theological reflection, since the task of theology is to serve the hearing of God's word, that strange truth that disrupts our ordinary world and moves us—and it—to a new place.

Speaking in Parables
Sally McFague TeSelle

4.1 *God is a particular agent that is known and revealed in his story.*

Agents, human and divine, are known in their activities. The act of creation is proper to God alone. History, or the universal story, begins with God's creative action and is sustained by it for the achievement of its purpose. God is known and revealed in his creation, his universal story, or history, which grounds and encompasses the totality of human life stories.

"Anyone who fails to love can never have known God ... since a man who does not love the brother that he can see cannot love God, whom he has never seen" (1 Jn. 4:8, 20). Later more philosophical reflection was to assert the same truth in metaphysical terms. To desire a particular good is to desire the likeness of God and God implicitly.[1] It is not a particular case of "love me, love my dog," as though God had commanded men to love their neighbors as the price of loving God; it is not that the love of neighbor is commanded *ab extrinseco*, as though God could have ordered the world otherwise, but that the love of God is actuated in the particular loving of man's neighbor. The love of neighbor is the very condition of the possibility of the love of God.[2]

Likewise, God's story is known as personal only in the particular stories of our neighbors. God acts in the universal and particular stories; consequently, he is known and revealed both in his all-encompassing story (history) and in every particular life story, however obliquely.

The sacred writer of Genesis (1:26) implies that the Supreme Agent is known and revealed in his created agents, when he puts into God's mouth the words: "Let us make humankind in our image, after our likeness, and let them have dominion. ..." The agency of God is known and revealed in and through the agency of each human person. The Supreme Agent constitutes the origin, ground, and destiny of every human agent. *Who* God is, consequently is obliquely known and revealed in the same human agency that obliquely makes known and reveals *who* we are as particular persons. As human agents, we are God's images, manifesting something of the reality and activity of the Supreme Agent. As such, our life stories are implicitly particular stories of God, particular signs of the sacred in the secular, necessarily answering or resisting the call of God in a grace-filled universal story (history) no matter how obliquely it is experienced. Our life stories implicitly tell the story— with varying degrees of truthfulness—of *the* Storyteller, *the* Supreme Agent, *the* Acting Person, who calls them into existence; they make known something of his identity and purpose.

4.11 *The transcendent Spirit of God is, and is known, where it acts in the self-transcending faith and hope and love through which it transforms our lives.*

Just as the human body cannot survive without supplies from its environment, so the human person cannot survive without something beyond itself. The self-defensive concerns of the human person are rooted in the tension between desire and limits; they derive from the threats posed by the hazards of life and the fact of death.[3] We are not self-sufficient. We experience the precariousness of our lives. We cannot ultimately be indifferent to our fate. We cannot live without some ground for our faith and hope, without basic trust, without some basic conviction about our own worth and well-being in the present and in the future. If this affirmation is accepted, at least as an approximate generalization, it means that there is no human life that can be entirely neutral from a religious point of view: what grounds our basic faith and hope, in biblical terms, is either God or an idol.

All idolatry is implicitly self-idolatry, a making of ourselves into a God, refusing to transcend ourselves in allegiance to the transcendent reality of the Supreme Good that is God alone. The worshiper of idols attempts to manipulate God, to make God serve his purposes.[4] (In Oriental thought the worship of an image was believed to give the idolator a power over the divinity represented; consequently, the Old Testament prohibited images of God.[5]) The tendency to idolatry reflects the temptation to self-sufficiency or self-fulfillment or egotism. Idolatry represents the divinizing of created realities in the service of self-divinization. It represents an attempt to cope with the problem of evil, a self-protective attempt to evade the painful tension between desire and limitation. It takes many forms. The search for "religious experience" may become tantamount to idolatry: using God as a means to satisfy one's desires. The search to establish a religious a priori, the too close identification of the transcendent God with feelings of numinosity and awe, may result in a dictating to God that he must appear in certain ways, speak in certain forms, be present in certain feelings. Then the manifold responses of human beings to the transcendent are mistakenly understood not as responses but as God and are worshiped as idols.[6] Moral self-righteousness can express itself as legalism; the concern for "righteousness" expresses the urge to self-justification rather than to self-transcendence. Knowledge may become an idol, may "puff up" the mind, as Paul remarks, in the form of ideological attempts to endow humankind and its historical range of action with the meaning of eschatological fulfillment. The tendency to idolatry is the temptation to make oneself the guarantor of one's present and future worth and well-being; to overcome by oneself and for oneself the fear of failure, suffering, and death; to be the master of one's own destiny.

If the human thrust to self-transcendence, which begins with the desire to know and extends to the desire to live responsibly, is to be brought to its fulfillment, there must be the hope of knowing Someone who transcends ourselves. If our willingness to know the truth (often unpleasant) and to accept responsibility and limitation (often difficult) is not to succumb to despair, then it must find an adequate source of freedom from the temptation to self-protection and pseudosolutions to the problems of life and death.

In religious conversion a person no longer stands at the center of his or her own world in terms of what he or she knows, hopes for, and loves. Religious faith, hope, and love derive from the love with which God floods our hearts through the Holy Spirit he has given us (Rom. 5:5). God is the loving source of our religious faith and hope and love through which we intend God in all our intending.[7] The Christian tradition makes explicit our implicit intending of God in all our intending by speaking of the Holy Spirit that he has given to us.[8] Through the gift of God's love, man must find his center beyond himself, surrendering himself to God in faith, hope, and charity, and leaving it to God to effect an ultimate solution to the tension between desire and limitation in human life. Faith, the knowledge born of love, is the apprehension of transcendent value, in whose light all other values are relativized. In the light of faith the divine love and light is the originating value of all created values, linking itself to all other values, transforming, transfiguring, magnifying, and glorifying them. As Augustine remarked, "in every man who is converted to God his delight is changed, his pleasures are changed (not taken away, but changed)."[9] With the hope born of religious love, the limit of human expectation ceases to be the grave.[10] Hope is the security and confidence of those to whom God has given his love. It liberates us both from despair as regards the fulfillment of our deepest desire and from the presumption of wishing to be the guarantor of our own fulfillment. God is love, says St. John (1 Jn. 4:8, 16), and that love overflows in creative and redemptive activity. So, too, the gift of God's love, the creation and communication of that love in our hearts, overflows into the love of our neighbor.[11] "There is nothing which so draws a man to return love," wrote Chrysostom, "as when he understands that he who loves him is urgently longing for his affection."[12] God's love floods our hearts and calls for our response; the gift of God's Holy Spirit, the gift of Love Proceeding, is graciously at work whenever we respond to God with an authentically self-transcending love for others.

The experience of God's gift of his love is a conscious experience of the mystery of transcendent intelligibility, truth, reality, goodness, and love. Authentic religious experience, the experience of grace, the experience of the God and Father of Jesus Christ, is not something known to the senses or to thought (cf. Hebrews 12:18ff), as though the experience of God were a higher form of looking or feeling, nor is it the recognition of God as a distinct object of sense or intelligence or love within a world of other objects, but rather it is an experience of attention to the stories told by creation, by others, by self, and an understanding and affirmation of those stories as gift, as stories told gratuitously by a Teller, and it is a decision to live by that understanding and that affirmation. It is a coming, as the Letter to the Hebrews affirms, to the city of the living God, a community of faith, hope, and love where the sign, missed by the evil and adulterous generation of the Gospels, is the acceptance of our own intelligence and intelligibility, our own lovableness and loving, our selfhood, as something we have not achieved but have been given. All human beings, as we argued previously in thesis three, are conscious of themselves as the subject of a verb. The man or woman who is converted to God (who may or may not be explicitly related to Christ) is conscious of himself or herself as a created and loved subject of a story told by Another. Robert Southwell expressed the gift quality of the subject so well when he wrote:

God is my gift, himselfe he freely gave me:
God's gift am I, and none but God shall have me.[13]

I am God's gift to myself. Christian faith reveals itself as the explicitation of God, Giver and Gift, Storyteller and Story told, as the deepest fulfillment of the human spirit.

4.12 Inasmuch as God is the Giver of all human life stories, they are the manifestations of his grace and are measured by the demands of his intention.

God alone creates. Because he freely creates human persons, their existence and becoming as life stories is gratuitous. He speaks his primary word in the grace or gift of every human life story. He is the measure of and the demand for their authentic meaning. The Giver of human life invests it with a meaning that is measured by his intention. Human persons, in their existence and becoming as life stories, implicitly "speak" of the grace of God and its demand for responsibility; they implicitly reveal the Giver and measure of their stories.

4.13 Human stories are implicitly coauthored with God and neighbor.

One cannot tell stories in isolation from other people. To talk to oneself, tell stories to oneself, is popularly a sign of madness. One tells one's story to somebody else. The Creator, he who is the Absolute Other present as the origin and term of all other others, endows each human person with an ability to listen, to hear the story we tell. To truly listen to someone tell a story is creative of a true relationship between the listener and the teller. Priests, nuns, psychotherapists, people who are spontaneously sought as a "good shoulder to cry on" reflect the creative love of God insofar as by their active listening they enable the other to tell his or her story. Frank Lake in a chapter on listening retells a story of Frieda Fromm-Reichmann.

> Almost immediately on her arrival in the United States as a refugee, on account of her international reputation as an analyst she was sought out by a wealthy American who insisted on consulting her. She registered a protest but was overruled and the interview was held. Some years later she was, if I remember rightly, raising money for a fund and received a generous donation from this grateful patient. He recalled how vitally he had been helped by this interview. In thanking him for his donation she made this significant comment, that, at the time of the interview, she hardly understood a word of English. She had evidently listened, interjecting only such reassuring sounds as enabled him to talk through his problem.[14]

Without a listener the story cannot be told. There is no life story that unfolds independently of other life stories and a heritage of stories. Storytelling implies a collaboration, a shared responsibility, a binding together of agents and events through the richness of an intentional activity that produces an intelligible pattern that can be expressed in narrative form. Our cooperation with other human beings is an intrinsic part of our attempt to make intelligible the muddle of things we have to do to become ourselves. We implicitly coauthor both our individual and collective stories.

4.2 *The story in which God is known and revealed is the Word of God.*

In Jesus the universal has become particular. The life story of the crucified and risen Jesus is that of the Word of God made flesh. The true meaning of the divine reality is contained in and belongs to his person, so that in his human existence we encounter God. As the

Letter to the Colossians puts it, the fullness of the Godhead dwells bodily in Jesus (2:9). The Supreme Agent expresses himself in his Word, in the historical particularities of the life story of Jesus Christ whose true meaning progressively emerges until it is fully revealed in his death and Resurrection. God takes time to speak his Word to humankind. His external Word assumed the nature of man, and in the life story of him who is God made man, Jesus Christ, the Good News of God for all humankind is revealed. This Good News constitutes the story of the Church's proclamation and reveals the ultimate meaning of the universal story.

4.21 *The universal story, together with every human life story, is God's primary word.*[15]

God speaks primarily in his creative act, which includes his Son Jesus and every event and life story from the beginning to the end of time. He speaks his primary word in a language proper to himself alone, through the events of all the life stories of history, whose meaning is measured by his intention and the capacity of the "expression" to carry that meaning. The primary word includes all that is, the very constitution of things, of all human events and life stories, of all events in the cosmos. God speaks in all his creation.

4.22 *The stories of God told by prophets, priests, apostles, evangelists, and others are God's secondary word.*

God speaks secondarily through his human agents, prophets, priests, apostles, evangelists, hagiographers, and his Son Jesus, all of whom interpret the primary word for his people. The secondary word is spoken in human language, verbal or nonverbal; its meaning is derivative because it receives and transmits the meaning of the primary word; its meaning also has the limits set by human language, and ultimately by the effective range of the human mind and heart.

4.3 *Jesus the Storyteller redeems all human storytelling.*

All storytelling is rooted in the imaginative or symbolic. A symbol may be described as an image that expresses a known unknown. Because it is an unknown known that is expressed, the reality symbolized may require more than one image, and these mutually exclusive. Thus arises the symbolic preference for the *coincidentia oppositorum*, the expression of a meaning in the tension between the predication of contradictory images about the same subject. This is true not only of those forms of storytelling that we more usually label symbolic or imaginative, but also of scientific, economic, historical, psychological, and theological explanations, which are, in themselves, a form of storytelling. Thus there arises in physics the need to attribute waviness and substantiality to the same phenomenon of light; in psychiatry one needs both topographical and economic models to describe the same psyche; in theology there is the *communicatio idiomatum*, where it can truly be said that "one of the (impassible) Trinity has died,' and there is the "now and not yet" of every Christian life.

Equally, the same image may symbolize more than one reality. All symbols are polyvalent. The night can be a symbol of the outer darkness, as in the gospel of John, or it can be the *vera et beata nox* of the Easter liturgy. The symbolic name Lucifer may be the personified evil of Milton's *Paradise Lost,* or it can be a title of Christ, as in the Easter *Exultet*. The same image can bring together (*symbollein*) or tear apart (*diabollein*). Water may herald the new birth in Christ or the catastrophic irruption of "unconscious" contents into waking life.

Man is born immersed in the sensible; the baby's world is a world of images. It is precisely the powerfulness of the symbolic that requires us to undergo a journey from a world mediated entirely by imagery to a world mediated by meaning. The attractiveness of the symbolic threatens to inhibit the passage through intellectual conversion to the real as affirmed by judgment. The repulsiveness of the symbolic threatens to dessicate the articulation of our insights and turn the pure and unrestricted desire to know into the pathways of what has sometimes been called a bloodless abstraction.

The power of Jesus' storytelling to redeem humankind's telling of its stories has seldom been more forcefully expressed than by Auden in his *Meditation of Simeon.* Echoing the declaration of Chalcedon, Auden remarks:

Because in Him the Flesh is united to the Word without
magical transformation, Imagination is redeemed from
promiscuous fornication with her own images . . .
Because in Him all passions find a logical In-Order-
That, by Him is the perpetual recurrence of Art
assured. . . .
Because in Him the Word is united to the Flesh without

loss of perfection, Reason is redeemed from incestuous
fixation of her own Logic . . .
Because in Him abstraction finds a passionate For-The-
Sake-Of, by Him is the continuous development of Science
assured.[16]

Because Jesus has told his story and tells his story in our stories,
humankind's wounded capacity to tell and hear story aright is redeemed and made whole.

4.31 *Every human life story will reflect the presence of evil in the world and in men's lives.*

If every human life story ends in failure, still not all failures are
the same. On the biological level there is the inevitable failure of
the organism to prolong its earthly existence, the fact of death. On
the level of understanding there can be failures of understanding
due to inattentiveness or culpable bias, and there can be failures to
understand because of a lack of native intelligence that, for this
person's concrete life, is a given of their existence. There may be
failures to understand because the opportunities for cultivation of
intelligence and the learning of skills have been given but not
grasped or have not, in the concrete, been given. On a higher level
there may be failures of judgment. Rash judgment and prejudice
may short-circuit the judicial process; excessive caution and lack
of nerve may sap the very ability to make up one's mind.

At a still higher level there is the level of decision and responsibility. People consciously are actors, the subjects of verbs. Consciously they decide, take responsibility for their decisions, for
their actions and for themselves, and call themselves to account for
their failures and inadequacies.

Each level of consciousness supposes for its effectiveness its underlying levels. Failure on one level has repercussions on succeeding and higher levels. Somatic functions and dysfunctions—fa-
tigue, aggression, and sexual passion; indigestion, toxemia and
narcosis—impair or destroy the ability to understand, to judge,
and to decide. A jury may judge correctly on the evidence, but if the
evidence is skillfully perjured the verdict may be logically and
morally unassailable but factually false: miscarriages of justice
may be "spontaneous" as well as induced. *In foro mentis* one may
culpably or inculpably overlook relevant evidence, and one may

attend to the relevant data but fail to understand the issue and thus one may conclude correctly from premises that are false. Where attentiveness, intelligence, and critical reflection have failed, one may end by doing the wrong thing for the right reasons. Thus one may keep faith with moral imperatives that are false and struggle with heroic virtue to serve aims that are misguided and ill conceived. There are few fates so sad as martyrdom for an illusion.

Each higher level not only presupposes the levels of consciousness beneath it, but it also affects and gives shape to the operations on the lower level. Thus, attentiveness to the data, understanding of the data as symptoms, clinical judgment, and decision will lead to operations to correct the dysfunctions of the somatic level. Understanding of the mathematical data will compel the astronomer to look for an as yet-unsighted planet. The later judgment *"intellectus prophetae Pii IX"* that Mary's Immaculate Conception *"esse a Deo revalatam"* would, it may surely be reasonably assumed, have led a resurrected St. Thomas to revise his understanding of the question as to what was signified by the keeping of the feast.[17] Decisions as to one's calling or profession will affect what one subsequently notices, understands, and judges to be the case.

Insofar as decisions initiate or retard authentically human operations on the somatic, intellectual, and rational levels, so the life stories of human beings will exhibit responsible and irresponsible performance on all levels of consciousness. My life story will testify not only to failures that are intelligible, as when I fail to grasp an author's meaning because of misprints that render the text unintelligible, but also to failures that lack all intelligibility and result in inhuman inauthenticity. Such failures stem from what David Burrell has felicitously decribed as "that terrible refusal to be human that admits of no explanation," in a word, sin.[18] It is the unintelligible failure to be authentically human that occurs when Cain murders Abel, not for any intelligible reason, but "simply for this reason, that his own life was evil and his brother lived a good life" (1 Jn. 3:12). Every human life story reflects not only understandable failure but also failure that is felt, understood, and judged to be evil.

4.311 *The guilt that attends every life story must not only be experienced but also understood and judged.*

Guilty feelings do not infallibly prove a person to be guilty. One may feel guilty about actions that one truly judges to be morally neutral or even meritorious. One may feel no unease about one's actions or omissions either because one is justified or because the sense of moral values has been stifled and deadened by a life of wrongdoing. Pangs of conscience may be absent because one's habits are virtuous or because one's habits are sinful. A concrete story may aid understanding here much as the diagrams in a book of geometry aid one's grasp of Euclid's meaning.

A woman was the seventh of eight children. Every morning the family ate oatmeal for breakfast. The paterfamilias was allowed the privilege of having a separate bowl for his cream in order to enjoy the taste of cold cream with the hot oatmeal. The mother of the family was prepared to wash one extra bowl but not eight or nine, and so the children were excluded from enjoying this prerogative. As a child the woman used to look forward to the day when she would be grown up and be able to have two bowls, one for her milk and one for her oatmeal. The mother died, the woman nursed her father through his last illness and, as a young married woman living in the same house in which she had spent her childhood and seen her father die, she decided to gratify her childhood desire. As she spooned her cereal she felt uneasy and guilty. Far from its being an enjoyable experience, she found it distasteful enough never to repeat. Whatever explanations might feasibly be offered for her feelings of guilt—unhappiness that her father was dead, nostalgia for childhood security, uneasiness about her new responsibilities as a wife and mother-to-be (and in the concrete case, too psycho-analytical an explanation would seem like using a sledge-hammer to crack a nut)—it is clear that real guilt would be an inappropriate category to apply in such a case.

The customs-officer's stare can make one feel and act as if guilty even though one knows that one is carrying nothing that one should have declared. Conversely, anyone who has listened to the tape recordings of mass murderers calmly pleading "nicht schuldig" at the Nuremberg trials will know something of the power of rationalization and the refusal to take responsibility for one's knowledge and actions to dull the sense of guilt and culpability. Consciousness is not the same as knowledge. The true guiltiness of any life story may be assessed only by attention to the relevant data, in this case the details of the story, insight into the meaning of that data, and a judgment as to whether one's understanding of the data is true or false. I am consequently as fallible in judging the guilt of my life story or the life stories of others as I am about all other knowledge. At the best one can only make a judgment that is beyond reasonable doubt.[19]

4.312 *Guilt is not absolved by observing that the person "meant well."*

There is a saying to the effect that one should not shoot the pianist, because he or she is doing his utter best. While it would be socially unacceptable to murder the pianist merely because he was murdering Chopin, it would not be unreasonable to declare one's dissatisfaction with his performance. In the world of literary criticism one does not equate Patience Strong with Shakespeare on the grounds that they are both doing their best. In the case of Patience Strong it would be reasonable to conclude that her best poem was not good enough and that it would be better for her to try her talents in some other medium. Michelangelo's sculpture is not the wonder of the world because he did his best but because his best (and even at times his worst) was superb. Insofar as any human life is a story and therefore falls under the rubric of what might be termed the product of dramatic consciousness, the judgment of excellence and the complacency in the presence of the beautiful (*"quae visa placent"*), which are proper to the appreciation of art, is a not unhelpful category in the (constructive) criticism of human life stories.

That a person's "heart was in the right place," or that "he or she meant well" is not an exhaustive response to the quality of a person's thought or action or life. The meaning of a person's life story is not exclusively a matter of what he or she intends, taking intention in a voluntaristic sense as a kind of wanting to do the good, as though the actual achievement of the good action was somehow accidental to its moral worth. That is precisely the problem Paul delineates in the seventh chapter of Romans: "I fail to carry out the things I want to." Paul's answer is not to excuse himself as one who "means well" but to argue for the necessity of the gift of the Holy Spirit. The experienced therapist and the canon lawyer will testify to the frequency with which the psychopathic personality who is incapable of authentic relationship with a wife will confess to an inability to understand his own behavior, his wanting to be loving, and his inability to turn his words and wishes into deeds. If loving is an art, as Erich Fromm so cogently argued,[20] then the criteria of excellence, right proportion of the means to the end, and authenticity, which are the proper categories of art criticism, may be applied *mutatis mutandis* to the art of making a life/love story. The aesthetic and the ethical are not mutually opposed, as Kierkegaard seemed to think, but mutually interpenetrate and circumincess.

The case histories of marital conflict, such as those that are published by the Tavistock Institute[21] bear witness to the importance of this thesis. Where a relationship breaks down and neither party seems able to understand either the reasons why or the appropriate means of redress, the invincibility of their ignorance does not prove that their ignorance is entirely free from blame. Even where good will exists, in the popular sense of that term, the incomprehension may be the result of previous habits of inattentiveness and thoughtlessness, years of refusal to try to understand, previous rash judgments, and refusals to affirm the truth about each other and about themselves. The confusing of consciousness with knowledge, the stubborn myth that knowing is somehow like taking a look, would seem to lie at the root of certain popular misuses of the concept of the "unconscious" as a rationalization for the avoidance of taking responsibility. The doctrine of purgatory, however difficult it may be to extrapolate its theological meaning from perhaps outworn imagery, is an affirmation of the truth that good intentions without effective performance are not enough to redeem a human life story. Faith without good works, if not totally dead, is in need of the purification and resurrection that brings new life.

4.32 *As storymaking animals we are responsible for our failure to tell our story authentically.*

The story is told that when Pharoah wished to impute guilt to the sons of Israel he gave orders that the daily quota of brick was to be maintained but the wherewithal was to be withheld. Such an exercise of realpolitik implies an understanding on his part that human beings may be held responsible and accountable for their failures. The correct judgment of the Israelite foremen that Pharoah's action is unfair implies an understanding on their part that Pharoah is responsible and accountable for his failure to produce the necessary straw for making bricks. His demands are judged to be unreasonable, and such unreasonableness, is judged to be reprehensible. The telling of the story in the fifth chapter of the Book of Exodus implies that the writer or writers are appealing to a universally accepted understanding that where the means are given and the demands are reasonable any failure is our responsibility.

To the question, "Why have the Israelites failed to produce today's quota of bricks?" the attentive, intelligent, and reasonable foreman will reply, "It is because there is too little time to both gather straw and make the bricks as well." The failure is intelligible as the result of a lack of time and materials. To the question, "Why should such be the case?" the dissident foreman might reply that such was the policy of the Pharoah and that it was perfectly intelligible as the most efficient method for making the lives of the slaves intolerable. To the further question, "Why should Pharoah wish to make the lives of his slaves intolerable?" the perspicacious Israelite might reply that the reigning Pharoah was less self-assured than his predecessor, who had known Joseph, and felt threatened by the presence in his kingdom of an alien people. The behavior of the Pharoah is perfectly intelligible as the prudent policy of a government that feels threatened. To the further question, "Why does Pharoah feel threatened," presuming that the Israelites had given no cause to suspect disloyalty, a psychoanalytically oriented Israelite might reply that the incestuous goings on of the ruling house of Egypt had resulted in a Pharoah who was mother fixated, had repressed his incipient homosexuality, and had fallen victim to paranoid delusions. A less Freudian and more Jungian or Adlerian Israelite might give a different interpretation, but all would claim to understand, that is, find intelligible, the cause of the Pharoah's unreasonableness.

From the viewpoints of the ergonomics of brickmaking, the sociology of race relations, the politics of empire running, and the psychopathology of behavior, the causes of the brick shortage can be traced and the situation can be understood as intelligible. The fact that there once was a Pharoah who was assured enough of his position to invite Joseph to settle his dependents in the kingdom, however, bears witness to the fact that oppressive policies are not inevitable and that Pharoahs can react in different ways. If the straw is not provided and the quota remains the same, the output of bricks necessarily falls. If the Pharoah wishes to make the lives of his workmen intolerable, some such strategem will inevitably be decided upon. If the Pharaoh is threatened by the presence of aliens, some policy to deal with the situation must necessarily be formulated. If the Pharaoh is paranoid, then his reactions will bear the imprints of his paranoia.

But to whatever underlying causes the oppressive policies of an oppressive regime may be traced—economic, cultural, psychological, religious, ideological—the situation could be otherwise, and the resulting behavior remains unreasonable. Insofar as the Pharaoh has failed to overcome the personal, familial, and societal defects in the material he was given to shape his life, his behavior is unreasonable and his conduct blameworthy. When the sum of all the factors that go to make up the unjust system has been analyzed and understood, there remains the surd, the unintelligibility of the failure to transcend psychic, economic, and political necessity by an act of creative freedom. There remains sin.

The narrative and mythic expression of this truth in the story of Exodus can be transposed into the abstract categories of scientific theological discourse by the classical understanding of sin as a *me on*, as a *non ens*. Insofar as the failure to produce bricks may be subsumed under the necessary laws of ergonomics, political and economic science, psychopathology and the like, thus may the failure be understood and reasons for its occurrence be found. But insofar as this particular historical failure to produce the required bricks is concerned, its occurrence is unnecessary and therefore unintelligible. Insofar as it is unintelligible, it is the product and the symptom of irrationality and ultimately of sin.

Complementary to the classical understanding of the lack of intelligibility of sinful situations, there is the statistical understanding of sin as a statistically inevitable but, in its particularity, irrational failure to sublate the intelligibility of lower levels of being by the higher intelligibility and reasonableness of ever-higher levels of being. It is a failure of successively higher levels of being and consciousness to respond to the innate call to self-transcendence. Thus, though the breakdown of my relationship with a spouse or friend may be perfectly intelligible to the psychiatrist or counselor as the transference of infantile needs and reactions to an inappropriate person or situation, my failure to transcend the reactions and behavior of childhood remains unintelligible and reprehensible. Though the psychiatrist may find reasons enough for the behavior that threatens the relationship, the behavior remains unreasonable, and thereby, because of its lack of intelligibility, illegitimate and blameworthy.[22]

The first letter of Peter uses the imagery of house building to describe the Christian life. Each person is called to be a living brick or stone making up a spiritual house. Every man and woman is called to make bricks. There may be many differing kinds of brick and many ways of firing them: for the rich young man of the Gospel, brickmaking consisted in selling what he owned and following Christ in poverty, but for the healed demoniac of Gadara brickmaking involved returning home and leaving to others the following of Christ (Mk. 10:17 – 22; Mk. 5:18 – 19). All are called to be brickmakers, and to each God gives the necessary time and straw. Failure to produce the required brick renders us accountable in the sight of God. To change the metaphor: brickmaking is storymaking. Each human person is called to make a sentence in a story told by God. God and humankind are the joint authors of the story. Each is given the required words and time. Failure to produce the sentence required is sanctioned by the penalty of the sentence of one's life not being written and thereby not appearing in the book of life. The meaning of our responsibility as storytellers is implied in what Pope Paul VI said of each person:

> In the design of God, every man is called upon to develop and fulfill himself, for every life is a vocation. At birth, everyone is granted, in germ, a set of aptitudes and qualities for him to bring to fruition. Their coming to maturity, which will be the result of education received from the environment and personal efforts, will allow each man to direct himself toward the destiny intended for him by his Creator. Endowed with intelligence and freedom, he is responsible for his fulfillment as he is for his salvation. He is aided, or sometimes impeded, by those who educate him and those with whom he lives, but each person remains, whatever be these influences affecting him, the principle agent of his own success or failure. By the unaided effort of his own intelligence and his will, each man can grow in humanity, can enhance his personal worth, and can become more a person.[23]

4.33 *The true meaning and value of a human story are precarious; it can be lost through a misinterpretation of the meaning and a noncommitment to its value.*

The authenticity of a tradition derives from the personal appropriation of the true meaning and value of its foundational story. Such authenticity is not a serene and secure possession of those who claim to belong to a particular tradition; the appropriation of the foundational story's true meaning and value cannot be taken for granted. It must always be achieved, and it can be lost. There is always the risk of knowing the words and of losing the meaning of a tradition's foundation story, of possessing its form and of losing its content, of being true to its letter and of betraying its spirit. When telling a funny story it is often not what you say that matters so much as how you say it. Though the actors in a drama may be word perfect in their knowledge of the script, their resulting production may entirely distort the playwright's intended meaning. The history of monastic orders and congregations testifies to the ease with which a founder's rules may be kept but his or her spirit evaporated: hence the repeated emergence of second founders and monastic reformers. Religious legalism or formalism within the Christian community represents a distortion of its foundational story of the Good News that is Jesus Christ. Although it retains the form or letter of the story, it loses its true meaning and value, its content, spirit, and purpose: the particular transformation that the story was originally meant to effect in the lives of those who make up the community.

A human story is open to misinterpretation and false evaluation. Getting the point of a story may require much time, patience, and maturity. Missing the point of the story is one way in which its true meaning is lost on its hearers. Immaturity, superficiality, distraction, inattention, and bias are some of the factors conducive to missing the point of a story, even the point of one's own life story. A true self-understanding implies the personal appropriation of the true meaning and value of one's own life story in relation to its ultimate context (God as our ultimate background, ground, and foreground) and precludes our grasp of the true meaning and value of our own life stories. Losing the meaning of one's own life story is the most radical human loss; it recalls the expression, "losing one's soul." Whatever profit one may obtain through the appropriation of whole worlds of meaning would be ultimately of no account in the event of losing one's own meaning, of missing the point of that God-given meaning.

A true understanding of our own life story is a lifetime's project that conditions the attainment of our true understanding of other human stories. And even when such understanding is attained, it is always partial or limited; we never know all that can be known about ourselves and others. Even such limited achievement requires time, patience, humility, courage, and preparation.

To understand my own life story (and thereby that of others) I must attend to the data of my life. The characters, scenery, and much of the plot are given. My attention to the data must be selective. I cannot recall all my past life in all its details. I cannot have total perception of all that goes up to make my present situation. I do not know what new characters or changes in scenery may appear before the story has been completed. We select from the data those things that, correctly or incorrectly, we judge to be significant and/ or full of promise. My attention to the data may be distorted through self-deception, bias, rationalization, deliberate inattention, laziness, indifference, discouragement, impatience, neurotic transferrals of one set of characters or events from one context to another, and by self-idolatry. The data by themselves are insufficient. To know myself I cannot just take a good look. My understanding of the data, my understanding of the story of my life may be distorted through lack of insight, through inexperience, inappropriate selection of the data, or deliberate self-deception. Finally, I must judge my self-understanding as correct or incorrect, remembering that no one can be the final arbiter in his or her own case, and that one's own judgments about the authenticity of one's life story are only a court of first instance whose judgments are open to reversal by other courts and, in the final instance, by a Judge who judges not appearances but the heart.

4.331 *Sin consists in the deliberate distortion of our life stories in order to take them out of their proper context in the universal story.*

We experience human limitation in our missing the point of human stories, in the difficulty with which we grasp the deeper meaning of stories, and in the facility with which we even unintentionally distort stories in our attempts to communicate them. We are not infallible storytellers. We further experience our human limitation by our attempts to claim sole authorship of our life story. Rejecting the characters, scenery, and plot as given, we can attempt to manipulate the given elements of our story so that it tells a different tale from the one intended by our coauthor. The characters who people our story have each their own stories to tell. Like an actor who steals the limelight from other players, or who speaks lines belonging to another player, we can willfully ignore the proper characterization of our fellows or seek to manipulate them into playing another and inappropriate part. We can insist on replaying out act one when the scenario had moved on to act five, or we can anticipate illegitimately the ending of the play by speaking later lines before our time. In the first case we neurotically distort our adult lives by acting the part once appropriate in childhood; in the second case we precociously pretend that we are maturer than we are. In neither case may all moral imputability be arbitrarily ruled out.

In living out our life story we can be tempted to invent "cover stories" to hide the real story we know to be inauthentically lived. We lie about ourselves and, when we have become practiced in deceiving others, we come to believe our chosen version of who we are. We can censor our stories, or the stories of others, by leaving out those bits that hurt us or show us in a poor light. We can rationalize our censoring of another's story by falsely claiming that we are being "charitable." We can use a false understanding of ourself as a charitable and guileless person to cover our refusal to confront the real evils that can be found in institutions, authority figures, and individuals.

Sin, in this context, can be regarded as our futile attempt to give our life stories a meaning that implies our radical rejection of their God-given meaning. We can futilely attempt to take our life stories "out of context" with respect to their ultimate background, ground, and foreground, who is God. We can attempt to make our own human egos the ultimate context of our human story. To take anything out of context is to lose its true meaning. The rationalizations of a bad conscience express the experience of such a taking-out-of-context. The discomfort and unease of a bad conscience is the voice of God recalling us to the true meaning of our life story. Our radical misinterpretation of the universal story and of its ultimate context (God) distorts our grasp of all human stories by taking them out of their true context, that which ultimately makes a story good to tell. Not only is our storytelling fallible, it is peccable as well.

4.34 *Jesus Christ's making and telling of stories summon all humankind to share his filial responsibility for the making of their stories.*

In a marvelous image, taken from the common experience of seeing the way children imitate their parents, John records Jesus as carrying on the work of the Father:

> The Son can do nothing by himself;
> he can only do what he sees the Father doing;
> and whatever the Father does the Son does too. (Jn. 5:19)

A loving father shows the child everything he himself does. We learn to be the persons we are by imitating those who show us how to live and work. We respond as children to the lessons we are taught by ourselves learning to comb our hair, to tie our shoelaces, to be grown up.

The Father is the creator. The heavens and earth tell his story. The poet who gave us Psalm 19 praises the One who creates the story and who brings its characters to life.

> Heaven declares the glory of God,
> the sky shows the work of his hands.
> Day utters to day,
> night shows knowledge to night
> without speaking and without language,
> and their voice is not heard.
> But their sound has gone out to the whole of the earth,
> and their words to the ends of the world.[24]

The night sky is a great storybook written and illustrated by God. When the psalmist sees the heavens, the work of God's fingers, he exclaims:

> What is the son of Adam, that you should trouble over him?
> Yet you have made him only a little less than a god . . .
> You have made him govern the works of your hands.[25]

The response of the child observing with wonder the work of his or her father is to acknowledge his or her own responsibility for creating, for telling the story in his or her own turn.

Jesus Christ, first-born and most perfect of all humankind, responds as Son of God made Son of Man by telling the story told him by the Father. The life story of the crucified and risen Jesus manifests and proclaims the summons of the Father to tell forth the universal story in terms of his filial relationship to God. Jesus experienced his sons in both as an already-given relationship and also as a responsibility to be fulfilled in obedient submission to the Father's will. Jesus is affirmed as the Son on the basis of his mission; the two are inseparable. He is already the Son from the beginning, but the Christian affirmation of his Sonship is the verdict of faith on his completed and vindicated mission of filial responsiveness to his Father. His mission is rooted in his being the Son, in his personal intimacy (loving responsiveness) with the Father. He is uniquely the Son in that through his Sonship others become sons (and daughters). We are sons and daughters in the Son: *filii in Filio.* Christ is the maker of a new story that grounds the new humanity. The story that he makes is unique in that others participate in the new humanity only by partaking in *his* new humanity. It belongs to the unique quality of his Sonship that it can, or rather, that it must be shared.

It is the imperative of his filial mission (and therefore essential to his Sonship) to mediate to others his own filial relation to God. His Sonship *means* this. Filial responsibility is filial love. As the divine Son he is God's existence in the world for humankind, the Son for other sons (and daughters). He manifests and proclaims the Father, who wills to be the Father of all other persons. He reveals God seeking other sons, creating new life stories, summoning all to filial responsibility, and enabling all to respond by sending the gift of his Spirit. An old paraphrase of St. Augustine puts it beautifully:

> He was the only Son of God and yet would not be alone;
> He longed for brethren and taught them to say "Our Father."

The divine Son opens his Sonship to all humankind as a human possibility in God's eschatological grace. In the Sonship of Jesus Christ God provides a new possibility of existence for humankind out of the resources of his own inner being.

4.341 *The divine Storymaker unifies all creation within his universal story.*

Everyone loves a good story. The Christian Church in our proclamation of the Good News (kerygma), our catechesis, whether of adults or children, in our homilies, and in our theological elaborations of the Christian faith has, naturally and correctly, given a centrality to the human story of Jesus. Jesus is he who lived, preached, healed, and died for our salvation. The ease with which the Christ story is narrated, its appeal as a great story, can, however, obscure the real value and importance of the story of creation. In a Docetist Christology, whether implicit or explicit, the garb of human nature becomes a costume the actor puts on. It is a bad production in which the costume designs are so captivating as to draw our attention away from the meaning and drama of the play. In a Docetist Christianity the costume in which the Word clothes himself is thought of, implicitly or explicitly, as at best a mere garment and at worst a mere distraction. In a Docetist sacramental theology the earthly elements—water, oil, bread, and wine, the touch of human hands—are accepted as necessary matter but are conceived as unimportant in their earthly reality. Consequently, the immersion of the whole man or woman in the saving reality of Christ's death is symbolized by a trickle of water, the breaking and sharing of the one loaf are symbolized by the administration of tiny plastic-looking hosts, preconsecrated and brought out of a tabernacle, and the gestures of reconciliation and welcoming forgiveness are performed in the semidarkness behind a grille and a purple curtain. The innate capacity to symbolize contained in earthly realities is used rather than sublated into the higher context of supernatural intentionality. A Docetic spirituality is ultimately manipulative. Alienated from himself or herself as enfleshed and world dwelling, the Docetist believer relates to himself or herself as to a ghost in a machine. Reality is otherworldly, "spiritualized," and ethereal.

In the 1935 edition of his *Art and Scholasticism,* Jacques Maritain added a corrective footnote to his text. In the original edition Maritain had written that creatures have no savor. Compared to God, the "Parthenon and Notre Dame de Chartres, the Sistine Chapel and the Mass in D" were as so much human straw that would be burned on the last day. Later, Maritain apologized for his thoughtlessness. "One must have little experience of created things," he wrote, "or much experience of divine things, in order to be able to speak in this way. In general, formulas of contempt with regard to created things belong to a conventional literature that is difficult to endure. The creature . . . exists only because it is loved."[26]

Even where the telling of the story of Redemption is neither explicitly nor implicitly Docetic, the narrative ease with which the story may be told may inadvertently lead to an oversight concerning the importance of the creation story. This may especially occur where the Redemption is conceived exclusively in terms of a repair job, where the story of Redemption is told as the reversal of a fall, the patching up of an old garment. The experience of salvation is the experience of being made a new creation. The myth of genesis, the eating of the tree of knowledge, the discovery of humankind's nakedness, and the expulsion of humankind from a garden of delight is a favorite symbol of many forms of psychotherapeutic thought. The state of original justice, the delights of Eden, are seen as the undifferentiated bliss of infancy and childhood before the separation from the maternal bond and the growing up to know pain and sin, right and wrong, truth and falsehood. While such may be the psychic origins of many of the myths of *Paradise Lost,* so that Redemption becomes a Paradise regained, and while the objectification of the story of Redemption in the symbolic consciousness of many or even most Christians may owe more to Milton than it does to the story as intended by Paul, the new creation, the new heaven, and the new earth, heralded by the gift of the Spirit, are *altogether a new creation*. Eye has not seen nor ear heard the delights God has in store for those who love him, delights that, through the gift of the Spirit, are already enjoyed inchoatively *in via*. The experience of Redemption is the experience of the joyousness of the new creation, a new creation that sublates and reaffirms the essential and inalienable goodness of the old. Sin may affect the ability of man to feel the goodness of his home and yet

> for all this, nature is never spent;
> There lives the dearest freshness deep down things.[27]

The story of the forgiving father (Lk. 15:11 – 32) is instructive in this regard. The father in the story is portrayed not as one who demands apology or satisfaction before welcoming his prodigal offspring to the fellowship of his table. The father is moved with pity, runs to clasp his son, and kisses him *before* the boy acknowledges his sinfulness. He appears to cut short the boy's apology: *"But* the father said . . . (v. 22)."* Carroll Stuhlmueller comments, "The remembrance of his father's goodness revives hope and compunction. The father first seeks the lost son by the memory he has instilled; he is seeking the boy before the lad thinks to return."[28] No doubt, in any such occurrence, the returning lost sheep would have to talk through his story with his father, but the accent in Jesus' story is firmly on the welcome shown the son by the father. In the redemption of the son the stress is on the new creation (re-creation) of the family and on the feasting and the joy that go with it and not upon the previous rupture of the father-son-brother relationship nor upon the sinfulness of the son nor the difficulty of his return. The same sensitivity to the value of creation as sublated and renewed by the new creation in Christ is shown forth in the *Romances* of St. John of the Cross. St. John tells the whole story of creation and Redemption without once mentioning sin or the Fall. The hard yoke (duro yugo) under which humankind labors (*Romance VII*) is not conceived in terms of sin, but in terms of the longing of humankind for the appearance of its Savior.

> Pero la esperanza larga
> Y el deseo que crecia

De gozarse con su Esposo
Continuo les afligía.[29]

The true conviction of one's own sinfulness, the permanent transcendence of the continuous temptation to trivialize sin, come as the fruit of conversion more than as its preparatory grace. Before conversion, the conciousness of sin and guilt appears often to be more neurotic in origin than that fear of the Lord that is the gift of God's Spirit and the beginning of wisdom. The conviction that one is loved and delighted in by God, and that God demands our love in return, is more truly conducive to an authentic sense of our unworthiness and of the distance between our hope and our performance than a premature harping on sin and damnation. Before his conversion Saul was too full of zeal and (self-)righteousness to acknowledge the depth of his sinfulness in as radical a way as the maturer Paul so acknowledges in the seventh chapter of Romans.

Once we have regained a sense of the revelatory power of the story told by God in creation we increase in awareness of the revelatory power of human stories. God creates not only the heavens that they may tell forth his glory but also the human subjects and the human materials with which the human race spins its story. God creates humankind out of love. It is the same love that undergirds us even when we are sinners. The story of humankind is a story made up of many stories. It is a story played out in the context of God's creative love. It is a story in which God's redemptive love causes him to send his word to become part and parcel of the context of other human stories so that they may be unified and brought into their proper focus when the Christ hands over the whole of his story to the Father and God is all in all.

4.4 *The way in which we envision God is always determined from the start by the way we love and treasure the things presented to us within the context of our life's story.*[30]

Human experience is both cognitive and affective. The truthfulness of our images of God, the authenticity of our knowledge of God, the maturity of our love of God, the way in which we understand or envision God, will always rest upon the truthfulness of our images of contingent realities (particularly, at least in the beginning, of our parents), the authenticity of our knowledge of contingent realities, the maturity with which we responsibly love finite things and persons, the way in which we understand or envision the things of this world. It is, as Karl Rahner has affirmed, not as though we first of all knew God in a *neutral* fashion, subsequently considering whether to adopt a loving or hating attitude toward this God.[31] Such neutral knowledge of vision, such "objectivity," is a philosophical abstraction.

The mother is experienced either as the provider of our needs or as the nonprovider. (In concrete cases, she will be experienced as both, and the interaction will usually be ambivalent.) It is impossible to remain neutral in the face of the mother. Indifference to the mother is a defense mechanism against the pain of rejection. In the same way it is impossible to remain neutral in the face of God. (An apparent indifference may perhaps best be understood as a flight from confrontation with the positive and negative aspects of the God image.)

The relationship with the parent is a "relation of opposition." The mother/father is constituted as mother/father by the relationship to the son/daughter. The son/daughter is constituted as son/daughter by the relationship to the mother/father. Whether God is imaged and conceived as Father, or Mother, or Creator, or Ground of Ultimacy, or Limit of Questioning, or whatever, God is always imaged and conceived as the other term in a relation of opposition. As Father or Mother, God constitutes me as son or daughter. As Creator, God constitutes me as created. He is the ground of *my* ultimate concern, the limit of *my* questioning. As the known unknown intended by my questions for understanding, reflection, and decision God can be intended only as the related term to myself as knower, understander, reflecter, decider, intender. To know God as my Father I must necessarily know myself as his child. To have any knowledge of God, or an image of God, I must have some knowledge and image of myself. But who I am, my knowledge and image of myself, is an amalgam of relationships of opposition to more than one term. I know myself (and love myself) as the subject of relations to parents, siblings, companions, associates, and so on. As a consequence we may affirm that our concrete knowledge of our self is born of our love or lack of love for the other terms of the relations that constitute us. Wherefore, we may also affirm that our concrete knowledge or vision of God is born of the love or lack of love with which we relate to the persons and things presented to us within the context of our life's story.

4.41 **The way that Jesus Christ loved and treasured the things presented to him within the context of his life story reveals to Christian faith the meaning of authentic love and the true vision of God.**

Jesus was formed by the community into which he was born. As Word of God he was constituted as subject by a relation of opposition to the Father. As man he was constituted by relations of opposition to God (as Creator), to Mary as Mother, to the persons and things presented to him within the context of his life story. He was born into a praying community, a community formed and maintained by the call to conversion and the gift of God's love. The story of God that emerges from his storylistening and storytelling implies how he loved the persons and things presented to him. The story that his life and death tell reveals the way in which he envisioned God, humankind, the world, himself, suffering, failure, evil, and death. The life story of the crucified and risen Jesus defines for the community of faith the true meaning of divine and human love. The authenticity of his love manifests the authenticity of his vision of God.

4.5 **The meaning of Jesus Christ is seen as the outcome of his life story.**

Jesus is described by Luke (2:40;52) as growing not only in years and in stature, but also in wisdom and in grace. He grew in the favor of God and of men. He grew within a family, within a village community, and within a religious congregation (the synagogue at Nazareth "where he had been brought up" (Lk. 4:16). He grew by making a life story as a particular man, born of a particular woman, born the subject of a particular Law, as part of a whole web of interpersonal and community relationships (as the genealogies of Matthew and Luke attest). He grew in wisdom by asking questions and by listening to and understanding the answers to those questions. He grew in wisdom and grace by listening to the stories of his people and by learning to tell the stories, and make that story, in his turn. The life of Jesus, in all its parts and in all its aspects, was an ever-increasingly more perfect communication and expression of his purpose. Newman remarks somewhere that to live is to change and that to be perfect is to have changed often. The life of Jesus was a life of continual change, a life of ceaseless movement toward the definitive revelation of its meaning in the hour of his glorification. Luke, by casting the form of his narrative as a journey to the holy city of Jerusalem, the city of peace and the place of sacrifice, reveals Christ's life as a continuous movement toward a final consummation when he can cry, as John records him crying, "it is accomplished" (Jn. 19:30).

In the second book of Luke, the movement is taken up again in the reverse direction. Acts records a second journey in which the meaning of Jesus' life is proclaimed, starting in Jerusalem and spreading to the farthest limits of the world. The events in Jerusalem, the death of Jesus, and his exaltation by the Father, are thus portrayed by Luke as the focal point where the meaning of Christ's life is manifested. It is because of these events that Jesus can be acclaimed as "Lord and Messiah" (Acts 2:36).

For Luke it is the Resurrection and exaltation of Jesus that allow him to communicate his Spirit. The Father's answer to the death of Jesus, his answer to the whole story of Jesus' life, is the gift of the Holy Spirit (Acts 2:31 – 34). It is this gift of the Spirit, a gift given in response to the life story of Jesus as accomplished and finished on the Cross, which allows his disciples to know him as Lord and Messiah.

John tells the story in a complementary fashion. In John, the lifting-up of Jesus is that which makes him known (Jn. 8:28). That lifting-up is both the death, the Resurrection, and the exaltation of Jesus. In his description of the death of Jesus, John speaks of his death as the giving up, the breathing forth of his Spirit. On the first Easter Day Jesus breathes the Spirit on his disciples. From the dead body, from the stilled heart of Jesus, there flow both blood and water, which together with the Spirit bear witness to the life story of the Son of God (Jn. 19:34; 1 Jn. 5:6 – 9). And these witnesses are not external pointers, signs that can be seen out-there-now, signs that are refused a wicked and adulterous generation, but are interior to the heart of each believer (1 Jn. 5:10). In describing the death of Jesus, John makes use of the prophecy of Zechariah: not only will men look upon the One whom they have pierced, but God will pour upon them a spirit of kindness and prayer (Zech. 12:10; Jn. 9:37). It is the same outpouring of the Spirit that Luke recalled had been prophesied by Joel (Acts 2:16 – 21). Both Luke and John, each in his own way, tell the story of Jesus as coming to completion in its ending. As Eliot remarks in "Little Gidding," "The end is where we start from."[32]

4.51 *The vision of Beloved Sonship symbolized in the baptism of Jesus is further revealed as the foundation of the Christian story by Jesus' Way of the Cross.*

Baptism into Christ is baptism into his death. Where Mark alludes to Jesus as the servant hymned by Isaiah, John further refines our understanding of Christ's baptism by proclaiming Jesus as the Lamb (Aramaic *talia* means servant or lamb) of God (Jn. 1:29, 36). The sacrificial death of Jesus, made effective for us by our baptismal soaking, is the image that communicates to us our status as fellow trusted ones of God.

A consideration of Aristotle helps us to appreciate the revolutionary character of the vision of Christian faith when he teaches that it is absurd to speak of the love that the gods have for human persons. Since they have no need of anything for their happiness they have no need to love. Likewise, argues Aristotle, it would be absurd if someone were to say that he loved Zeus.[33] For Plato, love is a movement for what is recognized to have value and that is recognized to be intrinsically lovable. Whoever loves seeks in the giving and receiving of love a self-enrichment through the value or excellence of the beloved. From this perspective God cannot love because he is perfect and possesses every good.

The Christian too affirms the perfection of God, and yet we equally affirm that God's gift involves a certain mutuality of giving:

> You have no need of our praise,
> yet our desire to thank you is itself your gift.
> Our prayer of thanksgiving adds nothing to your greatness,
> but makes us grow in your grace.[34]

The statement of faith that God is Love implies a new vision of love as being not necessarily a fulfillment of a need but a total self-investment in love for another that has overcome the fear of rejection. Perfect love casts out fear. Human claims to have achieved by ourselves a perfect love that has no element of need are a measure of the fear that unless we can deceive the other into believing that our regard for him or her is totally altruistic we shall suffer rejection.[35] In Mark's Gospel Jesus becomes progressively more unpopular, more unacceptable to others—to the miracle-seeking crowd, to the diffident and disconcerted disciples, to the hostile religious leaders—as he approaches the culmination of his life story in the revelation of love as the abandonment of self to God. Mark punctuates his narrative with prophecies of the Passion. After the first of these, Peter remonstrates with him. He earns the sharp rebuke: "Get behind me, Satan! Because the way you think is not God's way but man's" (Mk. 8:31 – 33). Peter's problem is that his faith is weak. After they had left for the Mount of Olives, Peter rashly protested his fullness of faith, "Even if all lose faith, I will not!" (Mk. 14:31). Just as he refused to listen to Christ's prediction of His Passion so now Peter refuses to listen to Christ's prediction of his coming denial. But he repeated still more earnestly, "If I have to die with you, I will never disown you." Peter's lack of faith entails that his "eye of love" is not yet sufficiently opened for him to accept and understand the new image of love being disclosed to him. His love for Jesus is still too bound up with his need to cut a *bella figura* in front of the other disciples.

The agape disclosed by the story of Christ's self-appreciation as one totally trusted by God and of his total trust in God discloses to our world the divine possibility of so totally abandoning one's self into the hands of God that one can transcend one's need to be loved by others enough to overcome the all-too-human fear of rejection. To offer love to another human is, by definition, to risk that offer being rejected as untrustworthy, as a sham, or as not worthy of notice. Even where our love is genuine and genuinely appreciates the loveliness of the beloved, it is always an offer of love to a finite, sinful person who, through stupidity, cowardice, or malice, may reject our love and hurt us at our most vulnerable. To partake in the self-transforming love of Jesus is to love the other so much that one can risk being hurt and misunderstood. The desire to love God is itself his gift. Our love for him is only possible because he has first loved us with a totally transforming love. To love God is to abandon oneself into the hands of one who has irrevocably promised that he will not reject our love; indeed, since our love is the fruit of the gift of his own love through the Holy Spirit, for God to reject our love would be to reject and to deny his own self. Insofar as my love for another human has been transmuted and given a new and supernatural intentionality by the gift of God's love, so my love for my neighbor will be an abandonment to the God who is disclosed in my neighbor as the God and Father of our common Lord Jesus Christ.[36]

4.52 The story of Christ's life reveals the necessity of suffering in every human life story.

There is no human story without other persons. Every human being is the child of a mother and father. Our story neither origi-nates nor exists in abstraction from our relationships to other sig-nificant persons; it cannot be understood or evaluated apart from them. We learn the possibilities for the behavior and actions that tell our life story from the stories that other lives are telling us. Our experiences, feelings, perceptions, and tendencies occur within a unique and shifting constellation of other life stories that form the living context for our own story. The quality of our story depends upon how well we discern our best possibilities within this living context. In the language of narrative, we depend on others for our characterization, motivation, description, and commentary, as well as for the plot of our life story. Parents, siblings, teachers, spouses, friends, and enemies make up the dramatis personae of our story. Our coming into and leaving of relationship with other persons mark the turning points in our story.

As infants we are naturally sympathetic. The feelings and moods of our mother are communicated to us by our mother's milk. We are fed by what Shakespeare called the milk of human kindness. We are warped and nearly destroyed by the soured milk of human discord and hatred. Spontaneously we move to pick up a falling child; without thought we touch the arm of a grieving fellow hu-man; spontaneously we put up our arm to ward off a hostile blow. The joys, griefs, sorrow, and laughter of our fellows communicate themselves spontaneously to our consciousness, and we often grieve and laugh without knowing why.

The dynamic thrust of our life, the upward vector of our devel-oping affectivity and intelligence, move us from a natural, sponta-neous and easy sympathy to an achieved, a deliberate, and an ever-precarious empathy. We learn to share the worlds and horizons of other persons, races, and nations. As children we learn to move out of the world of our immediate surroundings toward the far larger world revealed through the memories, meditations, scholarship, research, literature, common sense, and experience of others. Their lives and accomplishments expand our world; they bring new meanings that establish our world of meaning. Heart speaks to heart. By an act of creative imagination we pass over to the thoughts and feelings of others; we imagine what it is like to be in their shoes. We attend to our imaginative constructions of other lives and other subjects, we understand what those lives and those persons must be, we judge whether our understanding is correct, and we decide to shape our lives according to our enlarged understanding. The stories to which we listen shape the stories we tell.

The passage from the world of infantile spontaneity and immediacy to the mediated and freely chosen world of adult responsibility is attended by what might conveniently be named growing pains. Each new call to enlarge our own horizon unsettles the comfortableness of our own small world. The refusal to grow up, the failure to make the passage from one horizon of knowing and loving to a new and larger horizon, can be experienced as a threat to our security, as a shaking of the foundations. Various and manifold are the refuges for the threatened and fixated consciousness: xenophobia, class hatred, anti-intellectualism, religious obscurantism, misanthropy, sectarianism, and the like are all ways of refusing the enlargement of our horizons. Such refusals may be rationalized as patriotism, as defense of religious or political doctrinal purity, as down-to-earth, no-nonsense common sense, and the like. In and through all the particular calls to self-transcendence there occurs what Bernard Lonergan has aptly named the undertow of a dread call to holiness. Not only is each call to cognitive and affective self-transcendence attended by a fear of the unknown, but the way of developing intelligence and affectivity is blocked and hindered by the deliberate and indeliberate failings of others. Family, social, economic, and even religious ties may need to be overcome in the search for fidelity in doing the truth.

The life story of Jesus, as portrayed in the Gospels, is a model of all life stories. Christ learned to put religious claims above those of family life, to be faithful even at the cost of being misunderstood by those he loved (Lk 2:49). Jesus had to endure the rejection of the synagogue in which he had been brought up (Lk. 4:28), the incomprehension of those to whom he preached (Jn. 6:41, 52, 60–62), rejection by the leaders and teachers of his people. The physical agony of the garden, Christ's overcoming of physical and psychic fear by his devotion to the will of his Father, is a powerful symbol of a life lived out in continuous self-transcendence.

The story of Mary, as it may be legitimately conjectured from the Gospel accounts, is similarly a journey of self-transcendence and continuous enlarging of horizons. She treasures in her heart words she cannot as yet comprehend. The synagogue community where she took her Son as a child rejects him. The men she had been brought up to revere as sitting in the chair of Moses, the mediators to her of her symbols of God, her instructors in the Law, are represented in the Gospels as rejecting her Son. Mary's life was a life of continuous change in which the one stability was the inexorableness of God's call and her devotion to her Son.

There is a form of Pelagianism, of illegitimate self-reliance, which conceives the essence and value of religion as lying in the hardness and difficulty of the demands it makes. Such Pelagianism has amusingly been described as a "hardening of the oughteries." Such Pelagians talk much of sacrifice; for them religion is meaningless unless it is fraught with difficulty and hardship. One may be forgiven for suspecting a secret prayer of thankfulness that they are not as other people. Such Pelagians tend to identify sacrifice with an ethic of "giving things up"; pleasure *qua* pleasure is all but identified with sin. Such Pelagianism forgets that sacrifice is not measured by the hardness of what we are called to do but by the generosity and totality of our self-giving *whether the consequences are joy or pain.*

A story may illustrate the point. A man was asked to contribute a few pence to a farewell present for a person he disliked intensely. He begrudged the few pennies he gave. Later, on the same day, he bought a birthday present for one he loved. In his excitement at the pleasure he knew it would bring to his loved one he did not notice the cost. It was only days later, looking at the receipt, that he realized how much it had cost. We are called to give without counting the cost, a phrase that surely means not that we must "give until it hurts" but that in our excitement at finding the pearl we do not notice the loss of our other possessions. The point is beautifully illustrated by Metropolitan Anthony of Surozh who criticizes from the Eastern point of view the Western tendency to sympathize with the Mother of Sorrows.[37] How, he asks, could one so holy and so perfectly attuned to the Divine Will not experience a profound and unquenchable joy in observing the faithfulness of her Son even unto death? All true sacrifice disregards the shamefulness of the Cross for the joy that is set before it (Heb. 12:2). It takes no count of the cost. The story of the mother of the seven Maccabees (2 Macc. 7) more perfectly expresses the mind and heart of Mary than much Christian devotional literature and hymnody. The Gospels record the faithfulness of Mary and the faithlessness of the disciples; it is perhaps a legitimate eisegesis or midrash to see in the absence of any Resurrection appearance to Mary the recognition, conscious or unconscious, that the Virgin Daughter of Zion had no need for sensible reassurance.

The painfulness of the sacrifices we are called upon to make varies in direct proportion to our attachment to other things. Two children leave their mothers for their first day at school; the one tearfully clings to his mother in his fear of the unknown; the other joyfully runs to school in his excitement at growing up. Both children leave the familiar and embrace the unknown, but the joyful child's attitude is more pregnant with hope of future growth. The hardness of the demands God's call makes on us is the measure more of our sinfulness and of our distance from perfection than of the value and worth of our sacrifice.

4.521 *The Way of the Cross as disclosed in the story of Jesus reveals the nature of authentic suffering.*

A true story is told of a bishop who suffered from attacks of asthma. The asthma would attack at the most inopportune times, causing disruptions during parish visitations and the like. A priest, affecting to be ignorant of the bishop's disability, remarked to him one day that the cause of asthma was well known. It arose from seeking to be the center of attention and, to add concreteness to his imagery, the priest continued that it resulted from not having one's bottom smacked enough in childhood. The bishop was never known to have another attack from that day.

Not all suffering is authentic. The hypochondriac uses a supposed but really felt unwellness to manipulate the lives of others. Sore throats, headaches, angina pectoris, and a host of other ailments both great and small can be used to attract attention, get our way, manipulate other people's concern, and even to comfort ourselves by ensuring that others will nurse us.

Not all suffering is authentic, least of all the suffering that we bring upon ourselves. A particular temptation of those brought up in the Catholic tradition is to seek out suffering to offer it up. Paul's image of the athlete (1 Cor. 9:24 – 27) is easily misunderstood. Athletes train, diet, give up smoking and alcohol, and the like *not* because hardship is good in itself but because it is the necessary means if they are to win the race. Their fidelity to their "mission"— in this case, winning an Olympic Gold—brings about the hardships of training and the disappointments of many races in which they are the losers. They do not seek such hardships for themselves but have their hearts so set on the prize that they can endure them if they happen to occur. It is perhaps not unfair to suggest that much popular teaching on ascesis has intentionally or unintentionally given the impression that asceticism is a good in itself. The danger with all teaching that suggests that giving things up and offering things up is good training for the cross that we may one day be called upon to bear is that such teaching can often trivialize the meaning of carrying one's cross. Giving up sweets for Lent, enduring a headache for the sake of the Holy Souls, standing motionless while the Passion is sung on Good Friday are not really much use as training for the discovery that fidelity to one's mission to proclaim the Gospel will arouse the opposition of many whom one could have expected to rely on for support. In explaining the need for penance to children, it is probably far better to dwell upon faithfulness to God's will in little things as a stepping stone to faithfulness in big things rather than to run the risk of encouraging the growth of a Pelagian mentality.

Shortly after his ordination a young priest went on vacation with another priest and a married couple. All three were university professors of some distinction and were used to a style of life that was above anything their newly ordained companion had ever experienced. They stayed in the best hotels, ate at the best restaurants, and took taxis in preference to buses. Their young companion enjoyed the life immensely but, fired by a youthful and romantic ideal of what was the proper life-style of one dedicated to the preaching of the Gospel, felt a growing unease and dissatisfaction. On arrival at the railway station that marked the end of their holiday, the unease had turned to irritation at his companions. Looking for a porter to carry the luggage, the older priest chanced to remark that surely he wasn't expected to carry his own bags. His younger companion retorted with righteous indignation, "Take care! They might ask you to carry a cross." The older priest, a man who had suffered from self-appointed heresy hunters and guardians of orthodoxy, gently tapped his forehead and replied, "My cross is in here. Preach the Gospel without fear or favor, and you will know what it is to suffer."

The Christian eye of love, the understanding that comes from fidelity to the faith and love one has received, connaturally understands the Way of the Cross. One who had preached the Gospel in season and out of season, welcome or unwelcome, has no need for exterior training in carrying the cross. She or he knows the power of the Good News to arouse opposition. Suffering acts as an index to human authenticity and excellence. Only one who knows how a sonata should be played suffers when he or she hears it played badly. Only one who is tactful and genuinely thoughtful of others will suffer as the result of another's tactlessness or thoughtlessness. Only one who is authentically religious will suffer as the result of understanding the distortions of religion. Jesus suffered at the hands of a religious establishment that had distorted the faith of Israel; it would be surprising if his followers were never called upon to suffer similarly. To be called to incarnate authenticity within a religious family or institution that has become inauthentic (as so many monastic reformers have been called upon to do) is perhaps of all vocations the hardest cross of all. Only the eye of authentic love can begin to perceive the beatitude of being abused and persecuted and slandered on account of Christ (Mt. 5:11).

There is a bias against suffering that has perhaps characterized much spiritual direction in our history. It can conveniently be summarized under the heading "Fit in and don't make a fuss." Eccentricity, psychic pain, confrontation with others were to be avoided at all costs. Toleration of ecclesiastical abuses was preferable to "risking it getting into the newspapers." The attitude was beautifully displayed by a pastor who told his assistant not to read Scripture to the people when conducting the Way of the Cross because they had complained of being challenged and they came to church for comfort in a harsh world! Suffering, when seen from the viewpoint of such a syndrome, becomes an indication that there is something wrong with the sufferer's spiritual life. Suffering means "being too intense" or "being unbalanced." Equanimity is held up as the great virtue; not the true equanimity of the one who stood speechless before his accusers, but the equanimity of the one who stands speechless at the abuse and sufferings of others. At the close of the Matthaean beatitudes, Jesus reveals the essence of Christian suffering; it is the mark of the prophet, the one who truly speaks in the name of God (Mt. 5:12). Fidelity to the demands of the Good News may necessitate the use of anger. Jesus threw the money changers out of the temple and was harsh in his rebuke of those who had distorted religion. Inability to criticize and, where necessary, to be angry, is not the infallible sign of humility about one's own perceptions and judgments but a sign of fear at the suffering that fidelity to the Good News will entail. It was said of a bishop who had been five years in office that he had got along too well with everybody to have been an authentic and a credible witness to the love revealed in Christ's prophetic Way of the Cross. He had never once criticized anything or anyone.

Far from being a sign that something is spiritually wrong, a liability to suffer augurs well for human and Christian authenticity. The pastor whose preaching and praxis never arouse opposition should worry whether he is quite so molded in the image of Christ as he would like to imagine. The equanimity of the rich and powerful in the Third World or of the averagely rich and powerful in the Rich World is an index of the inauthenticity with which they live the Gospel. A failure to disturb the peace may be a sign of cowardice and spiritual deadness as much as it may be a sign of patient, long-suffering endurance.

Suffering is related to self-knowledge. When we willingly suffer for the values we proclaim, we have some assurance that we truly adhere to them. Similarly, our profession of friendship for others is authenticated by our voluntary self-sacrifice on their behalf. Claims of love and friendship must be authenticated by more than mere words. We learn the truth or falsity of our claims about ourselves as lovers and friends only when we gladly pay the price that authentic love and friendship demand; otherwise, the question of self-deception may not so easily be put to rest.

4.522 *The Cross reveals to Christian faith the extent to which the divine Storymaker is committed to the excellence of his universal story.*[38]

One commonly hears said by a certain sort of Christian that the fact that one is commanded to love one's neighbor does not entail that one must like him or her. A distinction is made between liking and loving. I may like or dislike whom I please but, if I am to be a Christian, I must love with a universal love. Such an affirmation overlooks the obvious, but seemingly overlooked is the point that I cannot by definition love that which is unlovable, and in any credible and normally accepted sense that which I do not like is that which I do not love. Love may commonly be regarded as an intense or as a superior form of liking (and here we are not making any judgment as to the adequacy or inadequacy of such a usage), but it can hardly be argued that men commonly love their wives while disliking them or that we commonly dislike our enemies while at the same time heroically loving them. There is a truth in the distinction between loving and liking to the effect that the call to universal love should move us to transcend our petty and, in the light of eternity, quite ludicrous likes and dislikes, but that is another matter. When someone is forced to bend language in so remarkable a way, we can suspect with reason the presence of a rationalization. When I grudgingly give a beggar a dime or a few cents "because he is Christ" and at the same time barely conceal my ill humor and dislike of the fecklessness of the "underserving poor," the hardness and ill grace with which I "love" Christ in the poor while at the same time disliking this intrusion upon my wealth and privacy are a measure not of the heroism of my charity but of the lack of perfection of my love. A fastidious woman who had a particular dislike of skin diseases was called upon to nurse someone with an unpleasant-looking skin complaint. When it was remarked that she had done various things that one would have expected to have caused her nausea, she replied that the suffering and distress of the patient made her quite forget the unpleasantness of her task. Authentic love causes us not to notice, let alone count, the cost.

When a child is cared for and responsibly given all that he or she needs in the way of physical sustenance, she or he may surprise the parent by complaining that the one thing he or she really needed was never given, namely, love. The child has, rightly or wrongly, understood himself or herself to have been unwelcome, disliked, unaffirmed as good and valuable. Conversely, a child may come from a poor home where the level of physical and educational care is low, perhaps because of the lack of understanding on the part of the parents or because of economic circumstance, but where he or she is made to feel precious in the eyes of his or her family. The teenager who complains that "no one loves me" feels disliked, unwanted, and of little value or account. Anorexics, who consistently expose a family background of uncommon rigidity and lack of love, doubt the likeability of their body image. Their supposed fatness, albeit bizarrely exaggerated, appears to them a barrier to their being attractive (likeable) enough to be loved. While it would be bizarre to suggest that love is not shown in caring and doing one's best for one's beloved, it would, nevertheless, appear that attractiveness and likeability are more closely asociated with loveliness (the ability to be loved) than some Christians would find it convenient to affirm. If I dislike the leper as I kiss him or her, far from showing my love for God, I am engaging in a more or less cynical use of the sufferer as an instrument for worship. I am degrading a fellow human being to the status of a thurible or candlestick. When a saint kisses the leper, he or she is proclaiming, if the sign is genuine, his or her true and honest welcome for the real presence of Christ in the real presence of a human being who is precious in

his or her own right. In his second *Romance*, St. John of the Cross
puts these words into the mouth of the Father as He addresses his
Son before the creation of the world:

> Y si algo me contenta,
> En ti mismo lo quería;
> El que a ti más se parece,
> A mí más satisfacía. . . .
>
> Al que a ti amare, Hijo,
> A mí mismo le daría,
> Y el amor yo en ti tengo,
> Ese mismo en éí pondría,
> En razón de haber amado
> A quien yo tanto quería.

The Father delights in the children of men because He sees in
them their family likeness to his Beloved. The saint, the person in
whom the love of God has been poured out by the gift of conversion,
reflects the intra-Trinitarian delight of the Persons of the Godhead.
The saint truly loves the leper as he kisses him or her because that
person in all his or her concrete humanity and individuality, and
because of that unique and irreplaceable individuality, reflects the
very face of Christ.

In the translation of Roy Campbell:

> But if aught please me, I as duly
> In You, Yourself, the cause construe.
> The one who satisfies Me truly
> Is him who most resembles You. . .
>
> The man who loves You, O my Son,
> To him Myself I will belong.
> The love that in Yourself I won
> I'll plant in him and root it strong.
> Because he loved the very one
> I loved so deeply and so long.[39]

Love delights in the presence of its beloved. The truth of this
argument may perhaps be confirmed by an act of creative imagination. The reduction of a counterposition to its absurdity may
sometimes express more forcefully the truth of one's position. What
Christian has ever imagined that at the particular judgment he or

she might hear Christ say, "I love you, I died for you, but I do not like you"? To posit the possibility of love without delight in the object of one's love is to give existential justification to the phrase "as cold as charity." Where charity is cold, it is not charity at all. The warmth of our love for our neighbor can never be divorced from the warmth of our love for God.

In all true forgiveness, affirms Sebastian Moore, the forgiven person is affirmed as good. True forgiveness is "the opposite of what we normally think forgiveness is. The normal understanding of 'being forgiven' is 'I am bad, *but* you forgive me.' I *am* no good, but *even so*, you're *so* good that you forgive me. Whereas true forgiveness means Mary's reawakening John's sense of *his own* goodness, which has taken a big knock from the way he's treated Mary. True forgiveness is love in action awakening the offender to the good he suppressed *in himself* in hitting out at the offended one."[40] In the most radical instance of forgiveness known to Christian faith, the atoning death of the Beloved Son of God, God affirms in the most radically possible way, the goodness of all humankind.

> I was angry with my friend:
> I told my wrath, my wrath did end.
> I was angry with my foe:
> I told it not, my wrath did grow.

Blake's verse, from "The Poison Tree," hints at the paradox of confession and forgiveness. When anger is unacknowledged (and in a sense all sin is anger inasmuch as every sin is the disruption of a personal relationship, a malice-filled offense against others and against God) and is repressed, it becomes anger against oneself. Depressive illnesses (leaving aside possible endogenous chemico-physical etiology) are largely a matter of repressed anger, an anger turned against oneself. When I repress my guiltiness and refuse to acknowledge my sinfulness, my self-understanding as bad festers and works out its poison below the surface. It is not without reason that Blake entitled his poem "The Poison Tree." When I acknowledge my sin, placing it in the context of other persons' life stories and, above all, in the context of the story told by Christ, I find myself reaffirmed in my essential and inalienable goodness.

> When I was silent, my bones withered away with groaning
>   all day long.
> Your hand was heavy on me day and night,

my moisture dried up like a drought in the hot season.
I will show you my sin, I have not covered my wickedness.
I said, I will confess my sins to God,
and so you forgave the wickedness of my sin.[41]

Moore expresses the same point in language more technical than
that of the psalmist: "confession of fault means a good self-concept.
Repression of fault means a bad self-concept."[42] When we say that
confession of sin restores a person's happiness, we are not saying,
as some perhaps naively would, that confession is a little like the
dentist's chair: it's great when it's over. We are affirming that ultimately one can confess only to a lover; in authentic love there is
a basic trust and confidence, a trust that perdures even through
temporary tiffs and quarrels, that allows us to be who we are. Love
affirms us as good and lovely even as it forgives and heals. The
forgiveness of a lover affirms us to be what we truly are: lovers,
both by nature and by grace.

In his second letter to the Christians of Corinth, Paul comes to
the heart of the matter: "For our sake God made the sinless one
into sin, so that in him we might become the goodness of God" (2
Cor. 5:21). The forgiveness of Christ's atoning death is achieved by
his sharing in the dread and loneliness of our guilt-ridden mortality *in order that we may be affirmed as good and precious in his eyes.*
Edith Stein, one who voluntarily accepted death as a witness to the
truth of her story, affirms in her study of the Cross that to be "pure
of guilt yet to feel the pain of it" is the inner meaning of Gethsem-
ane and Golgotha.[43] Christ stands speechless before his accusers,
refuses to defend himself at the bar of human justice, commits his
soul into the hands of his Father because he knows that the Father
has affirmed, does affirm, and will affirm him as the Beloved Son.
If all forgiveness is an affirmation of our loveliness, and if it is true
that to accept our own loveliness is the most self-transcending task
of all, the most difficult thing any human being is called to do, then
we can affirm that by his death Christ has experienced for us, in the
most radically possible way, the goodness-affirming forgiveness of
God.

The death of Jesus affirms the goodness of creation in two ways:
by his acceptance of the goodness of the created humanity of his
Son and by the Son's being as the goodness-affirming Word of God
made flesh. In Christ's created humanity humankind comes to perfection. In Christ's life of total self-transcendence, his life of loving

commitment to the value of his Father's story as told through the created lives of his fellow humans, he reveals God's Word as a word of goodness-affirming and goodness-creating love. "It is not easy," Paul tells the Romans, "to die even for a good man—though of course for someone really worthy, a man might be prepared to die—but what proves that God loves us is that Christ died for us while we were still sinners" (Rom. 5:7 – 8). To die for a friend, says the Christ of John's Gospel, is the greatest affirmation of the friend's loveliness. In a poem of startling beauty Samuel Crossman sings of the Savior's love for humankind. Jesus has

> Love to the loveless shown
> That they might lovely be.

By nailing our sinful estrangement to the tree, Christ has uttered the definitive word about the worthiness of men and women; we are worth dying for. An act of self-surrender by which I am affirmed in my goodness by the very act of affirming the goodness of another is a most potent symbol for understanding the depth of meaning shown by the Cross. Surely, it is for that reason that Augustine, in a daring metaphor, can liken the Cross to the bed of marriage: "Like a bridegroom Christ went forth from his chamber, he went with a presage of his nuptials into the field of the world. . . . He came to the marriage bed of the Cross, and there, in mounting it, he consummated his marriage. And when he perceived the sighs of the creature, he lovingly gave himself up to the torment in the place of his bride, . . . and he joined the woman to himself forever."[44]

4.6 *Because our faith is preconceptual our telling and listening to God's story will be a communication of the incommunicable and an expression of the inexpressible.*

Christian tradition asserts that God is and ever remains incomprehensible. The supreme knowledge of God, wrote St. Thomas, is to know that we do not know God.[45] The occupational hazard of theologians, affirms Karl Rahner, is to feel that they have been admitted to God's secret counsel and that they have grasped more about God than others have done, "whereas in reality the true theologians are those who have understood better than other men that God is inconceivable."[46] God remains unknown.

Though God remains ever unknown, it is as a known-unknown that he is conceived. When I look out to sea, I cannot see what lies beyond the horizon. I know the horizon as the limit of my sight. I have a concept of the horizon as that beyond which my eye cannot travel. The concept of a horizon contains a preconcept of what might lie beyond. I know and understand the horizon not as the limit of the world but as the limit of my knowledge. When, before Columbus, people imagined that to sail beyond the horizon would cause them to fall off the edge of the world, or that it might bring them directly to China, their preconcept of what lay beyond the horizon was wrong though their concept of the horizon, as a limit of sight, was correct. Preconceptual understanding is as prone to error as conceptual thought.[47] Nevertheless, it is our preconceptual understanding, our idea of what it is we are looking for, that allows us to form and to validate or invalidate our concepts. We have a conception of the unknown in the same way that we have a conception of a forgotten name; we attend to the known, not as it is in itself, but as a pointer to the unknown.[48]

The baby who has not yet learned to articulate experience in speech crawls happily away from the mother or climbs cheerfully out of the crib. The baby is attempting to explore the unknown. In the earliest stages the external world remains strictly unknown. Presented with a hitherto unknown experience the baby reacts, perhaps with delight or, alternatively, with fear. The child has a preconception of what lies at the end of his or her exploring as good or bad. The baby is faced with a known-unknown that, as a result of his or her exploring, becomes known. What before was a known-unknown, something preconceptual, becomes something known, something conceived.

When we affirm that faith in God always retains its preconceptual character we are not affirming that we can have no concept of God. Frederick E. Crowe has rightly criticized the latent epistemology of Edward Schillebeeckx in this regard.[49] According to Crowe, the act of insight grounds not only the concept that is understood but also the concept of what lies beyond. Consequently we have conceptions of sin (the surd beyond intelligibility), of nothing (what lies beyond existence), and of God (what transcends the limits of human understanding and imagination). Faith in the truth and goodness of God remains preconceptual insofar as the unknown always remains greater than the known. In affirming the transcendence of God over all the concepts we can have of him we are not affirming that we have no concept of God at all. Kant affirmed that the beautiful was that which was perceived without the aid of concepts, yet this did not mean that we can have no concept of the beautiful. Without some such concept it would be impossible to write a *Critique of Judgment*. Reality is never exhausted by the concepts we have of it; the existential and concrete can never be reduced exhaustively to a conceptual system *more geometrico.*

Nevertheless, conceptual knowledge is not to be despised. The logician, as Newman remarked, may well turn rivers full, winding, and beautiful into navigable canals, but without the admiralty charts we will never safely appreciate the winding beauty of the river as we sail along it.[50] There is an existential, a concrete, an experiential knowledge of God that is expressed by such concepts as knowing Jesus as one's personal Lord and Savior or, less happily, as a heart knowledge of God opposed to the knowledge of the head. Such a dichotomy between the reality and the concept of it (and concepts themselves are real entities) is not something exclusive to our conceptions of God. The conceptual framework of scientific discourse about bacteria, neuroses, sexuality, and nutrition never exhausts the reality of the hepatitis that attacks my liver, the addiction that ruins my life, the woman or man who becomes the very half of my soul, or the relish with which I attack the chocolate *gâteau.* Every being, however humble, eludes the complete mastery that humankind's intellectual hubris would sometimes like to claim as belonging to our conceptual knowledge.

But insofar as the being of an entity is more perfect, so its transcendence of our concepts will be greater. God is perfection subsistent, and the gap between the Supreme Reality, which is God, and the concepts that we can form thereof, is perhaps the source of the common illusion that our knowledge of God is altogether different from our knowledge of contingent realities. It is the same person who knows and loves God as knows and loves the universe that God created.

Insofar as the concrete reality that we love and know exceeds the concepts that we can have of it, in that much the object of our love and knowledge as known and loved by us remains incommunicable and inexpressible. The kerygmatic proclamation of God in Christ and the catechesis that builds on it will remain always the communication of an incommunicable love and knowledge. In the communication of faith it is always Apollos and Paul who tell the Story in human words, but it is God who, by the gift of his Spirit, gives the ability to hear and to make it one's own.

4.61 *The symbols with which we spontaneously express the life story of God are taken from our own unthematized expression of our own life story.*

Our knowledge and love of God are rooted in the imaginative. The material from which we construct our images is taken from the perceptions of our senses. We cannot imagine unseeable sights, nor hear unhearable sounds, nor imagine what lies beyond the realm of sense. The images with which we symbolize God must be taken from experience. Certain experiences and the images stemming from them, particularly those which may be described as affect laden, have a particular potentiality for carrying the image of God. Such images may be likened to what Rahner has called primordial words.[51] Such images or words may also be described as manifesting being or meaning rather than as carriers of being or meaning.[52]

1. Aquinas, *In Lib. de Div. Nom. c 1, 1, III ed Vivès, t XXIX, p. 394a.*
2. Cf. Karl Rahner, "The Order of Redemption within the Order of Creation," *Mission and Grace, I* (London: Sheed & Ward, 1963), p. 79.
3. We are indebted to Bartholomew M. Kiely for his basic hypothesis on the tension between the world of desire and the world of limits and the temptation to pseudosolutions, implied in the biblical concept of idolatry. See his book, *Psychology and Moral Theology: Lines of Convergence* (Rome: Gregorian University Press, 1980), pp. 173–227.
4. Thomas Cooper, "On Praying to God in English," *The Clergy Review* 65 (1980), pp. 41–51.
5. A useful overview of the anti-iconic strands in classical Yahwism is provided by Aidan Nichols, *The Art of God Incarnate: Theology and Image in Christian Tradition* (London: Darton, Longman & Todd, 1980), pp. 13–29.
6. On the feelings often identified a priori as sacred or religious as "poorly grasped aspects of living" experienced in the parataxic mode, see Harry Stack Sullivan, *The Interpersonal Theory of Psychiatry* (New York: Norton, 1953), pp. 163, 370.
7. Bernard Lonergan, *Method in Theology* (London: Darton, Longman & Todd, 1971), pp. 104–107, 291.
8. *Ibid.*, p. 291.
9. St. Augustine, *In Psalmos 74 n 1, PL 36,* 946; *Corpus Christianorum Series Latina XXXIX*, p. 1024.
10. Lonergan, *op. cit.*, p. 116.
11. Bernard Lonergan, "The Future of Christianity," in *A Second Collection* (London: Darton, Longman & Todd, 1974), pp. 153–156.
12. St. John Chrysostom, *Hom. 14, 1–2, PG 61,* pp. 497–499.
13. *The Poems of Robert Southwell, S. J.,* edited by James H. McDonald and Nancy Pollard Brown (Oxford: The Clarendon Press, 1968), p. 6. Reprinted by permission of the publisher.

14. Frank Lake, *Clinical Theology: A Theological and Psychiatric Basis to Clinical Pastoral Care* (London: Darton, Longman & Todd, 1966), p. 9.

15. The distinction between God's primary and secondary word, in theses 4.21 and 4.22, is taken from Frederick E. Crowe, S. J. "Theology of the Word of God: Structural Elements for a Treatise," informally published notes (Toronto: Regis College, no date given), p. 19.

16. W. H. Auden, "The Meditation of Simeon," in *Collected Longer Poems* (London: Faber & Faber, 1974 ed.), pp. 182f.

17. See fn. 8, p. 63, "Ineffabilis Deus," *DS 2803; ST 3a* q. 27, ad. 3.

18. David Burrell, "Indwelling: Presence and Dialogue," *Theological Studies* 22 (1961), pp. 1–17.

19. For a valuable discussion of conscience and consciousness from the standpoint of Lonergan's intentionality analysis and in dialogue with Freudian thought, see Walter Conn's unpublished thesis, "Conscience and Self-Transcendence," (Ann Arbor, Mich.: University Microfilms).

20. Cf. Erich Fromm, *The Art of Loving* (London: Allen & Unwin, 1957).

21. Lily Pincus, ed., *Marriage: Studies in Emotional Conflict and Growth* (London: The Tavistock Institute, 1973 ed.); K. Bannister and L. Pincus, *Shared Phantasy in Marital Problems; Therapy in a Four-Person Relationship* (London: The Tavistock Institute, 1971).

22. For a brief but incisive treatment of sin as the absence of intelligibility, see Bernard Lonergan, "The Redemption" in *3 Lectures* (Montreal: Thomas More Institute, 1975), pp. 1 – 28.

23. *Populorum Progressio*, 15.

24. The psalm is given in the translation by Peter Levi: *The Psalms* (Harmondsworth, Middlesex: Penguin Books, 1976), p. 28.

25. Psalm 8, Levi's translation, p. 11.

26. Jacques Maritain, *Art and Scholasticism and the Frontiers of Poetry* (New York: Charles Scribner's Sons, 1962), p. 36.

27. Gerard Manley Hopkins, "God's Grandeur," in *The Poems of Gerard Manley Hopkins,* 4th ed., edited by W. H. Gardner and N. H. MacKenzie, published by Oxford University Press for the Society of Jesus.

28. Carroll Stuhlmueller, *The Jerome Biblical Commentary* (London: Geoffrey Chapman, 1968, vol. II), p. 149.

29. The meaning and poetic intent of this verse are beautifully captured by Roy Campbell in his translation, *Poems of St. John of the Cross* (Harmondsworth: Penguin, 1951): "But the length of endless waiting / And the increase of desire / To enjoy the blessed Bridgegroom / Was to them affliction dire."

30. Karl Rahner, *Hearers of the Word* (London: Sheed & Ward 1969), p. 106.

31. *Ibid.*

32. T. S. Eliot, "Little Gidding," from *Four Quartets* (New York: Harcourt, Brace Jovanovich).

33. *Nicomachean Ethics*, 9, 1158, B, 35.

34. *Missale Romanum*, Preface for Weekdays IV, ICEL trans.

35. On the complexity of love, see Otto Bird, "The Complexity of Love," *Thought* 39 (1964), pp. 210 – 220.

36. Note that love of my neighbor as self-abandonment to God as disclosed by my neighbor is not a love of my neighbor to please God; that would be to use my neighbor as a means for my salvation. True supernatural charity for my neighbor is the elevation of natural love for my neighbor (and the making of that natural love possible, in many cases) to a new and supernatural intentionality that sublates the natural into a new order so that I intend God "through him/her, with him/her and in him/her."

37. Archbishop Anthony Bloom, *Living Prayer* (London: Darton, Longman & Todd, 1966), p. 15.

38. This thesis is brilliantly affirmed in an important article by Sebastian Moore, "Christian Self-Discovery," in Fred Lawrence ed., *Lonergan Workshop*, vol. I (Missoula, Montana: Scholars Press, 1978), pp. 187 – 219.

39. Roy Campbell, trans., *Poems of St. John of the Cross.*

40. Sebastian Moore, *op. cit.*, p. 191.

41. Psalm 32, Levi's translation.

42. Moore, *op. cit.*, p. 192.

43. Edith Stein, *The Science of the Cross: A Study of St. John of the Cross* (London: Burns & Oates, 1960), p. 12.

44. St Augustine, *Sermo Suppositus* 120, 8. The translation is that of A. S. B. Glover in C. G. Jung, *Collected Works*, vol. XIV (London: Routledge and Kegan Paul, 1966), p. 32.

45. St. Thomas, *De Potentia, q. 7, a. 5: "Ultimum cognitionis humanae de Deo, quod sciat se Deum nescire."* Cf. Bernard Lonergan, *De Verbo Incarnato* (Rome: Gregorian University Press, 1964), p. 448.

46. Karl Rahner, "Unity-Love-Mystery," *Theological Investigations VIII* (London: Darton, Longman & Todd, 1971), p. 243.

47. It is perhaps important here to stress that when we affirm faith to be preconceptual we are not affirming that the certainty of faith depends on its preconceptual quality. The certainty proper to faith rests upon its gratuity as a gift or grace. Our preconcepts are as fallible as our concepts, a point that sometimes appears to be overlooked in some discussions of "anonymous christianity" and "charismatic" or mystical experience of God.

48. Cf. Michael Polanyi, *Personal Knowledge: Towards a Postcritical Philosophy* (London: Routledge & Kegan Paul, 1968 ed.,) pp. 127 – 128.

49. F. E. Crowe, review of E. Schillebeeckx's *Revelation and Theology 2, Theological Studies* 29 (1968), pp. 779 – 781.

50. John Henry Newman, *An Essay in Aid of a Grammar of Assent* (London: Longmans, Green, 1939 ed.) p. 267. Cf. Simon Tugwell, "Faith and Experience: VIII. Beyond Reason and Language," *New Blackfriars* 60 (1979), pp. 384ff.

51. Karl Rahner, "Priest and Poet," *Theological Investigations III*, pp. 294 – 317.

52. The distinction is taken from J. P. Manigne, O. P., *Pour une Poétique de la Foi: Essai sur le mystère symbolique* (Paris: du Cerf, 1969), pp. 43, 57ff. Manigne distinguishes between words that are *ontophanique* and those that are *ontopherique*.

CHAPTER 8.

THE FIFTH MOMENT:

The gift of God's love through the Holy Spirit of Jesus Christ grounds the story of Christian conversion

Being in love with God, as experienced, is being in love in an unrestricted fashion. All love is self-surrender, but being in love with God is being in love without limits or qualifications or conditions or reservations. Just as unrestricted questioning is our capacity for self-transcendence, so being in love in an unrestricted fashion is the proper fulfillment of that capacity.

Method in Theology
Bernard Lonergan

5.1 *The telling and the hearing of the Gospel story are the work of the same Spirit working in both the teller and the hearer.*

Christianity is sometimes conceived as a "religion of the Book," as though the essential act of revelation were the publication of a book written by God. Fundamentalist accounts of Scripture and Inspiration are inadequate because they explicitly or implicitly overlook the fact that Scripture is, in a well-worn phrase, the Word of God in the words of men. Unlike Joseph Smith, founder of the Mormon Church, the Church did not discover the Word of God on plates of gold written by an angel. Some theories of direct inspiration of the Scriptures are not much different from Mormon accounts of finding their foundational scriptures as faits accomplis. Revelation occurs in the mind of the prophet; more radically, it occurs in the heart of the one who has been converted to God by the outpouring of the Spirit and who has been constituted as a spokesman or spokeswoman (*prophetes*), bearing witness to the Word that he or she has received in his or her innermost core. God reveals himself by the creation of love within us.

The four canonical versions of the Gospel story reflect the differ-

ent stages of achievement that each Christian must traverse in the
growing maturation of his or her response to the gift of God's love.
Each Gospel is the expression of its human author's personal appropriation of God's gift of his love. Just as the Word-made-flesh
grew in wisdom and grace, so, too, those who hand on that word,
whether as individual storytellers or as the communities in which
the story is told, are engaged in a lifetime's process of growing in
wisdom and in favor with God. The Gospels are neither tablets of
stone dropped down from heaven nor the sublime but solely human
expressions of a community's aspirations, hopes, and dreams. The
four Gospels are the authentic expressions of the God-given response of human beings to the gift of God's love. Paul's letters are
a privileged means of communicating God's revelation because the
writer could truly and authentically say that he lived no longer
with his own life but with the life of Christ that lived in him (Cf.
Gal. 2:20). The Gospel writer must live the story before he can write
it. Paul tells the Corinthian community that it itself is a "letter
from Christ . . . written not with ink but with the Spirit of the living
God" (2 Cor. 3:3). Paul writes letters to the Corinthian community
so that the community may itself become a letter. Likewise, the
evangelists could have said that they had written their Gospels so
that the communities in which and for which they wrote could
themselves become a "living Gospel for all men to hear."[1]

The same Spirit, whose gift to one is to be an evangelist and
whose gift to another is to be an elder, enables the leaders of the
community to recognize which Gospels are canonical. In recognizing the four Gospels as inspired, that is by judging their origin to
be from the Spirit by a judgment of connaturality, the Christian
community proposes these Gospels as the rule of faith, as the standard of revealed truth or doctrine, and as the norm of Christian
authenticity, maturity, and development. Each Gospel represents
the achievement and the demand of God's gift of his love according
to the four stages of Christian maturation.

The distinctiveness of the Christian response to God's gift of his
love lies, according to Bernard Lonergan, in the suprastructure of
religious experience.[2] The four Gospels belong to this suprastructure.

As infrastructure, Christian religious experience is the dynamic
state of being in love in an unrestricted fashion, a conscious content
without an apprehended object. Its suprastructure, however, is already extant in the Gospel account of Christian origins: God's loving of us so much that he sent his only Son to die and rise for us
and breathe upon us his Holy Spirit. The acknowledgment of the

presence of the Spirit in those who are what Rahner calls anonymous Christians does not contradict the affirmation of the universal salvific will of God with its implicit claim to a Christian universalism (such as we find in 1 Tim. 2:4) since, argues Lonergan, the
salvation of the Christian is in and through charity, and this gift of
charity as an infrastructure can be the Christian account of religious experience in any and all human persons.[3] Cardinal Newman's distinction between real and notional assent may help us to
understand the purpose of the Gospel writers. Christian conversion
may be expressed as the act of insight, an insight that is God-given
as grace, by which we understand that the promise of God in Christ
is *for me*. It is equally a God-given act of judgment that convinces
us beyond all the evidence (a conviction that many Christians
would more normally term an assurance) that our understanding is
correct. Such an act of understanding and judgment of the exterior
word as talking *about me* forces me to take a stand, one way or the
other, against this insight. Every act of conversion is always a "passionate" act, a real judgment that resonates upon every level of
human consciousness.[4] The Gospels may in some way be compared
to the famous British recruiting poster of the First World War: Lord
Kitchener, the Secretary of War, stared out at the passer-by with
his finger pointing at the viewer. The slogan read, "Your country
needs YOU." The Gospel story is God's way of pointing his finger
at the person and saying, "I am talking about YOU." When we
understand, judge, and responsibly react to the fact that God is
talking through Jesus about us, we may be said to pass from a
notional idea of God to a real idea; we may be said to be undergoing
a conversion.

The four Gospels are examples of the truth that heart speaks to
heart or, perhaps better, that Spirit speaks to Spirit. Just as God's
Spirit helps us to pray when we ourselves are at a loss for words,
so, too, God's Spirit enables us to hear when our hearing has gone.
The same Spirit of God is present in the hearts of the Gospel tellers
and the hearts of their hearers. Love seeks to awaken love. The gift
of God's Spirit seeks to lead the hearer of the Gospel to a full and
personal acceptance of what God has already given.

5.11 *Christian conversion is a gift of God that enables us to hear the story of Jesus and his Church.*

People who tell their whole life story uninvited to a stranger run
the risk of boring their listener. The wedding guest waylaid by the

Ancient Mariner was, at least at first, an unwilling listener. It was the storyteller's artistry and the strangeness of the tale that eventually had the wedding guest captivated and spellbound. Most of us are less competent at telling a good tale than Coleridge or his mariner. Snapshots of somebody else's holiday, the history of a stranger's illnesses, or the detailed retelling of the trivia of somebody else's children's lives bore us *unless we are interested, or become interested, in that person or persons.* It is being in love with our loved one that makes us ready and able to listen to the story of his or her life before our paths had crossed. The knowledge a man or woman gains of his or her loved one is a knowledge born of love. Love is most usually born of knowledge: *nihil volitum nisi praecognitum* (I cannot affirm as good that which is unknown). Nothing can be willed or desired unless it is already known. We cannot decide to do something unless we have decided what we can do. Actions demand plans of action. Things that are simply unknown, which lie totally outside our horizon, are unlovable and unwillable. That which is known, that which lies within our horizon, can be loved or willed. Knowledge precedes love.

The known-unknown, that which is sought but yet unfound, that which draws us on our lifetime's quest, that which is presented to our consciousness as mystery, is loved and desired before it is known. It is known as an unknown-known; it is affirmed as good and loved as a known-unknown. The knowing of the known-unknown is consequent to our loving it. We would not seek the mystery unless we had already found it. Psychologists tell us that the sexual drive is first undifferentiated; it is a drive with a content but no object.

Infantile sexuality, the general and suffused drive toward intimacy, closeness, union, symbiosis, is at first undifferentiated. In adolescence the drive centers more particularly upon the genital and procreative and yet remains contentful but objectless. Young men are attracted to girls and fantasize about their ideal partner long before they have met one who might become their life partner. Young women dream of handsome strangers and imagine themselves as wives and mothers long before they have met the one who delights their heart. Many an elderly unmarried has explained his or her single state by saying that the right person never came along. He or she has some knowledge of what sort of person the right person might be even though he or she has in a sense no knowledge of the opposite sex and no knowledge of who the right person was. When men and women meet and fall in love, it is their love for each other that opens their ears to hear the story the beloved tells. The mutual love of lovers turns them toward each other (*conversio*, conversion) and leads to a change of heart (*metanoia*) so that the other becomes one half, of their soul—*dimidium animae meae.* When I fall and remain in love, my heart—the center of my cognitive and affective subjectivity—so changes that I become as if the subject of my lover's life story, as she (or he) becomes the subject of mine.

Paul likens the bonds of sexual love to the bond that unites the Christian to Christ (cf. Ep. 5:21ff). Just as the sexual bond so unites two life stories that they become one flesh, one story, so Christ unites the Church so totally to himself that the two become one body. The conversion or metanoia that unites two human life stories reflects, as sacrament, the conversion and the change of heart that must precede all true knowledge of God in Christ. The inborn drive for self-transcendence, that is, the drive to know and to be known, the drive to love and to be loved, the drive to become oneself by union with the other, is at first undifferentiated. It has a content but no object. It is the resonance in the cognitive and responsible planes of consciousness of a natural, pure, unrestricted openness of the human spirit to God. It is the *naturale desiderium videndi Deum* of Aquinas.[5] It is the restlessness of the Augustinian heart. In Christian conversion the natural exigency for self-transcendence is itself transcended. The natural desire to know, though it may be temporarily satiated in the release of the tension of inquiry by a flash of insight, remains ever unrestricted and pointing to things unknown. The natural desire to love, the eros that is drawn out to possess the good, though it may temporarily be satiated by the joy of possession, remains ever unrestricted and a reaching-out to other particular goods. The natural desire for God is fulfilled beyond its expectations by the gift of a complacency (*complacentia*) that is none other than the gift of the Holy Spirit, who fills our hearts with his love.

Karl Rahner issues a timely warning against conceiving of beatitude as a motionless rest. Heaven, the beatific vision, the total and simultaneous possession of oneself in the act of totally possessing and being possessed by God, is, affirms Rahner, a continuous process of ever-deeper penetration into the mystery that is the God who holds our lives.[6] Nevertheless, the movement of eros requires, as Frederick Crowe has argued, a complacency in the beloved whereby already in germ we possess the term to which our whole being is striving.[7] Faith is the assurance of things hoped for, the conviction of things unseen (cf. Heb. 11:1). Just as faith can be described as an *inchoata visio,* so it could be described as the inchoate complacency or fruition of the things our hearts desire. Though I can never exhaust the unrestricted desire to possess my beloved, nevertheless already at any one moment I possess her or him totally.

We can be fascinated by a good tale well told even if the teller is a stranger. But even Homer can outstay his welcome. Once we have heard the story that someone has to tell we become bored with its needless repetition or unnecessary elaboration. Very often, no matter how well a novelist tells a tale, overly long narratives lead to a flagging interest in the reader. When an ill-advised theater company enacted the whole of Shakespeare's historical plays as a continuous drama over several days, the result was a monumental boredom. Symphonies have to be resolved. A tune may enter our head and stay there for days, but eventually even the most obsessive mind tires of it. When we are in love, the object of our love never bores us. The complacency of being in the presence of the beloved allows us to hear with delight a tale that never ends. By the supernatural gift of conversion, by the pouring into our hearts of the divine complacency, we are enabled to hear the tale told by Christ and his Church and to delight in its unending telling.

5.12 *Christian conversion is a gift of God that enables us to tell the story of Jesus and his Church.*

The story told by our beloved is a story that ever delights us. It is a story that never ends. It is a story that leads to a change of heart in the hearer so that the story of the beloved becomes our own story. The sexual bond unites two life stories so that they become one flesh, one story. The story of Jesus becomes the story of his listening Church. The Church is the Body of which Christ is the Head; the Church becomes the subject of a story told by our Beloved. In the marriage of true minds we become, as Donne said, "one another's best." Our stories intertwine and engraft themselves upon each other's so that we become the subject of each other's story or, better, we become the twin subjects of the one story. By the gift of conversion Christ gives us the ability to make his story our own. Not only do we hear his story, but we also tell that story ourselves. The Church becomes the twin subject of the Story told by the Whole Christ, Head, and members. With Christ I am nailed to the Cross; with Christ I am buried and rise to new life;

it is no longer I who live, but Christ who lives in me. I tell the tale I have heard from Christ, so that it is Christ who baptizes when I baptize; it is Christ who preaches when I preach; it is Christ who bears witness when I bear witness; it is Christ who becomes present when I identify the bread and wine with my body and blood.[8] Jesus was a listener before he was a teller. The humanity of Christ is eternally significant because Christ, in his humanity, ever remains the perfect listener to the story told by God. Christ, as God, remains ever the teller of the Story. In Christ the teller and the listener are one. By the gift of conversion we become the storylistening and storytelling Christ. Christ is the only subject of the human story, and we await the consummation when he hands the telling of the story over to the Father, and God is all in all.

5.2 *The materials of the Gospel story point to distinctive understandings of God's gift of his love manifested in Jesus and to the dimensions of discipleship associated with them.*

The Gospel story is a composite of miracle stories, sayings of Jesus, apocalyptic literature, and a Passion narrative. The canonical Gospels attempt to communicate a comprehensive and balanced understanding of God's gift of his love in Jesus and of the discipleship to which it summons us. Discipleship is understood in accordance with the different particular ways in which we apprehend God's gift of his love in Jesus.

Miracle stories are told to express God's gift of his love manifested in Jesus' extraordinary power to transform human lives. The response appropriate to disciples is grasped as that of receiving the benefits of God's gift of his transforming love for them and of subsequently becoming channels of the same power for others in the event and process of Christian conversion.

When Jesus is presented in terms of his sayings that instruct us on how to live and why we should live that way, God's gift of his love is understood as manifested in moral guidance. The authentic disciple, therefore, is one who lives in accordance with the wisdom of God made manifest in Jesus. The love and wisdom of God shown forth in Jesus determine the shape of authentic Christian discipleship, of the personal transformation that is Christian conversion.

When Jesus is depicted as the revealer of the divine secrets concerning our origin and ground and destiny, God's gift of his love is understood to be revelatory of both God and our true selves. It summons the disciple to the personal transformation of repentance or conversion: to live according to the truth that the gift of God's love reveals about our relationship to God, to others, and to ourselves; we are called to make ourselves ready for the ultimate outcome of history, for the Kingdom of God's love.

The Passion narrative points to a particular understanding of God's gift of his love made manifest in Jesus and to a distinctive view of discipleship. The self-transcending, self-investing, fellowship-creating mystery of God's love manifested in Jesus' Way of the Cross shapes the future that God wills for all humankind in his Kingdom. The Gospel of Mark, for example, has Jesus say that the Son of Man "did not come to be served but to serve, and to give his life as a ransom for many" (10:45). The Passion narrative functions as a declaration that God's self-transcending, self-investing, redemptive, and reconciling love constitutes the origin and ground and destiny of the story of Jesus, the Church's story, and the story of the world; it is the life that, for those who accept it, constitutes the Kingdom of God. Such love is the criterion of authentic Christian discipleship, the meaning of the "first and greatest" commandment, of the eternal life that transcends death in the Kingdom of God.

5.21 **In appropriating the story told by the four Gospels we appropriate our own life story.**

Diverse materials are used in telling the Gospel story to set forth a comprehensive understanding of the gift of God's love manifested in Jesus and the discipleship this gift should evoke. They are employed to communicate a true understanding of God's gift of his love in Jesus and in his community of faith; they help, therefore, to dispel a false understanding of discipleship. The diverse elements that enter into the formation of the four Gospels help us to avoid the tendency to reductionism in our understanding of God's activity in Jesus, in his community of faith, and in our basic self-others-world-God relationship. They help us to recognize that the experience of God's gift of his love is many faceted. When we read the Gospels we spontaneously and unwittingly pick out from the text those parts that appeal to us. If we systematically identify those parts of the canonical Gospels that go to make up "our own gospel," we discover how much richer is the gift of God's love than our own hearts could imagine. If we imagine the effect of a Christian Gospel that had been reduced to a bare account of miracle stories, or a collection of sayings,[9] or a bare apocalyptic, or a simple retelling of the Passion, we can appreciate the multifaceted nature of the evangelists' storytelling.

A most fruitful insight into the Gospels may be obtained by the experiment of writing a gospel.[10] Imagine that all the New Testaments throughout the world have been destroyed. Write a gospel that from henceforth will be the only written link between the generations to come and the original four Gospels. Write your own Gospel, "The gospel according to *Your Name.*" Use only the words of the four Gospels. Use not more than two thousand words and try to achieve an architectonic unity: you must have at least one parable, one miracle, one saying of Jesus, and between a fourth and a fifth of the Gospel must be concerned with the Passion and death of Jesus. If possible, do this in a group and, after you have written your gospel, exchange it with another member of the group. Write a commentary on his or her gospel. Try to discern the portrait of Jesus that comes through this particular telling of the story and also the portrait of the "evangelist" who is telling the story. You should attempt to answer the following questions in your commentary:

1. What picture of Jesus emerges? Make a list of the verbs that describe Jesus' actions. What does Jesus do for the writer? What does the writer expect Jesus will do for his readers?

2. What picture of the "evangelist" emerges? Make a list of the sayings of Jesus. What is Jesus saying to the writer? What does the writer expect Jesus will say to his or her readers?

3. What are the meaning and value for the "evangelist" of Jesus' story?

4. At what level of consciousness—emotional, intellectual, moral— does Jesus speak to the writer? Is Jesus regarded as more solitary than social, more receptive than active, more suffering than joyful, as more among women than among men, as more among friends than among adversaries, as more a speaker than a doer, as more often rebuking than encouraging, as more often criticizing than approving, as more demanding than accepting, as more human than divine, as more courageously confronting difficult situations than as being welcomed by admiring followers?

5. What does the "evangelist" expect of Jesus?

6. At what level of personal need does Jesus encounter the writer?

7. What is the writer's particular interest in and feeling toward Jesus?

8. Has the "evangelist" unwittingly incorporated nongospel material in her or his gospel? Have images and doctrinal interests from outside the gospels colored the "evangelist's" shaping of the story?

The value of such an exercise, whether in a group or on one's own (and in the latter case one needs a rare amount of honesty in writing the commentary), is twofold: first, the participants achieve an experiential grasp of how the original Gospels came to be written—like Luke, the "evangelists" must carefully go over the whole story as contained in the various accounts of eyewitnesses and write an ordered account so that others may come to learn how well founded Christian teaching is (cf. Lk. 1:1 – 4)—and, secondly, the participants achieve a greater understanding of themselves and others in the group.

The "gospels" that emerge from such an exercise reveal in large measure the spiritual development of the writers. They bear witness to the way in which our emotional and psychic development, far more than our intellectual development, determines what we "hear" when the Gospel story is proclaimed to us. Such "gospels" show how the writer's experience of life in large measure determines the shape of his or her image of Jesus. The individual writer of such a gospel is asked to select from the four original Gospels those miracles, sayings, theological statements, and parables that he or she considers the most important for handing on to future generations. The writer's choice reflects to an uncanny degree the character and expectations of the writer.

In one group of gospel writers, two contrasting gospels came from two women whose lives and expectations had been very different. The first woman, middle-aged and the wife of a police officer, had lived a life of religious conformity. She had never missed mass through her own fault, had kept the Church's fasts, and engaged herself in good works. The Jesus who appeared in her gospel was one who laid down a strict morality; he condemned divorce, adultery, murder, disobedience. Unlike the Jesus of the Synoptics he was not much given to criticizing the religious establishment. The second woman was in her early twenties, had played truant from school more often than she had attended, had ceased going to Church at an early age, been married to and divorced from a wife-battering husband before her twentieth year had ended, and had come to faith and the sacraments after contracting and as a fruit of a stable but uncanonical marriage. The Jesus of her gospel was a man who not only forgave but also demanded that we too should forgive, a man who made others feel loved and demanded that we too be loving people. Though the younger woman's gospel did not show Jesus as condemning immorality, he came through as a much more demanding person. The life experience and character of the two writers had determined their hearing of the story as told by the original evangelists.

5.22 *The Gospel story calls its hearers to return (be converted) to themselves in the process of being converted to God.*

Conversion to God is always a homecoming. The Hebrew word *sub*, which the Septuagint translates as *metanoia*, change of heart, and the Vulgate translates as *conversio*, conversion, signifies at root a homecoming, a return. The idea of a homecoming to God is at first found only in scattered instances in Scripture and becomes frequently used (1059 times in Kittel's *Biblia Hebraica*) only in the later prophets. It would appear that the experience of exile, of being estranged from the Holy Land, and thereby feeling in some way estranged from themselves, was instrumental in evoking in the minds and hearts of the prophets a sense of being in need of a return, a homeward journey, to the God who had first called them into existence.[12] Conversion is a turning from the wrong path on which one has been traveling in order to return home to the one who loves us. Although the concept of conversion includes ideas of repentance, sorrow for sin, purpose of amendment, and the like, its "essential meaning is a new relationship with God, a homecoming, a being at home with him who is Emmanuel, God-with-us."[12]

Let us consider the story of the homecoming of the youngest son (Lk. 15:11 – 32). The young man asks his father for his share of the estate. In effect, he wishes that the father were dead (he asks for what is due to him on the death of him to whom he is an heir). He cuts himself off from his roots in his family and in the land (he goes to a far country). He cuts himself off from the source of life. He lives off his capital, that which he has received from his father. Like many a young man before and after him he uses up his capital in attempting to enhance his life (the life he has cut off from its source in the father) in the arms of various women. No doubt he was a "big spender"; estranged from the true father, he makes himself into a sugar daddy, an alienated and inauthentic father-provider for his women. Once he has used up the capital, that is the life-buying power, received from his father, he finds himself estranged not only from his father and his country but also from himself. Like the poetic author of Psalm 136 – 137 he finds he can no longer sing the songs of Israel in a foreign land. Sitting among the pigs, he comes to realize that he has ceased to be who he was: he is no longer a son. Our post-Hegelian, post-Freudian world has charted as perhaps never before the destructiveness of alienation and estrangement from one's own self. His healing necessitates his returning home. His father refuses to treat him as a paid servant, as less than a son; that is, the father refuses to allow him to be estranged from his sonship. In returning to the father the son has returned to himself. As he sat among the pigs he knew one term of his journey: he would return to the one who had once been his father. What he never imagined was that in returning he would return to himself: he would be not a paid servant but a son. In all our journeying to God we are, whether we know it or not, journeying also to a meeting with our true self.

The Church communicates the Gospel story and its truths so that we may be returned to our own deepest mystery as human persons. Our conversion is a homecoming to God and to ourselves. The Gospel story is preached so that we may come to know, love, and serve ourselves as we come to know, love, and serve Christ. The knowledge, love, and service of Christ is not a master-slave relationship (the master-slave relationship is always an alienated and alienating one) but a relationship between friends. In coming to Christ I come to myself. The mystery of the Blessed and Undivided Trinity is a revelation of the roots of all equality and friendship. Only equals may be friends. Christ did not think equality with God a thing to be grasped or clung on to but emptied himself to achieve an equality with humankind that would allow him to mediate the eternal friendship of God (cf. Phil. 2:6 – 7). The absolution over the body at the end of the funeral mass in the Missal of Pius V asks that God not enter into judgment against one "who while he (she) yet lived was signed with the sign of the holy Trinity." In the Byzantine Liturgy the faithful give thanks to God for having received Holy Communion by confessing that their worship of the Undivided Trinity has saved them. The revelation of the doctrine of the Trinity is the revelation that bestows salvation; the revelation of the mutual circumincession of those who are to be adored as equal in majesty is the revelation of that which brings us to salvation.[13] The gift of the Spirit reveals us to be the temple where the Father and Son dwell each within the other (cf. Jn. 14:23; 15:4). Conversion is a homecoming in which we discover ourselves to be the home of the Triune God; it is a soaking (baptism) into the life of the Triune God whom we experience as Mystery, Revelation, and Love given to us through Christ in the Spirit.[14]

Although the a posteriori word of the Gospel is a necessary moment in the fulfillment of the a priori word, the inner word dwells at the recipient's core and reaches its fulfillment as his or her fulfillment. This coming to fulfillment is not only a movement from the outside (Gospel story) to the inside (God's love flooding our hearts), but also a movement from the inside to the outside. Just as a person who describes his or her experiences to a psychiatrist or psychotherapist is often told in different yet enlightening and liberating terms what she or he already somehow knew, experienced and lived, so, too, something similar occurs with the preaching of the Gospel. The Gospel story implies a form of graced therapy in which the recipient may come to realize more explicitly and freely what he or she has always known and experienced in some way. The effective preaching of the Gospel works a profound conversion and transformation by amplifying what was once only implicit, marginal, repressed, or hidden. In the light of the Mystery of God expressed in the Gospel story of Christ's life and death as a coming from and returning to the Father, we may experience and grasp this as our own story and salvation. The Gospel story throws us back upon ourselves, initiates a return to the self, evoking by means of the exterior word an intensified appreciation of God's saving presence and purpose at the core of our being.

The Gospel story finds its basis in its hearer insofar as every person is a mystery referred to Mystery. The Jesus story finds fruitful ground insofar as the hearer can taste the Mystery of Jesus Christ as dwelling within his faith community as the fulfillment of his or her own orientation as mystery to Mystery. Through the preaching of the Gospel story the Church invites us to demythologize ourselves, to excise the false or inadequate or inauthentic myths in which we try to express ourselves and our values and to find in the story of Jesus the true myth that anchors us in the reality of the Triune God.

5.3 *Four versions of the Gospel story serve the Church as four manuals for the attainment of Christian maturity.*

Being a Christian is about being converted. To become a member of Christ's Body is to surrender oneself to a lifetime process of turning (or, better, being turned) to God in a life that is a ceaseless journey home. If one undertakes a grand tour of Europe one needs to buy more than one *Michelin Guide Blue* if one is to be properly guided at all stages in one's journey. Each national frontier is like the ending of one stage and the beginning of another. A new guide is needed for each stage. Carlo Martini, biblical scholar and now the archbishop of Milan, sustains the working hypothesis that the four Gospels were written at four distinctive moments of the Church's history to meet the demands for a continuing spiritual growth and maturity.[15] Each Gospel corresponds to four stages of Christian maturation and perfection. They serve the Church as a pedagogical resource; as four manuals for articulating the meaning and for carrying forward the process of Christian conversion. The gift of God's love, which is the gift of a dynamic movement and not a static, "once for all" possession, is manifested in the hearts and behavior of the faithful in four discernible stages. The four Gospels both derive from the lived experience of these four stages and aim at leading us to the goal of each progressive stage.

From the start, the church felt its need for all four Gospels. The Syrian Church had collated the four Gospels into a continuous narrative by about the year A.D. 150. This collation, the *Diatessaron*, became the standard text of the Gospels until the fifth century, when it gave way to the four separate Gospels. The experience of the Syrian Church implicitly corroborates the functional utility of the four Gospels as four distinct "manuals" for four distinctive moments of Christian growth.

According to Martini, Mark is prebaptismal instruction for the catechumen—a preparation for the celebration of baptism, the sacramental celebration of the first moment of Christian conversion. Matthew is the manual for the catechist, a Gospel that aids the initiation of the catechumen into the fellowship of the Church. Luke – Acts is the manual for mission, the Gospel for aiding the Christian to witness beyond the confines of the Church community. In a slightly different context, it is the manual for the theologians as they attempt to mediate the meaning of Christian faith to the cultural matrix in which they live and move and have their being. John is the manual of the mature, contemplative Christian. It is the Gospel for one who has lived through the three moments of Christian initiation and conversion and who grasps their unity in terms of the foundational values of faith and love.

5.31 *The story as told by Mark prepares the catechumen for the sacramental celebration of the first moment of conversion.*

Mark's Gospel is the "beginning of the Good News about Jesus Christ, the Son of God" (1:1). Mark leads the baptismal candidate— usually a religious person of the Greco-Roman world—to break with former images of God. Mark leads us to accept the God of Jesus Christ, to reject the manipulable gods that are implicitly expressions of our own self-idolatry so that we may accept the saving rule of the god who demands our total self-abandonment to his will in the service of others. Unless the God and Father of Jesus Christ is the priority of our lives, self-idolatry will preclude our freedom to be of authentic service to others. At revivalist-type meetings the witness given about former lifestyles is usually a confession of addiction—narcotic, alcoholic, sexual, pecuniary—from which the person has been saved by acceptance of and giving of themselves to Christ as their Lord. Allowing for the dramatic quality of such confessions of salvation from addiction that might tend to overshadow other less dramatic testimony, it is interesting to note how frequently they are confessions of oral dependency, of what some depth psychologists would name primitive narcissism. The first moment of conversion is an abandonment of idolatrous centering of creation around the ego. The suffering Messiah reveals how costly it is to make God the priority of our lives in the service of others, the cost of discipleship that makes us overcome self-idolatry for the worship of the one true God. Mark's Gospel shows up the illusory nature of what Bonhoeffer called cheap grace. The catechumen cannot have a risen Lord without a suffering Messiah; he or she cannot come to enjoy the life that really counts without being willing to pay its cost. If we discount the long ending of Mark's Gospel, we find no recorded appearances of the Risen Christ. The Gospel ends with the women saying nothing to anyone because they were afraid (16:8). The awesomeness of the responsibility of being a witness to the risen Lord is stressed in the closing moments of Mark's story.

5.32 *The story as told by Matthew illuminates the way for the newly baptized to enter into fellowship.*

Matthew's Gospel starts with a genealogy. Jeus is depicted as the member of a people. Just as there is no Messiah without his people, so there is no Jesus present in history apart from his Church. Matthew loves to portray Jesus as a new Moses forming his people into a new Israel. The wealth of precepts and rules for Christian conduct that characterize Matthew's Gospel provides the catechist with norms for instructing the newly reborn Christian on the meaning of an authentic communion with God in the community of Christ's body. Matthew's Gospel provides the catechist with a manual for helping the newly baptized to enter into the fellowship-creating reality of Christ's Church. The catechist has a standard for determining the degree of authentic participation in the fellowship-creating reality of the messianic community: to have brought forth the fruits of the Kingdom (21:43), to have done the will of God (5:16; 7:21), to have attained to the higher righteousness (5:20), to have shaped one's life course so as to enter into the Kingdom by the narrow gate (7:13), to do good works that glorify our heavenly Father (5:16). Matthew's Gospel teaches us that Christ is Emmanuel, God-with-us, the Messiah Son of God in whom God is present among his people, the Church (1:23). God abides with his people in the person of Jesus, who is acting in their fellowship. Matthew's Gospel ends, not like Mark's in a holy fear, but in an assurance: "Behold, I (the risen Son of God) am with you always, even to the close of the age" (28:20).

Once again, experience of what is commonly called charismatic renewal corroborates the insights of Martini's working hypothesis. After the initial fervor of being saved from sin, from addiction to one's own quasi-spontaneous self-idolatry, commonly the task of the service committee or pastor is to help the newly converted integrate himself or herself into the diversely gifted structure of Christ's body. Salvation from sin can be a very individualistic affair. Being trapped by self-idolatry is ultimately to be imprisoned in our own self-love. There can be no community without the sharing that results from and calls us to self-transcendence. The well-known *Seminars* leading to what is often erroneously known as baptism in the Spirit rightly proceed from the individualistic acclamation of Jesus as *"my* personal Lord and Savior" to teaching on the way Christ's body is built up by the harmonious working together of the gifts the Spirit distributes among the members. Matthew edifies (builds up) the first moment of conversion into the second moment where our turning to God is strengthened by the common bonds of fellowship. Having broken the chains that bind us into ourself, Christ leads us to the new experience of making relationships with him through our relationships with others.

5.33 *The story as told by Luke, both in his Gospel and in Acts, aids the newly converted and mutually strengthened Christian into a life of missionary commitment.*

Luke writes his Gospel and his record of the Acts of the Apostles so that Theophilus, his reader, may learn how well founded the teaching is that he has received (Lk. 1:4). Luke – Acts serves as a two-volume manual for meeting the needs of the third phase of Christian maturity. It is written for Christians who already adhere to Jesus Christ and his community (Theophilus has received the teaching) and who are now seeking to grasp the meaning of this faith commitment and to express it to the world that lies outside the confines of their faith (Theophilus wants to consolidate his faith on its foundations). Persecution has made the Christian community aware of its impact upon the world; it has also created a need for the community to defend and explain itself. To explain oneself to others, one must first be able to understand oneself; one must be able to tell one's own story. The author of Luke – Acts, therefore, explains the roots of the Christian community in the Jewish world and relates the salvation promised to Israel to the entire world. The plan of Luke – Acts is hinged around the commission of the risen Christ to his disciples: "You will be my witnesses not only in Jerusalem but throughout Judaea and Samaria, and indeed to the ends of the earth" (Acts 1:8). At the end of Matthew's Gospel the risen Christ promises to be with his disciples (28:20); at the beginning of Acts, Christ calls the disciples to be with him. In Matthew's Gospel he promises to be where they are: to be with them in their community. At the beginning of Acts he calls them forth to be with him on his missionary journey.

Luke's work serves as a manual to meet the need for a dialogue with the Jewish, Hellenistic, and Roman worlds, to explain the relationship between salvation history and world history. Inasmuch as a theology mediates between a cultural matrix and the significance and role of a religion in that matrix, Luke – Acts serves as a manual to foster a mature theological reflection on the complexity of the Church's relationship to the world. The author envisions this complexity in a nuanced, existential way. The committed Christian cannot flee historical complexity; he or she cannot pretend that it is an illusion to be conquered by turning away from it. Christian maturation demands the courage and intelligence to confront the social, political, cultural, economic, and religious complexities of the times. Luke's writings represent the maturing Christian's response to the challenge of the world; to the questions, crises, and culture of the times.

When one has come home to the Ark of Salvation, come in from the cold of self-imprisoning isolation, and found onself at home within the warmth of Christian fellowship, the temptation is to cling to the faith community as if to a life raft. Pastors commonly experience the need to put before their communities, especially where the community is warmly welcoming and friendly, the need for outreach. The need for systematic catechesis, explanation of the foundations of Christian life, purification of the relics of outworn conceptions of God, and indications of the profound values that exist in secular and other religions' life experiences is a need that commonly surfaces after the initial stages of Christian conversion and incorporation into the Body of Christ. The experience of prayer-group leaders, parochial clergy, and others corroborates the needs addressed by the author of Luke – Acts.

5.34 **The story as told by John serves the mature and contemplative Christian as a manual for ascertaining and attaining the full development of the Christian life.**

John starts his Gospel by bearing witness to the fullness (maturity) of Christ from which we have, all of us, received—grace upon grace (1:16). John's Gospel locates the unifying principle that underlies the complexity of the three previous phases of Christian development in the gift of the Father's love we receive through the Son and in the Holy Spirit. Christian faith consists in the reception of this gift; whoever possesses it begins to love as Christ has loved us. Consequently, love is the only law. John's Gospel synthesizes the entire Christian experience in terms of the gift of God's love in Jesus Christ and his Spirit. The Church's confessions of faith, Eucharist, fellowship, gospels, prayers, precepts, proclamation, rites, service, and witness are called into existence and sustained by the gift of this love that alone constitutes their true meaning and value.

One of the present authors once asked his class of students which model of the Church most appealed to them. A student who had been received into full communion with the Church in adult life answered that he felt torn between the model of the Church as herald and the model of the Church as sacrament. He had been converted to Christianity by Fundamentalist preachers, and he would always be grateful for their vigorous "heralding" of the good news. As he had matured in his faith, however, he had increasingly been drawn to the sacramental system of Catholicism and felt more intellectual satisfaction within the Catholic tradition. Biblical fundamentalism had played an indispensable role in this convert's life. Analogously to Mark's "first manual," the Fundamentalist's preaching had been the sine qua non for finding the maturity of faith in sacramental worship.

Every Christian must first drink milk before he is weaned. The strong meat of doctrine is indigestible before our milk teeth have been cut. If we make the necessary distinction between kerygma and catechesis, we may legitimately wonder whether, in our actual Catholic practice we do not sometimes so concentrate on the cate- chesis that we fail to announce the kerygma. Within a month of writing these lines, one of the present authors has held long conver- sations with three different middle-aged Catholics who were find- ing themselves increasingly disenchanted with their Catholic life and increasingly attracted by Pentecostalism. Listening to their life histories, the present author increasingly suspected that they had missed a stage in their spiritual development. All that they found attractive in the Pentecostalist, Fundamentalist tradition was something that they should have found within the Catholic Church. Brought up in convents, prepared for confession and Com- munion, and later for confirmation, they appeared never to have heard the Gospel as Good News. Made to feel guilty before they had been made to feel loved, they had been sacramentalized without ever having been evangelized. Imagine a baby that has never been fully nourished by his or her mother's milk. Imagine further that there has been no alternative source of calcium and the teeth have never grown. For the child to eat the food of maturity, the meat would first have to be liquefied and strained: the meat would still be full of protein, but the meal would be unsatisfying. If we liquefy the meat of sacramental life (by too early an introduction to the thoroughly adult activity of confessing one's sins, for example) should we wonder if to many adult Catholics their sacramental life and their grasp of the Gospel are neither fish nor flesh nor good red herring? There is a kind of violence in forcing "meat" into the mouths of spiritual babes.

In a prison for young offenders, where one of the present authors once worked, many of the young men had been in a church perhaps only once or twice in their lives. The Sunday celebration of the Eucharist reminded the author of the words of Gregory Dix. In his description of the pre-Nicene liturgy as the "Mass in Maida Vale," Dix concluded his account with the following words: "That is all there is to it, externally. It would be absolutely meaningless to an outsider, and quite unimpressive."[16] The eating of bread and the drinking of wine are the most banal of ceremonies *unless* the gift of God's love has flooded the heart and we have heard the good news that liberation has happened. A young prisoner underlined this feeling. Asked what impression the Sunday mass had made on him, the prisoner, out of genuine puzzlement, replied, "Very nice, Padre; but why did we all queue up for bits of cardboard?" Motivated by this experience of prisoner's reaction to the mass, the chaplain argued strongly that the Eucharist should be replaced by a ministry of the word adapted to the preaching of the kerygma. The chaplain-general was sympathetic but pointed out that the state guaranteed the right of every prisoner to practice his religion, and the official stance of the Church was that every Catholic had the duty (and therefore the right) of attending mass. One could, of course, also ask about the right of every Christian to have the Gospel preached to him or her in a form that she or he could digest.

There is a rather silly slogan of ancient lineage to the effect that it is "the mass that matters." Profoundly, of course, it is true; but, like most slogans, it can become a talisman, an idol, which serves to obscure equally important truths. During a parish ministry a young priest sought to give effect to the instruction by the Second Vatican Council that "Pastors of souls should see to it that the chief hours, especially vespers, are celebrated in common in church on Sundays and the more solemn feasts."[17] Far from being commended for his zeal in following the collective wisdom of the world's bishops, the young assistant found himself reproved for distracting the faithful from the supreme importance of the mass. If special services were to be held they must always contain the celebration of the Eucharist. One sometimes gets the impression that the liturgical praxis of the Catholic Church is rather like a marriage where the couple are so dazzled by the delights of orgasmic union that they miss out on the joys of just wandering through the autumnal woods hand in hand. If we try to live all the time on the peaks, or to scale them before we have cleared the foothills, we shall faint from the rarefied atmosphere to which we have not become accustomed. In our hurry to bring children or adult converts to the grace of sacramental union, we perhaps too easily overlook that stable marriages are preceded by a reasonably lengthy period of engagement.

It will not have escaped the attentive reader that the Western Church in the readings that she customarily uses during Lent to instruct the catechumens (Cycle A) relies heavily on the Gospel of John. The Gospels used at the scrutinies of baptismal candidates put before them—the woman at the well (baptism), the man born blind (the stages of conversion), and the raising of Lazarus (humankind's sacramental sharing in the Passover mystery of Christ)—are pericopes taken from the Gospel of John. Far from invalidating our present thesis that the Gospel of Mark is the appropriate "manual"

for the instruction of catechumens, the Church's choice of pericopes reminds us that the celebration of the Word in the assembly
presupposes a prior preaching of the kerygma. As the catechumen
approaches his or her initiation into the sacramental sharing of
Christ's death and Resurrection, the Church puts before him or her
powerful symbols (the Johannine pericopes chosen are the more
picturesque passages of John rather than the more discursively
"theological" passages), which envision the maturity to which the
candidates aspire. Already in symbol the converts are being led to
the maturity in which their pedagogical catechesis should issue. In
his *Catecheses* for those who were to be illuminated by baptism and
in his *Mystagogical Catecheses* for those who have already partaken
of the mysteries, Cyril of Jerusalem is careful lest the strong meat
of Christian doctrine is given to those who are not yet prepared to
receive it. In his opening address to those who now stand on the
threshold of baptism, the bishop solemnly warns the candidates
from disclosing what they hear even to less well-prepared catechumens:

> When the instruction is over, if any catechumen tries to get out
> of you what your teachers told you, tell nothing, for he is out-
> side the mystery.[18]

"The spirit of mystery," writes Quasten, "pervades the entire
corpus" of Cyril's lectures.[19] It was only after their baptism, sealing
with the Spirit, and partaking of the thanksgiving, that the catechumens were fully instructed in the meaning of what had taken
place.[20] Edward Yarnold reminds us of the reasons, theological and
pedagogical, for this secrecy. "It was felt," he writes, "that a Christian needed to experience the sacraments of baptism and the Eucharist before he was ready to receive instruction about them."[21] In
order to truly experience the baptism as a real dying and burial
and rising with Christ to newness of life, there must be a patient
and thorough preparation. The concerns of Mark's Gospel precede
those of John's.

5.35 *Bernard Lonergan's theology of conversion allows us to un-*
derstand the progressive unfolding of the Christian story
from Mark through John.

Bernard Lonergan's theology of religious and Christian conversion throws considerable light upon Martini's working hypothesis

of a gradual unfolding of a conversion story through the stages implicit in the writings of the evangelists.[22] Conversion is none other than the gift of God's love mentioned in the fifth chapter of Romans as flooding the hearts of believers through the gift of God's Holy Spirit. In terms of God's self-investing love that the New Testament witness symbolizes, Mark can be understood to serve as the Christian community's manual for introducing the catechumen to the mystery and meaning of this love in Christ Jesus. Matthew appears as the "manual" for living according to the exigencies of this love within the Church. Luke – Acts is then seen as the manual for learning how to bear witness to its meaning and value for the world, and John becomes the manual that expresses the synthesis of the mature Christian who has lived out the demands of this self-investing love in following Jesus and his Church in the service of the world and who now asks what is at the heart of her or his Christian experience. In John's Gospel, the self-investing dynamic of God's gift of his love is understood to be the origin and ground and destiny of the Jesus story, the Church's story, and the story of the world. Not to have grasped this is to have missed the point of the dynamic of Christian conversion. Communion with God implies a participation in the dynamic of his self-investing love on a level prior to that on which doctrinal systems and organized institutions arise. The Gospels symbolize the unrestricted nature of God's love to which all humankind is constitutively oriented by presenting Jesus as God's self-revelation. They summon us to follow Jesus in his fundamental self-others-world-Mystery relationship for the authentic fulfillment of our life story.

Lonergan speaks of a multilevel conversion: psychic, intellectual, moral, and religious. Each conversion is a new moment in the dynamic self-transcending process of being a human being. Mark's Gospel shows the stage where God's power breaks down the walls that encapsulate me within myself. I come to place my trust and reliance in *another*. Intellectually, I move from a notional to a real assent: "Jesus is Lord." Morally, my life must be submitted to Jesus' rule and Kingdom. The Gospel of Matthew marks a further stage in the dynamics of self-transcendence. The Lordship of Jesus becomes incarnate, as it were, in submission to a body, a community of those in whom the Spirit has been outpoured. Intellectually, I submit to the judgment of the community my insight that Jesus is Lord: by the imposition of its rules and disciplines I allow the community to judge the truthfulness and authenticity of my claim to have surrendered my life to the Lordship of Christ. Morally, I transcend my pleasure-based morality. In my preconverted state of infantile narcissism, what was good was that which promised immediate pleasure. In the first moment of my conversion I moved to an acceptance that what brings true pleasure (the heady experience of liberation from all that entraps me) comes as the gift of another person. In the second moment, I transcend even that which truly liberates me in my submission of my ethical behavior to that which serves the common good of Christ's body.

Luke – Acts marks a further stage in the self-transcending process of conversion. My service is not confined to that which will build up the body of Christ but reaches out to serve the wider community. Intellectually, I move out to find the presence of Jesus outside the religious community in which I was brought up or which I entered through adult conversion. I transcend the limiting prejudices of my own time and place and culture as I reach out to express the Christian story intelligently, rationally, and responsibly in the cultures of other times and places. I am moved, like the apostles, to the point where I am no longer shocked that someone might eat pork and yet claim Jesus too as his or her Lord.

The Gospel of John marks a return to the self, an appropriation at a deep level where I come to acknowledge the presence of Jesus as the unifying presence who holds all the stages of conversion together. It is the same Lord who gently leads us, step by step, through change after change until we judge him Lord *because we know ourselves to be his children.* Intellectually, we transcend the subject-object, ego-other dichotomy as we judge the truth of Jesus by a judgment of connaturality. Morally, we love the good and do what we will with all the ease and spontaneity of the lover. Through our sharing in the baptismal death of Jesus and our sealing with the seal of the Spirit, that is, through our sacramental life, we are led to understand that it is right to call ourselves Christs.[23] The diaconal admonition before Communion, "Holy things for the Holy," is explained by Cyril as referring to the twofold holiness of what is offered and those to whom it is offered: "The offerings (Christ's Body) are holy since they have received the presence of the Holy Spirit, and you are holy because you have been accounted worthy of the Holy Spirit."[24] In the sacramental stage marked by John's Gospel we become one flesh, one body with Christ so that we understand God no longer as the wholly other but, with Augustine, we acknowledge him as *intimius intimo meo*, nearer to me than is my innermost self.[25]

5.4 *The death of Jesus outside the "camp" or "city" symbolizes Christian conversion as a breakout from our self-imposed imprisonment.*

In his novel *The Castle* Kafka tells the story of a young man arriving in a village dominated by a castle. The village exists to serve the needs of the *Herren*, the lords who govern from the castle. Nobody in the village ever sees them; contact is maintained by messengers who travel between the castle and the village. The young man spends the whole time attempting to get access to the castle but without success. The novel is lengthy, and nothing ever happens. The reader waits to enter the castle but is always frustrated. At the end of the book the reader comes to suspect that the whole point of the story is that the castle does not really exist. Human beings like to feel that they can enter the charmed inner circle.

Some popular British magazines publish a list each year of what is "in" and what is "out." Certain restaurants, certain areas of London, certain clothes, certain expressions, certain tastes in music or sports are declared to be "in," while others are declared to be "out." The idea is that conformity to a pattern mostly dreamed up by a writer in search of a little Christmas entertainment copy will identify the person as "one of the in crowd." In fact, of course, no such inner circle exists. The existence of the inner ring depends on making the majority of people feel excluded. If one succeeds in breaking into the inner ring, however, one discovers that its existence is really only an illusion because all those who, from the "outside," appear to make up the inner ring are themselves seeking to enter an "inner ring" and are desperate that they not be considered as outsiders.[26] Although such games may, in Christmas magazines, be a harmless parlor diversion, insofar as they are played out in the life story of an individual or a nation they can become deadly.

We can construct a prison for ourselves by idolizing certain behavior or possessions or lineage and base our whole self-image on not being like other people. In the end, our self-imposed prison becomes what the Book of Numbers (11:34) calls the Graves of Craving.[27] Imprisoned by our own quest for self-fulfillment we are trapped from achieving the fulfillment that comes from self-transcendence through relationship to others and to God. In the Gospel of John, Nathanael reacts to Philip's invitation to see Jesus with disparaging doubt, a reaction that Jesus will encounter all too often among those who believe in the Law and the prophets.[28] "Nazareth! Can anything good come from there?" (Jn. 1:46) The religious authorities of Jesus' time are represented by the New Testament as having distorted their religious tradition into an inner ring. Jesus is depicted as a reproach to them, precisely because they recognized his greatness, or at least his influence upon the masses. He should have been in the inner ring but chose rather to eat and consort with people in the outer ring.

The Letter to the Hebrews parallels the death of Jesus on Golgotha, a place outside the city walls, with the burning of the sacrificial animals outside the camp.

> Jesus too suffered outside the gate to sanctify the people with his own blood. Let us go to him, then, *outside the camp*, and share his degradation. For there is no eternal city for us in this life but we look for one in the life to come. (Heb. 13:12 – 13)

Eternal life is that which even now leads us outside the camp of self-involvement to find in the outer ring the self-investing love of God for humankind and humankind for one another. It leads us to reread our own personal "Old Testaments" and, in the Spirit, to transcend them, transforming their meaning into that of an all-embracing "New Testament" of universal love without limits. The entire Way of the Cross, the pattern of self-transcending love that is Jesus' way of life, is the way to the outer circle that achieves its fulfillment *outside the gates*.

5.41 *The Church employs the four stories of Mark, Matthew, Luke, and John as a means for communicating and cultivating its foundational experience of the love of God in Christ Jesus and in his Spirit that has been given us.*

The four Gospels are written to serve the purpose of grace and the demand of God's transcendent love in Jesus Christ and his Church. They articulate and objectify the meaning and value and demands of this love for us, both as individuals and as a community. The Church, by telling us the story of Jesus in its Gospels, summons us to put on his mind and heart in order that we may become what God intends us to be within his universal story of unfolding love. The authenticity of our response to Jesus' injunction to love God above all else finds its measure in the deeds by which we follow his way of self-investing love for our neighbor in self-surrender to the Father's universal salvific will for all humankind. The glory of the Father is the brotherhood and sisterhood of all human persons in his Son Christ Jesus. The Father's love for us is the source of our response-ability with regard both to the absolutely Other (God) and to all others. Fundamentally this is what makes us persons. What we have to give is God's love. Our receptivity is the ground of our productivity in sharing Christ's life of service, his shaping of the future into the form of the Kingdom of God. The greatest in the Kingdom, therefore, is the one most dependent upon and most responsive to the Father's love (cf. Mt. 18:1 – 7, 10): Jesus Christ, the Son of God, whose receptivity and response-ability make the fellowship-creating mystery of the Father's love available to all humankind.

The self-transcending love of the Father and Son is Eternal Life in the Kingdom of God. It is manifest in the suffering Messiah's service of all humankind in his total self-abandonment to God (Mark), in service of one another in the community of the suffering Messiah (Matthew), and in the service of all humankind (Luke – Acts). The Christian is called to mature in this love by following Jesus in his Church for his world. Mark underscores the christological dimension; Matthew the ecclesial; Luke – Acts the universal; and John the mystical, that is, the Trinitarian, interpersonal, mutual indwelling of the divine Persons one within the others and with us. The Father is self-transcending, self-investing love for the Son. The Son is self-transcending, self-investing love for the Father. Both are the self-transcending, self-investing love of God in their gift to humankind of the one Spirit who binds them and us in mutual, self-fulfilling love. We share in that love by transcending and investing ourselves in following Jesus. We participate in that love by the gift of God's Spirit. We come to fulfillment in that love by our self-abandonment to the Father, by our sharing in his unrestricted love for our fellow members of Christ's Body, and by our sharing in God's mission to all humankind.

5.42 *Basic to our experience of conversion is the felt judgment that we are loved.*

The fact that our judgment of faith is a judgment by connaturality necessitates that we must be on the road to conversion before we understand that to be the case. I was my parents' son before I knew myself to be so. By experience of conversion we mean, not some event, a being blinded on the road to our own personal Damascus, but the process by which we have an insight into the meaning of our life story, and thence understand and judge ourselves to be subjects drawn by the one whom Jesus called Father to our home where we will dwell in God and God in us. I am loved by God before I know what love is. To experience conversion is to judge with the eye of faith that I have been loved and am called to love in return. The story of the unmerciful servant (Mt. 18:23 – 35) brings home the prevenient nature of God's love where the king asks the rhetorical question: "Were you not bound, then, to have pity on your fellow servant just as I had pity on you?" We are called to forgive as we have been forgiven, to love as we have been loved, to relate to our neighbor (all others) as God himself has related to all humankind.

One of the best images for sin is that of the child (of whatever age) who stubbornly refuses to feel loved. Imagine a child who is loved, wanted, and cherished by his or her parents. Something upsets the child, perhaps justifiably. In a fit of pique the child perhaps refuses to eat dinner. She or he sulks. "Nobody loves me" is a good expression of his or her mood. After a time the parents perhaps try to cheer their child up. They offer their offspring a treat, something they know the child enjoys. In such a scenario one can often see the effort the child will go through to steel himself or herself against accepting the proffered token of friendship. The adult who has perhaps never felt loved by his or her parents may well take fright at the genuine love shown them by another adult (usually of the opposite sex) and refuse to feel loved.

The parable of the unmerciful servant says nothing about God loving us *only* if we love others; rather, it points to the ability to refuse to feel loved and loving. We can insist upon living under the demonic grip of our idolatries, though only at the cost of suffering the torment they mete out. God's love for us is not contingent upon our acceptance of it; it is not revoked because of its being unreceived. The feeling that we are loved is our reaction of *complacentia* to the judgment that another has *complacentia* in and desire for us. Ultimately, the feeling that we are unloved is a defense we erect against the demand that being loved makes on us. It has been said that the difference between patients who get well and those who do not lies in whether they have been loved by their doctors. More to the point, perhaps, is not whether they have been loved but whether they have allowed themselves to feel loved.

The temptation to reduce the process of conversion to an event can often be caused by a refusal to acknowledge that our reaction to the gift of God's love, our response to God's prior love of us, must be truly our reaction, our response. In uncovering the possible etiology of Pelagian emotional complexes, we may suspect that the desire to "make it on one's own," the grim determination to achieve salvation through one's own efforts may, paradoxically, be caused by resentment that we are called to make any response at all. In the earliest stages of infancy the satisfaction of our needs is relatively simple and comes to us as pure gift. Our hunger is satisfied, our bodies are kept warm, and when our needs have been cared for, we go to sleep. The bliss of satisfaction comes as the gift of another.[29] Psychically, the myth of the expulsion from the Garden of Eden is often interpreted, in its imagery, as an echo of the increasing differentiation of the growing personality as he or she discovers himself or herself to be separated from the mother. The expulsion from infancy involves the taking of responsibility for one's own living and life story. Just as the child who does not get his or her own way (instant satisfaction) may sulk and refuse other gifts, so the nascent personality may defend itself from the loss of the instant satisfaction of Eden by, as it were, saying to God, "If I cannot have the eschatological gifts *now*, then I will refuse to accept any gift from you at all and will make my own way."

Satisfaction is not then achieved as the goal of one's behavior but as the concomitant feeling of self-righteousness that one is beholden to no one else. Just as the stubborn child refuses to take pleasure in the love offered by her or his parents, so the Pelagian mentality refuses to take all pleasure in life (Puritanism) save in the knowledge that *I* (my ego with its own unaided powers) am doing God's will. The "god" in question is an idol who makes me morally superior to other human beings by validating my efforts to remain self-sufficient, unrelated, and a "martyr" to other people's lack of love. Conversion then becomes an event since, firstly, it must have already completely happened because I am morally (self-)justified and, secondly, an emotionally satisfying event stands as the symbol for the lost Paradise where humankind was not expected to earn its bread by the sweat of its brow.

Thomas C. Oden tells of an attitude in popular American Protestantism that implicitly reduces conversion to an event at the expense of process and maturation in response to God's gift of his love.

Popular Protestant Christianity is largely a conflation of (1) a *moralistic pietism* which has its roots in seventeenth-century

Puritanism and nineteenth-century frontier revivalism, in clandestine alliance with (2) a *liberal optimism* which emerged out of the spirit of the eighteenth-century Enlightenment and nineteenth-century bourgeois evolutionary idealism.

Moralistic pietism views the church as a converted community surrounded by an evil world. Salvation is reduced to a moral reformation in which one ceases to be irresponsible to social mores and joins the moral forces in their fight against immorality. The church's task becomes that of getting as many of the good people into its fold as possible and separating itself as much as possible from the world hastening toward corruption. It must build a wall to protect itself from the incursions and stains of the secular environment. In this way Victorian morality has become indissolubly wedded with an introverted, subjectively oriented religious pietism so as to produce a strange picture of the church as a community consisting not of sinners whom God has pardoned but of the morally straightlaced who rejoice in their own righteousness. Under these terms the basic function of worship becomes self-congratulatory. Worship is our time to get together to exchange signals about how good we are and ought increasingly to become.[30]

In such a mentality the world (not me, not like me), which has refused me the instant satisfaction I crave, becomes an evil world (the repository of my bad experiences) against which I must fight (by my own efforts). The paradoxical linking, in Protestant forms of Christianity, of such a mentality with an insistence on the principle of *sola gratia* can be interpreted as the symbol of the already-out-there-now-real satisfaction that was refused but that I explicitly claim has already been given me. Although liberalism and pietism have always existed in a certain tension, there is one crucial point at which they agree: serious confession of personal sin is unnecessary:

> *if* we are fundamentally the good community, and *if* history is inevitably on the upward road of progress, and *if* man's nature is on the side of goodness and social harmony, then we really have nothing to confess.[31]

Insofar as sin is, at rock bottom, a refusal to respond to the offer of friendship and the affirmation that one already possesses within oneself the resources necessary for satisfaction of all one's needs, the preaching of *sola gratia* can become a symbol for affirming the essential righteousness of one's present state, a state that covertly one has attained by one's own efforts.

5.421 **The world disclosed by Jesus in his Sonship of God defines each Christian storyteller as one who has been trusted.**

The baptism of Jesus is associated by all four Gospels with a vision of Jesus as the recipient of God's Spirit. The synoptic Gospels further link this gift of the Spirit with Jesus' status as the Beloved Son of God, the one on whom God's favor has rested. The vision of the world (*Weltanschauung*) that informs the story of Jesus is God's gift of his love that makes the Storyteller beloved. The story of Jesus' life is inseparably bound up with his mission to tell that story and to make it known to the ends of the earth. Matthew interestingly associates the telling of the story of Jesus with the baptism of each believer in his account of the appearance in Galilee with which he closes his Gospel. The story of Jesus discloses what it would mean to be the Son, the Beloved, the bearer of God's favor.

In normal circumstances the maternity of a child is never in doubt; one can witness the mother giving birth. Paternity is harder to ascertain; in many ways it depends on believing the word of the mother. Hence arises the importance of the naming of the child by the father. In Jewish law paternity was based on a man's acknowledgment that this was his child. According to the Mishnah, paternity was established by the man saying, "This is my son."[32] Implied in the acknowledgment of paternity is the promise to support, protect, and care for the child. The genealogies given by Matthew and Luke underline the Jewishness of Jesus; he is one sprung from the people of Israel. Jesus is a son of Israel because of his birth from a woman of Israel (Cf. Gal. 4:4). There was no doubt about Jesus' membership with the chosen people since he was the son of a virgin daughter of that people. In his Letter to the Churches of Galatia, Paul remarks that even where a child has actually inherited the estate of his father—presumably through the father's death—he is no "different from a slave . . . until he reaches the age fixed by his father" (Gal. 4:1 – 2). The final and definitive acknowledgment of sonship occurs at the appointed time when the son comes into his inheritance. A child who has already inherited his estate but who remains under the control of guardians and trustees is one who has not yet been entrusted with what is his own. Matthew pictures Joseph as deciding to repudiate Mary and therefore by implication the child, but he is bidden by the angel to support, protect, and care for the child and his mother (Mt. 1:19 – 25; 2:13, 20), that is, he is bidden to take the child on trust, to act as trustee for the Father. When the appointed time had come, God directly, no longer through a trustee, finally and definitively acknowledged paternity of the child: "This is my Son" (Mt. 3:17). God promises to support, protect, and care for the one who is his Son. Mark records the acknowledgment as addressed to Jesus himself: "You are my Son" (Mk. 1:11). God's disclosure of his paternity is not only a declaration to the world but a word of acceptance, acknowledgment, and trust addressed to the one he acknowledges. God reveals to the Son that he is trusted because now is the appointed time, the day when the Son can inherit his estate and be trusted with what is his own.

In the Yahwist account of creation the man has already been trusted with his inheritance—he is keeper of the garden (Gn. 2:15) and has accepted lordship of the animals by naming them (Gn. 2:19 – 20)—when God creates woman to be his mate. The moment of entering one's heritage, of becoming truly a son is linked by the Yahwist author with the leaving of father and mother, the leaving of a state of dependency, and the cleaving to another self (Gn. 2:24). Symbolic thought is not the single-minded pursuit of one particular image. Symbols are commonly contaminated—clusters of complimentary and even seemingly contradictory images. The symbolic accounts of the baptism of Jesus in all three synoptic Gospels are no exception to this rule. Not only is Jesus acknowledged as Son but also as Beloved: "This is my Son, the Beloved," "You are my Son, the Beloved."

The Gospel accounts of the baptism of Jesus mix filial and bridal imagery. The prophetic imagery of Hosea mixes the filial with the bridal. When Israel was a child God loved him: "and I called my son out of Egypt" (Hos. 11:1), yet when Israel has finally returned to Yahweh, she will call him not Baal (Master) or even Father but My husband (Hos. 2:16 – 18). At the baptism a voice is heard speaking from heaven and at that moment the deepest meaning of the prophetic parable of Hosea was fulfilled:

When that day comes—it is Yahweh who speaks—
the heavens will have their answer from me,
the earth its answer from them . . .

> I will love Unloved;
> I will say to No-people-of-Mine, "You are my people,"
> and he will answer, "You are my God" (Hos. 2:21–24)

> In the place where they were told, "You are no people of mine,"
> They will be called, The sons of the living God . . .
> To your brother say, "People-of-Mine,"
> to your sister, "Beloved." (Hos. 2:1 – 3)

Yahweh promises Israel

> I will betroth you to myself for ever,
> betroth you with integrity and justice,
> with tenderness and love;
> I will betroth you to myself with faithfulness,
> and you will come to know Yahweh. (Hos. 2:19 – 20)

Yahweh promises Israel a covenant relationship, the distinguishing characteristic of which is *'emeth*, faithfulness. Implicit in a declaration of love is an affirmation that the beloved is lovable. Since reciprocity is a necessary ingredient of all covenant relationships, an offer of betrothal and still more a wedding vow are an implicit affirmation of one's trust in the other that she or he will likewise be faithful to the pledged word. The painfulness of Hosea's vocation to knowingly marry a whore and beget children by her (Hos. 1:2) lies precisely in the fact that though he knows she will be faithless, there is an implicit assumption in his betrothing her that she ought to be faithful. The two great affirmations of our trustworthiness are the affirmation of a parent that we have grown up—think of the parent at a bar mitzvah or a bas mitzvah, a college graduation ceremony or an ordination: "This is my son/daughter and I am proud of him/her"—and that of the one who affirms us by vowing to make us joint partners in her or his life story. The affirmation by God that Jesus is his Beloved is a confirmation of his affirmation of him as his Son: Jesus is the Trusted One of God.

Further analysis of the Markan account of the baptism confirms this interpretation of the dual nature of God's affirmation of his trust in Jesus. "The heavens torn open" is an allusion to a psalm of Isaiah where it is asked that God would inaugurate the *eschaton* as a new exodus: "O that you would tear the heavens open and come down" (Is. 64:1). In that same psalm Isaiah speaks of God's Spirit coming down upon the Israelites at the Exodus (Is. 63:11, 14) just as at Sinai God had come down to form his people (Ex. 19:11, 18, 20). The Spirit was shown in the form of a dove, a biblical symbol for Israel (Hos. 11:11; Ps. 68:13; 74:19; 56:1 (LXX)). Jesus is thus designated as the New Israel of God. The voice coming from heaven reminds us of the first song of the servant of Yahweh from the Book of the Consolation of Israel (Is. 42:1):

> Here is my servant whom I uphold,
> my chosen one in whom my soul delights.
> I have endowed him with my spirit
> that he may bring true justice to the nations.

According to Mark all this took place "no sooner had he come up out of the water." Again we are reminded of Isaiah's linking of the Spirit with the Exodus across the Red Sea (Is. 63:11). The vision of Jesus at his baptism fulfills Isaiah's longing and recalls the passage of the Sea of Reeds, the crossing of the Jordan under Joshua (Jesus), and the new Exodus looked for by Isaiah at the start of the Book of Consolation (Is. 40:3 – 4, 10 – 11). The Markan account joins together the two affirmations that Jesus is the unique Son of God and the New Israel.

In many if not most cultures, the initiation into manhood and womanhood is linked with puberty, the beginning of the person's life as a sexual being capable of procreating new life. The neurotic fears of parents about their children are often linked with a fear of their offsprings' blossoming sexuality. The parents of childless couples will often, to their offsprings' intense annoyance, ask them when they are going to start a family. They long for their first grandchild. The grandparents' pleasure at the birth of a baby symbolically says, "This is my daughter/son. She/he is fully grown. She/he is fully in my image because she has given birth/he has begotten a child." Pleasure in the birth of one's grandchild is pleasure in the trustworthiness of one's child that she or he is now able to be trusted with the nurture of new life. The linking of Christ's status as the Son of God with his status as the Beloved of God implies God's trust in the maturity of Christ's sonship enabling him to become the founder and source of a new life, a new people, a new community. For Paul, to be baptized into Christ is to receive the gift of the Holy Spirit, the proof that we are sons (Gal. 3:23 – 27; 4:6 – 7) and to become one of "God's beloved" (Rom. 1:7). Christ's story as envisioned at his baptism is the foundational story for the community of God's beloved sons.

5.43 **The different ways of telling the story of Jesus correspond to the diverse ways in which God can tell us that we are loved.**

There is a kind of romanticism that makes an idol of unrequited love. The Duke opens Shakespeare's *Twelfth Night* in such a romantic mood:

> If music be the food of love, play on,
> Give me excess of it, that, surfeiting,
> The appetite may sicken, and so die.

Orsino thinks he is in love with Olivia; in reality he is in love with love. He enjoys being in love. The troubador loved his lady, and the more unattainable she was the more he loved her. Such lovers equate love with desire. The unrequitedness of their love-desire increases their self-given sense of worth. "I am worthy because I have loved without hope or promise of reward." The mother who enjoys being a martyr gives herself a sense of worth. "See how much I love them; I am so loving that I will slave for them even when they reject me." The heroic martyr-lover builds himself up in his own eyes by his Herculean labors to win the right to his lady's hand; the attainment of his heart's desire is largely irrelevant to his labors.

> When the One Great Scorer comes
>   to write against your name—
> He marks—not that you won or lost—
>   but how you played the game.[33]

For the Pelagian romantic, that which matters is not the prize (in love as in religion the "prize" is always unmerited and unmeritable) but the attempt to make oneself worthy of that prize; to give oneself worth in one's own eyes. Frederick E. Crowe[34] has drawn our attention to a neglected facet of love: love is not only desire but desire circumincessed with complacency. Love is the complacency felt and enjoyed in the presence of him or her who attracts our desire. Desire can be a powerful motivation. Moved by his desire for Beatrice, a desire that was never to be requited, Dante embarks upon a journey that will take him through hell and purgatory to heaven. The attraction of desire will lead him to the completion of love in the complacency of the vision where

> ma gia volgeva il mio disio e'l velle,
> si come rota ch'igualmente e mossa,
> l'amor che move il sole e l'altre stelle.[35]

Where love is equated with desire, love is equated with the natural thrust of created eros. There is a natural *desire* to see God, a desire that is changed and transformed and given a new intentionality by the supernatural gift of faith but is not taken away or replaced. We are created with a *potentia oboedientialis*, which is felt as desire. Dom Sebastian Moore argues that humankind is naturally in love with God. The flooding of our hearts by the gift of the Spirit, the gift of conversion, is not, he argues, the gift of being loving toward God but the knowledge that God has first loved us. For Moore the universal human condition is the desire to be desired by the one whom one desires.[37] When a man or woman falls in love, the experience we call and enjoy as "falling in love" is *not* the becoming aware that one has decided to love (we say "becoming aware that one has decided" because love is not a feeling but a decision, as Erich Fromm so cogently argues, but yet a decision on a level so deep that one becomes aware one has made it rather than that one is making it) but the moment of insight that one is loved by the beloved; the moment when one shouts, "Eureka—I have her/him." The complacency of love arises from the felt knowledge that I am loved; that my desire to love and be loved has found its mark (sin is that desire to love and be loved missing its mark—*harmatia*). At this point, perhaps, we begin to appreciate the profundity of the insight of John of the Cross:

> Y dice el Pastorcico: ¡Ay, desdichado
> De aquel que de mi amor ha hecho ausencia,
> Y no quiere gozar la mi presencia,
> Y el pecho por su amor muy lastimado!
>
> Y a cabo de un gran rato se ha encumbrado
> Sobre un árbol do abrió sus brazos bellos,
> Y muerto se ha quedado, asido de ellos,
> E pecho del amor muy lastimado.[37]

The real wound in Christ's side was placed there *before* he had been crucified and wounded by the lance. The blow from the centurion's lance was truly sacramental in that it opened to view the heart that had already been wounded by love. Honorius of Autun affirmed that it was Christ's love for his bride that had wounded his heart upon the Cross. The centurion's lance did not cause the wound but opened up a wound of love that was already there. Chrysologus makes the same point: "These nails do not pierce me with pain; they pierce me more deeply with love of you."[38] The Gospel story of Jesus, most especially as summed up in the image of the Cross, is the love story of God for humankind. "The Gospel is the proclamation," affirms Moore, "that our need to be desired by one we desire is met by the God whom we above all desire since he is our very reason for existing. Our Gospel-proclaimed desiredness in his eyes is the total fulfillment of that need to be in love which is the constitution of us as humans."[39]

Conversion is the flooding of our hearts with the knowledge that the One whom we have been intending, at first vaguely, confusedly, and implicitly and, later perhaps, more explicitly, in all our yearning and desiring and longing finds us precious in His eyes. It is the proclamation that He whom we desire has first loved us. We begin, perhaps, at this point to appreciate anew the radical denial of the Gospel in all preaching that aims at making the hearer feel guilty—whether it is the preaching in revivalist tent meetings or the similar, but thought to be so different, preaching of old-fashioned Catholic missions—and why such preaching has only a transitory effect. To appeal to the sense of guilt, to make the hearer feel unworthy and unlovable, is to appeal to the natural desire to earn love by a Pelagian-making of ourselves as worthy. The exigent god of the guilt-peddler is the tyrannical father who demands that we love first before he will deign to smile. The true conviction of sin comes as the gift of the Holy Spirit, the One whose gift floods our hearts with God's love (cf. Jn. 16:8ff). The Gospel proclamation is the gift of a divine complacency; the unalterable announcement that the One whom we have sought is pleased with us, a complacency that fulfills our desire and thus makes us feel and be altogether a new creature with an altogether new capacity to love.

The differing names of Jesus and the differing orthodox formulations of his meaning, the doctrines and dogma of the Church, derive from the conviction that we are persons whom God has loved; that we are graced and are to love as God has loved. Christianity does not claim that with the preaching of the Gospel humankind for the first time comes into contact with God. Rather it proclaims that what we are somehow confronted with as Absolute and as Holy Mystery in our subjectivity (with all its restlessness) is the very Absolute and Holy Mystery that we encounter in the Word at work in the life, death, and risen presence of Jesus. In Jesus a clue has been given that enables us to live responsibly with the mystery of existence, a clue that is a preview of the end, the goal, and the meaning of all history. In the words and deeds of Jesus an ultimate, absolute, holy, and transforming meaning and truth confront and encounter us: that Absolute or Holy Mystery that is the realm of transcendent love touches us on a level prior to that on which doctrinal systems and organized institutions arise. The stories told by such doctrinal systems and organized institutions are stories about someone whose story we have already heard. By communicating symbolically the meaning incarnate in Jesus, the New Testament supplies a basis of meaning upon which religiously converted subjects may and in fact do make common judgments and decisions. This is the community established by the response of those who accept the Good News of God's gift of his love in the crucified and risen Jesus and his Spirit given to us.

5.431 *The names of Jesus connote the ways that God's gift of his love transforms our lives and constitutes the life story of the Church.*

Vincent Taylor enumerates some fifty-five names and epithets applied to Jesus in the New Testament.[40] Jesus is addressed as Rabbi, as Teacher, and as Master. He is called Prophet, Savior, and Lord. He is the Christ, the Son of Joseph, the Root and Offspring of David. He is the King, the One Who Comes, the Holy One, the Righteous One, the Judge, and the Lion of the Tribe of Judah. He is the Servant, the Bridegroom, and the Shepherd. He is called the Only-Begotten Son, the Author or Pioneer, the Stone and the Head of the Body. He is the True Vine, the Lamb, the Light of the World, and the Door of the Sheepfold. He is the Paraclete, the Mediator, the High Priest, and the Radiance of the Divine Glory. He is the Bread of Life, the Way and the Truth, and the Life; he is the Resurrection and the Life. He is called the Expiation, the First-Born, the Last Adam, and the Alpha and Omega. Jesus is the Beloved, the Word, the Amen, and the Image of God. Each of these titles reflects a different dimension of the impact of the risen Christ on the lives of those who live within the community formed and shaped by the power of that impact. These titles also imply the different dimensions of the personal transformation that the Christ event or Jesus story effects in our lives.

The reality of our sonship-in-the-Son is reflected by the christological titles given to Jesus. He is the Son of God (cf. Mk. 1:1; 15:39) who has given rise to the messianic community and who defines it by his unique relationship of Sonship. His Sonship is the gift and summons of God, the foundation and orientation of the Christian community's relationship with God, the norm of Christian authenticity and maturity. Christian conversion entails the personal appropriation of this Sonship, the acceptance of what we have received in the gift and commitment of his Sonship, a gift that allows us to cry, "Abba, Father" and to call God our Father in the midst of his Church (Gal. 4:6; Mt. 6:9; Lk. 11:2; Rom. 8:15). In the absolute faith, trust, and dependence of the Son, we find the foundation and the norm of our own faith, trust, and dependency.

Christ's Sonship also has the quality of service. Christ is frequently called servant in the Synoptics (e.g., Mt. 12:18) and in Acts (3:13). Jesus is the one who must suffer to enter into his glory, one who must lay down his life for the salvation of many (Mk. 10:45; Mt. 20:28). Men commonly make a contrast between the role of a son and the role of a servant. The son enjoys the freedom of his father's house, whereas the servant is hired to do the master's bidding. The paterfamilias stands in a different relationship to each: to the one he is father; to the other he is master. Where the servant is lucky to get the pigs' leftovers, the son can expect to eat at his father's table (cf. the contrasted expectations in Lk. 15:17 – 19 and 29 – 31). The servant can expect no thanks for what he does since what he does is only his duty (cf. Lk. 17:10). The Letter to the Hebrews (3:5 – 6) contrasts the faithfulness of Moses with that of Christ: the former was faithful as a servant; the latter was faithful as a son. Paul uses the contrast between the status of sonship and the status of a servant as a model for Redemption: God's gift of the Spirit cancels our servanthood to make us sons (Gal 4:7). It is proper for servants to be fearful where the sons may confidently address the head of the household as father (Rom. 8:15). To become a friend is to lose the status of servant (cf. Jn. 15:15). Christ, the unique Son of God, lays aside his Sonship (that which makes him equal to God) to assume the condition of a servant (cf. Phil. 2:6 – 7). Christ's assumption of our servant condition raises those who have died and risen with him to assume by grace his condition of sonship. Christ, as the Church sings every Good Friday, *"factus est oboediens,"* became obedient and learned obedience through what he suffered (cf. Phil. 2:8; Heb. 5:8). In Jesus, sonship and servanthood circumincess. Christ reveals the true nature of service and obedience as rooted in sonship. Obedience is most often associated with childhood and inferiority of rank. Children and soldiers obey. The Letter to the Hebrews (12:5 – 7) seems to reflect this position:

. . . the Lord trains the ones that he loves and he punishes all those that he acknowledges as his sons. Suffering is part of your *training;* God is treating you as his *sons.* Has there ever been any *son* whose father did not *train* him?

Our sonship of God involves being made obedient through punishment and suffering. The history of the Church, as of other institutions, shows us the danger of setting up one model drawn from Scripture as though it needed no correction from other models equally found in the Sacred Writings. The image of God teaching his children obedience through punishment and hardship is a convenient model for those who wish to perpetuate an infantile understanding of Christian sonship. In context, the above passage must be understood as an encouragement: "Have you forgotten that encouraging text in which you are addressed as sons?" (Heb. 12:5) The writer reminds his readers that they have not as yet fully died as Christ has died (Heb. 12:4). We are not yet fully sons according to the measure of the maturity of Christ's Sonship. The Letter to the Galatians supplies us with a necessary corrective for our understanding of Christian childlikeness and obedience. Paul reminds us that a son, even if he has inherited his father's wealth and power through death, is no different from a slave for as long as he has not gained his majority (Gal. 4:1). True sonship comes into its fullness only when a man has attained his own autonomy. It is only when one can dispose of one's own property that one ceases to have in effect the status of a slave. As Christians we must live, says St. Paul, as people who have "come of age" (Gal. 4:3). Paul loves to describe Christian maturity by analogy with civil and legal coming of age. "When I was a child," he tells the Corinthians, "I used to talk like a child, and think like a child, and argue like a child, but now I am a man, all childish ways are put behind me" (1 Cor. 13:11). The fullness of Christian obedience is an affair of adulthood. A story may illustrate our meaning.

There was a young man of twenty-three, a student in a theological college. As can so easily happen in such places, there was a clash of models between the superiors and the students. Rightly or wrongly, the students considered that in general they were treated as children; they felt ashamed to meet their nonclerical friends who often were married and had responsible positions in industry and the public service and who marveled at the overprotective tutelage of the seminary staff. For their part the staff would speak of building a family, of the virtues of obedience, and of the need to "become as little children." The students were rebellious because they felt manipulated and untrusted.

For this young man, as for most of his fellow seminarians, obedience became a dirty word. Submission to rules and superiors was felt to be damaging as well as irksome. Over one Christmas period the student had worked late into the nights preparing himself for an examination at the university. The Christmas holidays were fast disappearing without his having taken any proper rest. One day a fellow student walked into his room, put down a sum of money on the desk, and ordered him to take a few days' break. At this moment the young man understood, perhaps for the first time, the nature of obedience. Obedience is submission in love to the better judgment of those who love you. Obedience is made perfect not in the submission of an inferior to a superior, but in the humility that allows a man or woman to accept that at some particular point those who love them, and who are their equals, may understand their needs better than they do themselves.

Paul frequently returns to the theme of wifely obedience in his writings. Many today see such Pauline injunctions as stemming from an outmoded cultural understanding of the relations between the sexes. One must admit that Paul was a child of his times; it would be strange indeed if Paul's thoughts on marriage betrayed no traces of first-century attitudes and cultural patterns. There are those, particularly in the movement often called charismatic, who would appear to wish to reimpose on Christians quaint notions of wifely and childish submission to the husband as head of the household—submissions that owe more to Victorian prejudice and machismo than to a nuanced and nonfundamentalist reading of St. Paul. Nevertheless, once we have understood obedience as an adult virtue, the humble submission of lovers to each other, St. Paul's meaning takes on a new profundity. Paul sets up the obedience between spouses as the model of Christian obedience, rather than the obedience of children to their parents. Wives submit to their husbands as to the Lord, just as husbands must love their wives on the pattern of Christ who sacrificed himself, that is *"became obedient even unto death"* (Eph. 5:21 – 25; Phil. 2:7). Both must give way to each other in obedience, an obedience that is a fruit of loving the other as much as one loves oneself (Eph. 5:21 and 33). Paul was no advocate of slavish obedience as he makes clear in the same letter:

> When Cephas came to Antioch, however, I opposed him to his face, since he was manifestly in the wrong. . . . When I saw they

(Cephas and his friends) were not respecting the true meaning of the Good News. . . . (Gal. 2:11 – 14)

Obedience is often seen as the road to love: if you want to love, then be obedient. Ethics then becomes, as in Kant, an ethic of duty. Obedience, on the contrary, is the fruit of love. I obey those I love. Servile conformity to the will of another always betrays, as Cardinal Wojtyla so cogently argues, a "weakness of personal transcendence of self-determination and choice."[41] The voicing of opposition to those in authority can be the voice of true obedience as it speaks out of love for the sake of the superior's or the community's good.[42] Jesus the unique Son of God becomes the unique human servant of God and reveals to humankind the true service as sons of him whose service is perfect freedom.

The diversity of names given to Jesus arises from the diversity of possible ways in which we can understand the transformation that his story has wrought in human lives. Although twenty centuries have elapsed since the story of Jesus was first told, we still have no completely satisfying overall explanation of the Christ event. The story of Jesus cannot be reduced to any one of its elements. We cannot separate Jesus from his mystery: his Incarnation of the Known-Unknown in human flesh. There is no doubt, however, among Christians about the reality of the personal transformation that the life story of Jesus effects in their lives. The various titles given to Jesus and the pluriformity of orthodox explanations of the Christ event derive from the multifaceted way in which the risen Christ makes an impact upon their experience. Here the Scholastic axiom holds good: *quidquid recipitur modo recipientis recipitur.* (That which is told is heard according to the capacity and understanding of the hearer.) The impact of the risen Lord upon a person's life is understood and expressed in terms of the life experience of each individual person.

The first generation of Christians strove to express their understanding of the Resurrection in the categories of thought current in their time. Resurrection and Ascension are complementary symbols for expressing the presence of the glorified Christ and the acceptance of his death by the Father. The ideas of being lifted up, exalted, made high, given a place next to a throne, and of being crowned with glory are part of a universal symbolism that associates rising with goodness and falling and the depths with badness. Xavier Léon-Dufour remarks that when the first Christians spoke in this way they "showed that they were the heirs of this ancient human symbolism."[43] In the Letter to the Ephesians (4:7 – 10) and in the Letter to the Romans (10:5–8) Paul uses categories derived from the Aramaic Targum (translation) on Psalm 68 to express the impact on the believer of the risen Christ in terms of a victor's triumph.[44] Christians of the second century sought to express the mystery of Christ in classical hexameters in the style of the pagan Sibyl. Later Thomas of Celano would use classical allusions side by side with scriptural ones:

> Dies irae, dies illa,
> Solvet saeclum in favilla:
> Teste *David* cum *Sibylla*.

The writings of the Greek Apologists, the first theologians of Christianity use the terminology and habits of thought of Hellenistic philosophy to express the mystery of Christ. Later, the two Alexandrines—Clement and Cyril—and Athanasius expound the effect of Christ's impact on the believer as an enlightenment. The fruits that Paul attributed to the inbreathing of God's Spirit—love, joy, peace, patience, kindness, goodness, fidelity, gentleness, and self-control (Gal. 5:22)—are spoken of by these Fathers as qualities produced by the impact of the risen Christ's enlightenment of the human spirit. The exemplarist tradition in theology tends to describe the impact of the risen Lord primarily in terms of moral regeneration or conversion or redirection of the human spirit, implying that God's gift of his love creates a new beginning for our lives both as individuals and in community. To express the gift given in baptism, the Western liturgical tradition makes use of more than the symbolism of washing. Baptism is a bathing of the candidate in light, a giving of new life, a call to discipleship, and a sending forth as witness, a setting free from original sin, a building of the candidate into a temple for God's glory, a sending of the Spirit, an anointing with salvation and a strengthening, an anointing as priest, prophet, and king, a becoming a member of Christ's body, a new creation and a clothing with a white garment, a reception of the light of Christ, and an opening of the ears to hear God's Word, together with an opening of the mouth to sing God's praise. Each one of these symbols and images used by the baptismal rite is necessary if the sacrament of baptism is to be understood in all its richness. The Western liturgical tradition tends to tell the story of Christ in terms of the personal transformation effected in the believer, whereas the Eastern liturgical tradition tends to tell the story in terms of a contemplation of the Christ-icon.

A brief comparison of the prayers surrounding the Communion of the faithful in the Eastern and Western liturgical traditions may illustrate the point. In the Liturgy of St. John Chrysostom the priest shows the chalice to the people and invites them to "approach with the fear of God, in faith, and in love." This corresponds to the Western priest's declaration that they are happy who are called to Christ's supper. To the invitation to partake of Communion the Westerner responds with a declaration of unworthiness: "Lord, I am not worthy to receive you, but only say the word and I shall be healed." The Greek Christian responds with a declaration of what has happened: "The Lord is God and He has appeared to us." The post-Communion collects of the Roman Rite tend to be prayers of petition for the sacrament to effect a transformation in those who have received it, whereas the Byzantine Liturgy calls the people to recite, "We have seen the true light, we have received the heavenly Spirit, we have found the true faith, worshiping the undivided Trinity who has saved us." While both liturgical traditions reflect the fullness and many-stranded nature of faith, it remains true that each tradition stresses and accentuates the various elements of the Christ story in different measure.

Cardinal Wojtyla speaks of the obligation to seek self-fulfillment.[45] Each person is called to fulfill himself or herself, to enjoy the fullness of life and love. The differing models that seek to shed light upon the transforming power of Christ's love serve to explain how we may enjoy life more fully. Each model serves to elucidate the way in which Christ's story calls us to self-fulfillment.[46]

5.5 *Christian conversion is worked out in a process of self-transcendence, in a lifetime's death in love and self-surrender.*

Stories of instantaneous conversion must be treated with caution. Paul's change of heart on the road to Damascus is neither the phenomenological paradigm of all subsequent Christian conversion nor in all probability as instantaneous as the Lucan accounts in Acts at first sight suggest. The three versions of what happened on the road to Damascus (Acts 9:1 – 19; 22:6 – 21; 26:12 – 23) show sufficient evidence of literary shaping to suit Luke's purpose to warrant extreme caution in treating the descriptions as a phenomenology of Christian conversion. The descriptions of Paul's subsequent activity in Acts are not easily reconciled with Paul's own description of the events in the first chapter of his Letter to the Galatians. Where Luke is eager to highlight the dramatic turn-

around in Paul's life—the persecutor has now become the preacher—
and so has Paul preaching in the synagogues after only a few days
in Damascus (Acts 9:19f), Paul stresses the need to assimilate the
story he has heard before he himself tells it to others. After Christ
had revealed himself to Paul he "did not stop to discuss this with
any human being" but "went off to Arabia at once" (Gal. 1:16f). A
period of reflection and prayer was required if Paul were to appropriate his call to be an apostle. Years later, writing to the Corinthians, he mentions the thorn in his flesh and his continuous reliance
on the sufficiency of God's grace (2 Cor. 12:7ff) and, to the Romans,
he bears eloquent testimony to the fact that the moral battle is not
yet definitively won (cf. Romans 7:21ff). Time is needed, perhaps
most usually a whole lifetime, if the healing power of Christ's Gospel is to reach down into the psychic roots of the personality.

A Damascus Road experience can be best understood perhaps by
analogy with the way we experience insight into data for understanding. We puzzle over a problem, wonder how it should be tack-
led, try various starting points, and explore various blind alleys in
our search for a solution. Commonly, we experience insights when
the tension of inquiry has been relaxed, when we abandon our in-
struments and calculators. In a flash we "see" the solution and
dance for joy that we have understood. When we stare at the diagram that accompanies a problem in Euclid, we suddenly see where
the perpendicular must be dropped; but doing Euclid is not merely
a question of gaining an insight into the diagram but also a question of subsequently working out the steps in the proof. Kékulé, it
is said, discovered the benzene ring while dreaming, but one flash
of insight was not enough to validate the hypothesis, let alone turn
a man or woman into a chemist. Insight into the cause of a neurosis
is not by itself sufficient to bring about or guarantee our cure.

Many people describe their conversion to Christ as an understanding that Jesus is Christ and Lord of *their* life. Before conversion, they tell us, they may have had what they call an intellectual
knowledge of the truths of faith but that after their experience of
conversion they know Christ to be what they call their *personal*
Savior. They have moved, Newman would say, from notional to
real assent. There exist too many accounts of human beings claiming that some event or insight changed their lives and brought
them to Christ to dismiss the possibility that the awareness of conversion may break suddenly into focus. But the notion that the
Good News of the Redemption may instantaneously engage a per-

son on every level of his or her consciousness is improbable beyond our wildest imaginings. The insight that Christ loves *me*, that *my* sins have been forgiven, that the promise is for *me* may indeed be more momentous, *sub specie aeternitatis*, than the insight that energy might equal mass times the square of light's velocity but, epistemologically, the insights are not so different, and the revelatory and overwhelming nature of the insight, or better of our reaction to the insight, must not blind us to the need, in both cases, to work out the implications and explanations by long and painstaking effort.

The suddenness of the insight that one has been converted (and many Christians report not a sudden conversion "experience" but a gradual growth) may be compared with the initial experience of falling in love, and even more with the initial judgment that the beloved loves us. When I fall in love it is though I had been reborn, I seem to know myself for the first time, and what before took effort I now do with spontaneity and ease. The story of my life seems transposed to a new key. But the initial rapture of *"Eureka—*I've got it! or her! or him!" must give place to the slow and lengthy task of building two life stories into one. Many who have been received into full communion with the Roman Church in adult life testify to the joy caused by their first confession; but first confessions are followed by other confessions and the rapture of being incorporated sacramentally and visibly into the union of Christ's Body, though never necessarily lost, gives way to the quiet appropriation at an ever-deepening level of the proclamation of sin's forgiveness.

The joy of baptism into Christ's Passover mystery is the prelude to mystagogical catechesis and a lifetime of increasing illumination. To be baptized is to be soaked in Christ. To be thrown bodily and without warning into a pool of water will make us feel wet all over, but only a lengthy immersion will soak us through and through. When we have heard a good story we will be quick to repeat it, but only repeated practice will bring our telling to perfection. The gift of God's love flooding our hearts, the gift of conversion, is a gift of a divine complacency that enables us to fall into love with God so that Christ's spirit may not only fill us with joy but also may convict us of sin (increase our self-knowledge) and fill us with a joy that can bear the terrors and hardships of ascesis. Authentic Christian conversion is a process that ends only with death, and because it is a process it can be rejected or abandoned and therefore, as Benedict clearly saw, may even need the safeguard of a vow.

5.51 **The truths of the Gospel story evoke Christian conversion both as event and as process.**

The Russian spiritual classic *The Way of the Pilgrim* is the story of one man's quest for religious understanding.[47] Going into a church, a man happened to hear the deacon sing the words of Paul: "Pray without ceasing." Leaving the church, the man started a pilgrimage in which he sought a starets who could teach him the meaning of these words. The Word of God can so strike a woman or man that she or he leaves all things and embarks upon a lifetime's quest. The pilgrim seeks an objectification of a story and a meaning that has already become the motivation for the story of his or her life.

The Gospel story is the exterior expression of the interior word that is God's gift of his love flooding our hearts. Religion is the prior word that God speaks to us by the grace of his love given through the Holy Spirit.[48] This inner and immediate experience of God's love is the light, depth, and horizon for understanding and experiencing the truths of the Gospel story. The exterior, a posteriori, saving word of the Gospel story awakens the inner, a priori, word of God found in the hearer's supernaturally elevated and Christ-affected self-transcendence. The Gospel story is a story that says, "This is who you already are; now act like who you are." The outer word of the Gospel story and its truth evoke the inner word of God's grace. Both the movements from the exterior to the interior word, and from the interior to the exterior word, involve an affective intuition, an experiential and connatural knowledge, an affective and hope-filled acknowledgement of the presence of one who loves us. The progressive interiorization of the truths of the Gospel story involves the graced person experiencing at his or her very core the inner word of grace—an inner word evoked by the outer, historical, saving Word of God. Inner sensitivity and receptiveness to God's grace are the prerequisites for hearing God's historical word of grace in Jesus Christ, the Scriptures, the liturgical worship and sacramental life of the Church, and preaching.

Gerard Manley Hopkins in his poem, "Spring and Fall," wrote of a young girl, Margaret, who cried because the autumn woods were turning to brown and losing their leaves.

> Margaret, are you grieving
> Over Goldengrove unleaving?

>Leaves, like the things of man, you
>With your fresh thoughts care for, can you?

The poet knows that increasing years are likely to dull her sense of the shock of death and decay and yet will bring the child a new insight into the reason for her grief.

>Ah! as the heart grows older
>It will come to such sights colder
>By and by, nor spare a sigh
>Though worlds of wanwood leafmeal lie;
>And yet you will weep and know why.

Though the child has never been told the cause, by exterior preaching, her heart already grasps, by an interior resonance or connaturality, the cause of her grief.

>Now no matter, child, the name:
>Sorrows's springs are the same.
>Nor mouth had, no nor mind, expressed
>What heart heard of, ghost guessed:
>It is the blight man was born for,
>It is Margaret you mourn for.

The exilic quality of human living, the sense of being the half of a lost partnership, the presentiment that one has been made for something or someone one knows not what or whom, is the ground in which the explicit preaching of faith will find a congenial soil.

The Gospel story is meant as more than an aid to Christians in internalizing a sublime value system. The Church presents the a posteriori truths of the Gospel story not only that we may grasp their "true essentials," but also that we may grasp the a priori horizon against which these a posteriori saving events are experienced precisely as God's ways and deeds. Hopkins was not only a great poet but also a priest and Jesuit. In "God's Grandeur," he says that the "dearest freshness deep down things" that the child with her fresh thoughts cared for were there

>Because the Holy Ghost over the bent
>World broods with warm breast and with ah! bright wings.

The Scotist theologian and preacher in Hopkins wished not only that Margaret would one day realize that she weeps for her own blight (that she is by nature a hearer) but that she would realize that her melancholy is a homesickness for the place to which the Gospel will call her, that she is by grace a hearer *of the Word*, and that her melancholy is the divinely created restlessness of the human heart without God. The a posteriori truths of the Gospel story are, therefore, valued not only in themselves, but also inasmuch as they awaken, intensify, and explain the Christ-affected character of our conscious horizon. The Church employs its Gospel story as a mystagogy into what is already hidden in the human heart, into what we continuously experience on the fringe or as the undertow of all our human experiences.

In "Leda and the Swan," the poet Yeats wrote of the classical image of the young girl Leda and her encounter with the swan.

> A shudder in the loins engenders there
> The broken wall, the burning roof and tower
> And Agamemnon dead.
>   Being so caught up,
> So mastered by the brute blood of the air,
> Did she put on his knowledge with his power
> Before the indifferent beak could let her drop?

The later details of the story—the siege of Troy, the death of kings, the wanderings of Aeneas—are all somehow contained within the original feelings of the heart. Rainer Maria Rilke wrote a "Mädchen-Klage," a "Girl's Lament," in which he gives voice to that growth of the heart's feeling that cries out for an answer to the barely understood or formulated question:

> Diese Neigung, in den Jahren,
> da wir alle Kinder waren,
> viel allein zu sein, war mild;
> andern ging die Zeit im Streite,
> und man hatte seine Seite,
> seine Nähe, seine Weite,
> einen Weg, ein Tier, ein Bild.
>
> Und ich dachte noch, das Leben
> hörte niemals auf zu geben,
> daß man sich in sich besinnt.
> Bin ich in mir nicht im Größten?

Will mich Meines nicht mehr trösten
und verstehen wie als Kind?

Plötzlich bin ich wie verstoßen,
und zu einem Übergroßen
wird mir diese Einsamkeit,
wenn, auf meiner Brüste Hügeln
stehend, mein Gefühl nach Flügeln
oder einem Ende schreit.[49]

The heart, to paraphrase Pascal's perhaps overused but nevertheless true remark, has its reasons unknown to (or only dimly guessed at by) the head. Yeats takes this understanding of heart knowledge and applies it in his poem "The Mother of God":

The threefold terror of love; a fallen flare
Through the hollow of an ear;
Wings beating about the room;
The terror of all terrors that I bore
The Heavens in my womb. . . .

What is this flesh I purchased with my pains,
This fallen star my milk sustains,
This love that makes my heart's blood stop
Or strikes a sudden chill into my bones
And bids my hair stand up?

Already in the Annunciation there is given to Mary's heart a knowledge of the sword that will pierce it (cf. Lk. 2:35). The exterior preaching of the Gospel reveals in retrospect the meaning and significance of such heart knowledge as the undertow in existential consciousness of a dread call to be holy as God is holy.[50] We may, of course, ignore, repress, flee from, or deny this haunting experience only to find, like Francis Thompson, that we are "Crushed in the fall of what (we) cast away."[51]

The Gospel story is used to awaken us to what is already present in the depths of our being, present not by nature but by grace, a grace that embraces every person as the inescapable setting of his or her existence.[52] Whether he or she knows it or not, the light of Christ illumines every man and woman born into this world (cf. Jn. 1:9—variant reading). A man or woman would never search for God, said Pascal, unless he or she had already found him. The inner word—the *lumen intellectus* supernaturally given a new intentionality as the *lumen fidei*, the light of faith and interior connaturality with God[53]—allows us to hear the exterior preaching of the Gospel story. God's historical word in the Gospel story expounds the inner word, intensifies it, explicates it, fulfills it, summons its recipient to take a stand in respect to it, and moves it from the domain of symbolic consciousness to the levels of intellectual, rational, and responsible consciousness before returning it mediated and critically founded to the second naivete of the mature and adult consciousness.

5.52 *The division of the Scriptures into Old and New Testaments and the Story told by Luke – Acts symbolize the presence of continuity and discontinuity in stories of Christian conversion.*

To understand the stories that men and women tell, especially stories told by storytellers from other ages, peoples, and cultures, it is essential that we should recognize something of ourselves in the characters who people the stories. Unless the story I tell strikes some resonance within my hearers' experience, it will appear altogether too strange and unbelievable. When we say of a theatrical play or a novel that the characters are unbelievable, we are appealing to our own experience of life and of ourselves and others that tells us that men and women just do not act in the way the playwright or novelist has made them act. If the stories told by the Old Testament writers evoked no echoes in our own experience, then we would be justified in considering them as stories badly told or, at the best, stories whose imagery had long since died. The story told by the two Testaments witness to the faith and experience of their human authors who share with contemporary believers a common humanity and a common faith that they have been filled by the Spirit of God's love. The fact that the Testaments are entitled, from the Christian standpoint, old and new, suggests that they witness respectively to something old and something new in us.

The Old Testament witnesses to the impact of God's universal love and offer of friendship in the hearts, minds, souls, and personalities of a particular people. It is the record of God's dealings with a particular nation or people; it is, according to Christian faith, a covenant of love and friendship that was brought to fulfillment by the new story or witness of Jesus Christ. The Old Testament witnesses to the dealings of God, to his universal call to friendship with all peoples—Melchizedek was a priest of God Most High, even though, as his name suggests, he was of Canaanite origin; in Luke's account of Jesus preaching in his home synagogue, Jesus points out God's dealings with a woman and man of Gentile origin (Lk. 4:25 – 27)—but the bulk of the Old Testament is a story about the felt impact of that call in one particular faithful and faithless people.

The story of Luke – Acts is the story of a journey to Jerusalem, a sojourning there, and an explosion of that journeying into many journeys to diverse parts of the world. It is a story of the continuity of the Church with Israel and the radical discontinuity entailed by the newness of Christ's Good News. Luke records the continuity of the new Christians with their old lives. Every day they went as a body to the temple (Acts 2:46), and the apostles are shown preaching to Israel and healing the sick in the same way that Jesus preached and healed. Peter's dream at Jaffa, his preaching in the house of Cornelius (Acts 9:43 – 10:48) chart the beginnings of the move away from their old lives. Peter's need to justify himself to the circumcised brethren in Jerusalem (Acts 11:2 – 3, cf. esp. the Western Text) and the difficulties that led up to the "Council of Jerusalem" (Acts 15) point to the inevitable tensions between their old and new lives.

Luke – Acts suggests a way of understanding the symbolic meaning of the Old Testament for all Gentile Christians. The pre-Christian past of every people and of each individual corresponds in its promise to the Old Testament. Their past, their life story before Christian conversion, is filled with a promise that Jesus Christ is meant to fulfill from the beginning of creation. All humankind has been created to be loved by God in Jesus and in his Spirit. There is a way of interpreting this "Old Testament" past of every people in a way that does not derogate from the uniqueness of God's revelation in Israel. What God revealed in his steadfast love for Israel was his pure, unrestricted, unconditional, universal desire to call all peoples into friendship. What Peter came to realize is that God, the God revealed in and to Israel, does not have favorites: "It is true, God sent his word to the people of Israel ... but Jesus Christ is Lord of all humankind" (Acts 10:34 – 36). God had shown his approval of the pagans by "giving them the Holy Spirit just as he had to us" (Acts 15:8). Peter's speeches symbolize the Christian church's transcendence of ethnic, sectarian, and particularist interpretations of Israel's story. The shift from Old to New Testaments is symbolized in Luke – Acts by the journey from Jerusalem to Rome. The Grail translation of Psalm 47 felicitously if somewhat inaccurately translates verse 2:

> Mount Zion, true pole of the earth,
> the Great King's city!

Just as the earth has two poles, so each Christian may be said to have two poles: Jerusalem and Rome. The Gospel of Luke reflects the journey to one pole: the holy city outside of which Jesus will die. Acts reflects the journey to the opposite pole: the city of all the nations. It is a journey that must be reflected in the life stories of all whose life stories are shaped by that of Jesus. Depth psychology teaches us that present in every human psyche are the images and symbols of its own archaic past. Ontogeny reflects phylogeny. The images of our dreams transcend our own personal histories and point to our future in symbols drawn from our past. The enormous importance attached by the liturgical tradition of Christendom to the chanting of the Psalms, the images and symbols of the Old Testament, points to a felt, if not necessarily conceptually understood, need to appropriate and express ourselves in the images and symbols of our own journey to Christ. Just as the human psyche, if it is to remain healthy, must keep contact with its roots, so, too, the new wine of the Spirit must keep some contact with the old wineskins that, in one sense, it has already burst. The two cities, the two poles of the earth, symbolize mind- and heart-sets in their interpretation of religious experience. They symbolize the tension present in every story of Christian conversion, the "already but not yet," the acceptance of salvation, and the need for ever-deeper healing through all the layers and strata of the human personality.

The tension between the Old and New Jerusalems, which characterizes every Christian story, reminds us that Christian conversion is ever precarious. Rome, which symbolizes in Luke the universality of God's offer of friendship, can become as exclusivist and ethnocentric as anything that has gone before. The battles of SS. Cyril and Methodius to allow their converts liturgical use of the "barbaric" Slavonic languages is not totally dissimilar from the battles of early Christians to relieve their gentile converts of the burden of circumcision and ritual impurity. A narrow interpretation of the principle *extra Ecclesia nullus salus* can conflict with the doctrine of the universal salvific will. The English poet Rudyard Kipling in his poem, "Recessional" asks the "Lord of our far-flung battle line" to Christianize "lesser breeds without the Law." The mission to universal domination, disguised as the civilization and Christianization of the heathen races, hymned by Kipling, is presented in ethnocentric symbols of converting what he calls the "Gentiles" to the civilized lifestyle of English country gentlemen. Some Fundamentalist Protestants, on the basis of OT texts, insist on an unqualified moral and financial and military support for whatever the government of Israel desires. Ironically, many of the same people believe that only the baptized can be saved. They support the *land* of the unbaptized, on the basis of OT teaching about the People of God and their land, even though they believe that the unbaptized are no longer the people of God. The same Fundamental approach may perhaps underlie the attempts of some theologians to understand the sacrificial nature of the Eucharist on the basis of a phenomenological approach that investigates the generic meaning and mode of sacrifice in archaic religions and thence seeks to prove that the eucharistic banquet fulfills the a priori conditions for sacrifice, forgetting that in the theological comparison of Christianity with other religions it is Christ's story and action that provide the prime analogate.

5.53 *The story of Jesus being in agony in the garden discloses the inescapable presence of tension in the life of Christian conversion.*

Underlying the Old Testament concept of conversion is the image of a people returning from exile. All conversion is a homecoming. In the Gospel of John, Jesus is described as knowing that the hour had come for him to go home to the Father (cf. Jn. 13:1). Luke records Jesus as entrusting himself into his Father's hands (Lk. 23:46) and as promising that the dying thief would be with him that day in paradise (Lk. 23:43). John and Luke in their separate ways clearly bring out the feeling of Jesus as going home. Mark accentuates a different feeling. "My soul is sorrowful to the point of death," Jesus tells the three who accompany him to the garden (Mk. 14:34). The different accounts of Jesus' Passion and the subtle allusions to his feelings are not contradictory but rather complementary to each other. Like all his fellow human beings, Jesus is subject to tension. Tension is not the same as having a problem. Problems can be solved or removed; the suffering of tensions is an inescapable dimension of human existence. Algebraic equations may serve as a model for all problems. Once the equation is solved there can be no more "mystery." Once I know that $x = 32$, I can pass on to the next equation secure in the knowledge that I will never have to return to the previous one again. Mark does not portray the approaching death of Jesus as a problem. As they walk to the Mount of Olives, Mark (14:27 – 28) records Jesus as saying:

> You will all lose faith, for the Scripture says: "I shall strike the shepherd and the sheep will be scattered, however after my Resurrection I shall go before you to Galilee."

Jesus is represented here as a man who knew where he was going; as one who knew the meaning of what was about to befall him, as someone who was in some sense in control of the situation. Nevertheless, Mark also portrays him as throwing himself on the ground and praying that, if it were possible, the hour of his death might pass him by (Mk. 14:35). Total fidelity to the truth does not of itself remove the fear and sorrow at the rejection that such fidelity will entail. Thomas Gray in his "Elegy in a Country Church-yard" describes as a characteristic of the great men of this world an ability "The threats of pain and ruin to despise."

There is a disdainful quality about the great woman or man who despises and thinks worthy of little notice the possibility of rejection and pain. To be insensitive to the fear of rejection, to be thick-skinned, is a form of pride. Jesus is not shown as one who despises the threat of pain and ruin. Rather, Luke shows him as one so sensitive to pain and fear that he suffers from a bloody sweat (Lk. 22:44). The fear of Christ, his anguish, his sensitivity to rejection and pain are disclosed to us as the reaction of one who is *sinless*, of one on the path of conversion (understood, not as conversion from sin but as homecoming to God). Christ's suffering is disclosed to us not as the sign that something is wrong but as the sign that he is on the right path. Mark's Gospel presents the *Via Crucis* as Good News, as the growing pains that attend the process of self-transcendence, as the birth pangs that herald the new creation. In a fine phrase, Dr. Frank Lake describes the culmination of Christ's life as a "paradox of suffering and glory." This, he writes,

> is God's final word to man about his own nature and destiny on earth. In order that no mistaken attempts should be made to dissociate these two [suffering and glory], as if the suffering

element could be alienated from man, as the ugliness he should shun, the pain he should avoid, or the emptiness he could abjure, Christ Himself inseparably binds the suffering with the glory. He does this in the most central act of His own Person, both as Son of God and representative man, in man, for man, and towards man. The preaching of the Cross does not allow us to forget this reconciliation, within the divine order, of suffering and glory, which in the human order can never come to terms with one another.[54]

Lake speaks of the Passion and Cross as indeed crowned "but not exceeded in essential glory" by the Resurrection and Ascension.[55] Insofar as all neurotic illness is the substitution of illegitimate suffering as an escape from "staying with" the real suffering, that is, a failure to confront the tension of "staying with the real," so the story of Christ as sharing our dread at the prospect of total commitment to the process of self-transcendence acts as an extraordinarily powerful image illumining the true pathway to glory. Lake speaks of Christ's "infinite courage of commitment."[56] If it is true, as many therapists of as many different schools affirm, that contemporary Western men and women suffer above all from a schizoid longing for commitment bound up with a fear of that commitment, then the image of Christ suffering at the felt demands of the pathway to universal and self-transcending friendship with God and with all humankind will, perhaps above all others, be the image in which contemporary women and men can intuit the beginnings of the answer to the deepest question of their lives.

In an interview on British television, part of a series entitled "God and the Scientist," John Polkinghorne, formerly professor of mathematical physics at Cambridge, implicitly warned against the too-easy preaching of the Christian understanding of suffering. The story of God's sharing in the dread and pain of humankind is not the total answer to the problem of suffering, but in contemplating it one can detect the *beginnings* of an answer, not in the brain, but in the heart.[57] The messianic secret of the synoptic Gospels implies that you may have heard the words of the story, but you may have missed the meaning of messiahship. One must not attempt to tell anyone of the meaning of suffering, as illuminated by the Cross of the Messiah, until one has, for oneself, appropriated the meaning by experiencing what it is to live out the self-transcending and costly love of the *Via Crucis*. The image of Christ crucified and wounded with love for humankind grasps our affectivity and beckons us to a life of commitment long before we can begin to hesitantly stammer something of what it can mean for the human race.

5.6 *Christian conversion is sacramentally signified by the grace of matrimony.*

Bernard Lonergan has described Christian marriage as the "real apprehension, the intense appetition, the full expression of union with another self."[58] In Christian conversion there are given to the human being a real apprehension, an intense appetition, and the full expression of union with God in and through Christ. The man or woman who is converted in Christ affirms really and not merely notionally the reality of things unseen. Faith is an *inchoata visio;* to have seen Christ is to have seen the Father, and to have accepted the testimony of those who have been sent *(apostoloi)* by Christ is to have accepted Christ himself. In telling the story of Jesus, his Body the Church effectively makes present the Word whom it proclaims. In conversion we are given a real hope in the promises made by God. We develop a taste for the things of God. By the gift of conversion we fix our eyes upon the "heaven, where Christ is." The intensity of his appetite for the things of God led Paul to wish his own dissolution and to be with Christ. By conversion the Christian man or woman enjoys the full expression of union with God in Christ. Bonded by the shared love of the Holy Spirit, the convert acknowledges the real presence of Christ in the poor, the community, the Word proclaimed, the ministry of the overseers and elders and, most excellently, in the Bread broken and the Cup shared.[59]

The life of the converted Christian is a life of union with Christ. It is a lifelong process by which each convert's story is taken up, sublated, and transformed into the story of Jesus Christ. To express the nature of the commingling of the divine and human stories in Christ and his Church, Christian tradition has made use of many images and symbols but especially the symbol and sign of Christian marriage.[60] In the joining of husband and wife the partners experience the outward and physical sign of the affirming love of God. In authentic marriage, writes Jack Dominian, there is an affirmation by the couple that each one is true, good, and beautiful, and this affirmation is a "second affirmation," an affirmation that has the power to heal the affective and emotional hurts suffered in childhood.[61] In the Book of the Consolation of Israel, Yahweh affirms the goodness of his people:

Do not be afraid, for I have redeemed you;
I have called you by your name, you are mine.
Should you pass through the sea, I will be with you;
or through rivers, they will not swallow you up.
Should you walk through fire, you will not be scorched
and the flames will not burn you. (Is. 43:1 – 2)

Yahweh will be with his people, for better or for worse, for richer or for poorer, in sickness and in health. And why?

Because you are precious in my eyes,
because you are honoured and I love you. (Is. 43:4)

It is perhaps the hardest thing in the world to love oneself. The Pelagian do-gooder assuages the pain of feeling unloved by proving his or her own worth by a self-deceiving pretense that he or she puts others before himself or herself. The joylessness that Nietzsche observed as afflicting so many Christians originates in a debilitating sense of worthlessness that issues most often in a conviction that one is unloved and unlovable. The work of John Bowiby and others on infancy and early childhood can leave little doubt that the loss of maternal affection results in a radical incapacity to give love to oneself in later life. *Nemo dat quod non habet.* It is a central Christian conviction that no one is unloved since God has first loved us. The whole of John's First Letter is dedicated to the proclamation of God's unmerited, prevenient love. In the love of parent for child and in the love of man for woman and woman for man, the prevenience and gratuitousness of the divine love are sacramentally signified and experienced. In the experience of being desired physically, emotionally, intellectually, morally, and responsibly, men and women are affirmed in their intrinsic goodness and lovableness and attain a real apprehension of the delight taken in them by Yahweh (Is. 62:4 – 5).[62]

The intensity of man's appetite for woman and woman's appetite for man, the extravagance of the sexual impulse in human beings, an extravagance that marks humankind off from the animal kingdom, have their ultimate ground in the restlessness of the heart without God.[63] The longing for union, experientially and sacramentally signified in the physical, emotional, intellectual, and responsible longing of the partners for intercourse, is a particular, and privileged, instance of the irrepressible urge of the human person to self-transcendence by union with another. Honorius of Autun,

commenting upon the ninth verse of the fourth chapter of the Song
of Songs

> You ravish my heart, my sister, my promised bride,
> You ravish my heart with a single one of your glances

tells us that it was the love Christ felt for his bride that wounded
his heart upon the Cross.[64] The powerfulness of eros, celebrated
incomparably by the Song of Solomon, a power that can move a
man to sell everything in his house for love, reflects the longing of
the Spirit and the Bride that the Bridegroom may appear (cf. Rev.
22:17).

Finally, in marriage there is the full expression of the union of
two persons, of two life stories. Just as in Christian conversion
there is a tension between now and not yet, an inchoate possession
of eschatological beatitude, so in the fleshly union of husband and
wife there is experienced the already but not yet fulfilled promise
of the total intertwining of two life stories. In the momentary return to the symbiosis of infancy the couple are strengthened in
their faith, hope, and love in each other; they are confirmed in their
conviction that the promises of Christ are not illusory and that the
human story, when authentically lived out, demands a happy ending.

The very powerfulness of the sexual urge and the experience of
the real possibility of disaster can lead to an un-Christian fear of
sexuality and a neurotic desire to control it by repression. At least
one strand of Jewish tradition sees in the commandment to keep
holy the Sabbath a divine command to celebrate the union of Yahweh and Israel by enjoying what the Christian liturgy calls the one
great blessing not taken away by the flood.[65] When the natural is
sublated by the higher context of the supernatural, its own laws
and character are not thereby abrogated or transgressed; the sacred and sacramental character of Christian marriage is not safe-
guarded, as some narrow Christian thinkers have sometimes seemed
to suggest, by removing the marital relationship from the fleshly
and "spiritualizing" it in an illegitimate fashion, but by whole-
heartedly affirming with the author of Genesis that all of creation
is good and that God may by his grace sublate sensual and earthly
passions, precisely as sensual and earthly, into the service of revealing the inner meaning of the human story. The love of God was
revealed in the bruised and battered flesh of one from whom the
people screened their faces; the suffering face of Christ can be dis-

cerned by faith in the faces of all who suffer. It would be a bizarre theology that restricted the human body to being an instrument for revealing God's love only when it is battered and broken. The writer of Proverbs prayed that his son would always look with delight upon the physical charms of his wife (cf. Pr. 5:18ff). The bodily, emotional, and spiritual experience of union in marriage is an outward and visible sign of the self-transcendence given and received in conversion.

5.61 *The charism of celibacy for the Kingdom reflects the narrative quality of our life in Christ.*

By the gift of Christian conversion the natural blessing of the marital relationship is sublated sacramentally into the higher context of a symbolic revelation of God's relationship to humankind. For those to whom it is given, the gift of being made eunuchs for the sake of the Kingdom functions as an effective sign of the intertwining of the human story with the story of God.

In a mistaken attempt to justify the Christian tradition of voluntary renunciation of marriage and childbearing for the sake of the Kingdom, some writers have attempted to extol the human fulfillment that can attend the lived-out renunciation of family life. A story may illustrate the point. Two priests, members of a religious order, were dining with a family. A young man at the table was seriously reflecting on what might be God's will for his own life: whether to marry and have a family or whether God might be calling him to receive the gift of eldership. He remarked that it seemed to him that the celibacy presently required of those who are ordained as elders must entail loneliness and lack of human fulfillment. Immediately the two priests denied that the celibate life was lonely. The lack of one's own family was more than compensated for by being welcomed as father by all the families of a parish. They talked of the marvelous fulfillment of being on intimate terms with hundreds of people, which more than made up for the lack of a family. When they had gone, the young man said, "If that is all there is to it, why bother to give up married life? There are many professions or callings that would give me all the things these men say their priesthood brings, and I could have a family as well." He believed that the two priests were fundamentally dishonest in their reply. Their denial of any loneliness or frustration reminded him that priests, like Hamlet's mother, can protest too much. Their denial of any human lack of fulfillment destroyed for him any sign value that celibacy might have.

The text of Matthew's Gospel repays careful study (Mt. 19:10 – 12). Jesus is not recorded as advocating sexual renunciation as an alternative way of living a fulfilled life. He is not recorded as advocating celibacy as a means for freeing a person from matrimonial and family cares to devote himself or herself full time to the preaching of the Gospel. He is recorded by Matthew as recognizing the hardness of the saying: "It is not everyone who can accept what I have said, but only those to whom it is granted." He is recorded as likening celibacy for the Kingdom to those who have been born handicapped or who have been castrated. Mardian, Cleopatra's eunuch, bears eloquent witness to the plight of the eunuch.

Cleopatra: I take no pleasure
            In aught a eunuch has: 'tis well for thee,
            That, being unseminared, thy freer thoughts
            May not fly forth of Egypt. Hast thou affections?

Mardian: Yes, gracious madam.

Cleopatra: Indeed?

Mardian: Not in deed, madam; for I can do nothing
            But what in deed is honest to be done;
            Yet have I fierce affections, and think
            What Venus did with Mars.[66]

In reply to Peter's urgent questioning, Jesus replies that the reward for those who have left houses, brothers, sisters, father, mother, children or land for the sake of his Name will be given "when all is made new"—in the eschaton (Mt. 19:27 – 30). The fulfillment of the one who has received the grace of celibacy lies only in the parousia, the end fulfillment of the last days. Insofar as the celibate receives fulfillment in this life, it is a fulfillment that is given only by faith.

The tradition of the Eastern churches is instructive in this regard. The gift of tears, the gift of total repentance, is said to restore lost virginity. A period of being left fallow allows the farmer to recover for his or her fields the productiveness of virgin soil. In the Eastern view virginity is not something that once lost can never be regained. It is not a biological or emotional fact about somebody's life. Virginity, or as the Western Christian would call it, celibacy, is a state of looking to God exclusively for fulfillment. Just as the physical attraction of sexual desire is sublated by the emotional value of *convivium* and in turn is sublated sacramentally into an outward and tangible sign of the love of God, a sublation that respects the autonomy of each lower level, so the gift of celibacy for the Kingdom sublates the natural frustration of the sexual function into the higher context of embodying in a human life story the perpetual task of the Church to be waiting on God.

The natural development of a human life leads the subject of each life story to affirm himself or herself in the passing on to a new generation the life that he or she has received. Spontaneously we hope that other subjects will come to existence so that our own life story may be continued in the stories of our children and our children's children. In the normal course of events a person looks for self-fulfillment in the joining of his or her life story to another's and the coming into being of new lives with new stories to tell. By the gift of celibacy for the Kingdom the person who has been given that gift lives as a "sign of contradiction," as one who in his or her life embodies the incompleteness of human beings without God. The sacramental sign of marriage signifies the here-and-now possession in promise of the total union of humankind with God. The quasi-sacramental sign of celibacy for the Kingdom signifies the here-and-now waiting for that promise to be fulfilled. Mary, the archetypal model for all Christian celibacy, is represented by Luke as one who was blessed because she "believed that the promise made her by the Lord would be fulfilled" (Lk. 1:45). The gift of celibacy for the Kingdom is the sign, for those who can accept it, that ultimately our life story is told and completed not by our own unaided telling but by the Christ who takes over and lives again in our lives.

5.7 *The story of Judas as portrayed by the Gospel writers discloses ultimate human failure as the betrayal of the divine offer of friendship.*

Mark's Gospel discloses the increasing rejection of Christ by those who should accept him. Mark's narrative is structured as a Way of the Cross. Christ's story as told by Mark underscores for us the truth that the path of love is not the way to easy popularity but the road to the acceptance of a true glory that can be achieved only through suffering.

Scholars of Hebrew tell us that *kabod*, which we normally translate as "glory," means not the outward show and tinsel of worldly pomp and glory, but the weightiness of a thing, its value and worth.

Thomas Gray gave us a classical expression of worldly glory when he wrote in the churchyard at Stoke Poges:

> The boast of heraldry, the pomp of power,
>   And all that beauty, all that wealth e'er gave,
> Awaits alike th'inevitable hour,
>   The paths of glory lead but to the grave.
>
> Can storied urn or animated bust
>   Back to its mansion call the fleeting breath?
> Can Honour's voice provoke the silent dust,
>   Or Flatt'ry soothe the dull cold ear of Death?

Gray later discloses a main source of worldly glory:

> Th'applause of list'ning senates to command.

The writer of Psalm 3, a psalm applied by the patristic writers to the death of Jesus, gives us the biblical understanding of true glory:

> Yahweh, more and more are turning against me,
> more and more rebelling against me,
> more and more saying about me,
> "There is no help for him in his God."
>
> But, Yahweh, my encircling shield,
> my glory, you help me hold up my head. . . .
>
> Now I can lie down and go to sleep
> and then awake, for Yahweh has hold of me.[67]

The supreme trust with which Jesus can lay down his life and "go to sleep" in an act of complete self-abandonment to and trust in his God and Father is, in John's gospel, the last and greatest sign of his glory.

   Judas betrays Jesus with a kiss. To kiss someone is to express one's concern for the other, one's need of the other, one's appreciation of the other, one's reverence for the other, one's friendship and one's love. Judas symbolizes ultimate human failure as the betrayal of friendship. Insofar as his kiss is a lie—it speaks of friendship when betrayal is its purpose—it symbolizes the betrayal of his true self. In Robert Bolt's *A Man for All Seasons*, St. Thomas More explains to his daughter the meaning of an oath. His daughter has urged him to swear the oath with his lips but intend something different with his heart. More replies that an oath is words we say to God.

> When a man takes an oath, Meg, he's holding his own self in his own hands. Like water (*cups hands*) and if he opens his fingers then—he needn't hope to find himself again.[68]

At the arrest Judas speaks to Jesus, the primordial sacrament who discloses God to the world: "Greetings, Rabbi." In the narrative as given by Matthew, Jesus calls Judas his friend: "My friend, do what you are here for" (Mt. 26:50). Quite possibly Judas used the customary greeting, "Shalom, Peace." Judas lies to God; he calls God friend while refusing his real offer of friendship. His subsequent suicide symbolizes the self-destruction already implicit in his destructive attitude toward Jesus.

Matthew charts well the dynamic of Judas's behavior. Judas goes to the chief priests and offers to betray his master. "What are you prepared to give me if I hand him over to you? (Mt. 26:14). They gave him thirty shekels, the price fixed by the Torah as compensation for the death of a slave (Ex. 21:32). The price suggests that Judas is interested in more than the money. The price fixed suggests that Judas has power over Jesus, and that he is in some way his owner. Jesus is reduced in Judas's eyes from the status of being a friend to that of being a slave. Judas, who is a nobody in the eyes of the chief priests, is allowed the illusion of being treated as a man of substance with rights over another person. Mark suggests a further motivation; he records that the chief priests were delighted to hear Judas's proposal (Mk. 14:11). Judas perhaps has succumbed to the temptation to think of himself as "being in" with the authorities, as one who has a part to play in the Councils of state, as one with access to the inner circle, and as a man of influence who has friends at court. For a brief while Judas feels esteemed; no doubt the authorities made a show of welcoming him when he came to put his proposal. Judas's behavior is the behavior of a person who wants to seem big in his own eyes and who welcomes the passing acclaim of others because it serves to strengthen his own illusions. To adapt the dictum of Descartes: I am applauded; therefore I am.

In Matthew's account of the Last Supper Jesus foretells his coming betrayal. Someone who has dipped his hand in the dish with him—someone who has shared his table, that is, a friend or guest—will betray him. Judas exclaimed, "Not I, Rabbi, surely?" (Mt. 26:25). True to his character as one who needs the esteem of whoever he happens to be with, Judas presents himself as one who could not possibly be a traitor. Like Thomas More in Bolt's play, Jesus knows that the speaker's very self is at stake. "They are your own words," answered Jesus (Mt. 26:25).

When Judas discovered that Jesus had been condemned, he was filled with remorse (Mt. 27:3). This perhaps suggests that the purpose of Judas had not been to encompass the destruction of Jesus but to *use* him—he had treated him neither as a friend nor an enemy but as a slave, that is, as a possession—in order to gain the esteem of those who seemed greater masters in the eyes of the world than did his master. The reply of the chief priests and elders to his return of the money finally discloses to him the poverty of his self-image. He tells the truth: "I have betrayed innocent blood." Now that they have no further use for him they exhibit their indifference: "What is that to us? That is your concern" (Mt. 27:4). The false self-image of one in control of the situation, the one who could deliver what the authorities wanted, the one whose services were valuable to those in positions of power and prestige, has been shattered, and the real self, the self who tells the truth, is accounted by those he sought to please a thing of no account. The one who wanted to be master discovers that it was he who was being used. His anger turns inward upon himself, and he tries to put an end to his own existence.

The story of Judas is the story of a man who tries to capture the position of master for himself. The story of Jesus is the story of one who knows he is the Master but who can assume the position of a servant in order to embody the happiness that comes from abandonment of self into the hands of God (cf. Jn. 13:13 – 17). True suffering comes from faithfulness to one's mission to bear witness to reality. One's self-esteem should be independent of one's outward success or failure; it comes as the gift of God's love, which convinces us that we are trusted and gives us the operative and effective grace to fulfill the demands of that trust.

1. *Missale Romanum*, Praefatio de Apostolis II.
2. Bernard Lonergan, "Prolegomena to the study of the emerging religious consciousness of our time," *Sciences Religieuses/Studies in Religion* 9 (1980), p. 15.
3. *Ibid.*
4. Although methodologically it may be convenient to split conversion into the differing moments of intellectual, moral, religious, and psychic conversion, nevertheless it is important to affirm that any intellectual change of belief that goes beyond the merely notional always involves a moral, religious, and psychic change. True insights are always passionate affairs (Archimedes leaps from his bath) and resonate on all levels of consciousness.

5. Cf. Bernard Lonergan, "The Natural Desire to See God," *Collection: Papers by Bernard J. F. Lonergan, S. J.* (London: Darton, Longman & Todd, 1967), pp. 84–95; for a brilliant discussion of sexual love as sacrament see *Id*, "Finality, Love, Marriage," *Collection*, pp. 16–53.
6. Cf. Karl Rahner, "The Hiddenness of God," *Theological Investigations XVI* (London: Darton, Longman & Todd, 1979), pp. 227–243.
7. Cf. Frederick E. Crowe, "Complacency and Concern in the Thought of St. Thomas," *Theological Studies* 20 (1959) pp. 1–39, 198–230, 343–395.
8. Augustine's famous phrase is, of course, primarily concerned with the presbyterate. The Christian elder acts *in persona Christi* because he (and perhaps in the future, she) is ordained to act *in persona Ecclesiae*. Since the baptismal priesthood of all believers is chronologically and ontologically prior to the ministerial priesthood or eldership, Augustine's words can be applied *mutatis mutandis* to all who share in the royal and prophetic priesthood of the Church.
9. Some years ago the Catholic Truth Society of London, spurred by the success of *Thoughts of Chairman Mao,* published the small book, *Thoughts of Jesus.* The banality of the published product, with its facile reductionism, well illustrated the folly of tampering with the stories as told by the evangelists.
10. See John Navone, "Write a Gospel," *Review for Religious* 38 (1977), pp. 668–678.
11. On biblical stories as stories of a homecoming, see John Navone, *Towards a Theology of Story* (Slough, England: St. Paul Publications, 1977), pp. 53 – 68, or *Id, The Jesus Story*, pp. 75 – 85.
12. Bernard Häring, *Free and Faithful in Christ* 1 (Slough, England: St. Paul Publications, 1978), pp. 418f.
13. Cf. the Preface for Masses of the Blessed Trinity: *"Vere dignum et iustum est, aequum et salutare. . . . Ut in confessione verae sempiternaeque Deitatis, et in personis proprietas, et in essentia unitas, et in maiestate adoretur aequalitas."*
14. The Church employs its Gospel story and its truth in much the same way that St. Ignatius of Loyola employed his *Spiritual Exercises*. See Harvey D. Egan, *The Spiritual Exercises and the Ignatian Mystical Horizon* (St. Louis: The Institute of Jesuit Sources, 1976), pp. 157 – 160.
15. Martini's hypothesis appears in several of his articles: "The Stages of the Formation of the Christian in the Primitive Community in the Light of the Four Gospels," in *Pontificium Consilium Pro Laicis Documentation Service* 5 (February 1979), pp. 1 – 10; "Riflessioni sull'ininerario dell'esperienza cristiana nel NT," unpublished mss. (Rome 1978), p. 15; "Vangelo della Passione ed Esperienza Mistica nella Tradizione Sinottica e Giovannea" in *Mistica e Misticismo Oggi* (Rome: CIPI, 1979), pp. 191 – 201; "Iniziazione Cristiana e Teologia Fondamentale: Riflessione sulle tappe della maturità cristiana nella chiesa primitiva," in R. Latourelle and G. O'Collins, eds., *Problemi e prospettive di Teologia Fondamentale* (Brescia: Queriniana, 1980), pp. 85 – 91.
16. Gregory Dix, *The Shape of the Liturgy* (London: Dacre: Adam & Charles Black, 2nd ed., 1964), p. 143.
17. *Sacrosanctum Concilium* 100, (Abbott trans.)
18. W. Telfer, *Cyril of Jerusalem and Nemesius of Emesa,* in *Library of Christian Classics* vol. 4 (London: SCM Press, 1955), p. 12.
19. Johannes Quasten, *Patrology*, vol. III, (Westminster, Md.: The Newman Press, 1963), p. 364.
20. *Mystagogical Catecheses*, 18, 33.
21. Edward Yarnold, *The Awe-inspiring Rites of Initiation: Baptismal Homilies of the Fourth Century* (Slough, England: St. Paul Publications, 2nd ed. 1973), p. 52. Cf. *Mystagogical Catecheses, 1, 1* (printed in Yarnold, p. 68: ". . . I well knew that visual testimony is more trustworthy than mere hearsay, and therefore I awaited this chance of finding you more amenable to my words, so that out of your personal experience I could lead you into the brighter and more fragrant meadow of Paradise on earth.")
22. Bernard Lonergan, *Method in Theology*, pp. 101 – 124.
23. Cyril of Jerusalem, *Mystagogical Catecheses, 3:1;* Yarnold, *op. cit.,* p. 79.

24. *Ibid., 5:19;* Yarnold, *op. cit.,* p. 92.

25. St. Augustine, *Confessions, PL* 32, 688: *"Tu autem eras interior intimo meo, et superior summo meo."* Cf. Johannes B. Lotz, *Interior Prayer: The Exercise of Personality* (New York: Herder & Herder, 1968), passim.

26. The "screen memories" of Freudian psychoanalytic theory witness to the powerful need for human beings to enter the inner circle, to see what is going on behind the (bedroom) door.

27. See John Navone, "The Graves of Craving and Self-Fulfillment," *Homiletic and Pastoral Review* (November 1980), pp. 29 – 32, 52 – 54.

28. Raymond E. Brown, *The Anchor Bible 29: The Gospel According to John (i – xii)* (New York: Doubleday, 1966, and London: Chapman, 1971), p. 86.

29. This nonnecessity to stand on our own feet perhaps accounts for the frequent tendency to associate religious feelings with the oceanic (no I, because no "not me," in H. S. Sullivan's terminology) feelings of early infancy; see Sigmund Freud, *Civilization and Its Discontents,* trans. Joan Riviere and James Strachey (London, The Hogarth Press & The Institute of Psychoanalysis, 1963 ed.), pp. 1 – 2.

30. Thomas C. Oden, *The Structure of Awareness* (Nashville, Tenn., and New York: Abingdon Press, 1969), pp. 117 – 118.

31. *Ibid.,* pp. 118 – 119.

32. Cf. Raymond E. Brown, *The Birth of the Messiah: A Commentary on the Infancy Narratives in Matthew and Luke* (London: Geoffrey Chapman, 1977), p. 139.

33. Grantland Rice, "Alumnus Football." Rice apparently overlooked the fact that in most if not all games, whether you win or lose depends precisely on how you play the game!

34. Frederick E. Crowe, "Complacency and Concern in the Thought of St. Thomas," *Theological Studies* 20 (1959), pp. 1 – 39; 198 – 230; 343 – 395.

35. Dante Alighieri, *La Divina Commedia, Paradiso,* XXXIII, ll. 142 – 145. "The love that moves the sun and the other stars had already turned my desire and my willing to roll like a stone with constant motion."

36. Sebastian Moore, *The Fire and the Rose Are One* (London: Darton, Longman & Todd, 1980), passim.

37. Campbell's trans., "Alas! Alas! for him," the Shepherd cries, / "Who tries from me my dearest love to part / So that she does not gaze into my eyes / Or see that I am wounded to the heart." / Then, after a long time, a tree he scaled, / Opened his strong arms bravely wide apart, / And clung upon that tree till death prevailed, / So sorely was he wounded in his heart.

38. Chrysologus, *Sermo 108, PL 52,* 499.

39. Moore, *op. cit.,* p. 44.

40. Vincent Taylor, *The Names of Jesus* (New York: 1953).

41. Karol Wojtyla, *The Acting Person,* in *Analecta Husserliana X* (1979), p. 289.

42. *Ibid.,* pp. 286f.

43. Xavier Léon-Dufour, *Resurrection and the Message of Easter* (London: Geoffrey Chapman 1974), p. 35.

44. Stanislaus Lyonnet, "Saint Paul et l' exégèse juive de son temps. À propos de Rom 10:6–8," *Mélanges A. Robert* (Paris 1957) pp. 494–506. Cf. M. McNamara, *The New Testament and the Palestinian Targum to the Pentateuch, Analecta Biblica* 27, (Rome: Pontificium Institutum Biblicum, 1966), pp. 70–81.

45. Wojtyla, *op. cit.,* pp. 163ff.

46. John Navone, *A Theology of Failure* (New York: The Paulist Press, 1974), pp. 31f.

47. *The Way of a Pilgrim,* trans. R.M. French, with an Introduction by Metropolitan Anthony of Surozh (London: S.P.C.K.), 1972.

48. Bernard Lonergan, *Method in Theology,* p. 112.

49. Cooper's translation: "Our childhood's inclination to be on our own was mild;/ others spent the time in quarrelling,/ and each had their own place,/ their own nearness and distance,/ their own way, animal, and image./ I used to think that life/ would always allow us to be with ourselves./ Is there something greater than I?/ Will my life no longer allow me/ the consolation and understanding I had as a child?/ Suddenly, it's as though I've been rejected,/ and my loneliness reaches to infinity,/ when, on the hillocks of my breasts/ my feeling stands up and cries out/ for wings or for an ending."

50. Bernard Lonergan, *Method in Theology,* p. 240.

51. Francis Thompson, "Ode to the Setting Sun: After-Strain."

52. Karl Rahner, "Nature and Grace," *Theological Investigations IV,* pp. 165–188.

53. Cf. Juan Alfaro, "Supernaturalitas Fidei iuxta S. Thomam," *Gregorianum* 44 (1963), pp. 501–542, 731–787.

54. Frank Lake, *Clinical Theology: A Theological and Psychiatric Basis to Clinical Pastoral Care* (London: Darton, Longman & Todd, 1966), p. 9., *op. cit.,* p. 1100.

55. *Ibid.*

56. *Ibid.,* p. 1118.

57. Interview with Ronald Eyres on BBC2, February 4, 1981.

58. Bernard Lonergan, "Finality, Love, Marriage," in *Collection,* p. 32.

59. Cf. II Vatican Council, Constitution on the Sacred Liturgy, 7.

60. Cf. Thomas Cooper, "The Wedding of the Lamb," *The Venerabile* 24 (1969), pp. 269 – 280.

61. Cf. Jack Dominian, *Cycles of Affirmation: Psychological Essays in Christian Living,* (London: Darton, Longman & Todd, 1975).

62. On the use of these texts by the liturgy, especially with reference to the Incarnation, see Thomas Cooper, "Celebrating the Word Made Flesh: Images of Christmas in the Liturgy," *The Clergy Review* 63 (1978), pp. 406 – 412.

63. Bernard Lonergan, "Finality, Love, Marriage," *op. cit.,* p. 50.

64. Honorius Augustoduniensis, *Expositio in Cantica Canticorum, PL 168,.* 419.

65. Cf. the material cited in Marvin H. Pope, *Song of Songs: A New Translation with Introduction and Commentary, Anchor Bible 7C* (Garden City, N.Y.: Doubleday & Company, 1977), pp. 171–178.

66. Shakespeare, *Anthony and Cleopatra,* act 1, scene 5.

67. *The Jerusalem Bible,* (New York: Doubleday & Co., 1966), p. 787.

68. Robert Bolt, *A Man for All Seasons,* act 2 (London: Heinemann, 1960), p. 83.

CHAPTER 9

THE SIXTH MOMENT:

Jesus Christ is the Sacrament who transforms human life stories

Beauty has a likeness to the properties of the Son. Beauty has three elements: wholeness, just proportion, and clarity. Regarding the first element, beauty has a likeness to the property of the Son, insofar as He is the Son having in Himself the true and perfect nature of the Father. . . . As regards the second element, beauty is like the property of the Son, inasmuch as He is the expressed image of the Father. . . . Regarding the third element, beauty has a likeness to the property of the Son, insofar as He is the Word, which signifies light and the splendor of the intellect.

Summa Theologia
St. Thomas Aquinas

If there is one divine attribute rather than another, which forces itself upon the mind from the contemplation of the material world, it is the glory, harmony, and beauty of its Creator. . . . out of the infinitude of His greatness, He has defaced His own glory, and wounded and deformed His own beauty—not indeed as it is in itself, for He is ever the same, transcendentally perfect and unchangeable, but in the contemplation of His creatures,—by the unutterable condescension of His incarnation.

Discourses to Mixed Congregations
John Newman

The very ground of being smiles upon us in the face of Christ.

Love Alone
Hans Urs von Balthasar

6.1 *The categories appropriate to a critical understanding of the Gospel story are aesthetic rather than classically scientific.*

The story of Jesus as told by the Christian community, both in its foundational documents collected in the New Testament and in its traditional teaching and sacramental life, is a love story coauthored by God and by humankind. Since love is a relation of the whole person, an engagement of the whole self at all levels of its being, it follows that any declaration of love must be expressed in terms that in some way point to the multileveled relationship that necessarily exists when any human being falls in love. When I say to someone, "I love you," I am saying more to that person than I can verbally know or say. I have no clear and distinct idea of who I am. I am a mystery to myself; my affirmation that I love is a statement about a self that is not clearly and distinctly known. It is the statement of a subject and, while subjects can be conceived and understood and judged, any reflection upon the subject as object of one's conceiving, understanding, and judging turns the subject into a self. The *I* becomes an *IT*. The lover is conscious as the subject of a verb. He or she rightly or wrongly understands that verb to be "to love." (A person can be mistaken about whether they are loving, as Cherubino and any psychotherapist will testify.) Even when the subject has rightly judged himself or herself to be loving, that self, as the object of understanding and judgment remains an object that is imperfectly comprehensible in human concepts. When I hear someone say to me, "I love you," I am hearing speak someone who remains to me a mystery and who, if it is a human person who speaks, remains a mystery to herself or himself.

While the pure unrestricted act of understanding whom we call God is not in his absolute self-possession and unrestricted self-understanding a mystery to himself, so that his perfect self-expression is that relation of Understood to Understander whom we call the Person of the Word, nevertheless, for God to speak to humankind he must express himself in such a mode as is understandable by human understanding. The affirmation of God's love for humankind must be experienced as mystery, as an offer of friendship that will transform a self who does not enjoy perfect self-possession nor perfect self-understanding. God's expression of his love for humankind must be such that the human hearer hears more than she or he can verbally hear or understand. Since the exterior word of the Gospel story is the grace-filled work of human minds as they struggle to verbalize the interior teaching of the Holy Spirit, the putting into words of the writer's experience of what it is to be loved and cherished by God, it will always, like every declaration of human love, mean more than the speaker or writer can say. Since the symbolic is that which best points to a reality whose object remains unknown and that best mediates between the different levels of consciousness—intellectual, moral, and psychic—and between those levels and the unconscious dimensions of human-embodied existence, the fullest expression of love will always take place by way of symbols.[1]

A major theme in the life work of Bernard Lonergan has been his charting of the shift from a theology conceived upon the pattern of an Aristotelian science proceeding *more geometrico* from clearly and distinctly defined axioms and definitions to an understanding of theology as a recurrent set of operations in the mind and subjectivity of a theologian. For necessary and immutable laws applicable to all concrete situations, the modern theologian, in Lonergan's view at least, must increasingly substitute a discussion of statistical and moral probabilities and possibilities. No longer is theology to be thought of as a science about God but as the reflection of a believer upon the place and meaning of religious experience within a particular time and culture.[2]

The human sciences—psychology, sociology, history, and the like—are sciences *by analogy* with the physical sciences and not by univocal predication. Mathematical physics can no longer be regarded as the pattern for all sciences, as though the validity of their methods rested upon their likeness or unlikeness to the work of an experimental physicist. The case histories of the clinician and the judgments of taste of the literary and artistic critic increasingly become fruitful models for understanding the work of the theologian.[3] If theology is to be sustained reflection on the role of the religiously converted within a cultural context, the stories of the religiously converted and the stories of those who claim to live Christian lives but who evidence inauthentic or partial conversion must be carefully analyzed and compared as evidence for the ways in which the gift of God's love can be appropriated or nonappropriated.

If beauty is the circumincession of truth and goodness, as the tradition stemming from Albertus Magnus and Aquinas asserts, and if taste, as Kant argued, is the connatural judgment of the critic affirming or negating the authenticity of a work of art's claim to universal validity and value, and if the authentic holiness that responds to the gift of God's love is the perfection of the dramatic pattern of human experience and living, then the authentic incarnation of the value of truth and the truth of value in the lives of those we call saints, and the inauthentic response of what might be called pathological defense mechanisms to God's offer of friendship, will provide a major datum for theological reflection. Insofar as the Gospel stories may be considered the external objectifications of the inner conversion of heart experienced and responded to by Mark, Matthew, Luke, and John, thus far the proper categories for sustained reflection upon their significance and meaning will lie in the theologian's critical and sympathetic appreciation of them as testimony to the perfection with which the Gospel writers appropriated in their own living the story of Jesus. The critical appreciation of the effect of the Gospels in the lives of subsequent readers will be, in such an aesthetical theology, a prime datum for theological reflection. A work of art that never moved its viewers or listeners would be *prima facie* a failure. Likewise, a foundational document for a religion (a gospel) that bore no discernible fruit in the life of even one follower would be an inauthentic gospel.

One cannot judge Islam by a study of the Koran alone, as though the lived experience of the Islamic community was irrelevant to its claim to be an authentic expression of the gift of God's love. The way in which the Jews of the Diaspora, deprived of temple worship and sacrifice, and often persecuted allegedly in the name of their own coreligionist, were held together as a community and produced great spiritual fruit by their devotion to the Torah and Prophets is important testimony to the authenticity of the Old Testament as an authentic expression of God's redeeming love. Chesterton somewhere wrote that Christianity had not been tried and found wanting but had been wanted and never tried. There is a truth in such a slogan, insofar as it testifies to the fact that Christ's message is not proved false by the sins of Renaissance popes or the fires of the Inquisition; but there is a falsity in such a slogan if it is used as a *deus ex machina* to avoid confronting the scandal of sin and institutionalized injustice in the life of the Christian community and its members.[4] "By their fruits you shall know them" applies equally to the foundational stories of Christianity as to individual Christians.

6.11 The claim to universal validity of the judgment of taste provides a fruitful analogy for understanding the claim to universal validity made by the Gospel story.

Paul Tortellier was once asked by a television interviewer whom he considered to be the greatest composer. The cellist replied that to deny the title to J. S. Bach was merely to prove that one was not a serious musician. Tortellier's reply is a concrete illustration of a phenomenon adverted to by Kant. "In all judgments by which we describe anything as beautiful, we allow no one to be of another opinion."[5] In all true judgments we attain a virtually unconditioned; that is, we correctly judge that the conditions that would make $x = a - b$ have been fulfilled and that therefore our judgment that $a - b = x$ is true and not false. It is a judgment that the relations between a, b, and x are such *quoad se* that a *must* equal $x + b$, though what their relationships *quoad nos*, the observers, might be remain unknown and, from the point of view of the equation, irrelevant.[6]

When I affirm that the virus herpes zoster must have caused the inflammation of your nervous system, I am affirming the fulfillment of a necessary condition for the blistered condition of your skin and am prescinding from your present feelings about suffering from shingles. Judgments are disinterested and claim a universal validity. Such are the commonsense judgments of fact and the judgments of science. Where the child makes a mistake in addition and gets his or her sums wrong, the teacher simply marks the exercise as wrong and rightly admits no debate about the correct answer. Indeed, it may even at times be appropriate for the teacher to punish the child for inattention or carelessness.

Kant correctly observes that the judgments of aesthetic taste share the same claim to validity as the judgments of mathematics; one allows no one to be of another opinion. But, unlike the judgments of science, we do not ground the judgment of taste on concepts, "but only on our feeling, which we therefore place at its basis, not as a private, but as a communal feeling."[7] The judgment that Bach's music is beautiful is not based upon a rigorous chain of logical reasoning, though we may very well be able to offer convincing arguments *ex convenientia*, but relies upon the conviction that it is indeed beautiful and that if you have a taste for the beautiful and an educated ear you will so agree. Kant remarks that the judgment of taste "does not say that everyone *will* agree with my judgment, but that he *ought*."[8] To teach a pupil algebra one needs little more than a book of examples and a large supply of paper. To instruct a learner in Latin syntax a copy of Kennedy's *Grammar* will suffice. Classes in Aristotelian logic require little more than a discussion of statements about Socrates' status as an animal. Though the pupils may find such teaching dull, philosophy may be taught entirely in the confines of a classroom. When one attempts to interest a pupil in music or the fine arts, however, one cannot conduct the classes solely from a text. One needs to play records and tapes, show films and slides, and visit concert halls, museums, and the like. One cannot persuade a person of the excellence of Mozart in the same way that one would perhaps convince a jury that the prisoner at the bar is the selfsame person who pulled the trigger. The educator of taste relies upon the feelings he claims ought to be present in the observer or listener.

Allowing for a certain exaggeration in Tortellier's remarks (Karl Barth, after all, might well have made the same claims about Mozart), they do illustrate the claim to univeral validity implicit in every affirmation that something or someone is beautiful. To debate one's preference for Leonardo as against Michelangelo can be a fruitful occupation, to affirm that El Greco leaves one cold whereas Giotto inspires awe is a reasonable witness to one's own reactions, but to declare that any of the four were incompetent dilettantes with no claims to artistic ability would be to invite justifiable exclusion from the company of those whose opinions about painting are taken seriously. One judges the beauty of a work of art or of a person's achievements in the field of dramatic living by a disinterested judgment of connaturality. The judgment is disinterested in that the primary reference is not to one's present mood or utility; I may judge Beethoven's Ninth Symphony to be a work of genius while not necessarily being at this moment in a mood for that kind of music or for any music at all. The affirmation of the beautiful is an implicit claim to an objective judgment. The judgment of taste is connatural in that the subjectivity of the one judging is more intimately bound up in the judgment than would be the case if one were judging that $2 + 2 = 4$. The judgment of taste declares that the perceived beauty resonates in the experience and subjectivity of the perceiver. It declares that the feelings aroused in the beholder of the work of art *ought* to be aroused in any onlooker. We say of someone who disagrees with our judgment of taste that he or she is a Philistine or "has no soul." Kant remarks of the judgment of taste that it is a subjective judgment "assumed as subjectively universal," which "thus can claim universal assent."[9]

In a letter he wrote to Cardinal Hanibald, Aquinas spoke of the natural love of the good that God has created in all his creatures. It is, says Aquinas, the distinctive feature of human beings (*rationalis natura*) that they can intuit the universal source of goodness through wisdom and can sweetly savor it (*suaviter degustare*) through the love of charity.[10] In writing to Pope Urban IV, the same doctor speaks of Christ in aesthetic categories.[11] In commenting on the sixth chapter of John's Gospel, St. Thomas speaks of the believer being drawn *"admirabile delectatione et amore veritatis quae est ipse Filius Dei."*[12] The judgment of faith is a disinterested judgment by connaturality; it is a being drawn by the "eye of love." In the seventeenth of his *Discourses to Mixed Congregations* John Henry Newman writes:

> I am not proving these doctrines to you, my brethren; the evidence of them lies in the declaration of the Church. The Church is the oracle of religious truth, and dispenses what the apostles committed to her in every time and place. . . . I am not proving then what you already receive, but I am showing you the *beauty* and the harmony, on one out of many instances, of the Church's teaching. . . .[13]

The preacher's task is not to proceed by means of rational demonstration but to arouse the judgment of taste in his or her hearers. A few pages earlier Newman had spoken of the Mother of God:

> It would not have sufficed, in order to bring out and impress upon us the idea that God is man, had His Mother been an ordinary person. . . . She would not have remained in the memory, or the imagination of men. . . . She must be made to fill the mind, in order to suggest the lesson. . . .[14]

The judgment of faith is a judgment by connaturality. Like the judgment of aesthetic taste the man or woman of faith judges the truth, value, beauty, and harmony of the Christ story by the perception of an inner resonance. It is the judgment of a subject that implicitly claims to be subjectively universal and thus can claim universal assent. In telling the story of Christ one does not expect that everyone *will* agree with one's judgment but that they *ought.* Lonergan frequently remarks that teaching is the apostolate of the obvious. Just as one can lead a pig to the acorns but cannot make him eat, so, too, in all teaching one can patiently set up the material conditions necessary and favorable to the pupil's having an insight, but one cannot have the insight for the pupil. To understand a theorem of Euclid one must first draw the figure and make the necessary constructions; insight is insight into the diagram or phantasm. In theology there is an equal need for imagination if we are to have the insights that ground understanding. The *"splendor formae Christi,"* the beauty of Christ, the beauty found *"per se et essentialiter''* in the contemplative life of Christians,[15] must be pointed to by the preacher and teacher if the pupils are to achieve an *affective insight* into the image of God in Christ. Chesterton wrote of fairy stories that, if we read, "And in the hour when the king extinguished the candle his ships were wrecked on the coast of the Hebrides," we discover that our imagination accepts the image before the reason has time to reject it. Such phrases, he wrote, seem to correspond to something deep in the soul.[16] Such imagery provides the material for an affective insight (*"per carita-tem intuere"* St. Thomas called it); the king's tragedy in losing his ships is linked with the simple, everyday action of snuffing out a candle, and we, who have snuffed out candles, resonate to the "deep sense of the dependence of great things upon small, some dark suggestion that the things nearest to us stretch far beyond our power."[17]

In hearing the story of Oedipus we discover the common feeling (the spontaneous natural sympathy that is the psychic ground of love) that grasps our imagination and leads to the insight that the story of Oedipus is the story or, at least, could be the story, of ourselves. To understand themselves to be daughters and sons of God, *filii in Filio*, the hearers of the Christian mysteries must be presented with the story that can so fire their imagination that they may grasp by an act of affective insight into the image of Christ what it would be to live as a son or daughter of God. The story of Jesus acts as the Euclidean diagram that triggers the insight into what our stories are and could be.

6.12 *The claim to universal validity implicit in the judgment of taste provides a fruitful if imperfect analogy for understanding how, through the Incarnation, we are brought to love the God whom no human has seen.*

In the first preface for the masses of Christmastide we affirm that through the mystery of the Word made flesh the eyes of our mind are flooded with a new light so that knowing God made visible we are caught up in the love of the God we cannot see.[18] In his letter to Pope Urban IV, Aquinas makes the same point:

> ... unigenitum Dei Verbum ... in fine temporum carnem su-mere voluit, ut sub tegumento naturae corporeae, splendorem eius, humanus intuitus posset inspicere, quem in celsitudine maiestatis divinae attingere non valebat ...[19]

St. Thomas uses the vocabulary of his aesthetic theory. The human story told by Christ's life is the medium through which we have insight into the *splendor et claritas* that are "hidden by the cloud of our mortality."[20]

If we were asked to write a scientific treatise on shoes, to define them by genus and specific difference, for example, or to decide what was and what was not a shoe for the purposes of the Sale of Goods Act or for assessment of purchase tax, we might arrive at a clear and distinct concept of what constitutes a shoe. We can imagine a pair of shoes in general. In his discussion of the *Origin of the Work of Art* Martin Heidegger discusses van Gogh's painting of a pair of peasant shoes.

> From the dark opening of the worn insides of the shoes the toilsome tread of the worker stands forth. In the stiffly solid heaviness of the shoes there is the accumulated tenacity of her slow trudge through the far-spreading and everuniform furrows of the field, swept by a raw wind. On the leather there lies the dampness and saturation of the soil. Under the soles there slides the loneliness of the field-path as the evening declines. In the shoes there vibrates the silent call of the earth, its quiet gift of the ripening corn and its enigmatic self-refusal in the fallow desolation of the wintry field. This equipment is pervaded by uncomplaining anxiety about the certainty of bread, the wordless joy of having once more withstood want, the trembling before the advent of birth and the shivering at the surrounding menace of death. This equipment belongs to the *earth*, and it is protected in the *world* of the peasant woman.[21]

The image discloses a world; a way of being in the world. A drawing of a pair of ballet slippers or a painting of Cinderella's glass slipper discloses a different world from that of the world of the peasant woman.

Later in the same work Heidegger speaks of how a Greek temple viewed today both "discloses a world, and at the same time sets this world back again on the earth." The Greek temple is not a copy "whose purpose it is to make it easier to realize how the god looks; rather, it is a work that lets the god be present and thus it *is* the God himself.[22] If we prescind from the particular meaning of these statements in the totality of Heidegger's philosophical position, they are, taken in themselves, extraordinarily suggestive of the way in which the Christ story functions as the discloser of a world. The stories we tell disclose a whole world. The world of Dante is not the world of Homer. Jane Austen inhabited and protrayed a different world from that of Dickens or Virginia Woolf. Implicit in the affirmation that the work of art or story discloses a world is the affirmation that it discloses a world to a world. A world in this sense is not the cosmos taken as a physical entity but the psychic, intellectual, and moral space bounded by each person's psychic, intellectual, and moral horizons. In this sense stones, plants, and animals have no world. World is where we make our stories.[23]

When you tell me a story you disclose to me your world. In your world men and women act in this or that way, have these or those values, worship this or that god. Your world becomes present in my world. The work of John S. Dunne is a model of how by listening to other people's stories we can enter their worlds or, perhaps better, how we can allow their worlds to enter ours. Homer's god is not my god and yet, as I hear Homer tell his story, the god of his world can in some sense become alive for me. Heidegger's Greek temple is the product of a whole world or *Weltanschauung*, and it discloses to my world something of the world in which it was a locus for worship. The power of the biblical story lies in its ability to disclose a world in which the God of the Jewish world can enter my world. The story of a covenanted people, redeemed from slavery, exiled and brought home, and expectant of an Anointed One, discloses to me a world in which Yahweh is God and, because of its claim to universal validity, it claims to be what my world should be. Yahweh is revealed in the world disclosed by the Yahwist writer of Genesis as distinct from the god revealed in the world disclosed by the writer of Gilgamesh. The life story of Jesus discloses a world in which the god is *Abba*, the Father of Jesus. If we consider Jesus as the temple of God, Emmanuel, the Tent of Meeting pitched among our tents, then we can understand, on the analogy of Heidegger's Greek temple, how the human life story thus *is* the life story of God. As I listen to the story of Jesus, his world becomes present to my world, speaks to my world, so that I come to put on Christ's mind and his God becomes my God.

A person's face and body disclose a world. Our body language indicates the kind of world in which we live and thereby discloses the kind of god we worship. Imagine, for example, the face of a woman who has spent her life in the service of the poor and outcast for the sake of Christ. Her face is lined; it tells of sufferings shared, of compassion shown, and of hurts forgiven. The lines around the eyes and mouth are creased from much smiling and laughter. The face discloses a world in which joy has leavened the tears, and compassion has mingled with the laughter. The eyes betray a serenity and a liveliness that suggests thankfulness for and enjoyment of all that life has brought, the sorrows as well as the joys. The hands reposing in the lap point to an inner quiet that comes from casting her anxieties upon God, but in their suppleness and lack of heaviness or rigidity they point to a lifetime's growing docility to the promptings of the Spirit and to a familiarity with service. Her face and her body disclose a world in which the God and Father of Jesus has poured out his love and his life.

More than once Moses complained of having to lead a stiff-necked people. The phrase is well translated. Alexander Lowen affirms the almost inevitability of stiffness in the neck and shoulders of the schizoid individual.[24] Grumbling at the hardness of the desert journey, complaining at the boredom of being fed with heavenly manna, the people refused to relate to the real God who called them to freedom and responsibility, putting their trust in the idols of their fantasy world—the misremembered delights of Egypt and the golden calf made by their own hands. Otto Fenichel talked about the organ neuroses and other physiologic complaints as a body language.[25] The way a person walks and talks, the way she or he holds the body—many seemingly organic complaints disclose the sufferer's emotional and religious world and thereby the kind of god they worship.

In telling a story the storyteller claims a universal validity for his or her story—otherwise he or she would remain silent. The storyteller relies on the communal feeling he or she implicitly claims ought to be present in the teller and the one told. In affirming that a story discloses a world to a world, we are affirming that there is a transcultural quality to beauty. Beethoven and Mozart are played in Japanese concert halls; African sculptures are displayed in British museums. Though art is an expression of a culture and discloses the world in which it was formed and which it expresses, nevertheless there is a claim to universal, that is, transcultural validity in every affirmation of the beautiful.

The symbolic content of a story must not only reflect its own world—a mirror held up to one's own nature or world—but must also be translucent, a window opening onto other worlds and other possibilities of worlds. Think of a lighthouse. The source of light is magnified by being reflected off a series of mirrors. The sailor on his ship calls out that he sees the Eddistone light—not that he sees the light reflected from the lamp. When Aquinas affirms that in every act of knowing the true and of willing the good we know and will God, he does not affirm that human expressions of truth or human acts of charity are in some way copies of the divine truth and charity, but rather that the truthfulness and loveliness of human life stories reflect the truthful loveliness of God.

It would be odd to refuse to speak of the "Moonlight Sonata" on the grounds that Beethoven's physics was not up to par. Moonlight is a reality and properly belongs to the moon, even though its source is the light of the sun.

In a similar way the truth and goodness disclosed by human stories are a reality and properly belong to the human subjects of those stories, even though without the truth and goodness of God those human stories would not exist. The human story of Jesus is a translucent symbol because it perfectly reflects the universal story. The true symbol, affirms J. P. Manigne, is *ontophanique*, an apparition of meaning, not merely *ontopherique*, a (conceptual) carrier of meaning.[26] He quotes part of a poem by Archibald MacLeish:

> A poem should not mean
> But be.[27]

The Incarnation, by analogy with a work of art, makes present the totality of Meaning or Being within the contingent world. It does not abolish the precariousness of our contingent existence nor dissolve religious faith into a vague *Stimmung*, reflecting our hopes and fears and wishes, but by the transparency of its symbolism it renders our contingent world totally significant by disclosing what each person's world could and should be.[28]

6.2 *Human life stories function as icons of the divine life story.*

The words and images we use in our speech are not copies or representations of some inner wordless or imageless activity. The faith values expressed in the biblical writings can be communicated *as* values only insofar as they "embody" the faith of their writers and arouse faith in their hearers and readers. Henry Duméry reminds us that no communication from God will be understood and responded to as sacred unless it is expressed in the way proper to any transmission of the sacred.

There is no *hierogeny* without *hierophany*, just as in the philosophy of values, every *axiogeny* calls forth an *axiophany*. This is the classical position: there is no value without expression, no thought without words, no idea without an image.[29]

Every true image of faith calls forth the appropriate response. Imagine walking down a street. The first building one comes to may have the small discreet sign "Doctor." Unless one is ill and perhaps desperate to find medical help, the sign has no "pulling power." One walks by indifferently. The sign may be called conceptual rather than imaginative. Unless one is already wanting to see a doctor the sign will leave one unmoved. If one is anxiously looking for medical help there will be no need for the doctor to employ people from Madison Avenue to make the signboard attractive because one is already motivated to seek medical help. Following a suggestive image by Cardinal Newman, we might say that the letters "John Doe, M.D." discreetly etched on a brass plate act as a logarithm does for a real number. The logarithm is a convenient indicator that, if we were to write a poem about visiting the doctor, we would have to convert to the concrete and particular.

Farther along the street we might pass a take-out food outlet. Pictures of hamburgers and cola signs will abound. The commercial artist wishes not only to convey the information that hamburgers and hot dogs are available but also to make the erstwhile indifferent passer-by possess in imaginative anticipation the delights of the foods on offer. The sign writer is not interested in the logarithm, or "bloodless abstraction," but in the evocation of a concrete and singular desire to eat a hamburger or a hot dog. The sign writer has succeeded when the sign makes a satisfied passer-by feel hungry.[30]

The translucent quality of the symbols that express a world or life story is illustrated by the way in which icons function as the focus for prayer in the Slavo-Byzantine tradition. Saint John Chrysostom instructs the worshiper to stand before the icon with closed eyes.[31] The icon, affirms Metropolitan Anthony of Surozh, is not a copy of a heavenly reality but a "focus of real presence." It is not meant as a visual aid to help one meditate about the reality it depicts but as a sacramental disclosing of or opening onto a world filled by the Spirit of God. The icon is not made to be a "mirror held up to nature," still less as a logarithm to aid conceptual analysis, but as a door opening to a new world whereby the saving activity of Jesus can become present in the world and story of the worshiper. The icon is a hierophany, a disclosure of the sacred.[32]

The biblical tradition employs the notion of image to express diverse aspects of the relationship between God and humankind. The priestly writer of the creation account affirms that men and women are made in the image of God (Gn. 1:27). Paul affirms that that image or icon is perfectly shown forth in Jesus, who is the "image" (icon) of the invisible God (Col. 1:15). In his Letter to the Church in Rome, Paul affirms that God intends that humankind should be conformed to the image of his Son, who is the image of God (Rom. 8:29). This is both an eschatological hope and, in some measure, a present reality because, as Paul tells the Corinthians, to behold the glory of the Lord is to be changed into his image (*eikona*) from one degree of glory to another (2 Cor. 3:18).

In the Gospel of John, Jesus affirms that to have seen him was to have seen the Father (Jn. 12:45; 14:9). The life story, the humanity of Jesus, was not a copy or representation or logarithm of the Father but the icon disclosing his God and Father to the world. The life story of the crucified and risen Jesus is the paradigmatic image for Christian faith. We are called to communicate the likeness of God by sharing the likeness of Jesus in whom God is rendered visible, authentically imaginable, and imitable as our way, our truth, and our life. Inasmuch as we cannot do what we can in no way imagine, Jesus as the icon of God, motivates faith to a new way of being-in-the-world as beings-with-others. Inasmuch as motivation is commensurate with the concreteness and vividness and beauty of an image, the life story of the crucified and risen Jesus has proved a historically compelling image of God that has radically transformed the lives of millions through the centuries.

William F. Lynch regards faith as the deepest reality of a person, as his or her imaginative center and constant way of envisioning the world and the divine at work in that world. Faith functions to unite memory, intellect, will, and emotion in response to the revelation of God in one's life. Faith thus transforms the subject as subject. It is the primary and most elemental force in human nature, a force that precedes what we ordinarily call knowledge and all our specific knowledge, a force that is uneducated and needs education.[33]

The developmental psychology of Erikson posits trust as the primary requirement for all human living. The baby who never learns to trust his or her parents, the infant whose cries are never answered, and the child who learns by bitter experience that the significant adults in her or his life are vacillating and untrustworthy, will find it difficult to trust in a Father God imagined after the image of his or her own parents. The difficulties in prayer experienced by many adults can be traced to their early experience of parents. How can we trust the Father whom we cannot see, if we cannot trust the father and mother whom we can see? Walter E. Conn, commenting on the relationship between Erikson's concept of primal trust and Lonergan's notion of self-transcendence, remarks that

> more than anything else it is the rudimentary trust or hope resulting from this first critical stage that forms the bedrock for adult faith, in many ways the very essence of self-transcendence.[34]

The ability to trust is the ground that understands all religious faith. The inability to trust, whether caused by the faults of others or by an inexplicable and unintelligible failure to grow, is the ground that understands the lack of religious faith in adults. The mixture of trust and distrust, which makes up most if not all actual concrete human beings, shapes and mishapes the whole life story of individuals and societies. Trust in others is inseparable from trust in oneself. Self-confidence is inextricably linked to our confidence in others. Where others have let us down we may come to believe that salvation lies in faith in ourself alone, a faith that, because of its precariousness, requires an ever-grimmer determination to keep faith (hence the set jaw and increasing stiffness of the Pelagian personality).

Alternatively, our bad experience of others may lead us to undervalue ourselves and to retain a poor self-image. Low self-esteem can be linked with a resistance of a loving God and with a defense against a compassionate ethical orientation even when both are stressed in a particular institutional setting. Proper esteem of one's own self is required if we are to accept the possibility of a loving, accepting God.[35] The varieties of neurotic behavior—the suppressed rage of the depressive, the hysterical need for constant reassurance, the inability of the schizoid to relate, and the positive distrust of the paranoid—are a continuum of imaginative failures to deal with the problem of trust.[36]

The primal impulse to faith precedes all the objects or persons in whom we place our trust. Characters enter onto the stage of our world, we trust or distrust them, and they stay or leave. Christ, as the definitive revelation of the trustworthiness of God, comes upon the preexisting stage of faith to define it, shape it, raise it to a new and supernatural intentionality, and to declare that he is the way, the truth, and the life. Each image that we form of the persons who play their part in our story is a form of faith; Lynch writes of the final forms that Christianity gives to faith, with the implication that Christ is the final and superb gift of God's self-investing love to faith.[37] Faith, as the inner dynamism of every person, is a form of imagining and experiencing the world. Lynch affirms that there is an equation between the imagination and experience. Our imagination and the images it forms are the way in which we experience and manage the world. Faith is our way of experiencing the world through imagination. Faith is not something opposed to experience; rather, it provides the structure or context for experience. It is the place of imagination and experience. Experience is not a separate, prior, and independent world, and neither is faith an external and later addition, in the relationship of relevancy to experience.[38]

Human growth is a process of shedding falsely imagined images of faith and their abolition, transcendence, or sublation by newer and more perfect images. To modify a dictum of Newman we could say that to become perfect is to have changed often one's images of God and of oneself. Stagnation, illness, despair, and fear are related to our inability to change our images. The imagination can become fixated at a particular stage of human and religious development or, under the influence of fear and anxiety, it can regress to stages that we had once transcended.

The maturity of our life stories depends on our ability to interpret correctly the content that we give to our images. The maturity of our religious faith depends on our ability to interpret correctly the content of our images insofar as they embody the truth about our relationship to the Mystery we encounter at the root depths of all our relationships. Our images express not the meaning of things as they are related to one another (conceptual expression), nor the self in isolation from the real, but the human dimension of things in their concrete individuality and the real dimension of the human. The images of faith grasp the self and the real together, that is, the existential relatedness of the self. William V. Dych remarks how

Images of the real represent not only our initial but also our primary knowledge of the real because they grasp the self and the real together in a single act of knowledge in a way that reflects and represents, as concepts cannot, our primary and lived relationship with the real. In images there comes to expression the dialectical unity of the self and the real, of subject and object, of awareness and affectivity, of knowing and desiring, of knowledge and interest, of intellect and will, of truth and value, all of which polarities reflect the real unity of human sensibility.[39]

An authentic image of ourselves, others, and the world implies an authentic image of God—the pure of heart shall see God, because they "see" him as he really is in relation to the complexity of their lives as beings-in-the-world-with others. A distorted image of self implies a distorted image of God.[40] The concrete images of faith urge us to understanding—*fides quaerit intellectum*—and call us back from a deepened understanding to a deeper expression of faith—*praedicatio praesupponit intellectum.*

A story may illustrate our point. A professed atheist of high intelligence once remarked to one of the authors that the only Christian churches he could take seriously were those that used incense in their worship. He argued that the use of incense—with its implication that one could worship with one's nose—indicated the real seriousness with which the church believed the doctrine of the Incarnation. Allowing for a certain rhetorical extravagance, there is a valid point being made. The incensing of the book of the Gospels (a gestural image) expresses in a very concrete fashion the reverence due to them as the Word of God. Without a sense of their venerable importance, the theologian would not be moved to wrestle with the complexities of scriptual exegesis. Once the theologian has wrestled with the "logarithms" of form criticism and the like, she or he "returns to the image," that is, converts back to the "real number" of Scripture as the Word of God to this particular congregation with a deepened respect for the Bible and, perhaps, a deeper impulse to cense and kiss the book of the Gospels.

While engaged in writing these pages, one of the authors assisted in the solemn dedication of a neighboring church. While the altar was being anointed and the brazier of incense was smouldering on the altar stone he noticed the rapt attention displayed by one of the guests, a minister in the Calvinist tradition, with all that that implies of devotion to the Scriptures. Afterward the minister expressed to the parish priest his gratitude for being allowed to witness the ceremony. He mentioned the clouds of smoke filling the Church as reminiscent of 1 Kings 8:10 – 13; "Now I understand," he said, "how seriously Catholics take the images of Scripture." The symbols we use, whether pictorial or gestural, disclose a world that is worthy of (conceptual) exploring; and the result of all our explorations is best summed up, not in a hundred volumes, but in a symbol that can disclose the whole world—emotional, intellectual, and moral—of our response.

Lynch rightly opposes the idea that the Spirit works merely from a spiritual, disembodied center; rather, with us and in us it makes history, a real atmosphere and sensibility of faith. The man or woman of faith is sensitive to a world of anxiety and hate, and to a world of grace and hope. We are sensitive to the inner events that pull and counterpull us, which invite us to life and seduce us to death. The imaginative power of human life stories both impels us on the path that leads us to greater understanding and calls us back to express our groaning for the Spirit in a way that is too deep to be put into words.

6.21 *The life story of every human storyteller functions as an icon of that storyteller's faith.*

Our life stories and the stories we tell reveal the coherence or incoherence of our motivating images of ourself, of others, and of God. Our stories act as icons of our faith. They are always implicitly religious inasmuch as they involve some presupposition of what for us is the ultimate reality or god. Harry Blamires, in a paper delivered to British prison chaplains in 1971, argued that to divide the world into believers and nonbelievers, religious people and nonreligious people or atheists, as though it were possible to have no God, is one of the false myths of contemporary Western society.[41] The real question, affirms Blamires, is not *whether* a person believes in God but rather in *which* god he or she believes. Atheism is not, as many commonly and mistakenly suppose, an intellectual denial of the existence of God (rejection of God may not be the rejection of Yahweh or of the God of Jesus but a rightful rejection of the god of some Jews and some Christians) but a godlessness in living—a living as if one's god had died, as if there were no ultimate concern. It is impossible to have no ultimate value in one's life, even if that value be as shallow as naked self-interest. Faith in the God of Jesus is largely a matter of living as though all one's value judgments were open to revision in the light of the life story of Jesus.

The life story of Jesus and his parables reveal the coherence of his images of faith. They reveal his interpretation of life: his own life, our lives, and the external life he encountered in the lives of others and himself. Conversion is the process by which the life of

Jesus, the story told by his life, so transforms our cognitive-affective core that our life stories become icons of the same God as his.

The parable of the Talents (Mt. 25:14–30; cf. Mk. 13:34; Lk. 19:11–27) throws light upon the coherence of our motivating images and the need for their transformation in response to the challenge of the Good News. The unproductive life of the wicked and lazy servant is explained in terms of fear—he believes his master to be a "hard man." His image of his master engenders fear and distrust that, in turn, render the servant's life unproductive both for himself and for others. Failure to live with a true image of the master precludes sharing in his happiness; he is thrown into the outer darkness not because his master is a hard and exacting man but because that is the place where he will be at home. The servant trusted in his own plan for being safe instead of risking all as his master would have done.

If we understand that we have been entrusted with gifts, we should understand that if we have been en*trusted* then we ourselves must be *trustworthy*. If we understand ourselves to have been presented with demands (as though God were "taxing" us, that is, appropriating for himself something rightfully ours) then we will imagine ourselves to be people laboring under a heavy burden. The graciousness or ungraciousness with which our parents provide for our needs, that is, whether we experience our parents as giving gifts or as making loans to be repaid by good behavior, will color our subsequent self-image and our relationships with others. We will imagine ourselves to be thankfully giving back to God out of love or as laboring to appear righteous in his eyes. Without a basic trust and thankfulness to God—we might call this a eucharistic disposition—the image of God disclosed by our life story will be at variance with the image we explicitly attempt to project in our prayers, our hymns, and our telling of the Gospel story.

6.22 *The life story of the crucified-risen Jesus is the primordial sacrament of God's gift of his love, experienced by the Christian as underlying and informing all human life stories.*

John's Gospel expresses the relationship between God and humankind in terms of a divine calling and a human hearing revealed in the life story of Jesus Christ. Christ's friends make up the branches of the one vine—himself. He has chosen the branches and has called them friends because through his story he has made known to them all that he has heard from his Father (Jn. 15:1,15,16). Christ is the primordial sacrament of the fellowship-creating mystery of divine friendship.

The oldest recorded eucharistic prayer gives thanks to the Father

> for the Holy Vine of David Thy servant,
> which thou hast made known to us through
> Thy Servant Jesus. . . .
> As this broken bread was scattered
> over the hills and then, when gathered, became
> one mass, so may Thy Church be gathered
> from the ends of the earth into Thy kingdom.[42]

The Sacrament of Christ's Body, a sacrament that brings about the unity in friendship of his Body the Church, celebrates and makes actual the gathering of all peoples and races into the friendship of God. The life story of the crucified-risen Jesus expresses the ground and conviction of Christian faith: that God, through the gift of his love, always has called and is calling and shall forever call all human persons his friends. As the origin, ground, and destiny of all human life stories, God pervades every level of these stories with his endless, unconditioned, unrestricted, universal declaration of love. Edward Yarnold points out that the prophetic affirmation, "You shall be my people, and I will be your God," is an adaptation of the Jewish marriage formula, "She is my wife and I her husband from this day forever."[43] Christ is the sacrament of God's wedding with humankind; he is the word of love spoken that binds the speaker and the one he speaks to in an endless *convivium* of intimate and indissoluble friendship. John of the Cross affirms that God creates the human race to be a bride for his son.[44]

The rejection of Christ by humankind implies that the divine call to friendship, a call that lies at the heart of every life story, may be freely resisted, repressed, ignored, refused, and rejected. The Resurrection of Jesus implies that God's love for humankind is invincible, unconditional, and forever abiding. Even more than the story of Hosea, the story of Jesus bears witness to God's purpose to love Unloved and to say to No-People-of-Mine "You are my people" (Hosea 2:23f). God is Eternal Love affirming us to be his well-beloved friends. At every level and stage of our life story, from its beginning to its end, God speaks to us as individuals and as communities, saying, "Come then, my love, my lovely one, come" (S. of S. 2:10). Athanasius considered the Song of Songs to be the greatest and last song because it celebrated the marriage of God with humankind.[45] The Song of Songs, insofar as it is the classic and unequaled celebration of a love story, points, as all stories do, to the eternal love story of God for humankind and humankind for God. The story of eternal love that transcends all particular love stories is the horizon in which every particular love story is played out. No human story is beyond the embrace and affirmation and call to friendship of the universal story of God.

When the Gospel of John presents Jesus as addressing his disciples as friends, it is not restricting his declaration of love to the historical moment of the Last Supper and to the individuals there present; rather, in the primordial sacrament, Jesus Christ, Christian faith affirms that the entire story of Jesus, from conception through Resurrection, is the outward and visible sign of the inward grace of love. Jesus calls each and every person to share in his personal relation of love to the Father. Guilt and sin are the inexplicable failure to respond to that call to loving friendship.

When the Christian affirms the sinlessness and guiltlessness of Jesus, she or he is affirming that Jesus is not only the sacrament of God's call to friendship but, too, the sacrament of humankind's acceptance of that friendship. Dom Gregory Dix used to distinguish two sorts of human beings: aquisitive persons and eucharistic persons. The acquisitive person stands upon his or her rights, demands attention, feels hard done by when what he or she dreams to be his or her due fails to materialize; the eucharistic person, on the other hand, is one who acknowledges and lives as though all things come as gifts, as though all happiness depended upon the presence and loving kindness of another. Eucharistic living is the recognition that to be human is to be for another, that to be worthy and valuable is to be of worth and value to another, that to be a person is to be a relation of opposition to another Person or persons. Our experience of living, the lessons of history, and the revealing word of God all conspire to convince the Christian that there is a radical strain of aquisitive, noneucharistic behavior that mars every human life story. Sin is self-estrangement, alienation, because it is a culpable failure to relate. Not all my failures to relate are culpable. Insofar as my nonculpable failures to relate reflect and are symptoms of culpable (lethal/mortal) failures, they may be termed as culpable by analogy (venial, pardonable, analogous sin). Sin may be termed the deliberate taking-up of a schizoid position in regard to one's fundamental relatedness, one's relation to God. Sin is the refusal to accept God's friendship. Christian faith affirms that by ourselves we can never break down our schizoid defenses; that we are impotent to establish a relationship of friendship with God. To hear the one whom our heart desires call us beloved is a liberating experience; it is to find oneself allowed to be what one is—a person related to *this* other. The affirmation of the sinlessness of Jesus is the affirmation that his thanksgiving, his eucharistic nature, has not been, is not, and never will be marred and made imperfect by any taint of aquisitiveness. Through the Incarnation God allows the perfect eucharistic nature of the Godhead to be told as a human story. Through the coauthorship of a divine-human story in the story of the Word-made-human, humankind can offer itself as a perfect eucharist, a perfect sacrifice of thanksgiving. In the Eucharist of Jesus we too make our eucharist. In his sacrifice we too become living sacrifices.

In the story of Jesus God speaks a Word of undying friendship and love. As efficacious, that word originates, sustains, and brings to completion a response of undying friendship and love. Christ Jesus is the primordial sacrament of God's call to friendship. He is the primordial sacrament of humankind's hearing of and response to that call.

6.23 *The Gospel stories function as sacramental symbols evoked by the feeling for Christ of their writers and evoking the feeling for Christ of their readers or listeners.*

A Russian archbishop tells the story of his conversion as a coming to acknowledge the presence of Christ through a reading of Mark's Gospel. As a young man he was an unbeliever and was forced through politeness to listen to a priest speaking about religion. He was appalled at what he heard; Christianity as expounded by the speaker seemed to him a monstrous aberration of humanity. He was so angered by what he had heard that he decided to read something of the New Testament himself, mostly to check for himself whether the Christian Gospel was really so terrible. He chose to read the Gospel of Mark as it was the shortest. Before he reached the third chapter, he tells us, he "suddenly became aware that on the other side of my desk there was a presence"; it was, he tells us, a feeling of the presence of Jesus that has never left him in all the years since his conversion.[46]

The primary value of the Gospel is not apprehended in terms of historical information about a first-century Rabbi nor in terms of a theology practiced in his name. The Gospel story functions as a sacramental symbol evoking a feeling for or sense of Christ's presence. When Raskolnikov opens a copy of the Gospels at the end of *Crime and Punishment*, Dostoevsky is suggesting that Raskolnikov needs a symbol of Resurrection to evoke the presence that will sustain him in imprisonment. Bernard Lonergan defines a symbol as an image of a real or imaginary object that evokes a feeling or is evoked by a feeling.[47] A sign is an equivalence. A traffic light, for example, is a mechanical police officer ordering us to stop. The purely cognitive nature of many signs, even those that are pictorial, can be easily acknowledged in the road sign of three circles, red, yellow, and green, which inform us that we will shortly arrive at some traffic lights. The picture in this case functions as a sign informing us about another sign. The symbol, on the other hand, functions as a *signum efficax*, a sign that effects that which it signifies. The symbol functions in the cognitive-affective realm.

In an attempt to convey the reality of the Eucharist one sometimes hears it said that "the Eucharist is not a *mere* symbol but is real." Such a way of talking betrays a misunderstanding of the nature of symbol. A symbol is not something unreal but, in a certain sense, the most real of all our possible modes of expression. The Gregorian chant *"Iam non dicam vos servos tuos, sed amicos meos"* has functioned as a powerful symbol for generations of ordinands and silver jubilarians because it functions as a symbol of a real offer of friendship with God and, sung at countless ordinations, has evoked in countless priests the feeling that God's presence and love has, does, and will support them in the living-out of their sacramental vocation. There is nothing unreal about a kiss—whether it be the kiss of one's spouse or the kiss of Judas—though it evokes something more than the mere physical sensation of the touch of someone's lips. To speak of Christ or of his Gospel stories as symbols is not to say anything "mere" about them; it is to speak of them as cognitive-affective realities.

Antoine Vergote defines a symbol as "an image which, because of its affective connotations, re-presents for us a reality whose depth of meaning will never be completely fathomed by the mind."[48] Jesus Christ is the symbol of the Christian community's cognitive-affective relationship to itself, to others, to the world, and to God. Rollo May affirms that there is a conative element in all symbols; some action is called for. He gives the example of the Cross; one has to take a stand one way or the other.[49] Christ symbolizes, for Christians, both the cognitive-affective relationship of God to all humankind and what humankind's cognitive-affective relationship to God should be. Jesus Christ, the Son of God, is a sacramental symbol who embodies, reveals, and communicates the felt meaning, goodness, and value of God. As the incarnate Son of God, that man who is Jesus Christ is the *felt* meaning, goodness, and value of God. Christ embodies the cognitive-affective relationship of God to humankind and the consummate cognitive-affective relationship of humankind to God. Jesus, one might say, is the locus where God knows humankind (in the Semitic fullness of meaning of the verb to know) and humankind knows God.

The positivist and reductionist concern of the nineteenth century for form criticism was directed to a secondary level: Did this or that really happen? Does this or that pericope reflect the theology of this evangelist? Redactional criticism was directed more to the totality of the work: How was the Gospel put together? What was the overriding purpose of the author? What was his theological intent? To ask such questions is a good and necessary function of exegesis; but, if our consideration of the Gospel texts is restricted (reduced) to only this level, then, with redactional criticism the particulars of the Gospel become blurred and, with form criticism, the whole is lost.

The primary value of the Gospel is the Gospel text as sacrament. The sacramental nature of the Scriptures is forcefully brought out by the Dogmatic Constitution of the Second Vatican Council on Divine Revelation.

> The Church has always venerated the divine Scriptures just as she venerates the body of the Lord (*sicut et ipsum Corpus dominicum*), since from the table of both the word of God and of the body of Christ she unceasingly receives and offers to the faithful the bread of life, especially in the sacred liturgy . . . . in the sacred books, the Father who is in heaven meets His children with great love and speaks with them; and the force and power in the word of God is so great that it remains the support and energy of the Church, the strength of faith for her sons, the food of the soul, the pure and perennial source of spiritual life.[50]

The sacramental nature of Scripture is likewise expressed in the same Council's decree on the liturgy:

> In the liturgy the sanctification of man is manifested by signs perceptible to the senses, and is effected in a way which is proper to each of these signs . . . .[51]

Among these signs is the solemn proclamation of the Gospel story: Christ

> is present in His word, since it is He Himself who speaks when the holy Scriptures are read in the church.[52]

The sacramental power of the Gospel is a force challenging, operating upon, and touching us. The risen Christ speaks to us through the gift of his Spirit in our experience of the text. Though exegetical, historical, and theological studies are vitally necessary to provide controls lest we manipulate the Gospels to our own ends, nevertheless, those very controls can become an evasion, an escape from encountering the moving, challenging power of the Gospel story in all its "strangeness."

A Gospel is an external expression of an internal reality; it is the narrative or literary expression (an extended symbol) of the cognitive-affective relationship that Jesus Christ evoked in its author. Jesus Christ, the primordial symbol of God's fellowship-creating mystery, the sacramental locus where God and humankind know each other in love, is the one to whom Matthew, Mark, Luke, and John were drawn (Cf. Jn. 6:44). The risen Christ was present to each evangelist, regardless of whether or not he had known him during his life, because through the eye of love that is faith each one was an eyewitness to the Resurrection. The apostles, affirms St. Thomas, were able to testify to the risen Lord as eyewitnesses (*etiam de visu*) because they saw him after the Resurrection with the eye of faith.[53] The story each evangelist tells is the story of that which he has heard, seen, touched, and felt (cf. 1 Jn. 1:1). His Gospel is the symbol, the *signum efficax*, whereby we too are drawn, hear, see, touch, and feel the presence of the living Lord *oculata fide*.

There is no sacramental sign without the word (the form of the sacrament). Word and sacrament are not two *entia quae* but *entia quibus;* in the words of a once-popular song, "you can't have one without the other." If the preaching of the Gospel, the telling of the Gospel story, is taken to mean, not just the preaching of the homily, or the reading of the Gospel, so that the eucharistic prayer is seen as the culmination of the Church's ministry of the word and if, on the other hand, the sacrament of the Holy Eucharist is understood to include the entire eucharistic liturgy, then the Gospel and other New Testament writings can be understood as the verbal or literary dimension of that sacrament.[54] Common to every part of the mass is the presence of the risen Lord.[55] The presence of Christ in the congregation, in his minister, in his word, and in his Eucharist is the symbol that really effects the cognitive-affective communion of all humankind with one another and with God through Jesus and in the Spirit.

The sacramental, symbolic power of Jesus Christ, in his Eucharist and in his word, is from God and for God. It is an expression of God's presence and activity among humankind that seeks to transform humankind by the gift of divine, redemptive friendship. To the extent that the Gospel and Eucharist of Jesus do not move us to the decisions and the actions that will shape our lives, they are acting neither as symbols nor sacraments. To hear the Gospel and to receive Communion presuppose a connaturality on our part. Love recognizes what unlove cannot grasp. In this respect, love is more comprehensive than intellect. It does not abstract from the concrete to achieve the universal but attains to the universal good in all its concreteness. Through the concrete and particular imagery of the Gospel story, and through the concrete and particular action of eating the one Bread and sharing the one Cup, the universal call of the known-unknown that underlies all our questioning and loving becomes a known, loved, and felt call to address the one whom Jesus taught us to call our Father.

6.24 *The Resurrection is the key to the Christian interpretation of the divine and human coauthoring of the Jesus story, the story of the Church and the universal story of the world.*

Unlike the raising of Lazarus or the raising of the son of the widow of Nain, the Resurrection of Jesus is not the bringing back to life of a corpse. It is not revivification or resuscitation. The distinction can be seen pictorially in the ancient mosaics that decorate the walls of Sant'Apollinare Nuovo in Ravenna. In the raising of Lazarus Jesus stands pointing at a tomb from which there is emerging the shrouded figure of his friend. In the mosaic of the Resurrection there is no figure of Jesus; an angel and two women point at an empty tomb. Lazarus returns to the bosom of his earthly family—his sisters, Martha and Mary. Jesus goes, passes over from this mortal life to immortal life with the Father. The raising of Lazarus is a coming back to earthly existence; the Resurrection of Jesus is his entering into his Kingdom. Lazarus is restored to fellowship with his human family. Jesus founds a new family by the outpouring of his Spirit.

Christian faith affirms the uniqueness of Christ's death as the death that founds and issues in a new heaven and a new earth. In the Gospel of John, the evangelist places a significant quotation from the prophets to explain the death of Jesus. Jesus in the Fourth Gospel announces the completion or consummation of his story and then, bowing his head, he gives up the *Spirit*. John refers us to the prophecy of Zechariah:

> When that day comes . . . over the House of David and the citizens of Jerusalem I will *pour out a spirit of kindness and prayer*. They will look upon the one whom they have pierced. . . . When that day comes, a fountain will be opened for the House of David and the citizens of Jerusalem, for sin and impurity. (Zech. 12:9 – 13. Cf. Jn. 19:37)

For John, Christ's death is the release of the Spirit. Before re-counting appearances of the risen Jesus the author of the Fourth Gospel talks of the experience of Peter and the other disciple at the empty tomb. The other disciple runs up and observes the linen cloths strewn about. Peter notices that the head cloth was lying separately from the other cloths. The other disciple then enters the tomb, at which point "he saw and he believed." This other disciple has had an insight, a Eureka experience; now he understands. The evangelist comments: "Till this moment they had failed to under-stand" (Jn. 20:3 – 9). Later that evening, writes John, the Lord ap-peared and *breathed on them his Spirit* (cf. Jn 20:22f). The death of Jesus is the completion of the story of his earthly life and the begin-ning of the story of those who have been given new life by the gift of his Spirit.

Conversion, the communication of new life to the convert, is nothing other than the gift of the Spirit. Conversion, therefore, is radically grounded in the death of Jesus. The Resurrection is the affirmation of faith that the death of Jesus is not an ending but the beginning of eternal life. The Resurrection is one way (the Ascen-sion is another) in which the Church can affirm her belief that Jesus now lives the life of the Kingdom and invites others to share that life. The affirmation that Christ is truly risen, that he has truly appeared to Simon, that he is recognizable as truly present in the breaking of the bread, is an affirmation that the one whom men and women have killed has been made by God to be both Lord and Christ. To ask the question: "Did it really happen?" or "Was it a sudden burst of high energy?" as some students of the Turin shroud persist in asking, is to be like those who, like the Pharisees in Mat-thew's Gospel, ask for a sign (Mt. 12:38). "It is an evil and adulterous generation that asks for a sign! The only sign it will be given is the sign of the prophet Jonah" (Mt. 12:39).

To insist on asking whether the Resurrection is historical (and such insistent questioning usually betokens a desperate need to believe that it is) is to demand an incontrovertible sign while overlooking the signs that we have. It is to ignore the fact that we know for certain that Christ has risen because we have been baptized into his death; it is to ignore the fact that we have eaten and drunk with the Lord after his Resurrection by our share in his communion-sacrifice; it is to overlook the fact that our hearts burned within us as we read the Scriptures. The empty tomb, like any sacramental sign, is lifeless until it has taken form from the preaching of the Word: "He is not here, he has risen!" To ask whether the Resurrection is historical is to confuse seeing with believing. It is to misunderstand that believing is not something like taking a look ("Lord, show us a sign that we may believe"), but that faith comes from understanding what we hear, and hearing comes from what is preached (cf. Rom. 10:17).

The experience of Paul is mirrored by the experience of revivalist preachers: Paul never refers to the empty tomb; the preaching of revivalist meetings is a pointing to the effects of the risen Lord in the hearer's life now and, rarely, if ever, proceeds to faith by arguments from the empty tomb.[56]

The Resurrection of Jesus is not a *deus ex machina* snatching comedy from the grip of tragedy. It is not a coming back to life that undoes the tragedy of the Cross. It was for the sake of the Resurrection, the communication of eternal life, that Jesus came into the world, as the tenor of John's whole Gospel makes clear. The life of Sonship that Jesus enjoyed from the first moment of his human conception is the same life of Sonship he communicates after his Resurrection by the gift of his Spirit. The life of the Resurrection cannot be understood apart from the gift of self-transcending, self-investing love that issues in each believer in his or her acceptance of death in the response of totally trusting self-abandonment into the Father's hands.[57] Resurrection happens wherever men and women respond to the gift of God's love.

Although resurrectional life includes immortality, the two are not to be identified. Our sharing in God's life of self-transcending and unrestricted love, the life proper to Jesus Christ in his unique filial relationship to his Father, is more than immortality; it is the Eternal Life that Jesus possessed by nature and into which we enter by graceful adoption.

This difference between mere immortality and the resurrectional life of those who live and die in Jesus is implied in Christ's affirmation that we are no longer servants but friends (Jn. 15:15). By nature we are created servants of God; by supernatural grace we become his friends. Immortality, a prolongation of our earthly existence, or revivification, a return to our earthly existence, would be a continuation of servanthood. Resurrection is not revivified servanthood but a divinization, a sharing in the interpersonal relationship of the Father, Son, and Spirit, which is the divine life of self-communicating agape. The Father's life is the life of Jesus, and he fully shares it with his friends by his breathing on them the Spirit. This life of resurrectional love is the unique significance of the entire life story of the crucified-risen Jesus. The meat and drink that sustain this resurrectional life is the doing of the Father's will. The life of the Resurrection is the origin, the narrative, and the goal of Christ's story and the story of all those who have life in him.

Jesus reveals as his Father that Absolute to which every human being is open in all his or her questioning. Christ reveals as his Father that Holy Mystery that is loved in all our loving of particular goods and values. The Father of Jesus is present always and everywhere as the Absolute term of our unrestricted desire to know and love. Because Christ's Father is present as Absolute and not as a particular truth or goodness; his presence can be ignored, overlooked, or rejected as an illusion. The Eternal Life of the Absolute, revealed as the interpersonal life of the Father, Son, and Spirit, is present and offered to every human person. The Good News of the Resurrection of Jesus is the announcement and proclamation of that offer that summons all humankind to eternal friendship in the Kingdom of God's love.

---

1. See theses 2.611 and 2.6111 on pp. 80 and 82.

2. Bernard Lonergan, *Philosophy of God, and Theology: The Relationship between Philosophy of God and the Functional Specialty, Systematics* (London: Darton, Longman & Todd, 1973), p. 33.

3. Cf. John C. Meagher, "Pictures at an Exhibition: Reflections on Exegesis and Theology," *Journal of the American Academy of Religion*, 47 (1979), pp. 3–20. According to Meagher, theology's "career is primarily as the curator, commissioner, and critic of icons" (p. 17).

4. To be totally fair to Chesterton, it should be said that since every Christian who has not received a special privilege is guilty of sin, the fruits necessary for validating the Gospel story are perfectly brought forth in the life story of Jesus Christ and, through her Immaculate Conception gained by the merits of her Son, in the life story of the Panagia, the All-Holy Mother of God. For a work of art to be authentic, it is not necessary that it be popularly acclaimed—only that it be appreciated by men and women of taste. Ultimately it is only Jesus who is the person of "impeccable taste" (cf. Jn. 1:18; 5:19); in his human response to the beauty of God, the fruits or merits of Jesus alone are sufficient to validate the authenticity of his gospel.

5. Immanuel Kant, *Critique of Judgment, Analytic of the Beautiful, Fourth Moment, § 22;* trans. J. H. Bernard, in Albert Hofstadter and Richard Kuhns, eds., *Philosophies of Art and Beauty* (New York: The Modern Library/Random House, 1964), pp. 280 – 343.

6. Bernard Lonergan, *Insight*, pp. 280ff. Cf. *Id, Understanding and Being: An Introduction and Companion to Insight; the Halifax Lectures* (Lewiston, N.Y.: Edwin Mellen Press, 1980), passim.

7. Kant, *op. cit.*

8. *Ibid.*

9. *Ibid.*

10. *D. Thomae Aquinatis Epist. Dedicatoria ad Hanibaldum Presby. Card. in Catenam super Marci evangelium editam,* Venetiis 1593.

11. *D. Thomae Aquinatis Epist. Dedicatoria ad Urbanum IV in Catenam super Matthaei Evangelio Aeditam,* Venetiis 1593.

12. *In Ioannum 6 Lect 5, (Marrietti § 935).*

13. J. H. Newman, *Discourses to Mixed Congregations* 17 (Westminster, Md.: The Newman Press, 1966), p. 356.

14. *Ibid.,* p. 350.

15. St. Thomas, *Summa Theologia IIa, IIae,* 180, 2, 3m. Aquinas's insistence on the common origin of poetry and theology in wonder is echoed by Victor Hugo, *Preface de Cromwell* (cf. Gerhardus van der Leeuw, *Sacred and Profane Beauty* (Nashville, Tenn. & New York: Abingdon Press, 1968), p. 126: "The point of departure of religion is always also the point of departure of poetry"; and by the Shakespearean critic J. Middleton Murray, "Literature and Religion" (cf. Henri Bremond, *Payer and Poetry* (London: Burns, Oates and Washbourne, 1927), p. 130: "Religion and literature are branches of the same everlasting root."

16. G. K. Chesterton, *The Everlasting Man* (London: Hodder and Staughton, 1925), p. 116.

17. *Ibid.*

18. *Missale Romanum:* "Quia per incarnati Verbi mysterium, nova mentis nostrae oculis lux tuae claritatis infulsit: ut dum visibiliter Deum cognoscimus, per hunc in invisibilium amorem rapiamur."

19. St. Thomas, Letter to Pope Urban IV, *op. cit.*

20. *Ibid.;* note the use of the words "splendor" and "claritas," words central to Aquinas's aesthetics.

21. Martin Heidegger, *The Origin of the Work of Art,* trans. Albert Hofstadter, in Hofstadter and Kuhns, eds., *Philosophies of Art and Beauty* (New York: Modern Library/Random House, 1964), p. 663.

22. *Ibid.,* p. 670.

23. *Ibid.,* p. 671.

24. Alexander Lowen, *The Betrayal of the Body* (New York & London: Collier Books/Collier Macmillan, 1967), p. 62.

25. Otto Fenichel, *The Psychoanalytic Theory of Neurosis* (London: Routledge & Kegan Paul, 1946), pp. 236 – 267; cf. Frank Lake, *Clinical Theology: A Theological and Psychiatric Basis to Clinical Pastoral Care* (London: Darton, Longman & Todd, 1966), pp. 540 – 552.

26. J. P. Manigne, *Pour une Poétique de la Foi* (Paris: Les Éditions du Cerf, 1969), pp. 43, 51, 57ff.

27. Archibald MacLeish, "Ars Poetica," from *New and Collected Poems 1917 – 1976* (Boston: Houghton Mifflin).

28. J. P. Manigne, *op. cit.,* pp. 138ff.

29. Henry Duméry, *Phenomenology and Religion* (Berkeley and Los Angeles: University of California Press, 1975), p. 82.

30. The phenomenological analysis of the differences between a doctor's nameplate and a hamburger sign has only limited validity. The traveler through Naples is bombarded with large billboards advertising the services of the city's numerous urologists. The British Medical Association lays down stringent regulations to prevent medical practitioners from advertising; implicit in their regulations is perhaps the idea that the nameplates of doctors should evoke (symbolize) respectability and sobriety. Thus the end may be different, but the function of the plate is analogous to that of a hamburger sign. Nevertheless Newman's distinction between the real number and its logarithm retains its usefulness.

31. Quoted by Metropolitan Anthony of Surozh (Archbishop Anthony Bloom), *Living Prayer* (London: Libra/Darton, Longman & Todd, 1966), p. 68.

32. It is a fact too often neglected in theological writings that the Latin word *sacer* means both venerable and execrable. A hierophany is not the unmistakable revelation of a God who should be worshiped, as though one could come to faith by merely taking a look at some unmistakable sign of God's presence (cf. Jesus' refusal to give a sign in Mt. 12:38f and parallels), but the concrete (ontic) expression of the attractiveness of a known unknown.

In a certain part of London one can see a Catholic church surrounded by brothels and strip-joints. The crucifix outside the church and the pictures of naked women outside the strip-joints are equally hierophanies or symbols of the sacred. Both invite the passer-by to (comm)union; both invite the passer-by to unknown but imaginable delights; both invite the passer-by to give and receive love. Where they differ is in what they affirm to be the true way of achieving communion, delight, and love—whether the sacred is to be embraced as coming from the God and Father of Jesus or execrated as demonic belongs to the *judgment* informed by faith and not to a sensory perception. Dostoevsky expressed the ambivalent nature of the sacred well when he wrote in *The Brothers Karamazov* (Book III, chap. 3): "Beauty is a terrible and awful thing! It is terrible because it has not been fathomed and never can be fathomed, for God sets us nothing but riddles. Here the boundaries meet and all contradictions exist side by side. . . . Beauty! I can't endure the thought that a man of lofty mind and heart begins with the ideal of the Madonna and ends with the ideal of Sodom. What's still more awful is that a man with the ideal of Sodom in his soul does not renounce the ideal of the Madonna, and his heart may be on fire with that ideal, genuinely on fire, just as in the days of youth and innocence. . . . Is there beauty in Sodom? Believe me, that for the immense mass of mankind beauty is found in Sodom. Did you know the secret? The awful thing is that beauty is mysterious as well as terrible. God and the devil are fighting there and the battlefield is the heart of man." (Everyman edition, p. 106). We neglect the demonic dimensions of the sacred at our peril.

33. William Lynch, *Images of Faith* (Notre Dame, Ind.: Notre Dame University Press, 1973), pp. 9 – 10.

34. Walter E. Conn, *"Conscience and Self-Transcendence,"* unpublished dissertation (Ann Arbor, Mich.: University Microfilms), p. 147.

35. Cf. Peter L. Benson and Bernard P. Spilka, "God-Image as a function of self-esteem and locus of control," in H. N. Maloney, ed., *Current Perspectives in the Psychology of Religion* (Grand Rapids, Mich.: Wm. B. Eerdmans, 1977), pp. 209 – 224.

36. C. S. Lewis in his novel *Voyage to Venus* resituates the Genesis myth in the context of a different planet. The primal Venusian couple are placed on floating islands in the middle of the sea. Instead of being forbidden to eat of a tree of knowledge, they are forbidden to live permanently on terra firma; inability to trust is the root of all subsequent evil.

37. Lynch, *op cit.,* p. 11.

38. *Ibid.,* pp. 4–8.

39. William V. Dych, S. J., *Through a Glass Darkly: Reflections on the Theology of Faith,* unpublished book manuscript, 1976, p. 18. Dych asserts that our images express not the meaning of things in themselves nor the self in isolation from the real, but our interrelatedness: "God and man are affirmed and known in one act of the imagination" (p. 65).

40. The use of the notion of a "self-image" is problematic in that it can suggest in some writings on psychology an epistemology of "knowing as taking a look." It is important to realize that the mature handling of our self-image occurs only after we have returned to that image by way of critical reflection upon our self-understanding. To control critically one's own self-image and one's image of God is a prime requirement for growth. Lest we be misunderstood to be saying that mature faith is possible only in one who is a doctor of theology, it is perhaps important to advert here to the fact that we can live on a symbolic plane that is higher than the intellectual one on which we happen to be. Indeed, the process of growing in our grasp of the Christ story is one in which our imagination leaps ahead faster than our conceptual thoughts can follow. Self-generated knowledge is very small, even in the genius, when compared to the vast amount of knowledge we must take on trust from other people (theology is a collaborative effort); what matters is that we put our trust in the right teachers and attain whatever level of conceptual understanding is at present within our capabilities—always remembering with Hamlet that there are more things in heaven and earth than are dreamt of in our present philosophical positions.

41. Harry Blamires, "The Nature of Christian Education," paper delivered at Bishop Grosseteste College, Lincoln, England, July 1971, and reproduced for private circulation in *The Prison Chaplain's Journal*.

42. *Didache,* trans. Quasten, *op. cit., I,* p. 32.

43. Edward Yarnold, *The Second Gift: A Study of Grace* (Slough, England: St. Paul Publications, 1974), p. 5.

44. St. John of the Cross, *Romance III.*

45. Cf. Marvin H. Pope, *The Song of Songs, The Anchor Bible 7C,* p. 118.

46. Archbishop Anthony Bloom, *School for Prayer* (London: Darton, Longman & Todd, 1970), p. 12.

47. Bernard Lonergan, *Method in Theology* (London: Darton, Longman & Todd, 1971), p. 64.

48. Antoine Vergote, *The Religious Man* (Dublin: 1969), p. 158.

49. Rollo May, "The Significance of Symbols," in *Id* ed., *Symbolism in Religion and Literature* (New York: George Braziller, 1960), pp. 11 – 49, p. 16ff.

50. *Dei Verbum* 21 (Abbot trans).

51. *Sacrosanctum Concilium* 7 (Abbott trans).

52. *Ibid.*

53. St. Thomas, *Summa Theologia* IIIa, 55, 2 ad 1: "Christum post Resurrectionem viventem oculata fide viderunt, quem mortuum sciverat."

54. It is worth noting here how the culmination of the Church's response of thankfulness to God, a word of thanks that is efficacious and is never pronounced without achieving that which it set out to do, is a telling of the story of what Jesus said and did "on the night before he died."

55. Cf. Paul VI, *Encyc. "Mysterium Fidei,"* AAS 57 (1965), pp. 743 – 744; pp. 762 – 763.

56. This is not to say that revivalist Christianity is not often fundamentalistic about the Resurrection accounts in the four Gospels. The initial preaching of such groups, however, starts from the experience of Jesus' power in the present. It may be that revivalists "preach better than they know." The sacramentality of the empty-tomb accounts may require a more Johannine stage of Christian conversion before it can be properly handled; Paul's preaching being, in terms of Martini's hypothesis, a Markan (or even pre-Markan) stage. On the historicity or nonhistoricity of the Resurrection, see Gerald O'Collins, *The Easter Jesus* (London: Darton, Longman & Todd, 1973), pp. 57 – 74.

57. No one who has seen a newsreel of the Jews singing the "Shm'a Yisroel" in the gas chambers of Germany or who has seen the moving reconstruction in the film *Holocaust* of the end of the ghetto uprising in Warsaw, when the freedom fighters went to their deaths singing the "Hatikvah," the Song of Hope, could doubt that the resurrectional life of Jesus is communicated and lived by those who would explicitly reject the name of Christian.

CHAPTER 10

THE SEVENTH MOMENT:

The Jesus story as foundation for the story of his community, the Church

> As our Christianity is more an aspiration than an achievement, we have to have recourse to the Christian community, to its share of experience, its traditional wisdom, to awaken in us what is latent in us, to stir our feelings even though our minds are only partly open, even though our wills are not yet ready. . . .[1]
>
> Bernard Lonergan

7.1 *Persons communicate and relate to one another by the stories they tell.*

The ancient people of Israel were molded into a people largely by their common sharing in the stories of the Exodus and the Exile. Their hope in a messianic future was largely conceived in terms of a future continuation of the story of the House of David. After the destruction of the temple and the expulsion of the Jews from Palestine, the sons and daughters of Israel were able to preserve their common identity through the stories of the rabbis and the study of the stories that made up their sacred writings. The Yiddish way of telling stories has not only provided the world with a great literature but has also helped preserve the identity of the community as a distinct people. In our own times, the story of the Holocaust has become a raison d'être for the state of Israel.

The common folklore of the English—Arthur and his knights, Alfred and his burned cakes, Canute and his attempt to turn back the sea—together with commonly accepted history of this island people—especially in its evocation of a bulldog people refusing to bow to armadas, or to the threat of Napoleonic or Nazi invaders—and the self-understanding of the English as the exporters of tolerance and democratic institutions throughout a whole empire, conspire to create a milieu in which the English can find their own identity.[2]

The Boston Tea Party, the sonorousness and almost poetic quality of the Declaration of Independence and the Constitution, the opening up of the West, the welcoming of the poor and oppressed of all nations to citizenship, the belief in the equality of opportunity for all, are some of the stories that have gone to make up the beliefs by which the United States lives.

The common story of the stab in the back by the generals, the commonly believed myths of Jewish malevolence, the myths of Nordic superiority, the myths expressed musically by Wagner were instrumental in the formation of the Germans' self-understanding that allowed them to believe in the historical necessity and need for a Führer. The tacit agreement among Germans of a slightly later generation *not* to tell the story of what happened and the still later demand of a still younger generation that the story be told have left their mark upon the kind of self-understanding of present-day German society.

Community life, the common political and social consensus and the common actions and decisions they take are in large measure the product of a nation's myths and stories. Storymaking builds communities.

Family life, too, is built up upon the foundation of a common fund of stories. Distant relatives who meet only infrequently at weddings or funerals have a certain fellow-feeling for one another because they know that the almost total stranger with whom they have to converse knows the story about Uncle George getting drunk at Cousin Mildred's wedding and that he or she knows who the Aunt Fanny is whom everyone thinks is slightly odd. Distant cousins will ask after each other's parents (will ask about the latest chapter in their mother's story) even though they may know, or in truth care, little about a relative whom they hardly know. Brothers and sisters share a common fund of stories about their childhood, and they can relate to one another's present storytelling as a variation upon their own version of the later chapters of a story with a common origin.

Churches, too, have their foundational myths. The story of Christ and of the early Church is foundational for the Christian faith. The stories of the recusants and the martyrs of penal times, at least until recently, helped mark off an English Roman Catholic from his or her Anglican brothers and sisters, who had their own stories of the Smithfield fires. The stories of the founder and of the first communities can shape a whole subsequent spirituality and help mark off a Jesuit from a Franciscan, the Sisters of St. Joseph from the

Trappistines, and a Benedictine from a Little Brother of Jesus. The place names of Ignatius's story—Manresa, Loyola, for example—have become the names of universities, retreat houses, and schools, lived in by later members of his Society; the religious community he founded preserves its identity by a common and frequent reference of itself to its foundational story.

Human beings relate to their fellows and assert their own self-identity as a result of the stories they commonly hear and tell.

> 7.11 **There can be no community life, no consensus, and thus no common action without participation in a common understanding of the meaning of a common story and without a common commitment to that story's value.**

When different understandings of the meaning of a common story become radically incompatible and irreconcilable, community life and the consensus about meaning and values, and the common actions and decisions that go with that life-style break down. Jewish Christians broke with Judaism because their interpretations of the salvific meaning of Israel's history diverged too radically to be contained in the one community. The story told by Western Christians became irreconcilable (or at least seemed to become irreconcilable) with the story told by Eastern Christians. Protestant and Catholic communites are driven apart from one another by their differing interpretations of the meaning of the story of Jesus and his Church. The inability to share the common meaning of the story that had once united the community leads to the formation of new "break-away" communities. Radical disagreement about the true meaning of the story, especially the foundational story, fosters division and separation. A radical disagreement about the story the Constitution was attempting to shape led to the War Between the States. Failure to agree to a common story is the beginning of and the sign of schism. The power of stories to shape the identity of communities is seen in the emotional (and at times physical) violence that greets those who challenge the community's common interpretation of its foundational story.

> 7.12 **The life story of a community is the common good of those who call to mind its meaning and value by memory, awareness, and anticipation.**

We participate in the life of a community by calling to mind the meaning and value of its story. We collaborate in the activity of calling it to mind and find our unity in the activity of memory, awareness, and anticipation that orient the community to decision and action. Communion in calling to mind and taking to heart the meaning and value of the story constitutes the common good of the community's existence. The life story of a community is actively shared as a common good in calling to mind a tradition (memories, stories) that entails what its members are to believe, what they are to become, what they are to do. The community recalls its story in the present because of its hopes for the future.

Belonging to a community is a question of calling to mind its story. We share in its life by sharing in its memories and hopes. In terms of the biblical tradition, we belong to a chosen people only if we remember that God has chosen us; we live in a promised land only if we remember that God had promised it. To forget the story that called the community into existence and continues to sustain its existence implies an alienation from it.

7.13 *The tradition of a community or society is the story of its life.*

Tradition is not merely a question of a collection of time-honored customs, accepted not on critical grounds, but merely because things have always been so. Growth and development are sometimes opposed in the name of tradition, understood primarily as a conservative force in society, safeguarding it against centrifugal and disintegrating forces. We speak of the traditions of a school or university, of the army or navy, of a religious order, or of a certain family. There are national and regional traditions. These traditions connote more than mere conservatism; they involve the continual presence of a spirit or attitude, the continuity of an ethos. Just as religious and secular rites express a profound religious or secular reality, so these traditions safeguard and communicate a certain spirit. The tradition is the continuation of the same spirit, understood as orientation to insight, understanding, judgment, decision, and action, through succeeding generations. To belong to a society is to appropriate or live by its traditions. To live by a tradition we must assimilate its past in order to understand its present. Only by so doing will we be able to seek a particular future for it without breaking with the essential unity of its life story or tradition. Tradition is like the conscience of the group or society; it is the principle of identity that links one generation with another and enables them to remain the same society or people as they mature and develop in time.

Tradition can be described as the orientation of memory toward the future, a cognitive and affective disposition that enables us to find meaning for our future action by reflection upon our experience. Without memory the lives of individuals and of societies would preclude growth and development. To assimilate a community's tradition implies a willingness to learn from others, both those who have gone before and those now living whom we recognize as authentic bearers of the tradition.

7.14 *Authentic storytelling is the creation of a community of love.*

Communication, as its etymology implies, is a making of the many into one, a communion, many members being made one body. All communication is a sharing of the communicator's life, ideals, dreams, values, aims, purposes, and understanding with those to whom he or she addresses herself or himself. To communicate is to act both cognitively and affectively. I must understand what I wish to communicate; I must love what I communicate and those to whom I address myself. I must understand my audience, their desires, fears, longings, aims, cognitive development, if I am to speak effectively to their condition.

In all my storytelling, wittingly or unwittingly, I will reveal my love or lack of love for the subject of my story. Wittingly or unwittingly, I will reveal my love or lack of love for those I address. Community is the fruit of love. Without the love of God poured into the hearts of both the storyteller and the storylistener, we may spin yarns with the tongue of an angel, but our efforts will come to nothing. Without the gift of conversion, both in the preacher and the hearers, the homily or the theological discourse will at best be like the compulsive talker whose flow of words is nothing but a disguise to hide the fact that the marriage is loveless, and that the spouses have ceased to communicate in all but name.

7.2 *The members of a society benefit from its common story only to the extent that they allow themselves to be governed by it.*

The members of a society or community benefit from their membership only to the extent that they submit to its rules, aims, basic meaning, and story. It is unusual to join a swimming club if one hates swimming. Philatelic societies are a bore to those who find no interest in collecting stamps. Membership in a library is of little avail to those who cannot and do not wish to read. Such obvious truths may become obscured the more complex and many leveled the community. Those societies into which we are born, the family, the state, the local community, may have aims and rules with which we do not concur. Where the family structure is psychopathogenic, it may be in the interests of the individual member to attempt to change the whole aim, rules, and structure of the family in order to develop fully as an individual or even to preserve his or her sanity. We may be called upon to leave father, mother, sister, and brother, for the sake of the kingdom of truth and goodness. Similarly, we may be called to flee our country and go into exile for the sake of preserving our freedom, our honesty, our goodness, and our integrity.

With those institutions that we enter as the result of the choice of others, principally our school and, if we become church members in infancy, our church, there may be aims, rules, and structures incompatible with our true or false understanding of what our aims, rules, and structures should be. The concrete community into which we are inserted may, on maturer reflection, be judged an inauthentic bearer of its own tradition. Our decision to leave the community in which we have been brought up may be affected by particular values present in that community that attract us but that, though authentic in themselves, become a "cover story" obscuring the lack of value inherent in the society. The members of Jim Jones's People's Temple, for example, seem to have enjoyed a higher standard of concern for the poor and underprivileged than those of many other faith communities. The warmth of the welcome experienced by socially marginal people, the real concern for the redemption of drug addicts, the alleviation of urban poverty, and the political effectiveness of the organization, particular values that in themselves were good, helped obscure from its members, and perhaps from Jones himself, the underlying megalomaniacal ideology, the hidden pathological biases, and the totalitarian disregard for freedom, which culminated in the suicidal tragedy of Guyana.

The Church is a community of faith. Full participation in the community is the fruit of conversion. Outward and visible membership of the Church is no guarantee that the person has been converted or that the gift of conversion has been responded to. The members of the Christian community benefit from the story of Jesus and his Church to the extent that they allow themselves to be governed and shaped by it. One may retain outward and visible membership of the Church, even though one's own aims, the rules by which one lives, the basic meaning of one's story, differ from the aims, the rules, and the basic meaning of the story of Jesus.

For example, a man was a regular churchgoer and prided himself on being a good Catholic. His daughter had had an adulterous affair that the father had discovered. He went to the priest. "Father," he said, "I was brought up a good Catholic; how could I ever welcome her to my table? I can never forgive her." For seventy years the man had joined with the community in the celebration of the sacraments of reconciliation, he knew the parable of the Father who forgave his son, but apparently he had never "heard" the Gospel of Forgiveness. He had "heard" what he had wanted to hear: that to be a Catholic was to be respectable. He had paid his tithes, kept the fast days, eschewed grasping, unjust, adulterous behavior. He was not like his daughter, and for that he thanked God. It can happen, as John reminds us, that we can say we "hear" the story of Jesus while our own life story shows that we have not. Our claim to have heard the story can be discovered to be a lie (cf. 1 Jn. 2:3 – 6).

Because the Church community functions on many levels, we can come into membership because we are attracted by subsidiary levels of the story, important in themselves, which obscure for us a deeper "hearing" of the story told by Christ. I may say that Jesus is Lord because it affords me the opportunity to do good works. I may join a prayer group and "feel saved" because I enjoy the warmth of singing songs in good company. I may take instruction in the faith because it will please my intended marriage partner or because I enjoy the attention of a one-to-one relationship with my teacher, a ray of comfort in the loneliness of my life. I may preach the Gospel because it affords me an opportunity to impress others with my rhetoric. I may embrace the celibate life because it affords me the opportunity to refuse the responsibility of a sexual relationship and the demands of love. I may give my body to martyrdom because it makes me feel a hero. Without the love of God that has been poured into our hearts, that is, without the Spirit of conversion, my Christian living is as nothing. Without the gift of the Spirit I can not call Jesus Lord, but we know, by the testimony of that same Lord, that it is not those who call out "Lord, Lord" who necessarily enter the Kingdom. The gift of conversion is a spirit of openness to change that allows us to hear the story of Jesus and to be shaped into a new creation by the aims and basic meaning of the Church.

7.21 **Every society has limits to its tolerance for the diversity of its members' interpretations of its common (foundational) story.**

When one tells bedtime stories to children one often finds that the child will ask for a particular bit to be read again. The child does not ask us to read the whole of *Little Red Ridinghood* but "the part where the wolf explains why its mouth and eyes are so large." If one asks the child why he or she wants that part read again and not some other bit, one will commonly be told, "It's the part I like." The child relates in some way to a particular part of the story. A similar phenomenon occurs with the stories of communities, whether they be families, churches, or nations. A part of the story may become so important in our eyes that we are tempted so to concentrate on it that eventually we end by sundering it completely from its context in the wider narrative to which it belongs. The word heresy, from the Greek hairesis, means choice. We choose to dwell upon some particular aspect of the story that seems important to us or that seems to us to be neglected (and in reality our judgment may be correct and it may be a part of the story the importance of which has been overlooked), and we stress that part so much that we end by making it too large in relation to its background. When one focuses a camera, one turns the lens until the various objects appear correct in their relations to one another. But if one continues turning the lens after the optimum point of focus has been reached, the picture goes out of focus "the other way." What before was neglected because it merged too much with the background is brought into focus but then distorted again as it is allowed to overshadow the other objects in its surroundings.

The meaning of a community's story admits of reconcilable understandings or interpretations. A conductor is entitled to make changes in the composer's score to bring out his own interpretation of the symphony. One conductor may slightly lengthen a note or ask for fortissimo instead of piu forte where another conductor will stick more closely to the score. There result differing and legitimate interpretations—Sargent's *Messiah* differs noticeably from Barbirolli's, yet both are recognizable as the work of Handel. Such a pluralism of interpretations is legitimated by the judgment of the critics. There comes a point, and the precise point is extraordinarily difficult to define, where the performance or production of the piece has lost all recognizable relationship with the composer's or playwright's work. Different film directors make different interpretations of the same book. In watching a "film of a book" we may notice the way in which the director has brought out some particular aspect of the writer's story. At other times, the direction may be so idiosyncratic or out of focus that we must conclude by saying that we have seen a new film, a new story, and not the story of the book. As in all aesthetic judgments, our judgment of the authenticity of a performance is open to question by our fellow-critics. Differing critics will prefer a different storytelling to others. If one compares a Gielgud Hamlet with one by Richardson or Olivier, one will find legitimate preferences expressed by differing critics. All critics, however, will agree that the three men are great actors and interpreters of Shakespeare. All communities, families, churches, nations, the scientific and academic communities, achieve a certain consensus of what is or is not an acceptable claim to be taken seriously as an interpreter. When one hears that Tolstoy has dismissed Shakespeare as a hack, one does not listen respectfully to Tolstoy as an acknowledged master of literature but concludes that he must have a blind spot about the merit of one whom all those with authority in the field acknowledge to be a genius. The community acknowledges the legitimate variations in the interpretations of its story and repudiates those interpretations it judges to be a betrayal of its true meaning.

Where there were no limits to the tolerance of a society with regard to the interpretation of the true meaning of its common story, the society would have no meaning and would cease to exist. The aesthetic judgment about the validity of an interpretation is exercised at different levels of the community's membership. In a parish several people were discussing how to decide between the varying interpretations of the Christian story offered them by their pastors. As an adult and reflective Christian, but with no formal training in theology, how do I judge a proclamation of the Gospel that seems to be at variance with the proclamation of the same Gospel by other pastors, or at variance with the proclamation I heard as a child? I wish to hold fast to the Gospel that was first preached, but how do I tell who of these concrete teachers is Paul and who is Apollos? When Paul's present teaching seems to be at variance with what Paul preached before, how do I know whether to trust my memory of childhood or to give thanks that my teacher is leading me from the milk of infancy to the solid nourishment of a maturer faith? How do I discern the spirits of my teachers? A question of vital importance in the hearts of many of today's post–Vatican II Catholics, it is a question that must have exercised the pious Jew when faced with the preaching of the Rabbi from Nazareth. *Plus ça change, plus c'est la même chose;* the questions men and women ask show more continuity than the answers they give.

A woman in the group put it this way: "Father X and Father Y are clearly teaching different things. How am I to tell which is right? I do not always agree with what Father X says, but I find that what he says so often makes sense that I always try to reexamine my beliefs when I disagree. Father Y, on the other hand, is well known to be a crank. I therefore disregard what he says." Drawing on her past experience of the two men and of how they related to her experience of life and of prayer, the woman made an aesthetic judgment: the first is an authentic teacher; the second is not. In essence, the woman was doing at the level of commonsense reflection what Lonergan and Polanyi claim occurs at the level of the scientific community.

By an act of inverse insight, the scientific community judges alchemy and astrology as beyond the pale of intelligent inquiry.[3] By an aesthetic judgment the taxonomist judges how plants and animals should be classified; taxonomy can be defined only by describing it as what a good taxonomist does.[4] Science is what scientists do, and who are scientists and who are not scientists is decided by the judgment of other scientists.[5] The limits of tolerance are often a matter of a society's unwritten law: there is no need to define them by law when they are universally accepted or taken for granted. The consensus of scientists repudiates alchemical literature as nonscientific not by rigorously delineating the boundaries between alchemy and chemistry but by refusing to take alchemy seriously, by implicitly proclaiming its wrong-headedness in refusing to falsify its claims, and by neglecting to elect its practitioners (if such there be) to fellowship in the Royal Society or to membership in other scientific organizations.

In the first of his letters, the disciple John tells his readers that he is telling the story of the Word so that they may enter into communion with him (cf. 1 Jn. 1:1 – 3). John's telling of the story founds the community. Later in his letter he goes on to warn his readers about false storytellers: those who "speak the language [story] of the world" must be rejected (cf. 1 Jn. 4:1 – 6). The communion between overseers and their elders, and between the overseers of one church and another, is a communion of storytellers. It is in his capacity as the chief storyteller of his Church that each overseer can acknowledge or refuse to acknowledge other storytellers as being part of his community. The (largely unwritten) laws that govern membership of this community are implicitly the limits of the community's basic faith with regard to the human good.

7.31 *Our experience of the Jesus story is conditioned by our experience of our own world.*

Experience here is to be understood as a process of attentiveness to the given of our lives, our understanding of it, our judgments concerning the truth or falsehood of our understanding and our emotional and ethical response to those judgments, a response shown forth by our praxis. We affirm that our experience—the totality of our response—of the story of Jesus is conditioned and colored by our experience of ourselves and of our world. This experience does not arise automatically but through a dialectic with other worlds and our journey through time. It arises from a dialectic with other worlds insofar as I experience my world, my horizons, and the tradition in which I stand precisely as mine in differentiation from the worlds of others. It arises as the result of a journey insofar as I have a personal history that has left its imprint upon me but that is not yet concluded. As I am more inclined to believe my story (history) than to subject it to a universal methodological doubt, it is better to take my stand on the journey past, with confession both of its achievements and of its failures and limitations, and to be open to new turns and vistas.

We do not listen to nor attend to the story of Jesus, the Good News, unless we have a reason to do so—an experience or a question for which we hope it will provide illumination. It is impossible to understand and answer unless we have already posed and understood the question. Insofar as the story of Jesus is an answer to the universal human question, we cannot listen to it unless we have already in some way attended to that universal question. A young man met by chance in a restaurant once asked one of the authors why the author believed the Gospel. The author replied that the Gospel convinced him that his sins had been forgiven. It was Good News because the Gospel convinced him that he was loved by a forgiving and an accepting God. The young man replied that he could not believe the Gospel, that it made no sense to him, because he was not aware of being sinful, and he was satisfied with the love of his wife and had no need of anyone else to love him. The news that we are justified is not Good News to anyone who has never thought that she or he was unjustified. We cannot understand the answer Jesus gives until we have asked the question. It is true that our failure to ask the right questions may run the risk of finding in the story only those elements that respond to our particular interests or needs. The new experiences and new questions that life brings may lead us to discover elements and relationships in the story of Jesus and his Church that the old questions never saw.

In a concrete teaching situation, the selection of a topic for a paper may be dictated by the student's interest, which in turn emerges from his or her experience. When we approach the Gospels, for example, it is good that the student be able to formulate, however vaguely, her or his presuppositions as she or he approaches the text and the experiences that inspire her or his interest in this particular text. There is no *quaerens intellectum* without some kind of *fides:* some personal faith that this is God's Word, his Good News for us. Abbot David Parry wrote a book entitled *This Promise Is for You.* His concern was to show that the promise of the Gospel was a promise made to the individual believer, that the Gospel story was a story told for every person. To hear the Gospel story we must have a faith that the story of Jesus is addressed to us. Only if we are open to a possible transcendence of our own self-conditioned world, only if the Gospel story resonates with our experience will we be moved to say "Amen." Our discovery of the connaturality of the Gospel story with our story transmutes our life into an affirmation, a saying "Amen" to the offer of friendship given in Jesus.

So long as it remains in the confines of the academic study, the Good News is not open to the possibility of falsification. Only if it is tested by lived experience can the truth of the Gospel story begin to be known. In the living life of the community—its life of prayer, both corporate and private, its sacraments, its teaching, its works of charity—is found the theater where the theory can be put to the test.

7.32 *Our understanding of the Jesus story, the Good News, is conditioned by our participation in the living communities of Christian faith that tell the story.*

The life story of the Christian community, a community created by the life story of Jesus and his gift of the Spirit, conditions our understanding of the Good News of Jesus Christ, the Son of God, who invites all humankind to friendship by participation in the way of his cross. Paraphrasing Bernard Lonergan's remark on the classics, we may say that the life story of Jesus grounds a tradition and creates the milieu in which it is studied and interpreted. It produces in its hearers, through the cultural tradition and mentality it creates, the *Vorverständnis* from which it will be read, studied, and interpreted.[6] In hearing the Gospel story we hear the story of one who has already shaped our lives, our judgments, and our images by calling us to exist within a community founded upon his story.

The tradition and culture created by the Jesus story are often a counterculture to the environment, a counterculture that tests the validity of the word for authentically human life, against the unquestioned assumptions of the prevailing culture. Someone once said that it was the function of the Jew in our society to listen to the statements of fact and opinions that are common among us and then to stand up and say, "That ain't necessarily so." The Gospel image of the leaven leavening the lump of dough discloses how the Christian Church, the community founded upon the Jesus story, must be a sign of contradiction within the societies in which it finds itself. The Gospel story acts also as a leaven even within the Church; the story of Jesus is a sign both within and without the Christian community that much of what that community may believe or affirm "ain't necessarily so." The tradition in which we come to Jesus may be authentic or inauthentic or, more usually, a blend of the authentic with the inauthentic. It is always open to challenge to a greater authenticity both by the Word and by the world. The Good News may sound strange to the point of incredibility if we cannot experience its goodness enfleshed in the community. The experience of community often alerts us to the meanings of the Gospel that, as individuals deprived of the experience, we would never have expected.

Discernment of the true meaning of the Good News, the judgment phase of our cognitional process, is greatly facilitated when it is done in a community striving to find life through the Gospel. The Christian community provides a corrective and supportive matrix for our authentic hearing of the story of Jesus. Occasionally the judgment of a community is wrong, and one's personal judgment—assuming a conflict in interpretations—is right; still, the risk of solipsism that the isolated individual runs would seem to be a greater risk than when she or he is actively guided by the communal interpretation even when she or he has some objective linguistic controls for interpreting the Good News. The community's celebration of the Good News—particularly its liturgical celebration: *lex orandi, lex credendi*—appears to be a primary context for its authentic interpretation. The Good News is understood when it is celebrated.

According to Scripture, God's word is understood only when it is lived (cf., e.g., Jas. 1:22 – 25). The praxis of the community is a key to understanding its foundational story. Like a scientific hypothesis, the Good News may not be validated but must be subjected to the possibility of invalidation by the repeated experiment of living it.[7] The story of the two houses (Mt. 7:24 – 27; Lk. 6:46 – 49) reveals that our effort to live the Good News will influence our interpretation of its true meaning. David Lockhead underscores the importance of community praxis for hearing the Good News of Christ's story:

> We have a "problem" of private interpretation because we see hermeneutics as a primarily individualistic activity. Under the impact of the dominant liberal ideology of Western society, the insistence of the reformers on the freedom of conscience of the interpreter has led to a view of hermeneutics in which an interpretation is a matter of opinion of the individual and in which one opinion is as good as another.
>
> Against this we need to insist that interpretation is not a matter of "opinion" but of *praxis*. Interpretation does not end when we draw the "moral" of a text, but when we act upon it. Secondly, the *praxis* which is the end of interpretation is not individual but corporate. In the last analysis, it is the involvement of the interpreter in a community of interpretation, in a community of *praxis*, which makes interpretation a meaningful activity.[8]

The Good News concerns a community's way to the Kingdom of God, its Way of the Cross as the way of self-transcending love for all others. It concerns a fullness of meaning that by its very nature can never be exhausted; it calls into play the consciousness of its hearer-interpreters, a consciousness that is effectively historically structured and that is, therefore, not identical with that of any other hearer-interpreter. Every authentic hearing and interpretation of the Good News are, for Sandra Schneiders, a unique actualization of meaning, in which the text functions like a musical composition. A musical composition cannot be performed except with a genuine fidelity to the score, but it will be performed differently by each artist; and both the fidelity and the originality of the particular performance increase in proportion to the educated talent of the artist.[9] Heidegger remarks that Beethoven's Quartets, in their pure, unsullied, unplayed "thingness," "lie in the storerooms of publishing houses like potatoes in a cellar."[10] For the Quartets to exist in their fullness they must be played, but the "thingly" or given nature of the physical score remains normative for the musician and for her or his performance. The player's performance is always judged by the score and by the history of the interpretation of the piece. The interpretations of the exegete and the lived-out interpretations of each Christian believer remain always under the judgment of the text and of the living tradition of faith (the life story) of the Church. It is the whole Judeo-Christian revelation as lived in the Judeo-Christian communities of believers that tells us that the Parable of the Good Shepherd does not mean that God prefers evil people to good ones. And it is the same tradition (the life story of the Church) that validates the interpretation of the text as a statement about the saving identity of God as self-giving Love for all.[11]

The Constitution of the United States was composed by persons whose names we know. Nevertheless we do not read it as the thought of Benjamin Franklin or George Washington but as the foundational document, the common property and possession of a community, the United States of America. Ultimately, the Constitution can be understood only as the collective expression of a people. It is theirs because they have accepted it and have endeavored to live by it. The correct interpretation of its meaning is not the prerogative of the historical or political exegete (valuable though his or her contributions will be) but the prerogative of a Supreme Court that interprets in the light of the American experience the meaning of a particular passage in the life story of the American people. The court's authority as the source of definitive interpretations derives both from the Constitution itself and from the prestige and respect continuously granted to the court by the people. In an analogous fashion, the Scriptures function in the Church as the constitutional document. Scripture, taken as a whole, is a collective book. The names of some authors are known though, when the whole editorial history is considered, the authorship of the whole corpus is for the most part unknown. The canonicity of the Scriptures, that which makes each separate piece a part of Scripture and not merely a letter written by Paul or a history composed by Luke, is the judgment of the living community. The interpretation of the meaning of a particular passage is not exclusively a matter for the exegete in ascertaining, if it is indeed possible, the thought of the

Gospel writer, but ultimately lies in the Supreme Court of the ecclesial community.

7.33 *The tradition of the Church is the life story of Christians.*

As in other communities, the tradition of the Christian Church is
not merely a question of uncritical acceptance of customs and habits merely because they are customs and habits. The tradition of
the Christian Church is the continuous presence of the same Spirit.
The principle of continuity between generations of Christians, the
principle of Christian unity, is the gift of God's love that has been
poured into our hearts by the gift of his Holy Spirit (Rom. 5:5). The
Church is a communion of saints, that is, a communion of those
whose hearts have been filled with the Spirit of God's Love. The
tradition of the Christian community—its life story—results from
the outer communication of Christ's message (the suprastructure
of Christian belief) and from the inner gift of God's love (the infrastructure of faith).[12]
Tradition involves a doctrine. That which God communicates to
his Son, the Son in turn communicates to his disciples so that they
may communicate it in their turn throughout the generations. To
translate the infrastructure of Christian consciousness that unites
all believers on the prior level of faith into the explicit suprastructure that best objectifies that faith, is the ecumenical challenge.
Learning to live with the tensions that arise from an incomplete
translation is part of the Christian Way of the Cross.
Doctrinal tradition involves dogma: the decisions about how this
tradition is to be objectified as the norm for all subsequent objectifications. Tradition involves not the repetition of what John or
Paul said but the retelling of the story in such a way that subsequent generations may *"propriis cordibus ita propriis suis mentali-
tatibus ea credant quae suis credebant tum Paulus tum Ioannes."*[13]
That in which Paul and John believed and communicate as tradition is essentially the fellowship communicated by God's gift of the
Spirit, objectified in the life story of Jesus, and that binds the generations, separated by time, place, and culture, into one body.

Our message concerns that Word, who is life; what he was from
the first, what we have heard about him, what our own eyes
have seen of him; what it was that met our gaze, and the touch
of our hands. Yes, life dawned; and it is as eyewitnesses that we
give you news of that life, that eternal life, which ever abode

with the Father and has dawned, now, on us. This message about what we have seen and heard we pass on to you, so that you too may share in our fellowship. What is it, this fellowship of ours? Fellowship with the Father, and with his Son Jesus Christ. (1 Jn. 1:1 – 3)

The story of the Church is basically the story of a fellowship that is served by its Scriptures, doctrines, sacraments, structures, ministry, rites, laws, and customs, and formed in response to God's gift of his love in Jesus Christ and his Spirit given to us. Catholic teaching affirms the unity between the Church that transmits revelation and the revelation that is transmitted in the Church.[14] The story of the Church (its tradition) is manifested in and, thereby communicated, by its being a fellowship of the Holy Spirit. The history of the Church is its success and failure in responding to that gift of fellowship in the concrete and particular lives of its members.

We live within the Church tradition or story before we objectivize it. We are consciously participating in the fellowship of the Church before we have knowledge of it. The Church's self-knowledge is articulated in its doctrines, and by its councils it brings its experience to judgment. The Church is a communion that exists to bring all persons into communion (fellowship) with God and thereby to open them to communication with one another. Its tradition or life story, is both a communion and a communication. The community exists in order to communicate its message; and its message is that salvation is participation in its community. The fellowship of the Church is perhaps the best example of a rather tired slogan: The medium is the message. The Church's task is communication—*communi-catio*—the making or bringing into being of communion. The story of the Church is the story of the success and failure of its mission to bring about the explicit communion of all men and women in the embrace of God's universal love.

1. Bernard Lonergan, "Transcendental Philosophy and the Study of Religion," Lectures at Boston College, 1968, p. 3.20.
2. The historian's history, critical and scientifically sober, is often of far less account in the commonly accepted history of a people than what people thought happened but the historian knows did not.
3. Cf. Bernard Lonergan, *Method in Theology* (London: Darton, Longman & Todd, 1971), pp. 235ff.
4. Cf. Michael Polanyi, *Personal Knowledge: Towards a Post-Critical Philosophy* (London: Routledge and Kegan Paul, 1968), pp. 348ff.
5. The treatment of Mesmer by the scientific community is a reminder that the judgment of the scientific community is not infallible; *mutatis mutandis*, the caution that such ex-

amples should arouse in us, must be applied to analogous situations in the life of the Church.

6. Bernard Lonergan, *Method in Theology,* pp. 161–162.

7. Scientific theorems can never be definitively validated but, to be scientific, must always remain open to the possibility of falsification. However, it must be well noted that every experiment that fails to work is not prima facie overwhelming evidence for the invalidity of the hypothesis. Extraneous factors may have affected the result. If I set up an experiment to prove Boyle's law and the experiment fails, I presume that I have set the experiment up wrongly, not that Boyle's law must be immediately revised. The corporate experience and judgment of the scientific community condition what I will expect to happen and act as the *Vorverständnis* for my interpreting my own experiment. The recognition of sin within the Christian community is not an immediate reason for rejection of the Christian tradition.

8. David Lockhead, "Hermeneutics and Ideology," *The Ecumenist* 15 (1977), pp. 83–84.

9. Sandra M. Schneiders, "Faith, Hermeneutics, and the Literal Sense of Scripture," *Theological Studies* 39 (1978) pp. 734–735.

10. Heidegger, *The Origin of the Work of Art,* trans. Albert Hofstadter, in Albert Hofstadter and Richard Kuhns, eds., *Philosophies of Art and Beauty* (New York: Modern Library, 1964) p. 651.

11. Schneiders, *op. cit.,* p. 733.

12. Bernard Lonergan, *Method in Theology,* p. 361.

13. Id, *De Deo Trino II: Pars systematica seu Divinarum personarum conceptio analogica (editio tertia et recognita)* (Rome: Gregorian University Press, 1964), p. 10.

14. Dogmatic Constitution *Dei Verbum* 8.

CHAPTER 11

THE EIGHTH MOMENT:

The Jesus story reveals that human beings are ever to be "surprised by joy"

Hope springs eternal in the human breast;
Man never is, but always to be blest.

An Essay on Man
Alexander Pope

Surprised by joy—impatient as the wind
I turned to share the transport.

William Wordsworth

8.1 *The Gospel stories witness the amazing quality of God's grace.*

Archimedes, it is said, jumped from his bath and ran naked through the streets of Syracuse, shouting "Eureka! I've got it!" New discoveries, even if afterward they become commonplace and obvious, fill their discoverers with a surprised elation. What is true of the intellectual life is true also of the life of grace. The sudden understanding that we have been graced can be likened to the moment of insight. Conversion in its first moment can be likened to the moment of insight; we understand and judge that we have been loved. We are amazed that the One whom our heart has always, wittingly or unwittingly, sought, the One whom the Litany calls the desire of the eternal hills, the One who is obscurely sensed in every act of willing and desiring and loving and knowing, loves us.

The Gospel stories are witness to the amazing quality, the surprising nature of God's gift of his love. In his narrative of the Annunciation to Mary, Luke shows us the mother of Jesus as one surprised. "How can this come about," she asks, "since I am a virgin?" (Lk. 1:34). At the Visitation, Luke speaks of Elizabeth as one who has been surprised by joy: "As soon as Elizabeth heard Mary's greeting, the child leapt in her womb," and she tells Mary that the child's leaping was caused by joy (Lk. 1:41, 44). At the birth of

Jesus, Luke tells us that those who heard the shepherds' story were astonished at what they had heard (Lk. 2:18). As Luke draws his Gospel of the infancy to a close he speaks of those who heard Christ in the temple being astounded at his intelligence and replies (Lk. 2:47).

At the start of Jesus' public ministry, Luke records him as preaching in the synagogue of his home town. "And he won the approval of all, and they were astonished by the gracious words that came from his lips" (Lk. 4:22). Again in the synagogue at Capernaum we are told that Christ's hearers were seized with astonishment (Lk. 4:36). Those who witnessed miracles of healing "were all astounded . . . saying, 'We have seen strange things today' " (Lk. 5:26).

It is not only the secondary characters of Christ's story who are characterized as surprised by what they hear and see. The central character, Jesus himself, is portrayed as astounded, amazed, surprised, and overjoyed by the marvelous, wonderful works of God. Luke tells us that he was astonished at the faith of the centurion whose servant lay sick (Lk. 7:9). When the seventy-two return, astonished that even the devils submit to their invocation of Christ's name, Luke pictures Jesus as sharing their joy and amazement: "It was then that, filled with joy by the Holy Spirit, he said, 'I bless you, Father, Lord of heaven and earth, for hiding these things from the learned and the clever and revealing them to mere children' " (Lk. 10:17 – 21). The story of Jesus as told by the Gospel writers, especially Luke, discloses the universal story, the story of every man and every woman, as a story of amazing and unexpected grace.

8.2 *Christ's story of the Good Samaritan challenges our a priori assumptions about the mode in which God will reveal himself to us.*

On the modern road from Jerusalem to Jericho the bus driver will point out to the tourist-pilgrims the traditional site of the Inn of the Good Samaritan. Without departing in so Fundamentalist a way from our duty not to read our own concerns into Scripture, it is perhaps not illegitimate to consider Christ's parable from a broader base than strict exegesis might allow.

The polemical needs of the evangelists, especially of John, have perhaps colored too black the picture we should have of the Pharisees, the Scribes, the Priests, and the Levites. The history of the Church certainly teaches us that Christian prejudice can easily misread the Gospel and engender an anti-Semitism blasphemous in one who acknowledges a Jew to be the very Son of God. On the other hand, those who rightly seek to redress the balance and to recover for Christians the riches of their Judaic inheritance can often seem to err in the opposite direction. To be unable to accept any criticism of another religion and to have nothing but condemnation for the history of one's own are as unchristian and uncritical as to have nothing but condemnation for another's religion and to have nothing but praise for one's own. An ability to see the warts and the good points of Judaism and Christianity is a necessary prerequisite for being able to enter the world of first-century Judaism and for relating that world to our own. No one can come to the understanding of a story with an "empty head," allowing the text to "speak for itself." All interpretation of a text or story presupposes our own experience of life and storytelling. Our Christian-Catholic experience of what it is to be a member of a church allows us to understand something of what it would be to be a member of a synagogue. If that is not true, then it is impossible, humanly speaking, for Jesus' experience of being formed by the synagogue to say anything to our experience of being formed by the Church.

The Priest and the Levite were not necessarily bad people. In a poem about Eichmann, Leonard Cohen beautifully expresses the ordinariness of evil.

ALL THERE IS TO KNOW
ABOUT ADOLPH EICHMANN
EYES: .... Medium
HAIR: .... Medium
WEIGHT: .... Medium
HEIGHT: .... Medium
DISTINGUISHING FEATURES: .... None
NUMBER OF FINGERS: .... Ten
NUMBER OF TOES: .... Ten
INTELLIGENCE: .... Medium
What did you expect?
Talons?
Oversize incisors?
Green saliva?
Madness?[1]

Eichmann's story illustrates Hannah Arendt's "sheer banality of evil," the unintelligibility of sin. It is a crucial mistake to think that the Priest and Levite of Christ's story were some kind of monsters. They were probably no better and no worse than the average Catholic priest and deacon. To think that the evils of Nazi Germany or those that can afflict organized religion "couldn't happen here among such nice people" is one sure way of making it possible that they will.

A Catholic priest might leave his church taking Communion to the sick. He passes a person sitting on a wall. He doesn't give that person a second look; he is intent on taking God to a housebound person. He doesn't notice, because he doesn't properly look, that the one sitting down has been taken ill and is in need of attention. Even if he did notice he might presume that someone had already called the ambulance and proceed on his way to perform his spiritual duties. The point of Jesus' parable is not to give us an exact agenda for dealing with all situations in life but to act as an image for understanding the amazing quality of grace. At the end of the story in the Gospel, Jesus asks his listener, "Which of these three (the Priest, the Levite, and the Samaritan), do you think, proved himself a neighbor to the man who fell into the brigands' hands?" The answer, of course, was the Samaritan (Lk. 10:36 – 37). Jesus' question suggests another question: Where was God disclosed? Much popular preaching centers upon the extraordinariness of its being a Samaritan, a heretic and foreigner, who showed (God's) love when the professional men of religion did not. The power of the parable lies in the hearers being led to expect that the holy men would show mercy and being surprised that God's love was mediated through an unexpected person. This is to see the events from the point of view of the injured man. Salvation comes to him from an unexpected source. If we make a Copernican revolution and view the events through the eyes of the three passers-by, then we can ask where it was that these travelers hoped to find God. A certain type of religious mentality, a mentality that looks for God in the extraordinary and strange and that institutionalizes the extraordinary and strange in a churchy image of God, misses the presence of God in the ordinary things and events of life, which to that person seem an extraordinary and unexpected locus for God's self-revealing activity. The Samaritan found God in the ordinary and even banal sight of an injured man lying crumpled in the road. Humankind is well practiced in the art of imagining a priori the ways and possibilities through which God may mediate his grace. We dictate to God that he will communicate with us, and that he could communicate with us only in this particular style of church building, or through this particular style of liturgical worship, or through people who behave in this particular kind of way, or through this particular religion or religious community, or through this particular book or author. We can so expect to find God in church or synagogue, in the reading of the Torah or the recitation of the breviary, in the pronouncements of the chief rabbi or the homilies of the pope, that we miss his presence in the little ones who claim a cup of water.[2]

The story of the Good Samaritan stands as a powerful symbol of the unexpectedness of the places and the people through whom God will speak to us. It implies that we can never be sure where and when the goodness and the loveliness of God will enter into our lives. The offer of redemptive friendship is always an amazing grace; a grace so amazing and unexpected that it transcends any of the a priori conditions for its possibility that humankind can imagine.

1. Leonard Cohen, *Selected Poems 1956–1968* (London: Johnathan Cape, 1969), p. 122.
2. Thomas Cooper, "On Praying to God in English," *The Clergy Review* 65 (1980), pp. 41–51, esp. p. 49.

CHAPTER 12

THE NINTH MOMENT:

The Blessed Trinity and Undivided Unity of God is the beginning, the middle, and the end of all our storytelling

Tout beauté créée est un reflet de la splendeur trinitaire, comme une irradiation de sa gloire.

La Trinité et le mystère de l'esistance
Cardinal Daniélou

*9.1 **The mystery of the Blessed Trinity and Undivided Unity, symbolically present in human consciousness, points to God as the deepest fulfillment of the human spirit.***

In an article first published in 1942, C. G. Jung subjected the Christian doctrine of the Trinity to a psychological analysis.[1] Approaching the Trinitarian dogma from the viewpoint of analytical psychology and not from a theological perspective, Jung attempted to show by a comparison with other religious and psychological symbols, the essential incompleteness, from the standpoint of psychological symbolism, of a threefold symbol for the Godhead. In Jungian thought the process of individuation, the growth of mental, moral, and emotional maturity in the human person, was incomplete without a resolution of what he termed the problem of the fourth. From his study of the imagery found in art, alchemy, gnostic speculations, contemporary dreams, and the like, Jung argued that the quaternity, a fourfold symbol, was the best symbolic representation of the wholeness and integrity of the God image. As a consequence he welcomed the dogmatic definition of the Assumption as paving the way for the recognition of Mary's divinity and as a step toward finding a more satisfying symbol for the Godhead than that of the Trinity.[2]

Even a passing acquaintance with the problematic of Nicaea and with the Augustinian psychological analogy would be enough to show up what Moreno has called the deep cleavage between the Christian dogmatic truth on the Trinity and Jung's psychological approach.³ Nevertheless it is a mistake to parallel the methodologies of classical Christian theology and Jungian psychology, as Moreno does, as though they were rival methods for investigating the same phenomenon. Jung was not engaged in writing theology, as he frequently explicitly states, and it would be a mistake to dismiss Jung's argument out of hand as though it had nothing to teach the theologian about the way in which the mystery of God is apprehended by and responded to by the psyche. The psychological analogy of classical Nicene theology is an attempt to achieve a fruitful if imperfect understanding of the facts of revelation. Jung's psychological analysis of the Trinity is an attempt to achieve an understanding of the pictorial representation of the Trinity as it is found in art and dreams. The fact that St. Patrick thought he had found an analogy between a shamrock and the Trinity would still be of interest to the historian of catechesis even if the theologian pronounced it more misleading than helpful. It is a mistake to set up the psychological analogy of Augustine and Aquinas and the depth psychological approach of Jung as an either-or choice. If, as Lonergan maintains, one must practice introspective rational psychology if one is to understand what Aquinas conceived the created image of the Trinity to be, one must also practice depth psychology to uncover the meaning of Jung.⁴

Insofar as one rigorously excludes all vestiges of dualistic thinking and refuses to restrict the created image of the Trinity to a "ghost in a machine," one must allow for the possibility of images of the Trinity at all levels of human consciousness. If the inanimate firmament can remind the psalmist of God, then it is arbitrary to exclude the possibility that images of God may be present in the inchoatively conscious visions of the night. Christian tradition has not hesitated to see in the sexual division of the human race a *vestigium vitae Trinitatis.*⁵ However profound and nuanced one's understanding of the analogy between the inner word of the intellect and the procession of the Second Person, it remains an analogy. Our knowledge of God remains an imperfect knowledge. *Magis similitudo, magis dissimilitudo.* One cannot a priori rule out, as some theological critiques of Jung appear to do, that an image of God on the psychic level might be imperfect. It would, on the contrary, be in line with the Scholastic notion of a hierarchy of being to expect that the image of God as mirrored in the psychic and emotional life of human beings would be less perfect as an image than the image of God as mirrored by the intellectual and volitional levels of human consciousness.

Jung claims to have found in all triform images and symbols a human need to complete the symbol by the addition of a fourth. In the Christian Trinitarian image of God he claims to have uncovered a psychic need to complete that image by the addition of a fourth, specifically Mary, the Mother of God. Moreno rightly points out that the spontaneous images produced by the psyche, dreams, and symbols, "express psychic needs, not necessarily the nature of God."[6] While the classical Trinitarian theology starts from the *quoad nos* and proceeds to the *quoad se*, it nevertheless remains an expression of God as conceived by a finite human mind. Furthermore, God's revelation of Himself as Father, Son, and Spirit remains always a truth revealed *propter nos et propter nostram salutem*. If God's revelation is a revelation of truth in and to human minds, then its expression must, if it is to be heard, be in some way proportionate to the minds that hear it. God's revelation is always a call to union. An image of God that is imperfect and that calls for completion is not by the fact of its imperfection alone to be considered as expressing a mere psychic need and not in some way the nature of God.

If we accept Jung's psychological findings as more or less correct, it would seem perfectly orthodox to see in the imperfection (in human psychic terms) of the number three a revelation of God as the term of a human process of growth. Insofar as Mary is the archetype of the perfect Christian, the one portrayed by Luke as a hearer and doer of the Word, and insofar as every Christian is called to share in the divine nature of him who shared our humanity, it is perhaps possible to see the Mother of God as an archetypal symbol for the self. In such a case, the Jungian understanding of the psychological implications of the Trinitarian dogma can be interpreted as the felt unease of the human self when it is not united to the Godhead. The psychological incompleteness of the Trinitarian symbol would then be understood as the resonance on the psychic level of the natural desire to see God; it would be the felt restlessness of an Augustine who knew that God had made him for himself. Insofar as the Jungian hypothesis has validity, it can be seen as a pointer to God's creation of the human listener as incomplete and as satisfied only by a listening to and a sharing in the story told by God. God so creates the hearer that he or she is perfectly realized only as the hearer of God's tale. God reveals himself symbolically in such a wise that he draws all men and women to himself.

9.2 **The human experience of telling and listening to stories provides a fruitful if imperfect analogy for the Blessed and Undivided Trinity.**

Men and women delight to tell stories. They put themselves into
their stories.[7] When the teller tells a story well, his or her listeners
hear not only the words of the story but the storyteller's own story
too. Christ is the story of God. To have heard Christ is to have heard
the Father (cf. Jn. 14:8f). At the end of his life on earth Jesus was
able to say, "Father, I have made your Name [that is your person]
known" (Jn. 17:6). Christ has not only made known the Name of the
Father but also promises that he will continue to make it known
(Jn. 17:26). The Father tells the story and his story is the Son. In
the letter to the Church at Colossae, Paul speaks of Christ as the
icon of the Father (1:15) and immediately goes on to point out that
the Church is the body of which Christ is the head (1:18). To have
seen Christ is to have seen the Father, and to have seen the Church
is to have seen Christ. The community of believers, a body inseparable from its head, as the branch is from the vine, is the icon, the
image, the story told by Christ. John records Jesus as promising the
gift of his Spirit: "the Holy Spirit, whom the Father will send in
my name, will teach you everything and remind you of all I have
said to you" (Jn. 14:26). The Spirit will call to our minds the story
as told by Christ. A few verses before, John links for us the storytelling of Christ and the storytelling of the Church. The words that
Christ speaks are not his own words, but it is the Father living and
working in him (Jn. 14:10). In Jesus the Father is the storyteller.
Those who believe in Jesus, who authentically hear his story and
keep it, will not only tell the tale themselves but will also perform
"even greater works" (Jn. 14:12). The Church will be an even
greater teller of the story than Christ.

In the First Letter of John, the writer tells the story as told by
Christ. "What we have seen and heard we are telling you" (1 Jn.
1:3). Why does he tell the story? To make our joy complete (1 Jn.
1:4). We delight, take joy, in a story well told. The Ancient Mariner
delighted to tell his story. Coleridge delighted to tell the story. The
Ancient Mariner and Coleridge are one. When an actor recites the
story, he becomes that Ancient Mariner and he becomes Coleridge.
He delights to tell the tale. We, the audience, are enraptured by the
tale as it is told well. The delight and joy of Coleridge and the actor
in telling the tale are communicated to their audience. So rapt do

we become that for the space of the story we too become the Ancient Mariner. At the origin of every story there is delight. Hopkins put it well in his sonnet "To R. B."

> The fine delight that fathers thought: the strong
> Spur, live and lancing like the blowpipe flame,
> Breathes once and, quenchèd faster than it came,
> Leaves yet the mind a mother of immortal song.[8]

The singer is in the song, and the same delight and joy fill the singer as the song, and those sung to. The rhythm of the singer's voice communicates itself to the dancing and tapping feet of the listeners. We beat time to the music, and joyously we join the song. "You are the music, while the music lasts."[9] In a prayer attributed to St. Ambrose and printed in the *Missale Romanum* of Pius V, the priest is bidden to prepare himself to celebrate the mysteries by asking the Father to send the Holy Spirit.

> Let your good Spirit enter my heart, there to utter his silent music, his wordless declaration of all truth.[10]

The Spirit of God is the joy that inspires the Father to tell the Story. He is the joy that fills the Story told. He is the joy that fills that same Story told when it is expressed *ad extra* in the Story-made-Flesh, the Story told in another medium. He is the joy that fills the hearers as they listen to the Story and make that Story their own. He is the expectation of hidden delights that makes us listen to the Story. He is the joy in the telling that keeps us fascinated by the tale. He is the joy that quietly fills our hearts with a satisfaction too deep for words. He is the joy that bids us join in the telling.

Eliot wrote of being the music "while the music lasts." Christ promises at the end of Matthew's Gospel that he will be with us to the end of the age. Unlike the drama of Aristotle's *Poetics*, God's Story has no beginning, no middle, and no end, though it brings about the unity of all times and all places. God's music never stops; it lasts forever. The same joy fills the Teller, the Tale, and the told. We who hear become the Teller and the Tale for as long as the music lasts, and the music lasts forever. In the experience of telling and listening to stories, imperfectly but fruitfully we enter the mystery of God.

9.3 *The interpersonal dynamics of the life story of Jesus Christ as disclosed in his life of universal friendship function as a fruitful model for understanding the interpersonal dynamics of our life in Christ.*

When the liturgy is celebrated according to the Byzantine usage, the faithful, immediately after making their Holy Communion, confess the Trinity as the source of their salvation: "We have found the true faith, worshipping the undivided Trinity. This has saved us." This accords with the story of Christ's last discourse as told by John: "Eternal life is this: to know you, the only true God, and Jesus Christ whom you have sent" (Jn. 17:3). Salvation can be described as the revelation of God as the Community that founds and undergrounds the community of humankind, so that, in an apt sixteenth-century expression, the Church becomes a Christian commonweal where faith is experienced as interpersonal, as the response to an offer of universal friendship. Since grace builds on and perfects nature, sublating the interpersonal, relational nature of human existence into the higher context of a participation in the interpersonal, relational nature of God, it will be as well if we briefly turn aside from our discussion of the Trinitarian nature of the life of the Christian community to consider the dynamics of Christ's human life insofar as they can be a model for our own before returning to the main theme of our ninth moment.

For the Christian the human life of Jesus Christ must be the norm and pattern and model of all Christian and, indeed, human life. We are to model ourselves on Paul, as he modeled himself on Christ (1 Cor. 11:1). Emile Mersch, in his seminal work *The Whole Christ*, affirmed that the manner of being that God willed for humankind was an

> *esse in Christo*, an existence in Christ. Human ontology, viewed in its origins, was in reality a supernatural ontology, an ontology of members destined to be joined together in a body.

In a luminous phrase, Mersch goes on to declare that "we have existence in order that we may become members of the Savior."[11]

If, as Karl Rahner asserts, the humanity of Jesus is of eternal significance for his fellow-humans, then all that we can discover of the way in which Jesus lived a fully human life will provide precious pointers to the way in which we are called to live out our human life stories precisely as *human* life stories.[12]

Certain modern critics find that the Christ of St. John is not a living Christ. The reason is that they view Him through a metaphysical theorem. In reality . . . [John's] Man-God is supremely alive. We see Him weary; we sense His indignation; we can even feel the tears welling to his eyes. . . . Throughout the Fourth Gospel we are put into contact with the very interior of Jesus, with His life, with his "Ego."

However, this "Ego" is not one of those narrow, ever-hateful personalities of which Pascal speaks. Rendered imposing by the very qualities that make it invading, it takes its rightful place within every man. This is the marvel, and for some, the mystery and the scandal of the "Johannine" Gospel. This Jesus, whose history it traces, whose actions and psychology it portrays with perfect clearness, is at the same time and without contradiction, a mystical reality. That is, while He is supremely alive in Himself, He is also living within us.[13]

Explicitly invoking these texts of Mersch in his support, the psychiatrist Frank Lake has extrapolated from the Fourth Gospel what he believes should be the model for the healthy development of the human personality.[14] While the construction in the human sciences of any model as normative for human behavior is fraught with great dangers, the alternative of a purely statistical description of how human beings in general behave (if, indeed, such a "pure" description is in fact possible) would be of little practical use, especially if Fromm is correct in asserting the possibility that a whole population can be pathologically disturbed. Lake's procedure is, in effect, little different in principle from Freud's use of his self-analysis in *The Interpretation of Dreams* to construct a general theoretical understanding of human psychic mechanisms.

Lake identifies four basic stages in the development of the human personality. The first two stages (input) concern acceptance and growth. The last two stages (output) concern status and achievement. These four stages make up what Lake calls the dynamic cycle of being and well-being that arises out of and expresses presumptively normal personal relationships in infancy and in later years.

The emergence of selfhood and the capacity to transcend one's self in giving to another is conditioned by one's status, that is, by the concepts and ideals that one has of oneself and for oneself. If I lack confidence in myself as a person, in my capacity to give and to be of service to others, then I will be impaired in my giving to and servicing of others. This status (who I believe myself to be) is in turn conditioned by the two prior stages of input. The personal source (mother, father, family, society) comes down to me in my need and accepts me. This acceptance is characterized by Lake as the "primary ontological requirement" for all human development. Without acceptance by significant others (parental others), the baby dies, if not physically, at least emotionally and spiritually. The parental other not only must accept the developing personality but must also sustain it. "Whoever *enjoys* relationships of a generous and gracious kind is enhanced by them in his power of 'being.'" Having achieved status I am then able to achieve in the self-transcendence of accepting and sustaining others. This achievement in its own turn reinforces my acceptance by others (my "parents," those who "bear" me up), and the circuit is thus complete.

Having set up his model, Lake then applies it to the life of Jesus as portrayed in the Gospel of John. Lake concentrates exclusively on the Father-Son relationship, whereas in the following we broaden the model to include reference to the Spirit. The Spirit might be viewed, from the point of view of our analogy, as somewhat analogous to the internalization of the father, of his life, acceptance, and sustenance, by the growing personality.

Jesus is accepted by the Father. At his baptism God affirms him to be his beloved Son (synoptic accounts; the Baptist sees the Spirit come down on Christ, Jn. 1:32ff); such a birth through water is also a birth through the Spirit (Jn. 3:5). Christ knows himself to be acceptable to the Father because he has constant access to the Father in prayer (Jn. 11:41f). The Father sustains the Son by his giving him the Spirit without reserve (Jn. 3:34); Christ's sustenance, his meat and drink, is to do the will of the Father; he has food to eat that the "world" knows nothing about (Jn. 4:32ff). The Father sustains the Son in love by showing him all that he does (Jn. 5:20). Because he has been accepted and sustained, Jesus is able to pronounce more fully than others the words, "I am." This self-confidence in his own identity, this security that is the fruit of the Father's gift of the Spirit, allows the Son to remain confident of his own status when it is questioned by others: "You are from below; I am from above" (Jn. 8:23); his opponents are wrong to accuse him of blasphemy because he says "I am the Son of God" (Jn. 10:36). He is the light of the world, the bread of life, the good shepherd, the Resurrection and the life. From the fullness of his status as Son of the Father, Christ has achieved the completion of the work God gave him to do (Jn. 17:4); that is, the Father who is the source of life has made his Son the source of life for others (Jn. 5:20), from his breast flow the living waters that well up to eternal life (Jn. 4:13f; 8:37f): the Spirit that those who believe in him were to receive (Jn. 8:39). Because he had achieved the work he was given to do, the cycle of being and well-being is completed by the Father's giving glory to the Son (Jn. 17:5).

Such a model for the essential relatedness of human subjects functions as a useful corrective to the overemphasis on the intellectual that seems to many to mar the account of the relationship between the commonsense dramatic patterns of living and theory given by Bernard Lonergan, an account, incidentally, that Lake considers to be the "most competent study" he knows.[15]

In considering the model of Christ's relationship to God outlined above, it would be easy to fall into the trap of privatizing the human experience of Christ, and thence the Christian's, by considering the words of Christ recorded by John as exclusively the outer expressions (outer word) of an interior, ineffable experience (inner word) communicated directly by God to the human soul of Christ. Lake guards against such a privatization by remarking that

> although the "kenosis," or "humbling," involved our Lord in laying aside all the trappings of kingship and much else besides, this did not include the ultimate kenosis of being born in a brothel from a sluttish woman who would bring Him up to know the seamy side of infancy. Tradition affirms the special holiness and godliness of the Blessed Virgin Mary. From this it is not unreasonable to infer that God the Father was making provision for His Son's human spirit to come to "being" and "well-being" by response to a woman whose character was like His Own, in loving kindness, holiness, and graciousness. Can we then regard the Godlike mothering of Jesus Christ as a normal pattern and expect to find that divergences from it in the direction of unloving or unGodlike behavior toward the child will cause disturbances and distortions of the nascent spirit within the foundation years?[16]

Frank Sheed remarked somewhere that Mary, like any human parent, had to teach her Son about God. In teaching the Word to speak, she taught him how to verbalize his experience. Insofar as the ability to differentiate one thing from another is dependent upon our ability to call things by different names, insofar, that is, as language is essential to thought, thus far is it significant that it was other human beings, presumably chiefly Mary, who taught Christ the meaning of the words "Eli" and "Abba." In concentrating upon the theophanic aspects of the synoptic accounts of the baptism—the Father's voice, the descent of the dove—we must not overlook the fact that John the Baptist was chosen to be the means whereby Christ would be submerged in the Jordan.

Lonergan adverts us to the universal and often irritating habit of children asking an unending series of questions.[17] But, as Bartholemew Kiely rightly points out, there is more to life than a desire to raise questions.[18] While this was being written, the final redactor interrupted his task, to celebrate the Eucharist. A young child who has just learned to talk and whose mother brings him with her to daily mass spent the whole time, as is his custom, calling out "daddy, daddy." After mass the priest, who had noticed over the weeks that this seemed to be the only word the child knew, asked if that were so. The little boy's mother replied that he did know some other words but that "daddy" was by far his favorite. When a child moves from infancy with the discovery of language, his or her first activity is not usually to ask questions but to call out to mother or father, that is, to express a relationship. The use of language to express the stirrings of love is prior to the use of language to inquire about the nature of the world. When Lonergan affirms that God's gift of his love is at the heart of religious conversion, he appears to overlook the way that this gift is given to us. John's insight is valid in both directions: if I cannot feel loved by the other I can see, how can I feel loved by the other I cannot see? Christ's way of being with his disciples was such that it gave rise to one of them earning the title "the beloved disciple." Christ's experience of human friendship was not accidental to his ability to become the efficacious symbol of God's offer of universal friendship to the whole human race.[19] In Christian conversion God's gift of his love is communicated in and through a community. During his conversion experience on the road to Damascus, Saul is told to go into the city where he will be told—by a human person—what he must do (Acts 9:6; 22:10). That human person was to be characterized by Paul's speech to the Jews of Jerusalem as one who was "a devout follower of the Law and highly thought of" (Acts 22:12). Paul was then instructed to waste no time and be baptized, that is, submit himself to the sacramental practice of the community (Acts 22:16). As Mersch affirms:

The incorporation of mankind in Christ is, before all else, a work of unity: unity of all men with God, unity of all men among themselves . . . .[20]

Lonergan's proper appreciation of the precariousness of human intellectual and moral development, the difficulties that stand in the way of intellectual, moral, and religious conversion, seems to have blinded him to the essential role that the community plays in the concrete experience of falling in love with God. His keen awareness of the universality of general bias has, as its dark side, the scotoma of neglecting the role of the group and human society in aiding what Lake calls the "potentially isolated and, as such, anxious individual" to escape from intellectual, moral, and religious alienation from God. If the accounts of the Exodus, surely one of the most privileged images for conversion, suggest a motley crew of stiff-necked and irritating people finding salvation together, the account of conversion given by Lonergan, profound and important though it is, seems more like the emergence of a single, beautiful butterfly from its chrysalis, or the unfolding of a single bud from a self-pollinating tree. Those who are *actually* in love with God (sacramentally making the sacred, transcendent Love present to us in endlessly surprising and encouraging ways) seem to have little or no part in Lonergan's explanation of the prior word of religious conversion. There is a strange paradox in Lonergan's achievement. While he has been in the forefront of those who have understood the historically conditioned nature of the objectification of faith in its outer word, nevertheless, the inner communication of that word, the gift of God's love flooding our hearts, has been privatized and abstracted from the concrete, social relationships in which we live, move, and have our being. In *Method in Theology* Lonergan writes:

Before it enters the world mediated by meaning, religion is the prior word God speaks to us by flooding our hearts with his love. That prior word pertains, not to the world mediated by meaning, but to the world of immediacy, to the unmediated experience of the mystery of love and awe. The outwardly spoken word is *historically* conditioned: its meaning depends upon the human context in which it is uttered, and such contexts vary from place to place and from one generation to another. But the prior word in its immediacy, though it differs in intensity, though it resonates differently in different temperaments and in different stages of religious development, *withdraws man from the diversity of history* by moving out of the world mediated by meaning and towards a world of immediacy in which image and symbol, thought and word, lose their relevance and even disappear.[21]

Lonergan here distinguishes the prior and interior word of God, spoken within the intimacy of the human mind and heart from the subsequent and exterior word; only the latter is historical. Lonergan here falsely assumes that the subject of Christian conversion is in some way transhistorically in a community-transcending relationship with God prior to the expression of the interior word to the community in objectivized exterior speech. One must ask whether there can be an unmediated experience of love. The baby at the breast may not be able to objectivize in words his or her experience of being loved and may well feel at one with the mother's body so that any division into *I* and *Thou* has not yet appeared; nevertheless, whatever the baby is experiencing is most certainly being mediated by the body of the mother. When mother is absent, the baby cries. Although Lonergan correctly affirms the inescapable concreteness and singularity of the good, nevertheless, when treating of the interior word of conversion, he illegitimately abstracts from the concrete, particular, and social nature of all our responses to value.

Classical Catholic theology, when speaking of the baptism of desire, understood that a man or woman could be saved by "extraordinary means." He or she could do the truth and do the good even though they had not been granted to hear the exterior word of the Gospel. The "anonymous Christian", to use Rahner's term, is not someone who, cut off from the ordinary means of salvation in the Christian community, is thereby someone cut off from all community. Rather, the justified man or woman who has not heard the Gospel is someone who has remained faithful to the demands of a conscience (whether erroneous or not) that has been shaped by his or her experience of the community in which he or she has been formed. Insofar as the anonymous Christian has experienced being loved and loving, she or he has been loved by someone and has loved someone in return. When Jesus spoke to the woman of Samaria he told her that her community worshiped what they did not know, whereas his own community worshiped what they did know (Jn. 4:22). In Lonerganian categories we may say that the same love of God (interior word) flooded the hearts of both Jew and Samaritan, whereas their exterior words about God were different. The

Samaritan woman was not a lonely individual possessed by a trans-historical, unmediated love but someone whose love had been mediated by her fathers who had "worshiped on this mountain," and perhaps one may legitimately wonder if her experience of having had five husbands was not totally unconnected with whatever love she had experienced!

If the interior gift of God's love resonates differently in different temperaments, as Lonergan asserts in the passage we have just quoted, then whatever side we take in the "nature versus nurture" controversy, we must remember that our temperaments are mediated and historically transmitted by our genes and our cultural traditions. An understanding of Christ's life story as a story growing out of the web of interpersonal relations that made up his community is essential for an understanding of our own life stories as Christians and for an understanding of the way in which our own life stories are incorporated into his universal life story.

9.4 *The interpersonal life of Jesus Christ—his relationships to God and to his fellow humans, to divine and to human persons—is the prime analogate for the Christian community's experience and understanding and judgment of its own interpersonal relationships with divine and human persons, and of the relationship between the universal story and the Blessed Trinity.*

Since the personal is interpersonal, we cannot grasp the significance of Jesus Christ apart from his relationships with the persons—both divine and human—who enter his life, *from* whom he receives his life, and *for* whom he gives his life. The life of Jesus Christ, like all interpersonal existence, is rooted in the giving and receiving of love, in knowing and being known, in reciprocal intercommunication between persons.

St. John of Damascus, in an ode sung every Easter night by the churches of the East, says of Christ:

> He was born a real man,
> and yet did not open the womb that remained virginal;
> He is the Lamb, and he is human;
> He is the All-Pure One because all-blameless;
> He is real because He is the very God.[22]

St. John affirms not only that Jesus Christ is really human, but also that he alone is really human because his humanity is united to the Godhead. In his sinlessness Jesus Christ discloses the perfection of what it is to be human. From the pages of Mark's Gospel Jesus puts the question to every Christian: "Why do you call me good? No one is good but God alone" (Mk. 10:18). In reply each Christian sings with Damascene:

> Let us adore the all-holy Lord Jesus,
> He alone is without sin.

Sin is the failure to be truly human because we are in some measure separated from God. Sin is the failure to be fully personal, culpably to fail to be related. Sin is lack of love. There is an impersonal quality to all sin and evil. The diabolic in its root meaning is something that tears apart. Real evil is uncannily impersonal.

A young mother of two small children, pregnant with her third baby and suffering from toxemia, called a priest to her house at midnight. The snow was quite thick upon the ground. She was a Catholic, and her husband, who had been an Anglican, had been converted to membership of an extreme Fundamentalist sect on the fringes of Christianity. All during her marriage she had had a crucifix in her home. Her husband had come to believe that the crucifix was a blasphemous idol and kept throwing it into the garbage can from where she would rescue it. She had been faced by an ultimatum that if she did not destory the crucifix she could leave that instant with her children. The ultimatum was presented yet again, in the presence of the priest, by the minister of her husband's newfound faith. What struck the priest about the minister was the coldness with which he presented his demands. Asked point blank whether he was prepared to see a seriously ill and pregnant mother and her two children put out on the street into the snow in the middle of the night, he answered, without a trace of emotion, that he was. There could be no compromise with idolatry. It is fortunately a rare experience, but it left on the priest's mind a lasting impression of the sheer impersonality of evil, the coldness of total uncompassion.

Ultimate human fulfillment is participation in the interpersonal life of Being-in-Love without limits. To be or not to be, for persons, is to be in love or not to be in love, to be personally related or not to be related. For Christians, the possibility of that boundless, limitless being in love is grounded in the incarnate Being-in-Love that communicates itself in the life and story of Jesus Christ.

Jesus Christ is an existing person whose interpersonal Love-Life embraces all persons, human and divine. His life is the integration of all the individual strands of loving relationships that go to make up the universal story with the interpersonal Love-Life of the Blessed Trinity. Human persons are free to accept or to reject the interpersonal Love-Life that He reveals and communicates as the integration of all persons, human and divine, in one life of interpersonal love and friendship whose eschatological fulfillment is the communion of saints in the Kingdom of God.

The Father sends his Son incarnate to incorporate the universal story into one body, its members relating one to the other; both the Father and Son send their Spirit to divinize all that the Son incorporates so that "God will be all in all" (1 Cor. 15:28). We are not alone, therefore, or left to ourselves; we belong to one another in the Son of God whose Spirit has been given to us. All persons, human and divine, ontologically belong to the interpersonal life of love that is Jesus Christ; all are interpersonal—have a personal love life—in and with him. Salvation and damnation, heaven and hell, imply respectively the acceptance or rejection, the love or hatred of the gift of God's all-embracing and integrating Love-Life, which Christians affirm to be Jesus Christ, the person whose interpersonal Love-Life is the community-creating revelation of God and of what he is doing for the universal story of humankind.

The Christian community exists where persons recognize and proclaim that the interpersonal Love-Life of Jesus Christ is their own; that they belong to him, to his Father, and to his Spirit with the intimacy of both friendship and family (cf. Jn. 15:15; 1 Jn. 3:1; Rom. 8:28f). The Christian missionary enterprise is based on the conviction that all human persons belong to the Blessed Trinity and that all are summoned to enter into the fullness of their interpersonal love and life in Jesus Christ and his community of sisters and brothers.

Jesus tells his disciples that belonging to the interpersonal Love-Life of God (Lk. 10:20) is a deeper motive for their rejoicing than whatever power they possess over evil: ". . . rather rejoice that your names are written in heaven." Luke envisions Jesus as *the* person whose interpersonal Love-Life embraces both the world of his Father in heaven and that of his disciples on earth. This is the ultimate basis of all Christian rejoicing. Our interpersonal life with Jesus Christ assures us of our interpersonal life with the Father; consequently, we should rejoice in knowing that we are loved by the Father, thanks to our life of friendship with his Son. This foundational experience communicates our assurance of our ultimate interpersonal fulfillment. In our interpersonal life with Jesus we hear the Word of God's love for us and for all who partake with us in the universal story. Our mutual love in Jesus Christ and his Spirit expresses our reception and acceptance of the interpersonal Love-Life of Jesus Christ with his Father and their Spirit.

Jesus Christ *is* an interpersonal Being insofar as he *is* Being-in-Love without restrictions in the Blessed Trinity.[23] He reveals interpersonal Life insofar as he is God's "Son, the Beloved," through whom the Holy Spirit of their Eternal Love-Life is given to enable all persons within the universal story to become interpersonal-beings-in-their-Love-Life. He communicates his interpersonal Life of Being-in-Love insofar as he historically invests himself in his disciples, in his Church, and in the universal human story. He is the subject of the Life that he receives from his Father and communicates through their Spirit to all humankind in order that all persons might become interpersonal beings-in-their-Love-Life. To accept Christ's life-story as our own is to enter into the interpersonal Love-Life of the Blessed Trinity, which embraces all humankind in its creative, sustaining, redemptive, and integrating activity. Therefore, to make Jesus Christ's life story our own is to enter into the interpersonal love life of all humankind with the Blessed Trinity, as the bearers of its Love-Life for all.

To be in love as Jesus Christ is in love is to accept Being-in-Love, God himself who is love, and the interpersonal life that is being given us in the universal story. Being-in-Love, the Blessed Trinity, is the Supreme Goodness of interpersonal life that Christians affirm to be revealed in Jesus Christ as the meaning and purpose of the universal story. The Cross represents the total self-investment of Being-in-Love for the achievement of this purpose. God is Love, investing his interpersonal life in the universal story.

The "I" that is Jesus Christ is the Being-in-Love whose interpersonal existence is that of addressing every "You," both divine and human, with the love that is the Supreme Goodness at the heart of the universal story. At the burning bush God revealed himself as "I am (*Ehyeh asher ehyeh*)" (Exodus 3:14). The ancient Hebrews referred to God as "He is (Yahweh)." The "I am" (*Ego eimi*) of Jesus before the high priest (Mk. 14:62) and elsewhere in the New Testament is the "I" who sends another "I" so that we will know that he is in us and we in him (Jn. 14:16, 20). It is that other Paraclete who allows us to cry out, as Jesus cried out, "Abba, Father." In other words, no longer do we call God "He is," but can call him "You are," just as he has called us "You are."

The prime analogate for Christian interpersonal life (or authenticity or perfection or love or fulfillment) is the interpersonal life of Jesus Christ and his Church. The Jesus story and the story of the Church, not a philosophical system nor an ideological system nor an abstract catalogue of propositional truths, are the prime mode in which we situate our own life stories. The concrete good valued in the narrative flow of the story of Jesus and his Church is the point of departure and return for all responsible Christian reflection and decision-making. It is the symbol, that which draws together, from which our insights into the meaning of our own life stories arise and to which we return to express those life stories to ourselves and to others. The story of Jesus become the story of ourselves is the beginning, the middle, and the end of all our striving.

1. C. G. Jung, "A Psychological Approach to the Trinity," *Collected Works XI* (London: Routledge & Kegan Paul, 2nd ed., 1969), pp. 109 – 200.
2. *Ibid.*, p. 171.
3. Antonio Moreno, *Jung, Gods, & Modern Man* (London: The Sheldon Press, 1974), p. 118.
4. Bernard Lonergan, *Verbum: Word and Idea in Aquinas* (London: Darton, Longman & Todd, 1968), p. 11.
5. Josef Fuchs, *De Castitate et Ordine Sexuali* (Rome: Gregorian University Press, 3rd ed., 1963), p. 10.
6. Moreno, *op. cit.*, p. 118.
7. See Thomas Cooper, "Christ and the Self: Symbols of Psychological Individuation and Religious Conversion in the Work of a Contemporary Artist," *Irish Theological Quarterly* 44 (1979), pp. 187 – 201. Among other things, the article investigates the way the artist is in his or her art.
8. In *The Poems of Gerard Manley Hopkins*, 4th ed., edited by W. H. Gardner and N. H. MacKenzie, published by Oxford University Press for the Society of Jesus, 1967.
9. T. S. Eliot, "The Dry Salvages," from *Four Quartets* (New York: Harcourt, Brace Jovanovich).
10. *Missale Romanum (Pii V),"Oratio S. Ambrosii Episcopi (Dominica)"*: "*Intret Spiritus tuus bonus in cor meum, qui sonet ibi sine sono, et sine strepitu verborum loquatur omnem veritatem.*"
11. Emile Mersch, *The Whole Christ: The Historical Development of the Doctrine of the Mystical Body in Scripture and Tradition* (London: Dennis Dobson, 1949), p. 22.
12. Karl Rahner, "The eternal significance of the humanity of Jesus for our relationship with God," *Theological Investigations III* (London: Darton, Longman & Todd), pp. 35 – 46.
13. Mersch, *op. cit.*, pp. 165f.
14. Frank Lake, *Clinical Theology, A Clinical and Psychiatric Bases to Clinical Pastoral Care* (London: Darton, Longman & Todd, 1966), pp. 132 – 141.
15. Frank Lake, "The Work of Christ in the Healing of Primal Pain," *Theological Renewal* 9 (June-July 1978), p. 33.
16. Lake, *Clinical Theology*, p. 137. A clinical psychologist, critical of Lake, told one of the authors that she was converted to Catholicism in the middle of delivering a university lecture by a sudden insight into the *convenientia* of the dogma of the Immaculate Conception for the mothering of the infant Christ.
17. Bernard Lonergan, *Insight: A Study of Human Understanding* (London: Longmans,

Green and Co., 1958), p. 173. Cf. *Id, Understanding and Being: An Introduction and Companion to Insight*; the Halifax Lectures (Lewiston, N.Y.: Edwin Mellen Press, 1980).

18. Bartholomew Kiely, *Psychology and Moral Theology: Lines of Convergence* (Rome: Pontifical Gregorian University, 1980), p. 128; cf. p. 157.

19. The researches of Kennedy and Heckler (reported by Kiely, *op. cit.*, pp. 40 – 43, pp. 241f), suggesting that the experience of true friendship was rare if not nonexistent for three quarters of the Catholic priests investigated, raise the sobering question of how far those who are entrusted by the community with the chief responsibility for communicating the meaning of the Gospel are in fact capable of communicating it.

20. Mersch, *op. cit.*, p. 21.

21. Lonergan, *Method in Theology*, p. 112, italics ours.

22. *The Easter Canon*, Ode IV, trans. by Raya and de Vinck.

23. Bernard Lonergan affirms that one can speak of three distinct and conscious subjects of divine consciousness. In his lecture "Christology Today: Theological Reflections" (in *Le Christ hier, aujourd'hui, et demain*, Quebec City, Les Presses de l'Université Laval, 1976, pp. 63-65), Lonergan affirms that to do so one must take the psychological analogy of the trinitarian processions seriously, one must be able to follow the reasoning from processions to relations and from relations to persons, and one has to think analogously of consciousness:

"The psychological analogy, then, has its starting point in that higher synthesis of intellectual, rational, and moral consciousness that is the dynamic state of being in love. Such love manifests itself in its judgements of value. And the judgements are carried out in decisions that are acts of loving. Such is the analogy found in the creature.

"Now in God the origin is the Father, in the New Testament named *ho Theos,* who is identified with *agape* (1 Jn. 4, 8:16). Such love expresses itself in its Word, its Logos, its *verbum spirans amorem,* which is a judgement of value. The judgement of value is sincere, and so it grounds the Proceeding Love that is identified with the Holy Spirit.

"There are then two processions that may be conceived in God: they are not unconscious processes but intellectually, rationally, morally conscious, as are judgements of value based on the evidence perceived by a lover, and the acts of loving grounded on judgements of value. The two processions ground four real relations of which three are really distinct from one another; and these three are not just relations as relations, and so modes of being, but also subsistent, and so not just paternity and filiation but also Father and Son. Finally, Father and Son and Spirit are eternal; their consciousness is not in time but timeless; their subjectivity is not becoming but ever itself; and each in his own distinct manner is subject of the infinite act that God is, the Father as originating love, the Son as judgement of value expressing that love, and the Spirit as originated loving.

"Perhaps now we can begin to discern, however imperfectly, the possibility of a single divine identity being at once subject of divine consciousness and also subject of a human consciousness.

"For though this implies that a man lived a truly human life without being a human person, still the paradox of this implication is removed by the distinction between identity and subjectivity. Though his identity was divine, still Jesus had a truly human subjectivity that grew in wisdom and grace and age before God and men (Lk. 2:52) and that was similar to our own in all things save sin (DS 301). Nor is the timeless and unchanging subjectivity proper to the divine identity in conflict with the developing subjectivity of a human life. For as Chalcedon would put it, though the identity is without distinction or separation, still the subjectivities are without modification or confusion (DS 302).

"Moreover, the human subjectivity of Christ conforms to the divine. For the eternal Word is Son, and it is that very Son that introduced into human language prayer to God not simply as Father but as a child's Father, as Abba; and as the Son prayed to Abba, so we in the Spirit of the Son also cry, Abba! Father! Again, as the eternal Word is the eternally true expression of the value that God as *agape* is, so the Word as man by obedience unto death again expressed that value by revealing how much God loved the world (Jn. 3:16). Finally, in his resurrection and exaltation he beckons us to the splendor of the children of God for which up to now the whole created universe groans in all its parts as if in the pangs of childbirth (Rom. 8:22). In that beckoning we discern not only the ground of our hope but also the cosmic dimension in the new creation of all things in Christ Jesus our Lord."

God's Word of Love: Mark, Model Christian Storyteller

Mark's opening statement declares his purpose; Mark is not placing on record the complete story of Christ's Gospel in all its historical extension, but is announcing the *"beginning* of the Good News
about Jesus Christ, the Son of God" (1:1). Jesus begins his ministry
by proclaiming the Good News that the Kingdom of God is at hand,
a Kingdom that will encompass all who are converted (*metanoeite*)
and who believe (1:15). At the beginning of Mark's Gospel a heavenly voice affirms Jesus as the Beloved of God (1:11). The beginning
of the Good News is a word of love: "You are my Beloved." The
Good News is Jesus as the Beloved of God, the one in whom God's
rule and Kingdom are present and at work. Mark presumes that the
Good News is still in the process of being communicated in the life
of the community of those who bear the name of Christ. The Kingdom comes when human minds and hearts discover that in Jesus
they too have become the beloved of God.

In common with the other New Testament writers, Mark is concerned to elicit an authentic response to the word of love spoken by
God in Jesus. He interprets Christian responsiveness to that word
in terms of the mystery of the Cross. The norm of Christian authenticity, the law of love, is the Way of the cross traversed by God's
Beloved Son. Mark's Gospel enjoys canonicity because the Church
("God's Beloved in Rome" and elsewhere, cf. Rom. 1:7) believes
that it truly expresses the meaning and demand of God's love for
every age and for every culture. It presents us with the agenda for
the coming of the Kingdom in Jesus and for the community that
follows him on his *via crucis.*

Love affirms the concrete goodness of its objects. God's word of
love, in Mark's narrative, is not an abstract concept but the affirmation of the concrete, particular, historically conditioned and interpersonal goodness of the Beloved. In addressing Jesus as Beloved, God addresses all humankind. Jesus, in his concrete and
particular humanity, is the word of love addressed by God to us.
What is good about the Good News is its concreteness; the teacher
and healer from Nazareth is already doing what he will do at the
end of time: uniting his human sisters and brothers with himself

and with one another by drawing them into his filial relationship under the lordship of his Father's love.

Baptism, Transfiguration, the Cross:
Three Signs of Acceptance

That Jesus is the Beloved of the Father is the basic assumption of Mark's Gospel. Although explicit reference to the Father occurs only later in Mark's narrative (8:38, 11:25; 13:32, 14:36), it is clearly the Father who speaks at the baptism of Jesus. God's declaration, spoken as the heavens open and the Spirit descends, should control our reading and interpretation of all the complete and incomplete, successful and unsuccessful attempts to identify Jesus that follow throughout this Gospel.

Historicist criticism reduces the understanding of the baptism to the question of whether it was an objective occurrence, a subjective vision of Jesus, an "experience," or an early Christian myth. Editorial analysis, in contrast, seizes on the theological importance the baptism had for Mark. For Mark, the marvelous reality of the Father's love for his Son, and the revelation of that reality, is the key to grasping the story of Jesus as Good News for all.

Mark presumes that his reader believes that what he relates is true. There is no provision for countering the skeptic who would object, "Jesus *says* that when he came out of the water...." To doubt the truth of the baptismal theophany is to range oneself with those who did not understand who Jesus was (cf.2:7; 3:21–30; 6:2–3, etc.). At a deeper level it is to range oneself with those who do not know the Father. We judge the truth of God by connaturality. Born again with Christ (cf. *connaître:* to know, to be *con-naître,* born with), we recognize the voice of Christ's Father because we recognize it as the Good News about Someone whom we already know—that we receive it as the expression of a reality we have already experienced.

In a parallel passage, Jesus is identified as the Beloved Son of him who speaks from heaven at his Transfiguration and, in parabolic form, Jesus identifies himself as the Beloved Son who will be killed by the evil vintners (12:1–12). Who is Jesus, and from whence does he come? Heaven gives its answer in the baptism and Transfiguration. The only human being in Mark's Gospel to give the full answer is the centurion at Golgotha. The centurion is the only one to acknowledge Jesus as the "Son of God," to recognize the Beloved Son of him who speaks from heaven (15:39). The Father's recognition of his Beloved, Mark implies, is now finally shared by a human person, a representative of all the Gentiles who will follow him by making the same full confession of Christian faith.

Mark's narrative is structured around three authentic and full affirmations of Jesus' identity. In all three, Mark implies that only the Lover authentically and adequately recognizes and knows the Beloved. At the beginning (1:11) and during (9:7) the life story of Jesus, the Lover explicitly identifies him as the Beloved. Only through the death of Jesus for "the many" (10:45; 14:24) is the Gentile centurion, the archetype of the many, able to share the Lover's recognition of the Beloved.

In recounting Jesus' consistent repudiation of the apparently true confessions of demons and demoniacs, Mark implies that only the Lover can authentically and adequately confess the Beloved. The diabolically afflicted confess Jesus as "the Holy One of God" (1:24), the "Son of God" (3:11), and the "Son of God the Most High" (5:7). Mark might well be implying here that Christians who confess Jesus with their tongues but have no love for him in their hearts are really no different from the devils in their meaningless affirmations of Jesus as Lord. As the old English prayer affirms, the only adequate invocation of the name of Jesus is as a prayer that he truly be a Jesus, the One who saves. Only the one who is himself Beloved (and those to whom that Beloved chooses to reveal the Lover as their Lover—cf. Lk. 10:22) can authentically and adequately acknowledge the saving love of God.

The same relationship of the Lover to the Beloved appears in traditions already known to Mark. The same word that Mark employs for beloved *(agapetos)* is used in the Pauline corpus with the same intention. No one, affirms Paul, is able to confess Jesus as Lord unless she or he has the Spirit (1 Cor. 12:3), a Spirit who has poured out God's agape into our hearts (Rom. 5:5), a gift that has made us God's *agapetoi*, God's beloved (Rom. 1:7).[1] Through the Beloved *(en to egapemeno)* God purposed that we should be holy and blameless, predestining us in love, *en agape* (Ephes. 1:1–7).

Mark sums up the story of Jesus in these three affirmations of his divine Sonship; affirmations that make up the beginning, the middle, and the end of his life story. Jesus is fully awakened to his God-given meaning and value, mission and purpose from the beginning to the completion of his life story. Aware of the Lover who has called him Beloved, Jesus is enabled to transmit to the "many," symbolized in the Gentile centurion, the transforming and saving reality of that love. Confessions that Jesus is the Son of God, which are purely notional and which do not proceed from the real apprehension and intense appetition of the love of God appropriated by the gift of his Spirit, are as worthless and meaningless as the confessions of the demons whom Jesus silences.

Baptism and Transfiguration

At the baptism the heavenly voice affirms Jesus as the Beloved Son. Why does Mark's narrative repeat this affirmation at the Transfiguration? Why does Mark recount the Transfiguration at all? Why does Mark not postpone his presentation of the glorious Son of God until after the Resurrection?

Every life story requires an initiating vision. Just as Michelangelo "sees" the Pietà in the stone before he starts to sculpt, so the Marcan Jesus sees the meaning of his life's story in the moment he starts to tell it. Jesus's life and mission begin with the major statement of the vision from which all else springs. Mark presents Jesus' knowledge and vision of his own beloved Sonship as the energizing source and dynamic principle that binds the disparate elements of his life story together. We can in no way do that which we cannot envision. The baptismal affirmation of Jesus as the Beloved Son of God gives Jesus the vision of who he is and what his story should tell.

Mark structures his story so that the vision that initiates the life of Jesus is present throughout his entire life story. The appreciative voice of the Father is heard by Jesus throughout the length of his saving mission. The baptismal affirmation of Jesus as Son can be likened to the flash of insight that, when understood and judged to be authentic, becomes the ever present principle of a continuous response. The baptismal voice defines Jesus as one who at core is in relation to the Father; it defines the character of the favor and authority he enjoys from heaven. The baptismal account seems to imply that it was Jesus alone who heard the voice; the voice testifies to the ontological basis of Jesus' ability to communicate the concrete goodness of being loved by God. It is because Jesus is the unique Beloved of God that he can make us beloved. It is from this that all else flows.

At the Transfiguration, the heavenly voice comes almost as a response to Peter's exclamation. Peter and heaven are represented as speaking. At the Transfiguration the representatives of the new people of God share the vision and hear the voice. Jesus is represented as transforming; the Beloved is making us beloved. This impression is reinforced by Mark's portraying Jesus as being in dialogue with Moses and Elijah. Peter responds by wanting to hold the feast of tabernacles; to reenact the honeymoon period when God's people dwelt with him in the wilderness. God's affirmation of his Son as the Beloved is the basis for the foundation of a community, when God shall say to no-people, "You are my people" and shall call Unbeloved "my Beloved" (cf. Hos. 2:23f). At the baptism the heavenly voice declares, "You are my Son, the Beloved; my favor rests on you." At the Transfiguration a command is added, "This is my Son, the Beloved; listen to him." In the narrative of the baptism the accent is on the Lover's favor resting on the Beloved; the accent in the Transfiguration narrative is on the Lover's authority that is invested in the Beloved. The Lover not only loves the Beloved but also demands that others listen to the Beloved.[2] Ortega y Gasset has written that when a man truly loves a woman he loves all women in her. We may broaden his remark to say that when a lover truly loves his or her beloved, then he or she loves all humankind in him or her.[3] At the Transfiguration the Father reveals the depth of authenticity of his love for Jesus; in loving his Beloved the Father-Lover reveals himself as the Lover of all humankind.[4] To be converted and to believe the Good News is to experience the concrete goodness of being loved through and in one's God-given acceptance of the Lover's Beloved.

If the baptismal narrative reveals Jesus as the person whose very existence is that of being loved by God, the Transfiguration narrative reveals that love as constituting Jesus as the sacrament of God's love for all humankind. The transfigured humanity of Jesus is the outward and visible sign of the inward and invisible favor that infallibly brings about that which it declares. Mark would not be writing the story of the Beloved Christ if he and his hearers had not themselves already heard the voice that calls them "my Beloved." Mark is writing the story of the One who is the supreme Symbol (sacramental sign) of the Lover-Beloved relationship, the efficacious Symbol (*signum efficax)* that draws together (*symbollein)* all humankind to become that which they contemplate. Christ affects us as sacrament by communicating to us the faith, the inner eye of love, which enables us to apprehend our basic self-others-world-God relationship. Unlove, like the unclean spirits, apprehends that relationship in a radically different way. Unlove-made-loved (to create a new Hosean character) apprehends himself or herself as beloved in the Beloved.

The Cross, Locus of Divine Love

In a daring metaphor, the Fathers would speak of the Cross as the marriage bed of humankind and God. The Cross is the consummation of the sacrament of the Transfiguration. The Transfiguration narrative is placed in the context of the predictions of the Passion. The Transfiguration represents how the transcendent Son, the Beloved, who is apparently "only Jesus" (9:8) is effectively communicating his relationship with God through his Way of the Cross. The Beloved must suffer many things and be put to death (8:31; 9:31; 10:33) before he can become the source of love for all other human persons. By his life-giving, love-giving death Jesus enables others to recognize him fully and authentically as the Beloved in whom they are beloved. No full confession of Christian faith is possible for Mark except as the fruit of Christ's death; otherwise, Jesus' passion and death would be implicitly interpreted as superfluous for the fulfillment of God's will. Jesus' rebuke to Peter for failing to grasp that the way is the Way of the Cross (8:33) is addressed by Mark to the readers of his Gospel lest they forget the costly demands of God's love for those he calls to become his beloved. If love costs God what is most dear to him, so love will cost us what is most dear to us.

The Gentile centurion stands for the many for whom Christ's blood was poured out (14:24). "Truly," he declares, "was this man the Son of God" (15:39). Christ's death becomes the sacramental sign by which the many may know themselves to be the beloved in the Beloved. The centurion's confession of faith represents for Mark a full confession of faith in the divinity of the crucified and risen Son of God. It expresses the Easter faith of Mark's readers. There are no appearances of the risen Christ in the Markan narrative when it is shorn of its longer ending. The response of the women to the theophany is to say "nothing to a soul, for they were afraid" (16:8). The original Mark represents the women as being told to tell the disciples to go to Galilee (of the nations)—it is there they will find him. The affirmation of Jesus' Sonship is elicited in Mark not by an appearance of the risen Lord but by the outward appearance of the failure of a criminal's execution. There is an exquisite irony in the Jewish women being told to tell the disciples to look for him in Galilee of the Gentiles and their telling no one, when contrasted with the centurion of the Gentiles who confesses the Beloved Sonship of the Christ.

Jesus' instructions on discipleship implicitly articulate the word of God's love that is the giving up of his own life. His first instruction defines discipleship as suffering: we are to take up our cross (8:34). His second instruction defines discipleship as service: we must be last of all and servant of all (9:35). His third instruction combines suffering with service: "Whoever would be great among you must be your servant, and whoever would be first among you must be slave of all. For the Son of Man came not to be served but to serve and to give his life as a ransom for many" (10:43–45). Jesus

Christ is the Good News that we, by sharing his suffering and service, may become for ourselves and for others the beloved of God. In human terms the news of Christ's death is bad news; the goodness of the Good News is Jesus as the Beloved who can and does pour out his life.

Mark leaves no doubt about the fact that it was not possible during the historical ministry of Jesus to recognize his true Sonship from his miracles alone. Jesus was more than a miracle worker. Mark's account of Jesus' Way of the Cross is an implicit rebuke to those who think that God reveals himself only in miracles. Even the wonder of the stone being rolled away is insufficient to elicit the obedience of the women. Fascination for miracle working implies a misguided esteem for self-sufficiency that would be an obstacle to recognizing the divine sufficiency of the Son who can lay down his life in failure. In response to the scribe's question, Jesus prays the *Sh'ma Yisroel*, the recognition of our obligation to love God and adds to it the obligation to love our neighbor (12:28–31). The three affirmations of Jesus' Sonship show Jesus as the living fulfillment of the divine demand to be loved. As the Beloved Son Jesus reveals what it is to love God as much as he reveals what it is to be loved by God. Mark's Good News is the news that the *Sh'ma Yisroel*, the *summa legis* of the Jew has been perfectly and completely fulfilled in the life-giving Cross of Jesus. Our justification lies not in the keeping of the law but ultimately in the gift of God's Beloved.

Mark's narrative as a Way of the Cross is the implicit condemnation of all temptations to idolatry—the ever-to-be-frustrated attempts of humankind to control its own destiny by controlling and manipulating God.[5] To contextualize the only fully authentic human confession of faith in the Cross of Jesus is the most radical condemnation of all our human refusals to let God be God and to let God's Beloved be *God's* Beloved. Mark structures his narrative to present Jesus as the One in whom all our inclinations to idolatry have been defeated. Jesus lives by God's approval and not by humankind's approval. The final words of Jesus on the Cross express his recognition of the supreme goodness of God. "My God, my God, why have you forsaken me?" (15:34). In the midst of pain, betrayal, and failure, Jesus, like the just man of the psalms, cries out to God. Jesus cries out his prayer at the ninth hour, when the trumpets called the people to the evening sacrifice and prayer at the temple. Mark implies that Jesus is with the people of God for the fulfillment of their worship. The bystanders do not consider the words of Jesus' prayer as a cry of despair because they had to distort them to mock them, hearing "Eloi" and saying "Elijah" (15:36). If it had been a cry of despair they would have welcomed it as a vindication of their condemnation of Jesus for blasphemy. The bystanders deliberately misquote Jesus to make of his words not a psalm of trust but a cry of anguish.[6] The death of God's Beloved is the supreme example of the just man who, though all things fail, even then gives praise to God.[7] On the Cross Jesus abandons himself totally into the hands of God, an act of such total self-transcendence that, in Mark's narrative, it elicits the fullness of Christian faith: "Truly this man was the Son of God."

Christian Conversion

The three affirmations of Sonship around which Mark structures his narrative suggest a Markan model for the entire event and process of Christian conversion. The relationship of human persons to the Beloved Son moves from nonrecognition (baptism) through incipient recognition (Transfiguration) to full recognition (Golgotha). Mark's readers will experience the goodness of God's affirming love in their lives only as they allow themselves to be drawn to him along the Way of the Cross. In the self-gift of his Son, God wills to make us the locus of his own self-giving to the whole human race. In the measure that we allow ourselves to be totally receptive to God—as, in Bartholomew Kiely's phrase, we become eccentric, that is, finding our center outside of ourself—in that measure can God make us the fountain from which his love will flow to our sisters and brothers. Mark's Good News, the concrete goodness of his news, is the same news that Paul gave to the Corinthians: that "for our sake God made the sinless one into sin, so that in him we might become the goodness of God" (2 Cor. 5:21).

Mark's narrative is an extended symbol of God's self-investment in his Son, the Beloved, a self-investing love that calls forth and creates love in all who receive the Spirit of the Son. Mark's Gospel summons each reader to hear the words of God: "You are my Son, the Beloved. My favor rests on you." Mark is engaged in the cognitive-affective transformation of his readers, a transformation that issues from the felt meaning of God's loving self-investment in their lives. Mark wants his readers to accept as the integrating center of their lives the Supreme and Beloved Goodness whose life has been poured out for them. Letting God be God means letting him invest in our lives the fulfilling goodness of his Beloved Son and Spirit.

---

1. *Agapetos* is the Greek translation of *Yahīd* in Genesis 22. *Yahīd* is Hebrew for "one and only" or "uniquely Beloved." The context of the vision and the definite article preceding *ho huios* (*the* Son) indicate that *agapetos* should be translated in the sense of *Yahīd*. Cf. with the Hebrew *Dôd*, which indicates 'beloved' or 'delight' in a more inclusive sense. Mark employs the one Greek word *agapetos* to imply both Hebrew words—the exclusive or singular Beloved *(Yahīd)*, Jesus, and the inclusive *(Dôd)* Beloved who are all Christians incorporated into Christ. Paul uses *agapetos* in the inclusive sense of *Dôd*; Mark extends the use of *agapetos* to the exclusive sense of *Yahīd* by putting it into the context of *the* vision and *the* Son. Mark underscores the fact that it is through this unique reality of *the* Beloved that we become the Beloved in the Pauline sense.

2. The common human experience of falling in love may help us here. At first the attention is exclusively focused on the beloved; the spouse's eyes are only for the other. Subsequently there arises the desire to tell the whole world the wonder of one's beloved. Thirdly there arises that daily intercommunion that founds and issues in a family. Aquinas taught that the most excellent end of marriage was as *sacramentum,* whereby the partners have *conversatio cum Deo* and, we might add, with all humankind. (Cf. *In IV Sent.* d. 33, q. 1, a. 1 = *Suppl.* 65, 1.)

3. Such is the theme of St. John of the Cross in his Romance II, *De la communicación de las tres Personas.*

4. Cf. the conclusion of the Collect in the Byzantine Liturgy, when the Presiding Celebrant asks that the Church's prayer be heard *"oti agathos kai* philanthropos *Theos iparchis"*: because you are a good God and lover of humankind.

5. On idolatry, see Bartholomew M. Kiely, *Psychology and Moral Theology: Lines of Convergence* (Rome: Gregorian Press, 1980), pp. 199, 221; H. Schlier, *Der Römerbrief* (Freiburg-in-Briesgau, W. Ger.: Verlag Herder, 1977), pp. 47–61; Thomas Cooper, "Christ and the Self," *The Irish Theological Quarterly* 46 (1979), p. 185; Thomas Cooper, "On Praying to God in English," *The Clergy Review* 65 (1980), *passim.*

6. Ernest Martinez, "The Gospel Accounts of the Death of Jesus," unpublished doctoral dissertation (Rome: Gregorian University, 1969), pp. 386–389.

7. The Office of Morning Praise on Good Friday (Lauds) beautifully brings forth this point by making each Christian recite the words of Habakuk: "For even though the fig does not blossom, nor fruit grow on the vine, even though the olive crops fail, and fields produce no harvest, even though flocks vanish from the folds and stalls stand empty of cattle, yet will I rejoice in the Lord and exult in God my Savior. The Lord my God is my strength. He makes me leap like the deer, he guides me to the high places" (Hab. 3:17–19). The Liturgy of Good Friday draws us to "put on the mind" and feelings of Christ and to experience his loving abandonment to the Father for himself and only for himself.

A Brief Guide to Storytelling

Listening to stories no less than telling them is an art. An art or skill is something that ultimately one cannot learn from a book but that is largely picked up by imitating the masters. The storyteller's art is an implicit injunction: Go and do likewise.

The following brief guide is a list of practical suggestions—really little more than hints—to aid the reader in his or her task of learning to hear and tell stories—most especially the story of Jesus. The suggestions are tabulated under the headings of the transcendental precepts: Be attentive, be intelligent, be reasonable, be responsible. These precepts are the four levels of our response to the love that God has created in our hearts. No one can fully attend to the story of Jesus unless he or she is drawn to it by the Father's gift of love (cf. Jn. 6:44). No one can adequately comprehend the Jesus story unless he or she experiences a certain connaturality with it. The judgment as to the truth of the Jesus story is a judgment of that inner eye of love we call faith. Though the Scholastic adage *"nihil volitum nisi praecognitum"* generally holds good, in the case of the Jesus story the opposite is true: *"nihil cognitum nisi praeamatum."* If the first three transcendental precepts are a response to the prior love with which God has loved us, the last precept—be responsible—is itself a response to the experienced, understood, and judged fact of being in love with God. A man in love with a woman or a woman in love with a man is attentive, understanding, and convinced of the rightness of his or her loveliness. The response is a lifetime commitment to that love; love as commitment and as decision follows on that initial, almost intuitive judgment that we call finding ourselves to be in love.

Telling the story of Jesus takes as many forms as there are storytellers. As storytellers we tell the story in different ways—through our living, informally through our relationships, formally in our families, classrooms, or churches. Just as the rules of artistic composition—concern for form and shape, structure and proportion, excellence and execution and performance, truthfulness and goodness—are shared but differently achieved by music, sculpture, painting, architecture, pottery, embroidery, furniture making, literature, engineering, and the like, so too the different forms of storytelling are different applications of the same fundamental principles to the different contexts, materials, and immediate purposes with which we tell our stories.

A. Be Attentive

1. Listen to stories.
   - 1.1   *Nemo dat quod non habet.* No one speaks who has not heard.
   - 1.2   Allow time for listening.
2. Listen to all stories.
   - 2.1   Listen to the stories around you.
   - 2.11   Listen to the stories (myths) of your people.
   - 2.111   Listen to the Judeo-Christian stories that ground our tradition.
   - 2.112   Listen to the Greek and Roman stories that historically grounded most Christian storytelling.
   - 2.113   Listen to the stories of your race, your nation, your religion.
   - 2.114   Listen to the stories of your family.
   - 2.115   Listen to the stories of the institutions (schools, universities, religious orders and congregations, armed forces, political parties, trade and professional associations, etc.) that formed you and your families.
   - 2.1151   In the case of religious orders or congregations, pay special attention to the stories of the founder or foundress.
   - 2.116   Listen to the stories of the Church—both Church history and the stories of the particular parish communities that have formed you and in which you now worship and minister.
   - 2.1161   Listen to the other ways in which Christians tell the Jesus story, within your own and other Christian denominations.
   - 2.2   Give priority to the stories that the most ordinary circumstances of your life disclose to you.
   - 2.21   Do not look for strange and "interesting" stories—as though God spoke only in heaven or at the ends of the earth. God speaks to men and women "where they are."
   - 2.3   Listen to contemporary stories—newspapers, magazines, television, cinema, theater.
   - 2.4   Listen to the stories told by the literature—poetry, drama, novels of your people and of your language.
   - 2.41   Listen to the stories told by literature and history of other peoples and other languages.

2.411   Listen to the stories told by the opposite sex.
3. Listen to the stories told by those you meet.
    3.1   Attend to the body language of those who are talking to you.
    3.11   How does the speaker hold himself or herself? At this moment? Habitually?
    3.12   What does the speaker do with his or her hands?
    3.2   Listen to the tone of voice, the inflections, the speed of talk, the hesitations, the punctuation of those who talk to you. Which words do they stress?
    3.3   Attend particularly to the eyes of those to whom you talk.
    3.31   Do they look at you or avoid your gaze?
    3.32   Are they wide or narrowed? Are they warm or cold? Lively or dead?
    3.4   What imagery is habitually used? What clusters of images are used?
4. Attend to the difference between the stories of those you love and those you hate or are indifferent to.
    4.1   Attend to the difference between the stories of those who love you and those who hate or ignore you.
5. Listen to the story *you* are telling.
    5.1   Listening to (being aware of) the story you are telling is usually better done in retrospect rather than at the time of speaking: self-consciousness changes the story (for example, thinking about how you wield a hammer usually stops you from driving the nail straight).
6. When listening to the explicit telling of the Jesus story:
    6.1   Attend to the context—liturgical, exegetical, personal witness, etc.
    6.2   Notice which stories spontaneously delight you—they may indicate areas to build on.
    6.3   Notice which stories are "hard sayings"—they may indicate areas that need healing or, alternatively, areas that can be left till later time (God's mercy is largely shown by patience).
7. Never stop listening even when you are telling.
    7.1   When teaching or preaching or reading the Scriptures liturgically, attend to the feedback from your audience—both oral and visual.

B. Be Intelligent

8. Insight cannot be forced; it happens quasi-spontaneously. Use your imagination.

8.1   Contemplate the image, as you might stare at a diagram of Euclid.

8.2   Try moving your perspective; imagine yourself in the storyteller's shoes.

8.21   Imagine yourself to be the different characters in the story or parable.

8.22   If insight into the story is delayed, "sleep on it." Insight often occurs after relaxation of the tension.

9. Growth in understanding occurs when we "stretch our minds." Listen to stories that are slightly above your head.

9.1   Use all the tools available for understanding stories—psychology, economic and political history, exegesis, etc.

9.12   Do not confuse hermeneutical tools with the prime matter for storytelling; homilies, for example, are not lectures in exegesis.

C. Be Reasonable (Critical)

10. Choose the right storytellers as your masters or models.

10.1   Which storytellers are "friends of God"?

10.2   Which storytellers are generally considered to be masters of storytelling (the classics)?

10.3   Which are the models I resonate with, which I spontaneously choose. Are they the right ones? Be critical of your own spontaneity.

11. Which stories are *not* told by your nation, local church, family, this particular storyteller?

11.1   Compare stories told by different storytellers and societies.

11.11   Compare the same story as told by different storytellers.

11.2   Why are certain stories not told by certain storytellers? Should they be told?

D. Be Responsible

12. Take responsibility for your own life story.

12.1   God does not deny his grace to those who are doing what is in their power to respond. *(Facienti quod est in se Deus non denegat gratiam.)*

12.11   Know your own limitations. Do not presume that you are completely free to shape your own story.

12.12   Within the limits of your own freedom, strive to achieve the *optimum* response to God's love; the *ideal* is an eschatological reality.

12.13   Be patient with yourself. Impatience with self leads to impatience with others.

12.131 Be patient with your listeners; it takes time to tell and to listen to stories.

12.14   Take responsibility for the stories you tell. Be willing to accept the consequences of your storytelling.

13. Tell your *own* life story

13.1   Your story is a unique expression of the universal story. Without your life story, the universal story will not be complete.

13.2   Telling the story of Jesus is not so much an imitation of Jesus as an allowing Jesus to tell his story through *your* story.

13.21   "Christ plays in ten thousand places,
Lovely in limbs, and lovely in eyes not his
To the Father through the features of men's faces."[1]

14. Tell the Jesus story in your *own* way.

14.1   Paul never quoted the stories or sayings of Jesus—Christ lived again in Paul's story.

14.2   Do what the evangelist did.

14.21   Use exegetical tools, biblical theology, etc., to aid you in your critical appropriation of the Gospel and then witness to your appropriation of the Good News.

14.211 For example, at Christmas, do not merely retell the infancy narratives—especially do not conflate them as if they were newspaper reports. Understand and judge what Matthew and Luke were trying to do for their audience and then do likewise.

15. Do not dilute the Gospel imagery.

15.1   A Buddhist monk once said: "Christianity is the most perfect and demanding Tao, but most Christians water it to taste."

15.11   Do not assume that the Gospel imagery is too powerful for children or for less theologically informed audiences. People can live symbolically on a higher level than they can think.

15.12   "Suffer the little children" does not mean "Translate the Gospel story into baby language," but draw them into the death and depths of Christ.

15.121 Remember, in the case of children, that images and symbols can start to work before they can be conceptually grasped.

15.2   Conversely, do not rarefy the Gospel, imposing your own prejudices and idealism on others; imitate the Council of Jerusalem (Acts 13) in letting people meet Christ where they are.

16. Tell the story for its own sake.

    16.1   Do not degrade the Gospel by using it as a tool to manipulate yourself and others.

    16.11   Like every work of art and every human person, your story and the Jesus story have an intrinsic worth.

    16.2   Be convinced of the worth of the Jesus story; its worth does not depend on its hearers' applause.

17. Be prepared to suffer.

    17.1   When you are truly telling the story and others won't listen, remember this was how their ancestors treated the storytellers of old.

    17.2   If there is *never* any opposition to your telling of the Jesus story, check to see if you have watered it down.

18. Accept none of these precepts with blind faith; check them out in your experience.

1. Gerard Manley Hopkins, excerpt from untitled poem beginning, "As kingfishers catch fire, dragonflies draw flame," in *Poems 1876–1889*.

Some Responses from Our Fellow Storytellers

A draft edition of *Tellers of the Word* was used during the early summer of 1981 as the basis for a course on the intentionality analysis of religious experience in the context of life stories and stories of God, which John Navone taught at the Gregorian University in Rome. As a class exercise the students were asked to write a paper detailing the theses that in their opinion the authors had left out. Faithful to their own injunction to listen to the stories around them (Appendix II, 2.1) the authors record here some of the suggestions they received.

Suggested Additions to Appendix II

Before the draft was printed and distributed to the students, the Reverend Bartholomew M. Kiely, S.J., professor of psychopathology at the Institute of Psychology of Gregorian University, suggested the following further questions with regard to understanding a life story.

1. What is the person's vision of the ideal state of the world?
2. What is the person's vision of the ideal conditions of life for himself or herself? Or in related terms, what role would he or she play in the ideal scheme of things?

    Is the ideal positive end-state of existence something like an endless condition of excitement, power, and applause, while the feared negative end-state is something like one of routine and anonymity? Is the ideal positive end-state a completely undisturbed life of stoic impassibility, in which life will not be agitated by anything as uncomfortable as compassion or anger? Is the desired end-state one of omniscience or omnipotence, of having everything perfectly under control and in order and a corresponding intolerance of "messy" things such as feelings, friendship, anxiety? (Needs, defenses, and behavior are pointers to the end-state desired.)
3. What battles is the person fighting?
4. Does the person know what he or she is in favor of? It is easy to be general and negative; it is very hard to be concrete and positive. Some are led by bitterness and grudges all their lives. A

strong character implies a person of strong desires. All motivation, all action, represents some form of desire. One cannot learn without *wanting* to learn. What, therefore, does the person want out of his or her life? What does he or she feel responsible for? What does he or she do about it?

People can be happy only by doing *something*. What that something fulfills is needs or values; but people cannot just "be happy." What do they desire and choose and commit themselves to? They define themselves by their choices and attitudes and expectations. A sense of identity in the original meaning of "identity" (sameness) means a constancy, stability, and therefore consistency in one's choices, attitudes, and expectations. If we say that we don't know who we are, we really seem to mean that we don't know what we want to do with our lives.

5. Out of what history of development do the answers to the above questions come? A privileged situation in a quiet family (Therese of Lisieux), illegitimacy (Leonardo da Vinci, Martin of Porres), a very sick family (Beethoven), a traditional and kindly society (Bergamo/John XXIII), the intellectual snobbery of Paris (Sartre), the experience of life in Poland during and after World War II (John Paul II), the life of the boondocks (Abraham Lincoln), a symbiotic relationship with a mother?

6. What word of hope does the person bear for others? What did it cost in terms of personal suffering? What the great people seem to have in common is that all suffered and all managed to find some word of hope for humankind, of which the individual was the bearer (like the mule carrying the sacred relics) but not the source, nor even particularly important in the context of history.

Responses: The Theses the Authors Missed

1. Stories speak to different levels of human knowing (interiority) revealing what we *can* or *will* not see on a conscious level.

   One student adverted to the many levels on which stories affect us. He used the customary iceberg image to remind us that most of our personal and interpersonal life lies below the surface. We are often our own worst enemies; insight may be blocked not only by our habits of thinking and relating so that we fail to understand what is strange to us, but also by our own unwillingness to enlarge our cognitive and affective horizons. The story can often disturb our complacency on a level different from our conscious knowing and willing. King Solomon appeals to the deeper instinct to protect new life, undercutting the shallower, jealous possessiveness of the two whores (1 Kings 3:16–28). The David-Nathan story (2 Sam. 12:1–15) is an example of how story can be a "fifth column," breaking David's resistance when a frontal assault, a direct accusation, would be repelled. The remoteness, the apparent anonymity and distance of Nathan's story, allows David to listen at a deeper level than his conscious or subconscious ego defenses. Nathan's story allows David to make the connection for himself.

If the story is to achieve its purpose, then the listener must have a willingness to hear what she or he does not always want to hear. The Delphic oracle speaking to Socrates and the witches speaking to Macbeth both disguised their truth with irony— but what a difference in the interpreters and the interpretations. It is illuminating to compare the reactions of David to Nathan with the reactions of the religious authorities in Luke's Gospel (20:1–20). Jesus forces the men of deception into silence. The refusal by the chief priests, scribes, and elders to answer the question posed by Jesus is shown up by the parable of the wicked husbandmen as a guilty, inauthentic silence, refusing to get the point of the story.

2. Prayer is a means of appropriating the Jesus story into the life of the storyteller.

Several students wrote variations on this theme. Prayer, it was said, is the act of appropriation of the Jesus story into the personal life of the storyteller. In prayer we tell our story to Jesus, and we listen to hear where the Jesus story resonates in our lives. Prayer is the connecting act with Jesus as storyteller and storylistener. In a paper too long to be given except in outline here, one student went through the nine moments of story showing how for storytelling and storylistening the word "prayer" could be substituted. Prayer is the interpersonal and mutual sharing and mingling of the life stories of two lovers.

In a parallel way another student adverted to the liturgy as the "summit toward which the activity of the Church is directed; at the same time it is the fountain from which all her power flows." *(Sacrosanctum Concilium* 10) The dramatic nature of liturgical celebration makes it a key element in a theology of story. In the liturgy we bring to mind *(anamnesis)* and make present the past and future moments of the universal story of Jesus: we proclaim his death until he comes. The second part of the thrice-holy hymn in the mass, "Blessed is he who comes in the Name of the Lord," sums up the point. In condemning the unbelief of Jerusalem, Jesus promises: "You shall not see me till the time comes when you say: Blessings on him who comes in the name of the Lord" (Lk.13:35). It was popularly thought that that blessing would be sung when the Messiah, the Day of the Lord, came. By its unvarying use at every Eucharist, the Christian church proclaims that we have seen him come, he is coming *now*.

3. One of the women students focused on the need to be loved before we can hear the Jesus story. The affective insight that we are loved by God is the genesis of our own telling of the Jesus story just as the prior creating love of God was the genesis of our being. She summed up her point by quoting from a song: "You're nobody till somebody loves you," perhaps a more contemporary version of Augustine's "Lord, you created me lovable because you loved me." In the same vein, another student wrote: "I like the idea of the universal story because it means you belong even when you feel you don't belong."

4. Among other, undeveloped, suggestions we found the following:

   The language of story: systematics :: the language of poetry: discursive prose. Story prefers multiple meanings, that is, connotative ambiguity, to univocity, that is, denotative precision.

   Stories embody a vital fabric of lived and pursued values; as in life, intellectual systematization follows.

   The theology of story more closely approximates, though less precisely, analyses of mystical consciousness than does systematic theology.

   Stories are almost universally told in the past tense. We might add that when they are told in the present tense for dramatic effect, it is a "present-historic tense." We are more comfortable with the completed gestalt of past events than with the ambiguities of the present.

   Contemporary literary criticism's understanding of poetry as language that "re-creates experience" throws light on the theology of story's key insight into the personal-spiritual encounter of meaning (subject-object union) as a holistic experience.

Bibliography

I. WORKS CITED IN TEXT

Alfaro, Juan. "Supernaturalitas Fidei iuxta S. Thomam." *Gregorianum* 44 (1963):501–542, 731–787.

Balthasar, Hans Urs von. *Love Alone: The Way of Revelation*. London: Geoffrey Chapman, 1968.

Bannister, K., and Pincus, L. *Shared Phantasy in Marital Problems: Therapy in a Four-Person Relationship*. London: The Tavistock Institute, 1971.

Becker, Carl. Review of H. G. Wells's *Outline of History*. *American Historical Review* 26 (July 1921).

Benson, Peter L., and Spilka, Bernard P. "God-Image as a Function of Self-Esteem and Locus of Control." In Maloney, H. N. (ed): *Current Perspectives in the Psychology of Religion*. Grand Rapids, Mich.: Wm. B. Eerdmans, 1977.

Bird, Otto. "The Complexity of Love." *Thought* 39 (1964):210–220.

Blamires, Harry. "The Nature of Christian Education." *The Prison Chaplains' Journal* (HMSO for the U.K. Prison Department, for private circulation), 1972.

Bloom, Archbishop Anthony (Metropolitan Anthony of Surozh). *Living Prayer*. London: Darton, Longman & Todd, 1966.

———. *School for Prayer*. London: Darton, Longman & Todd, 1970.

Bonhoeffer, Dietrich. *The Cost of Discipleship*. London: SCM Press, 1964.

Bremond, Henri. *Prayer and Poetry*. London: Burns, Oates and Washbourne, 1927.

Brown, Raymond E. *The Birth of the Messiah: A Commentary on the Infancy Narratives in Matthew and Luke*. London: Geoffrey Chapman, 1977.

———. *The Gospel According to John (i-xii)*. In *The Anchor Bible 29*. Garden City, N.Y.: Doubleday, 1966.

Burrell, David. "Indwelling: Presence and Dialogue." *Theological Studies* 22 (1961):1–17.

Butterfield, Herbert. *Man on His Past*. Cambridge: At the University Press, 1955.

Chesterton, Gilbert Keith. *The Everlasting Man*. London: Hodder and Staughton, 1925.

Conn, Walter E. *Conscience and Self-Transcendence*. Columbia University dissertation. Ann Arbor, Mich.: University Microfilms, 1973.

Cooper, Thomas. "The Wedding of the Lamb." *The Venerabile* 24 (1969):269–280.

———. "Communicating the Incommunicable: Remarks on the Relation of Theology to Art." *The Clergy Review* 62 (1977):186–193.

———. "Celebrating the Word Made Flesh: Images of Christmas in the Liturgy." *The Clergy Review* 63 (1978):406–412.

———. "Christ and the Self: Symbols of Psychological Individuation and Religious Conversion in the Work of a Contemporary Artist." *The Irish Theological Quarterly* 46 (1979):185–201.

———. "On Praying to God in English." *The Clergy Review* 65 (1980):41–51.

Crowe, Frederick E. "Complacency and Concern in the Thought of St. Thomas." *Theological Studies* 20 (1959):1–39, 198–230, 343–395.

———. Review of E. Schillebeeckx's "Revelation and Theology 2." *Theological Studies* 29 (1968):779–781.

———. *Theology of the Word of God: Structural Elements for a Treatise.* Informally published, Toronto: Regis, n.d.

———. *Theology of the Christian Word: A Study in History.* New York: Paulist Press, 1978.

Dix, Gregory. *The Shape of the Liturgy.* London: Dacre/Adam & Charles Black, 1964.

Dominian, Jack. *Cycles of Affirmation: Psychological Essays in Christian Living.* London: Darton, Longman & Todd, 1975.

Doran, Robert M. "Psychic Conversion." *The Thomist* 41 (1977):200–236.

Dulles, Avery. *Models of the Church.* Garden City, N.Y.: Doubleday, 1974.

Dumery, Henry. *Phenomenology and Religion.* Berkeley and Los Angeles: University of California Press, 1975.

Dunne, John S. *The Way of All the Earth: An Encounter with Eastern Religions.* London: Sheldon Press, 1973.

———. *The City of the Gods: A Study in Myth and Mortality.* London: Sheldon Press, 1974.

———. *A Search for God in Time and Memory.* London: Sheldon Press, 1975.

———. *The Reasons of the Heart: A Journey into Solitude and Back Again into the Human Circle.* London: SCM Press, 1978.

———. *Time and Myth: A Meditation on Storytelling as an Exploration of Life and Death.* London: SCM Press, 1979.

Duska, Ronald, and Whelan, Mariellen. *Moral Development: A Guide to Piaget and Kohlberg.* Dublin: Gill and Macmillan, 1975.

Dych, William V. *Through a Glass Darkly: Reflections on the Theology of Faith.* Unpublished manuscript, 1976.

Egan, Harvey D. *The Spiritual Exercises and the Ignatian Mystical Horizon.* St. Louis: The Institute of Jesuit Resources, 1976.

Eliade, Mircea. *Patterns in Comparative Religion.* London: Sheed and Ward, 1976.

Fenichel, Otto. *The Psychoanalytic Theory of Neurosis.* London: Routledge and Kegan Paul, 1946.

Fitzpatrick, J. "Lonergan and Poetry." *New Blackfriars* 59 (1978):441–450, 517–526.

Flanagan, Joseph. "Transcendental Dialectic of Desire and Fear." In *Lonergan Workshop I.* Edited by Fred Lawrence. Missoula, Mont.: Scholars Press, 1978.

Frankl, Victor E. *Man's Search for Meaning: An Introduction to Logotherapy.* London: Hodder and Staughton, 1964.

French, R. M. *The Way of a Pilgrim.* London: SPCK, 1972.

Freud, Sigmund. *Civilization and Its Discontents.* Translated by Joan Riviere and James Strachey. London: Hogarth Press/The Institute of Psychoanalysis, 1963.

Fromm, Erich. *The Art of Loving.* London: Allen and Unwin, 1957.

Fuchs, Josef. *De Castitate et Ordine Sexuali.* Rome: Gregorian University Press, 1963.

Godin, A., and Hallez, M. "Parental Images and Divine Paternity." *Lumen Vitae* 19 (1964):253–284.

Gooch, G. P. *History and Historians in the Nineteenth Century.* London: Longmans Green and Company, 1958.

Görres, Albert. *The Methods and Experience of Psychoanalysis.* London: Sheed and Ward, 1962.

Häring, Bernard. *Free and Faithful in Christ: Moral Theology for Priests and Laity,* vol. 1. Slough, U.K.: St. Paul Publications, 1978.

Heidegger, Martin. "The Origin of the Work of Art." English translation by Albert Hofstadter. In *Philosophies of Art and Beauty.* Edited by Hofstadter and Richard Kuhns. New York: The Modern Library/Random House, 1964.

Hillman, James. "A Note on Story." In *Loose Ends: Primary Papers in Archetypal Psychology.* Zurich: Springer Verlag, 1975.

Hofer, Walther. "Toward a Revision of the German Concept of History." In *German History: Some New German Views.* Edited by Hans Kohn. London: George Allen and Unwin, 1954.

Jung, C. G. *The Structure and Dynamics of the Psyche.* In *The Collected Works,* vol. 8. 2d ed. Translated by R.F.C. Hull. London: Routledge and Kegan Paul, 1969.

_____. *Researches into the Phenomenology of the Self.* In *The Collected Works,* vol. 9, ii. 2d ed. Translated by R.F.C. Hull. London: Routledge and Kegan Paul, 1968.

_____. "A Psychological Approach to the Trinity." In *Psychology and Religion: West and East.* In *The Collected Works,* vol. 11. 2d ed. Translated by R.F.C. Hull. London: Routledge and Kegan Paul, 1969.

_____. *The Spirit in Man, Art, and Literature.* In *The Collected Works,* vol. 15. 2d ed. Translated by R.F.C. Hull. London: Routledge and Kegan Paul, 1968.

Kant, Immanuel. "Critique of Judgment: The Analytic of the Beautiful." English translation by Albert Hofstadter. In *Philosophies of Art and Beauty.* Edited by Hofstadter and Richard Kuhns. New York: The Modern Library/Random House, 1964.

Kiely, Bartholomew M. *Psychology and Moral Theology: Lines of Convergence.* Rome: Gregorian University Press, 1980.

Klein, Charlotte. *Anti-Judaism in Christian Theology.* London: SPCK, 1978.

Lake, Frank. *Clinical Theology: A Theological and Psychiatric Basis to Clinical Pastoral Care.* London: Darton, Longman and Todd, 1966.

_____. *Clinical Pastoral Care in Anxiety and Related Conditions: Phobic Reactions, Automatic Reactions, Dissociative Reactions, Depersonalization and Conversion Reactions.* 2nd ed. Nottingham, U.K.: The Clinical Theology Association, 1970.

_____. "The Work of Christ in the Healing of Primal Pain." *Theological Renewal* 9 (June/July 1978):30–34.

Leeuw, Gerardus van der. *Sacred and Profane Beauty: The Holy in Art.* Nashville, Tenn.: Abingdon, 1963.

Leon-Dufour, Xavier. *Resurrection and the Message of Easter.* London: Geoffrey Chapman, 1974.

Leveque, Jean. "Interiorité—I." *Dictionnaire de Spiritualité, Ascétique et Mystique* 7. 2nd ed. Paris: Beauchesne, 1971.

Lockhead, David. "Hermeneutics and Ideology." *The Ecumenist* 15 (1977).

Lonergan, Bernard J. F. *Insight: A Study of Human Understanding.* London: Longmans, Green, 1958.

_____. *De Verbo Incarnato.* Rome: Gregorian University Press, 1964.

_____. *De Deo Trino I: Pars Dogmatica editio secunda et recognita.* Rome: Gregorian University Press, 1964.

_____. *De Deo Trino II: Pars Systematica seu Divinarum personarum conceptio analogica editio tertia et recognita.* Rome: Gregorian University Press, 1964.

_____. "Finality, Love, Marriage." *Collection: Papers by Bernard J. F. Lonergan, S. J.* London: Darton, Longman and Todd, 1967.

_____. "The Natural Desire to See God." *Collection: Papers by Bernard J. F. Lonergan, S. J.* London: Darton, Longman and Todd, 1967.

_____. *Verbum: Word and Idea in Aquinas.* London: Darton, Longman and Todd, 1968.

_____. *Transcendental Philosophy and the Study of Religion.* Lectures at Boston College, 1968. (Obtainable from the Lonergan Center, Regis College, Toronto.)

_____. *Method in Theology.* London: Darton, Longman and Todd, 1972.

_____. *Philosophy of God, and Theology: The Relationship Between Philosophy of God and the Functional Speciality, Systematics.* London: Darton, Longman and Todd, 1973.

_____. "The Future of Christianity." *A Second Collection: Papers by Bernard J. F. Lonergan, S. J.* London: Darton, Longman and Todd, 1974.

_____. "The Redemption." *3 Lectures.* Montreal: Thomas More Institute, 1975.

_____. "Religious Experience." In *Trinification of the World: A Festschrift in Honor of Frederick E. Crowe.* Edited by Thomas A. Dunne and Jean-Marc Laporte. Toronto: Regis, 1978.

_____. *The Philosophy of Education.* Transcribed and edited by James and John Quinn. Toronto: Lonergan Center, Regis College, 1979.

_____. *Understanding and Being: An Introduction and Companion to Insight (The Halifax Lectures).* Lewiston, N.Y.: The Edwin Mellen Press, 1980.

_____. "Prolegomena to the Study of the Emerging Religious Consciousness of our Time." *Sciences Religieuses/Studies in Religion* 9 (1980):3–15.

Lotz, Johannes B. *Interior Prayer: The Exercise of Personality.* New York: Herder and Herder, 1968.

Lowen, Alexander. *The Betrayal of the Body.* New York: Collier, 1967.

Luca, Anthony de. *Freud and Future Religious Experience.* Totowa, N.J.: Littlefield Adams, 1977.

Lynch, William. *Images of Faith.* South Bend, Ind.: University of Notre Dame Press, 1973.

Lyonnet, Stanislaus. "Saint Paul et l'exegese juive de son temps: A propos de Rom. 10:6–8." In *Melanges A. Robert.* Paris: Beauchesne, 1957.

McBride, Denis. "The Unity of Time in the Human Story." *The Month* 12(7) (1979):229–232.

McNamara, M. *The New Testament and the Palestinian Targum to the Pentateuch.* In *Analecta Biblica,* vol. 27. Rome: Apud Pontificium Institutum Biblicum, 1966.

Manigne, J. P. *Pour une Poétique de la Foi: Essai sur le mystère symbolique.* Paris: Du Cerf, 1969.

Maritain, Jacques. *Art and Scholasticism and the Frontiers of Poetry.* New York: Charles Scribner's Sons, 1962.

Martinez, Ernest. *The Gospel Accounts of the Death of Jesus.* Ph.D. dissertation, Gregorian University, Rome, 1969.

Martini, Carolo. "Vangelo della Passione ed Esperienza Mistica nella Tradizione Sinottica e Giovannea." In *Mistica e Misticismo Oggi*. Rome: CIPI,
1971.

_____. "Riflessioni sull'itinerario dell'esperienza cristiana nel NT." Un-
published manuscript. Rome, 1978.

_____. "The Stages of Formation of the Christian in the Primitive Com-
munity in the Light of the Four Gospels." *Pontificium Consoilium Pro
Laicis Documentation Service* 5 (1979):1–10.

_____. "Iniziazione Cristiana e Teologia Fondamentale: Riflessione sulle
tappe della maturità cristiana nella chiesa primitiva." In *Problemi e Pro-
sepettive di Teologia Fondamentale*. Edited by R. Latourelle and
G. O'Collins. Brescia, Italy: Queriniana, 1980.

May, Rollo. *Symbolism in Religion and Literature*. New York: George Braziller, 1961.

Mayer-Gross, W., Slater, Eliot, and Roth, Martin. *Clinical Psychiatry*. 3rd
ed. London: Ballière Tindall, 1977.

Meagher, John C. "Pictures at an Exhibition: Reflections on Exegesis and
Theology." *Journal of the American Academy of Religion* 47 (1979):3–20.

Mersch, Emile. *The Whole Christ: The Historical Development of the Doctrine of the Mystical Body in Scripture and Tradition*. London: Denis Dobson, 1938.

Metz, Johannes B. "A Short Apology for Narrative." *Concilium* 85 (1973):84–
97.

Milburn, R. L. P. *Early Christian Interpretations of History*. New York:
Harper & Brothers, 1954.

Mooney, Christopher. *Teilhard de Chardin and the Mystery of Christ*. London: Collins, 1964.

Moore, Sebastian. "Christian Self-Discovery." In *Lonergan Workshop I*. Edited by Fred Lawrence. Missoula, Mont.: Scholars Press, 1978.

_____. *The Fire and the Rose Are One*. London: Darton, Longman and Todd,
1980.

Moreno, Antonio. *Jung, Gods, & Modern Man*. London: Sheldon Press, 1974.

Murtagh, J. "Animus and Anima in St. Peter and St. John." *The Irish Theological Quarterly* 37 (1970):65–70.

Navone, John. *A Theology of Failure*. New York: Paulist Press, 1974.

_____. *Everyman's Odyssey*. Rome: Gregorian University Press, 1974.

_____. *Towards a Theology of Story*. Slough, U.K.: St. Paul Publications,
1977.

_____. *The Jesus Story: Our Life as Story in Christ*. Collegeville, Minn.: The
Liturgical Press, 1979.

_____. "Write a Gospel." *Review for Religious* 38 (1979):668–678.

_____. "Four Gospels: Four Stages of Christian Maturation." *Review for
Religious* 39 (1980):558–567.

_____. "The Graves of Craving and Self-Fulfillment." *Homiletic and Pas-
toral Review* (November 1980):29–32, 52–54.

Newman, J. H. *An Essay in Aid of a Grammar of Assent*. London: Longmans,
Green, 1939.

_____. *Discourses to Mixed Congregations*. Westminster, Md.: The Newman
Press, 1966.

Nichols, Aidan. *The Art of God Incarnate: Theology and Image in Christian
Tradition*. London: Darton, Longman and Todd, 1980.

Novak, Michael. "Philosophy of Fiction." *The Christian Scholar* 47 (1964).

———. *The Experience of Nothingness.* New York: Harper & Row, 1970.

———. *Ascent of the Mountain, Flight of the Dove.* New York: Harper & Row, 1971.

O'Collins, Gerald. *The Easter Jesus.* London: Darton, Longman and Todd, 1973.

Oden, Thomas C. *The Structure of Awareness.* Nashville, Tenn.: Abingdon Press, 1969.

Palazzoli, Maria S. *Self-Starvation: From the Intrapsychic to the Transpersonal Approach to Anorexia Nervosa.* London: Chaucer, 1974.

Persson, P. E. *Sacra Doctrina: Reason and Revelation in Aquinas.* Oxford: Basil Blackwell, 1970.

Pincus, Lily, ed. *Marriage: Studies in Emotional Conflict and Growth.* London: The Tavistock Institute, 1973.

Polanyi, Michael. *Personal Knowledge: Towards a Post-Critical Philosophy.* London: Routledge and Kegan Paul, 1968.

Pope, Marvin H. *The Song of Songs: A New Translation with Introduction and Commentary.* In *Anchor Bible*, vol. 7C. Garden City, N.Y.: Doubleday, 1977.

Quasten, Johannes. *Patrology III.* Utrecht-Antwerp: Spectrum, 1963.

Rahner, Karl. "The Order of Redemption within the Order of Grace." In *Mission and Grace.* London: Sheed and Ward, 1963.

———. *Hearers of the Word.* London: Sheed and Ward, 1969.

———. *Theological Investigations.* London: Darton, Longman & Todd, 1961 on.

"The Eternal Significance of the Humanity of Jesus for our Relationship with God." Vol. III, pp. 35–46, 1967.

"Priest and Poet." Vol. III, pp. 294–317, 1967.

"Nature and Grace." Vol. IV, pp. 165–188, 1966.

"Unity-Love-Mystery." Vol. VIII, pp. 229–247, 1971.

"The Problem of Genetic Manipulation." Vol. IX, pp. 225–252, 1972.

"The Hiddenness of God." Vol. XVI, pp. 227–243, 1979.

Roth, Cecil. *The Haggadah: A New Edition with English Translation, Introduction, and Notes.* London: The Soncino Press, 1959.

Schlier, H. *Der Romerbrief.* Freiburg, W. Ger.: Herder, 1977.

Schnackenberg, R. *Vision of God.* London: Sheed and Ward, 1970.

Schneiders, Sandra M. "Faith, Hermeneutics, and the Literal Sense of Scripture." *Theological Studies* 39 (1978):734–735.

Stein, Edith. *The Science of the Cross: A Study of St. John of the Cross.* London: Burns and Oates, 1960.

Strack, H., and Billerbeck, P. *Kommentar zum NT aus Talmud und Midrasch.* Munich. 1922–28, 1956, 1961.

Sullivan, H. S. *The Interpersonal Theory of Psychiatry.* London: Tavistock Publications, 1955.

Taylor, Vincent. *The Names of Jesus.* New York: St. Martin's Press, 1953.

Teselle, Sallie McFargue. *Speaking in Parables: A Study in Metaphor and Theology.* London: SCM Press, 1975.

Tillich, Paul. "The Religious Symbol." In *Symbolism in Religion and Literature.* Edited by Rollo May. New York: George Braziller, 1960.

Tolkien, J. R. R. "On Fairy-Stories." *The Tolkien Reader*. New York: Ballantine, 1966.
Tugwell, Simon. "Faith and Experience: VIII. Beyond Reason and Language." *New Blackfriars* 60 (1979):376–392.
Vergote, Antoine. *The Religious Man*. Dublin: Gill and Macmillan, 1969.
Wojtyla, Karol. *The Acting Person. Analecta Husserliana* X. Dordrecht, Holland: Reidel, 1979.
Yarnold, Edward. *The Second Gift: A Study of Grace*. Slough, U.K.: St. Paul Publications, 1974.
_____. *The Awe-Inspiring Rites of Christian Initiation*. Slough, U.K.: St. Paul Publications, 1972.

II. SUGGESTIONS FOR FURTHER READING

The following suggestions for further reading are made in the knowledge that only a small selection can be given from the vast amount of material relevant to the theological study of story.

A. Historians on History

Ausubel, Herman. *Historians and their Craft: A Study of the Presidential Addresses of the American Historical Association, 1884–1945*. New York: Columbia University Press, 1950.
Barnes, Harry Elmer. *A History of Historical Writing*. New York: Crofts, 1935.
Barraclough, Geoffrey. *History in a Changing World*. New York: Oxford University Press, 1955.
Becker, Carl. *Everyman His Own Historian*. New York: Crofts, 1935.
Berlin, Isaiah. *The Hedgehog and the Fox*. New York: Simon and Schuster, 1953.
_____. *Historical Inevitability*. New York: Oxford University Press, 1954.
Bloch, Marc. *The Historian's Craft*. Translated by Peter Putnam. New York: Knopf, 1953.
Burckhardt, Jacob. *Force and Freedom: Reflections on History*. Edited by James Hastings Nichols. New York: Pantheon Books, 1953.
Butterfield, Herbert. *The Englishman and His History*. Cambridge: At the University Press, 1944.
_____. *History and Human Relations*. London: Collins, 1951.
_____. *The Origins of Modern Science*. London: G. Bell & Sons, 1949.
_____. *The Whig Interpretation of History*. London: G. Bell & Sons, 1950.
Carr, Edward Hallett. *What is History?* New York: Knopf, 1962.
Geyl, Pieter. *Encounters in History*. New York: Meridian Books, 1961.
_____, Toynbee, Arnold J., and Sorokin, Pitirim. *The Pattern of the Past: Can We Determine It?* Boston: Beacon Press, 1949.
Gottschalk, Louis. *Generalization in the Writing of History*. Chicago: University of Chicago Press, 1963.
Hexter, J. H. *Reappraisals in History*. Evanston, Ill.: Northwestern University Press, 1961.

Jameson, J. Franklin. *The History of Historical Writing in America.* New York: Antiquarian Press, 1961.

Oman, Sir Charles. *On the Writing of History.* New York: E. P. Dutton, 1939.

Shotwell, James. *The History of History.* New York: Columbia University Press, 1939.

Smith, Page. *The Historian and History.* New York: Knopf, 1966.

Thompson, J. W. *A History of Historical Writing.* 2 vols. New York: Macmillan, 1942.

Wish, Harvey. *The American Historians.* New York: Oxford University Press, 1960.

B. Philosophers on History

Arendt, Hannah. *Between Past and Future.* New York: Viking Press, 1961.

———. *On Revolution.* New York: Viking Press, 1962.

Aron, Raymond. *The Nature of Historical Explanation.* Translated by George Irwin. Boston: Beacon Press, 1961.

Gardiner, Patrick. *The Nature of Historical Explanation.* New York: Oxford University Press, 1955.

Heard, Gerald. *Is God in History?* New York: Harper and Brothers, 1950.

Heilbroner, Robert L. *The Future as History.* New York: Harper & Bros., 1960.

Hempel, C. G. "The Function of General Laws in History." *Journal of Philosophy* 39 (1942):35–48.

Hook, Sidney. *The Hero in History: A Study in Limitation and Possibility.* New York: John Day, 1943.

Jaspers, Karl. *The Origin and Goal of History.* New Haven, Conn.: Yale University Press, 1953.

———. *Man in the Modern Age.* New York: Anchor Books, 1957.

Knowles, David. *The Historian and Character.* New York: Columbia University Press, 1955.

Mandelbaum, Maurice. "Historical Determinism and the Gospel of Freedom." *Journal of General Education* 6 (1951):7–16.

———. *The Problem of Historical Knowledge: An Answer to Relativism.* New York: Liveright, 1938.

Marcel, Gabriel. *Homo Viator: Introduction to a Metaphysic of Hope.* Chicago: Henry Regnery, 1951.

Maritain, Jacques. *On the Philosophy of History.* New York: Charles Scribner's Sons, 1957.

Oakley, Hilda H. "The World as Memory and as History." *Proceedings of the Aristotelian Society* 27 (1926–1927):219–316.

———. "Perception and Historicity." *Proceedings of the Aristotelian Society* 38 (1937–1938):21–46.

Popper, Karl. *The Poverty of Historicism.* Boston: Beacon Press, 1957.

Rotenstreich, Nathan. *Between Past and Present: An Essay on History.* New Haven, Conn.: Yale University Press, 1958.

Rule, John C. *Bibliography of Works in the Philosophy of History, 1947–1957,* compiled for *History and Theory.* The Hague: Mouton and Co., 1961.

Weiss, Paul. *History, Written and Lived.* Carbondale, Ill.: Southern Illinois University Press, 1962.

Widgery, Alban. *Interpretations of History from Confucius to Toynbee.* London: George Allen and Unwin, 1961.

Wollheim, Richard. "Historicism Reconsidered." *Journal of Philosophy* 52 (1955):269–277.

Zucker, Morris. *The Philosophy of American History.* 2 vols. New York: Arnold Havard, 1945.

C. Religion and History

Augustine, St. *The City of God.* New York: Modern Library/Random House, 1950.

Brunner, Emil. *Christianity and Civilization.* Parts I and II. The Gifford Lectures. New York: Charles Scribner's Sons, 1948.

Butterfield, Herbert. *Christianity and History.* New York: Charles Scribner's Sons, 1950.

Connolly, James M. *Human History and the Word of God: The Christian Meaning of History in Contemporary Thought.* New York: Macmillan, 1965.

Cullman, Oscar. *Christ and Time: The Primitive Christian Conception of Time and History.* Translated by Floyd V. Filson. Philadelphia: Westminster Press, 1950.

D'Arcy, Martin. *The Sense of History.* London: Faber, 1959.

_____. *The Meaning and Matter of History: A Christian View.* New York: Farrar, Straus and Cudahy, 1959.

Dawson, Christopher. *The Dynamics of World History.* New York: Mentor Books. 1962.

Löwith, Karl. *Meaning in History.* Chicago: University of Chicago Press, 1949.

Marcel, Gabriel. *The Mystery of Being: Reflection and History.* The Gifford Lectures. London: Harvill, 1950.

Niebuhr, Reinhold. *Faith and History.* New York: Charles Scribner's Sons, 1949.

_____. *The Irony of American History.* New York: Charles Scribner's Sons, 1952.

_____. *The Self and the Dramas of History.* New York: Charles Scribner's Sons, 1955.

_____. *The Nature and Destiny of Man.* The Gifford Lectures. New York: Charles Scribner's Sons, 1948.

Niebuhr, Richard R. *Ressurrection and Historical Reason.* New York: Charles Scribner's Sons, 1957.

Pieper, Josef. *The End of Time: A Meditation on the Philosophy of History.* London: Faber and Faber, 1954.

Richardson, Alan. *History, Sacred and Profane.* London: SCM Press, 1964.

Rougemont, Denis de. *Man's Western Quest: The Principles of Civilization.* New York: Harper & Bros., 1957.

Schweitzer, Albert. *The Quest of the Historical Jesus.* New York: Macmillan, 1948.

Tillich, Paul. *The Interpretation of History.* New York: Charles Scribner's Sons, 1936.

_____. *The Courage to Be.* New Haven, Conn.: Yale University Press, 1953.

———. *The Protestant Era*. Chicago: University of Chicago Press, 1948.
Toynbee, Arnold J. *An Historian's Approach to Religion*. New York: Oxford University Press, 1956.

D. Philosophical and Theological Works

This section includes works that, although not primarily about aesthetics or the theology of story, contain material relevant to such a theology.

Balthasar, Hans Urs von: *Herrlichkeit: Eine Theologische Ästhetik*. Einsiedeln in der Schweiz, W. Ger.: Johannes Verlag, 1961.
———. *Word and Revelation: Essays in Theology 1*. New York: Herder and Herder, 1964, especially pp. 121–163.
———. *Word and Redemption: Essays in Theology 2*. New York: Herder and Herder, 1965.
———. *A Theology of History*. New York: Sheed and Ward, 1963.
Barr, James. "Story and History in Biblical Theology." *Journal of Religion* 16 (1976):1–17.
Battaglia, Anthony. "Autobiography and Religion." *Horizons* 2 (1975):61–74.
Baum, Gregory. *Religion and Alienation*. New York: Paulist Press, 1975.
Bernard, Charles André. "Symbolisme et Conscience Affective." *Gregorianum* 61 (1980):421–447.
Borowitz et al. "What is Shaping My Theology?" *Commonweal* 108 (January 30, 1981):41–54. Eleven theologians, including Braxton, Novak, and Shea, take part in this contemporary theology issue.
Braxton, Edward K. "Bernard Lonergan's Hermeneutics of the Symbol." *Irish Theological Quarterly* 43 (1976):186–197.
———. *The Wisdom Community*. New York: Paulist Press, 1980.
Brown, Schuyler. "Exegesis and Imagination." *Theological Studies* 41 (1980):745–751.
Buckley, James J. "On Being a Symbol: An Appraisal of Karl Rahner." *Theological Studies* 40 (1979):453–473.
Buechner, Frederick. *Telling the Truth*. San Francisco: Harper & Row, 1977.
Burrell, David. *Exercises in Religious Understanding*. South Bend, Ind.: Notre Dame University Press, 1974.
Bush, Bernard. "Prayer and Experience." *The Way* 10 (1979):199–210.
Cameli, Louis. *Stories of Paradise*. New York: Paulist Press, 1978.
Campbell, Joseph, ed. *Myths, Dreams, and Religion*. New York: E.P. Dutton, 1970.
Cannon, Dale W. "Ruminations on the Claim of Inerrability." *Journal of the American Academy of Religion* 43 (1975):560–585.
Capps, Donald, and Capps, Walter H. *The Religious Personality*. Belmont, Calif.: Wadsworth, 1970.
Carnell, Corbin Scott. *Bright Shadow of Reality: C. S. Lewis and the Feeling Intellect*. Grand Rapids, Mich.: Wm. B. Eerdmans, 1974.
Carr, Ann. "Theology and Experience in the Thought of Karl Rahner." *Journal of Religion* 53 (1973):359–377.
Cary, Norman R. *Christian Criticism in the Twentieth Century*. Port Washington, N.Y.: Kennikat Press, 1975.

Crites, Steven. "Myth, Story, History." In *Parable, Myth and Language.* Cambridge, Mass.: Church Society for College Work, 1968.

_____. "Myth: The Narrative Quality of Experience." *Journal of the American Academy of Religion* 39 (1971).

Crossan, John D. *The Dark Interval.* Niles, Ill.: Argus, 1976.

_____. *Cliffs of Fall: Paradox and Polyvalence in the Parables of Jesus.* New York: Crossroad Books/Seabury, 1980.

Cunningham, Adrian. "Metaphor, the Self, and the Language of Religion." *New Blackfriars* 62 (1981):261–272.

Daly, Gabriel. "History, Truth and Method." *Irish Theological Quarterly* 47 (1980):43–55.

D'Arcy, Martin. *The Mind and Heart of Love: Lion and Unicorn: A Story in Eros and Agape.* London: Collins/The Fontana Library, 1962.

Dillistone, F. W. *The Novelist and the Passion Story.* New York: Sheed and Ward, 1960.

Dorna, Robert M. "Aesthetics and the Opposites." *Thought* 52 (1977):117–133.

_____. "Aesthetic Subjectivity and Generalized Empirical Method." *The Thomist* 43 (1979):257–278.

_____. "Psyche, Evil and Grace." *Communio* (Spokane) 6 (1979):192–211.

_____. "Jungian Psychology and Lonergan's Foundations: A Methodological Proposal." *Journal of the American Academy of Religion* 47 (1979):24–45.

_____. *Subject and Psyche: Ricouer, Jung and the Search for Foundations.* Washington, D.C.: University Press of America, 1977.

Drury, John. "The Spirit of Storytelling." *Theology* 79 (1976):78–83.

Dulles, Avery. *Myth, Biblical Revelation, and Christ.* Washington and Cleveland: Corpus Books, 1968.

_____. "The Symbolic Structure of Revelation." *Theological Studies* 41 (1980):51–73.

Egenter, Richard. *The Desecration of Christ.* Translated by Edward Quinn. London: Burns and Oates, 1967.

Eliade, Mircea. *The Quest.* Chicago: University of Chicago Press, 1969.

_____. *The Myth of the Eternal Return.* Translated by W. R. Task. Princeton, N.J.: Princeton University Press, 1971.

Eliot, T. S. *Notes Toward a Definition of Culture.* New York: Harcourt Brace, 1949.

English, John. *Choosing Life.* New York: Paulist Press, 1978.

Estess, Ted. "The Inerrable Contraption: Reflections on the Metaphor of Story." *Journal of the American Academy of Religion* 42 (1974):415–434.

Evdokimov, Paul. *La Teologia della Bellezza: Il senso della bellezza e l'icone.* Roma: Edizioni Paoline, 1971.

Fawcett, Thomas. *The Symbolic Language of Religion.* Minneapolis: Augsburg Press, 1971.

Ferlita, Ernest. *The Theatre of Pilgrimage.* New York: Sheed and Ward, 1971.

_____. *Film Odyssey.* New York: Paulist Press, 1976.

Fox, Matthew. "Hermeneutic and Hagiography." *Spirituality Today* 30 (1978):263–271.

Fromm, Erich. *The Forgotten Language: An Introduction to the Understanding of Dreams, Fairytales and Myths.* New York: Holt, Rinehart and Winston, 1951.

Fuller, Reginald H. (ed.). *Essays on the Love Commandment*. Philadelphia: Fortress, 1978.

Galot, Jean. *Who Is Christ?* Rome: Gregorian University Press, 1980. Especially chapter 10: "Meaning and Importance of the Unity of the Person," pp. 255–318.

Goetz, Joseph. "Symbole et Mythe." *Gregorianum* 61 (1980):449–460.

Gold, Arthur R. "Exodus and Autobiography." *Commentary* (May 1976):46–51.

Greeley, Andrew. *The Jesus Myth*. New York: Doubleday, 1973.

———. *The Mary Myth*. New York: Seabury Press, 1977.

———. *The Sinai Myth*. Garden City, N.Y.: Doubleday, 1975.

Hardy, Barbara. *Tellers and Listeners*. London: Athlone, 1975.

Harper, Ralph. *The Seventh Solitude*. Baltimore: Johns Hopkins Press, 1965.

Hart, Ray L. *Unfinished Man and the Imagination: Toward an Ontology and a Rhetoric of Revelation*. New York: Herder and Herder, 1968.

Hartt, Julian N. *Theological Method and Imagination*. New York: Seabury Press, 1977.

Hauerwas, Stanley. *Character and the Christian Life: A Study in Theological Ethics*. San Antonio: Trinity University Press, 1975.

———, and Bondi, Richard. "Memory, Community and the Reasons for Living: Theological and Ethical Reflections on Suicide and Euthanasia." *Journal of the American Academy of Religion* 44 (1976):439–452.

———; Bondi, Richard, and Burrell, David. *Truthfulness and Tragedy*. South Bend, Ind.: Notre Dame University Press, 1977.

———, and Burrell, David. "Self-Deception and Autobiography: Theological and Ethical Reflections on Speer's *Inside the Third Reich*." *Journal of Religious Ethics* (Spring 1974).

———. *Vision and Virtue*. South Bend, Ind.: Notre Dame: Fides/Claretian, 1974.

Haught, John. *Religion and Self-Acceptance*. New York: Paulist Press, 1976.

Haughton, Rosemary. *The Drama of Salvation*. London: SPCK, 1975.

———. *Tales from Eternity: The World of Faerie and the Spiritual Search*. London: George Allen and Unwin, 1973.

———. "Unless You Become as Little Children." *New Blackfriars* (Nov/Dec 1973).

———. *The Passionate God*. London: Darton, Longman and Todd, 1981.

Hefling, Charles. "Liturgy and Myth: A Theological Approach Based on the Methodology of Bernard Lonergan." *Anglican Theological Review* 61 (1979):200–223.

Holmes, Urban T. *Ministry and Imagination*. New York: Seabury Press, 1976.

Hultgren, Arland J. *Jesus and His Adversaries: The Form and Function of the Conflict Stories in the Synoptic Tradition*. Minneapolis: Augsburg Publishing House, 1979.

Jennings, Theodore W. Jr. *Introduction to Theology: An Invitation to Reflection Upon the Christian Myths*. Philadelphia: Fortress Press, 1976.

Jensen, Richard A. *Telling the Story: Variety and Imagination in Preaching*. Minneapolis: Augsburg Publishing House, 1980.

Johnson, Luke, ed. "Theology as Biography." In *Teaching Religion to Undergraduates: Some Approaches and Ideas from Teachers to Teachers*. New Haven, Conn.: The Society for Religion in Higher Education.

Johnston, William. *The Mysticism of the Cloud of Unknowing*. Religious Experience Series 8. Wheathampstead, U.K.: Anthony Clark, 1978.

———. *Silent Music: The Science of Meditation*. London: Collins/The Fontana Library, 1976.

———. *The Inner Eye of Love: Mysticism and Religion*. London: Collins, 1978.

Jones, Hugh. "The Concept of Story and Theological Discourse." *Scottish Journal of Theology* 29 (1976):415–433.

Kasin, Alfred. "Autobiography as Narrative." *Michigan Quarterly Review* (Fall 1964).

Keen, Sam. *To a Dancing God*. New York: Harper & Row, 1970.

Kelber, Werner H. *The Kingdom in Mark: A New Place and a New Time*. Philadelphia: Fortress, 1974.

———. *Mark's Story of Jesus*. Philadelphia: Fortress, 1979.

Kelsey, Morton T. *Myth, History and Faith*. New York: Paulist Press, 1974.

Kermode, Frank. *The Sense of an Ending: Studies in the Theory of Fiction*. New York: Oxford University Press, 1967.

Kort, Wesley A. *Narrative Elements and Religious Meaning*. Philadelphia: Fortress Press, 1975.

Krentz, Edgar. *The Historical-Critical Method*. Philadelphia, Fortress, 1975.

Krieg, Robert. "The Theologian as Narrator: Karl Barth on the Perfections of God." Ph.D. dissertation, Notre Dame, 1976.

———. "Cardinal Ratzinger, Max Scheler and Christology." *Irish Theological Quarterly* 47 (1980):205–219.

Kümmel, W. G. *Promise and Fulfillment: The Eschatological Message of Jesus*. Translated by Dorothea M. Barton. Studies in Biblical Theology 23. London: SCM Press, 1957.

Küng, Hans. *Art and the Question of Meaning*. New York: Crossroad, 1981.

Lerner, L. D. "Puritanism and the Spiritual Autobiography." *Hibbert Journal* (July 1957).

Lotz, Johannes B. *Aesthetica Philosophica*. Rome: Gregorian University Press, 1964.

Lynch, William F. *Christ and Apollo: The Dimensions of the Literary Imagination*. South Bend, Ind.: Notre Dame University Press, 1974.

———. *Christ and Prometheus: A New Image of the Secular*. South Bend, Ind.: Notre Dame University Press, 1973.

———. *Images of Hope*. South Bend, Ind.: Notre Dame University Press, 1973.

Mackey, James P. *Jesus: The Man and the Myth: A Contemporary Christology*. London: SCM Press, 1979.

Malits, Elena; Burrell, David; and Hauerwas, Stanley. "Theology as Biography." *Horizons* 1 (1974):81–87.

Malone, Peter. "Prayer and Poetry: Henri Bremond and Modern Developments." *Irish Theological Quarterly* 36 (1969):151–168.

May, John. *Toward a New Earth: Apocalypse in the American Novel*. South Bend, Ind.: Notre Dame University Press, 1972.

McAfee Brown, Robert. "My Story and 'The Story' " *Theology Today* (July 1975).

McArthur, Harvey K. *Understanding the Sermon on the Mount*. New York: Harper, 1960.

McClendon, James William Jr. "Biography as Theology." *Cross Currents* 21 (1971):415–431.

——. *Biography as Theology.* Nashville, Tenn.: Abingdon, 1974.

——and Smith, James. *Understanding Religious Convictions.* South Bend, Ind.: Notre Dame University Press, 1975.

McDonagh, Enda. *Doing the Truth.* Dublin: Gill and Macmillan, 1979.

Michie, Donald, and Rhoads, David. *Mark as Story.* Philadelphia: Fortress, 1981.

Mink, L. O. "History and Fiction as Modes of Comprehension." *New Literary History* 1 (1970):545.

Navone, John. "The Christ Story of the Christ-Self." *Irish Theological Quarterly* 43 (1976):171–185.

——. "Bipolarities in Conversion." *Review for Religious* 40 (1981):435–450.

——. *Communicating Christ.* Slough, U.K.: St. Paul Publications, 1976.

——. *Themes of St. Luke.* Rome: Gregorian University Press, 1970.

——. *Personal Witness.* New York: Sheed and Ward, 1967.

——. *History and Faith in the Thought of Dr. Alan Richardson.* London: SCM Press, 1966.

——. "Christ, the Beatitude of God." *The Furrow* 29 (1978):698–703.

——. "Freedom and Transformation in Christ." *Spiritual Life* 21 (1975):3–7.

——. "Myth, Man, and the Gospel Message." *Doctrine and Life* 25 (1975):859–868.

——. "The Divided Self and Its Healing." *Sciences Religieuses/Studies in Religion* 6 (1976–1977):651–663.

——. "Theologian as Interpreter of Dreams." *Spiritual Life* 22 (1976):115–124.

——. "The Search for the Self: The Christ-Self and the Christ-figures." *Review for Religious* 34 (1975):132–139.

Nedoncelle, Maurice. *La Reciprocité des consciences: essai sur la nature de la personne.* Paris, 1942.

——. *Love and the Person.* New York: Herder and Herder, 1966.

——. *The Nature and Use of Prayer.* New York: Sheed and Ward, 1964.

Neill, Stephen. *Jesus Through Many Eyes: Introduction to the Theology of the New Testament.* Philadelphia: Fortress, 1976.

Noon, William T. *Poetry and Prayer.* New Brunswick, N.J.: Rutgers University Press, 1967.

Novak, Michael. *"Story" in Politics.* New York: The Council on Religion and International Affairs, 1970.

O'Collins, Gerald. "Theology and Experience." *Irish Theological Quarterly* 44 (1977):279–290.

O'Donovan, Leo. "Orthopraxis and Theological Method: Rahner." In *Catholic Theological Society Proceedings,* vol. 25. Edited by Luke Salm. New York: Manhattan College, 1980.

——. "The Mystery of God as a History of Love: Eberhard Jüngel's Doctrine of God." *Theological Studies* 42 (June 1981):251–271.

O'Leary, Joseph Stephen. "The Hermeneutics of Dogmatism." *Irish Theological Quarterly* 47 (1980):96–118.

Olney, James. *Metaphors of Self: The Meaning of Autobiography.* Princeton, N.J.: Princeton University Press, 1972.

Olson, Alan M. *Myth, Symbol and Reality.* South Bend, Ind.: Notre Dame University Press, 1980.

O'Meara, Thomas F. "Of Art and Theology: Hans Urs von Balthasar's Systems." *Theological Studies* 42 (1981):272–276.

Page, Ruth. "The Dramatization of Jesus." *Theology* 81 (1978):182–188.

Palazzoli, Maria Selvini; Cecchin, Gianfranco; Prata, Guiana; and Boscolo, Luigi. *Paradox and Counterparadox: A New Model in the Therapy of the Family in Schizophrenic Transaction.* New York: Jason Aronson, 1978. Especially pp. 83–97, where the authors discuss ritual as leading to affective and effective insight.

Pascal, Roy. *Design and Truth in Autobiography.* Cambridge: Harvard University Press, 1960.

Pfeiffer, Heinrich. "Religiose Symbole und symbolsiche Darstellungsweisen in der christlichen Kunst." *Gregorianum* 61 (1980):507–536.

Powers, Joseph M. "The Art of Believing." *Theological Studies* 39 (1978):656–678.

Rahner, Hugo. *L'Ecclesiologia dei Padri: Simboli della Chiesa.* Rome: Edizioni Paoline, 1971. Rahner's exhaustive treatment of ecclesial symbols excellently conveys the polyvalent character of symbolism.

Rahner, Karl. *Theological Investigations.* London: Darton, Longman and Todd, 1961 on.

   Vol. III. " 'Behold this Heart': Preliminaries to a Theology of Devotion to the Sacred Heart," pp. 321–330, 1967.

   Vol. III. "Some Theses for a Theology of the Sacred Heart," pp. 331–352, 1967.

   Vol. IV. "The Theology of the Symbol," pp. 221–252, 1966.

   Vol. IV. "Poetry and the Christian," pp. 357–367, 1966.

   Vol. VII. "Holy Night," pp. 127–131, especially 127–128, 1971.

   Vol. VIII. "The Theological Meaning of the Veneration of the Sacred Heart." pp. 217–228, 1971.

   Vol. XIV. "Introductory Observations on Thomas Aquinas' Theology of the Sacraments in General," pp. 149–160, 1976.

Ramsey, Michael A. *The Glory of God and the Transfiguration of Christ.* New York: Longmans, Green, 1949.

Rigali, Norbert. "Human Experience and Moral Meaning." *Chicago Studies* 13 (1974):88–104.

———. "Faith, Hope and Love." *Chicago Studies* 13 (1974):253–264.

Ruland, Vernon. *Horizons of Criticism: An Assessment of Religious-Literary Options.* Chicago: American Library Association, 1975.

Scott, Bernard Brandon. *Jesus, Symbol-Maker for the Kingdom.* Philadelphia: Fortress, 1981.

Sewell, Elizabeth. *The Human Metaphor.* South Bend, Ind.: Notre Dame University Press, 1964.

Shea, John. *Stories of God.* Chicago: Thomas More Press, 1978.

———. "Theology and Autobiography." *Commonweal* 105 (1978):358–362.

Shideler, Mary McDermott. "Philosophies and Fairy-Tales." *Theology Today* (April 1973):14–24.

———. "The Story-makers and the Story-tellers." *Religion in Life* 45 (1976):351–360.

Simon, Ulrich. *The Trial of Man.* London and Oxford: Mowbrays, 1973.

———. *Story and Faith.* London: SPCK, 1975.

Simpson, Michael. "Savior of the World." *The Way* 10 (1970):336–343.

Spidlík, Tomás. "L'Icone, Manifestation du Monde Spirituel." *Gregorianum* 61 (1980):530–553.

Stack. "The Being of the Work of Art in Heidegger." *Philosophy Today* 13 (1969):159–173.

Stauffer, Ethelbert. *Jesus and His Story*. Translated by Richard and Clara Winston. New York: Knopf, 1960.

Stroup, George. "A Bibliographical Critique." *Theology Today* 32 (1975):133–143.

Tannehill, Robert C. *The Sword of His Mouth*. Philadelphia: Fortress, 1975.

Tiede, David L. *Prophecy and History in Luke–Acts*. Philadelphia: Fortress, 1980.

Tenynson, G. B. *Religion and Modern Literature: Essays in Theory and Criticism*. Grand Rapids, Mich.: Wm. B. Eerdmans, 1975.

TeSelle, Sallie McFargue. "The Experience of Coming to Belief." *Theology Today* 32 (1975):159–160.

Toliver, Harold. *Animate Illustrations: Explorations of Narrative Structures*. Lincoln, Neb.: University of Nebraska Press, 1974.

Tracy, David. *Blessed Rage for Order*. New York: Seabury Press, 1975.

———. *The Analogical Imagination*. New York: Crossroad, 1981.

Vergote, Antoine. "Le symbole paternel et sa signification religieuse." *Archiv für Religionpsychologie* 9 (1967).

Weddle, David L. "The Image of the Self in Jonathan Edwards: A Study of Autobiography and Theology." *Journal of the American Academy of Religion* 44 (1976):229–308.

White, Hayden. "The Structure of Historical Narrative." *Clio 1*, 2 (June 1972).

Wicker, Brian. *The Story-Shaped World*. London: Athlone, 1975.

Wiggins, James. *Religion as Story*. New York: Harper & Row, 1975.

Wilson, Colin. *The Outsider*. London: Victor Gollancz, 1956.

Woodward, Kenneth. Interview with John S. Dunne in "The Emergence of a New Theology." *Psychology Today* (January 1978):46.

Zuck, John. "Tales of Wonder: Biblical Narrative, Myth, and Fairy Stories." *Journal of the American Academy of Religion* 44 (1976):299–308.

E. Works on Psychology

Bodkin, Maud. *Archetypal Patterns in Poetry: Psychological Studies of Imagination*. London: Oxford University Press, 1963.

Brown, Norman O. *Life Against Death*. New York: Vintage, 1961.

Dominian, Jack. "The Capacity to Love: I. Love of Self." *The Tablet* (February 28, 1981):197–199.

Doran, Robert M. "Christ and the Psyche." In *Trinification of the World: A Festschrift in Honour of Frederick E. Crowe in Celebration of His 60th Birthday*. Edited by Thomas A. Dunne and J.-M. Laporte. Toronto: Regis, 1978.

Erikson, Erik. "Ego Development and Historical Change." In *Childhood and Society*. New York: W. W. Norton, 1952.

Fordham, Frieda. *An Introduction to Jung's Psychology*. 3rd ed. Harmondsworth, U.K.: Penguin Books, 1963.

Fromm, Erich. "Selfishness and Self-Love." *Psychiatry* 2/4 (November 1939).

Heydt, Vera von der. *Prospects for the Soul: Soundings in Jungian Psychology and Religion*. London: Darton, Longman and Todd, 1976.

Jacobi, Jolande. *The Way of Individuation*. Translated by R. F. C. Hull. London: Hodder and Staughton, 1967.

———. *Masks of the Soul*. Translated by Ean Begg. London: Darton, Longman and Todd, 1976.

Jung, C. G. *Memories, Dreams, Reflections*. Translated by R. Winston and C. Winston. Edited by Aniela Jaffé. London: Collins/The Fontana Library, 1967.

Kopp, Sheldon. *If You Meet the Buddha on the Road, Kill Him! A Modern Pilgrimage Through Myth, Legend, Zen and Psychotherapy*. Palo Alto, Calif.: Science and Behavior Books, 1972.

Lake, Frank. *Tight Corners in Pastoral Counseling*. London: Darton, Longman and Todd, 1981.

Lowe, Walter James. "Psychoanalysis and Humanism: The Permutations of Method." *Journal of the American Academy of Religion* 47 (1979):135–169.

Lynd, Helen Merrell. "The Nature of Historical Objectivity." *Journal of Philosophy* 47 (1950).

———. *On Shame and the Search for Identity*. New York: Science Editions, 1961.

May, Rollo. *Love and Will*. London: Collins/Fountain Books, 1972.

Marcuse, Herbert. *Eros and Civilization*. Boston: Beacon Press, 1955.

Mazlish, Bruce, ed. *Psychoanalysis and History*. Englewood Cliffs, N.J.: Prentice-Hall, 1963.

Meissner, W. W. *The Paranoid Process*. New York: Jason Aronson, 1978.

Rabut, O. *L'Experience Religieuse Fondamentale*. Tornai: Casterman, 1969.

Roheim, Gexa, ed. *Psychoanalysis and the Social Sciences*. 3 vols. New York: International Universities Press, 1947–1951.

Rulla, L.; Imoda, F.; and Ridick, J. *Psychological Structure and Vocation*. Dublin: Villa Books, 1979.

Siirala, Aarne. "Theology and the Unconscious." *Sciences Religieuses/Studies in Religion* 6 (1976–1977):607–623.

Wollheim, Richard. *Freud*. London: Collins/The Fontana Library, 1971.

Zilboorg, Gregory. *Psychoanalysis and Religion*. Edited with an introduction by Margaret Stone Zilboorg. London: George Allen and Unwin, 1967.

F. History and Sociology and Metahistory

Berger, Peter L. *Invitation to Sociology: A Humanistic Perspective*. New York: Anchor Books, 1963.

Kroeber, Arthur L. *Style and Civilization*. Ithaca, N.Y.: Cornell University Press, 1957.

Mannheim, Karl. *Freedom, Power and Democratic Planning*. New York: Oxford University Press, 1950.

———. *Ideology and Utopia*. New York: Harcourt Brace, 1949.

Mills, C. Wright. *The Sociological Imagination*. New York: Oxford University Press, 1959.

Pareto, Vilfredo. *Mind and Society*. 4 vols. New York: Harcourt Brace, 1935.

Salvemini, Gaetano. *History and the Scientist: An Essay on the Nature of History and the Society Sciences*. Cambridge, Mass.: Harvard University Press, 1939.

Spengler, Oswald. *The Decline of the West*. 2 vols. New York: Knopf, 1944.

Toynbee, Arnold J. *A Study of History*. 12 vols. New York: Oxford University Press, 1940–1961.

Voegelin, Eric. *Order and History*. 6 vols. Baton Rouge, La.: Louisiana State University Press, 1956.

G. Works on Storytelling

Caldwell, Eileen. *A Second Storyteller's Choice*. New York: Henry Z. Wick, 1965.

Chambers, Dewey W. *Storytelling and Creative Drama*. Dubuque, Iowa: Wm. C. Brown, 1970.

Cundiff, Ruby, and Cundiff, Webb. *Storytelling for You*. Yellow Springs, Ohio: Antioch Press, 1957.

Emerson, Laura S. *Storytelling: The Art and the Purpose*. Grand Rapids, Mich.: Zondervan Publishing House, 1959.

Hegarty, Edward J., ed. *How to Tell a Story*. Englewood Cliffs, N.J.: Prentice-Hall, 1963.

Sawyer, Ruth. *The Way of the Storyteller*. New York: Viking Press, 1949.

Shedlock, Marie L. *The Art of the Storyteller*. New York: Dover, 1951.

Tooze, Ruth. *Storytelling*. Englewood Cliffs, N.J.: Prentice-Hall, 1959.

H. On the Parables

Cadoux, A. T. *The Parables of Jesus: Their Art and Use*. London: James Clarke & Co., 1931.

Dodd, C. H. *The Parables of the Kingdom*. New York: Scribner's, 1935; rev. ed., 1961.

Glen, Stanley J. *The Parables of Conflict in Luke*. Philadelphia: Westminster, 1962.

Hunter, A. M. *Interpreting the Parables*. Philadelphia: Westminster, 1961.

Jeremias, Joachim. *The Parables of Jesus*. Translated by S. H. Hooke. New York: Scribner's, 1954; rev. ed., 1963.

———. *Rediscovering the Parables*. Translated by S. H. Hooke. New York: Scribner's, 1966.

Jones, G. V. *The Art and Truth of the Parables: A Study in Their Literary Form and Interpretation*. London: SPCK, 1964.

Jüngel, E. *Paulus und Jesus*. Hermeneutische Untersuchungen zur Theologie 2. Tubingen: J. C. B. Mohr, 1964.

Linnemann, Eta. *Jesus of the Parables*. Translated by John Sturdy. New York: Harper & Row, 1967.

Perkins, Pheme. *Hearing the Parables of Jesus*. New York: Paulist Press, 1981.

Perrin, Norman. *Rediscovering the Teaching of Jesus*. New York: Harper & Row, 1976.

Ramsey, Ian T. *Christian Discourse: Some Logical Explorations*. New York: Oxford University Press, 1965.

Via, Dan Otto. *The Parables: Their Literary and Existential Dimension*. Philadelphia: Fortress, 1967.

Wilder, Amos. *The Language of the Gospel*. New York: Harper & Row, 1964.

INDEXES

SUBJECT INDEX

INDEX OF NAMES

INDEX OF BIBLICAL PASSAGES CITED

About the Authors

European theologians have associated the development of the theology of story with the work of Johannes B. Metz and John Navone, S.J. Fr. Navone, professor of theology at the Gregorian University in Rome and author of nine books, published the first of his five books on the theology of story in 1974: *Everyman's Odyssey: Seven Plays Seen as Modern Myths About Man's Quest for Personal Integrity*. Doctoral dissertations are being written in Europe on the relevance of Fr. Navone's work for the renewal of fundamental, moral, and ascetic theology. On the basis of his theology of story, he was chosen to be the keynote speaker and facilitator for an Anglican clergy conference at Windsor Castle in 1978. His first book, *History of Faith in the Thought of Dr. Alan Richardson* (1966), which contained seminal ideas for the theology of story, analyzed the achievement of an Anglican theologian and appeared in the Contemporary Theology Series of the SCM Press (London). His book *Themes of St. Luke* (1970) has served as a text both in Rome and in Protestant seminaries in the United States and Scotland.

In *Towards a Theology of Story* (1977) and *The Jesus Story: Our Life as Story in Christ* (1979)—an incipient theology of story—Fr. Navone provided a statement of the questions: What is the theology of story? Who are the contributors? What are their aims? *Tellers of the Word*, written with the collaboration of Thomas Cooper, systematizes and carries forward these previous efforts to create an original, and the first systematic, theology of story.

Fr. Navone was born in Seattle, Washington, in 1930. He entered the Society of Jesus in 1949 and was ordained in 1962. He received his master's degree in philosophy from Gonzaga University, Spokane, in 1956. From 1959 to 1963 he studied theology at Regis College in Toronto, Canada. Since 1963, Fr. Navone has resided in Rome, where he received his doctorate in theology from the Gregorian University. For over a decade he has taught summer courses in theology at Seattle University.

More than 100 articles by Fr. Navone have appeared in such journals as *Chicago Studies, Concilium, Dizionario della Spiritualità, Gregorianum, Irish Theological Quarterly, Philosophy and Phenomenological Research, Revue de l'Université d'Ottawa, Studies in Religion, Scottish Journal of Theology, Thought*, and *Theology*. Other books by Fr. Navone are *Personal Witness: A Biblical Spirituality*

(1967), *A Theology of Failure* (1974), and *Communicating Christ* (1976).

Thomas Cooper was born in Bedford, England, in 1946. He was educated at Bedford School and at the Gregorian University in Rome, where he was awarded his licentiate in philosophy in 1967 and his licenciate in sacred theology in 1971, receiving the approbation *summa cum laude* for his dissertation on the theology of art. Ordained in 1970, he spent six years in the parochial ministry and was engaged in training seminars in clinical psychology during this time. Fr. Cooper has published in *Clergy Review, The Furrow, Irish Theological Quarterly,* and *Catholic Herald.* Recently he completed a liturgical hymnbook based on the texts of the Roman Missal and Lectionary. At present he is writing a doctoral dissertation on the symbolism of conversion in the work of Bernard Lonergan. A member of the council of the Henry Bradshaw Society for the Editing of Rare Liturgical Texts and chaplain of the Society of Catholic Artists, Fr. Cooper spends much of his time giving retreats and study conferences.